THE CAMBRIDGE COMPANION TO AMERICAN THEATRE SINCE 1945

The Cambridge Companion to American Theatre since 1945 provides an overview and analysis of developments in the organization and practices of American theatre. It examines key demographic and geographical shifts that American theatre after 1945 has experienced in spectatorship and addresses the economic, social, and political challenges theatre artists have faced across cultural climates and geographical locations. Specifically, it explores artistic communities, collaborative practices, and theatre methodologies across mainstream, regional, and experimental theatre practices, forms, and expressions. As American theatre has embraced diversity in practice and representation, the volume examines the various creative voices, communities, and perspectives that prior to the 1940s were mostly excluded from the theatrical landscape. This diversity has led to changing dramaturgical and theatrical languages that take us into the twenty-first century. These shifting perspectives and evolving forms of theatrical expression paved the ground for contemporary American theatrical innovation.

JULIA LISTENGARTEN is Pegasus Professor and Artistic Director of Theatre at University of Central Florida's School of Performing Arts. Her books include *Russian Tragifarce: Its Cultural and Political Roots, Theater of the Avant-Garde, 1950–2000, Playing with Theory in Theatre Practice*, and *Modern American Drama: Playwriting 2000–2009*.

STEPHEN DI BENEDETTO is Professor and Chair of the Department of Theatre at Michigan State University. Among his numerous publications are *The Provocation of the Senses in Contemporary Theatre, An Introduction to Theatre Design*, and the coedited *Designers' Shakespeare*.

THE CAMBRIDGE COMPANION TO AMERICAN THEATRE SINCE 1945

EDITED BY

JULIA LISTENGARTEN

University of Central Florida

STEPHEN DI BENEDETTO

Michigan State University

CAMBRIDGE
UNIVERSITY PRESS

CAMBRIDGE
UNIVERSITY PRESS

University Printing House, Cambridge CB2 8BS, United Kingdom

One Liberty Plaza, 20th Floor, New York, NY 10006, USA

477 Williamstown Road, Port Melbourne, VIC 3207, Australia

314–321, 3rd Floor, Plot 3, Splendor Forum, Jasola District Centre,
New Delhi – 110025, India

103 Penang Road, #05–06/07, Visioncrest Commercial, Singapore 238467

Cambridge University Press is part of the University of Cambridge.

It furthers the University's mission by disseminating knowledge in the pursuit of
education, learning, and research at the highest international levels of excellence.

www.cambridge.org
Information on this title: www.cambridge.org/9781108480260
DOI: 10.1017/9781108648134

© Cambridge University Press 2021

First published 2021

A catalogue record for this publication is available from the British Library.

Library of Congress Cataloging-in-Publication Data
NAMES: Listengarten, Julia, 1967– editor. | Di Benedetto, Stephen, editor.
TITLE: The Cambridge companion to American theatre since 1945 / edited by Julia
Listengarten, Stephen Di Benedetto.
DESCRIPTION: Cambridge ; New York, NY : Cambridge University Press, 2021. | Series:
Cambridge companions to theatre and performance | Includes bibliographical references and
index.
IDENTIFIERS: LCCN 2021008466 (print) | LCCN 2021008467 (ebook) | ISBN 9781108480260
(hardback) | ISBN 9781108727211 (paperback) | ISBN 9781108648134 (ebook)
SUBJECTS: LCSH: Theater – United States – History – 20th century. | Theater – United States
– History – 21st century.
CLASSIFICATION: LCC PN2266.5 .C36 2021 (print) | LCC PN2266.5 (ebook) | DDC 792.0973/
0904–dc23
LC record available at https://lccn.loc.gov/2021008466
LC ebook record available at https://lccn.loc.gov/2021008467

ISBN 978-1-108-48026-0 Hardback
ISBN 978-1-108-72721-1 Paperback

Contents

Notes on Contributors

Editors

JULIA LISTENGARTEN is Pegasus Professor, Artistic Director, and Director of Graduate Studies at University of Central Florida's School of Performing Arts. Her books include *Russian Tragifarce: Its Cultural and Political Roots* (2000), *Theater of the Avant-Garde, 1950–2000* (2011), *Playing with Theory in Theatre Practice* (2011), and *Modern American Drama: Playwriting 2000–2009* (2018). She has contributed essays to publications including *Semiotic Inquiry, Stanislavski Studies, Scene,* and *International Journal of Arts Education*; coedited the eight-volume series *Decades of Modern American Drama: Playwriting from the 1930s to 2009* (with Brenda Murphy); served as the editor of the *Stanislavski Studies* journal (2013–20); and is currently the series coeditor of Reflections on Contemporary Performance Process.

STEPHEN DI BENEDETTO is Professor and Chairperson in the Department of Theatre at Michigan State University. Among his numerous publications are *The Provocation of the Senses in Contemporary Theatre* (2010), *An Introduction to Theatre Design* (2012), and also the coedited *Designers' Shakespeare* (2016). Additionally, he is a Performance + Design Series Editor (Bloomsbury), was formally a convener of the Scenography Working Group of the International Federation for Theatre Research, an Associate Editor (Drama) for *ASAP/Journal,* an Associate Editor of *Scene,* and Book Review Editor (North America) for *Theatre Research International.*

Contributors

SUSAN C. W. ABBOTSON is Professor of English at Rhode Island College, where she teaches mostly drama. She is the author of *A Critical*

Companion to Arthur Miller (2007) and *Student Companion to Arthur Miller* (2000) and of numerous articles on Arthur Miller. She also authored *Thematic Guide to Modern Drama* (2003), *Masterpieces of Twentieth Century American Drama* (2005), and *Modern American Drama: Playwriting in the 1950s* (2018). She has published articles on Sam Shepard, Tom Stoppard, Mae West, Tennessee Williams, Thornton Wilder, August Wilson, Eugene O'Neill, Lillian Hellman, and Paula Vogel in a variety of books and journals.

ARNOLD ARONSON is Professor Emeritus of Theatre at Columbia University in New York. His books include *The History and Theory of Environmental Scenography* (revised 2nd edition); *The Routledge Companion to Scenography* (editor); *Ming Cho Lee: A Life in Design*; *Looking into the Abyss: Essays on Scenography*; and *American Avant-Garde Theatre: A History*. Professor Aronson is a former editor of *Theatre Design & Technology* and currently coeditor of the journal *Theatre and Performance Design*. He has a long history with the Prague Quadrennial of Performance Design and Space and served as General Commissioner in 2007.

JESSICA SILSBY BRATER is Assistant Professor of Theatre and Coordinator of the BA and MA programs in Theatre Studies at Montclair State University, where she also oversees a graduate certificate in Theatre of Diversity, Inclusion, and Social Change. Publications include her book *Ruth Maleczech at Mabou Mines: Woman's Work* and chapters in *Contemporary Approaches to Adaptation in Theatre* and *Women, Collective Creation, and Devised Performance*. Her writing has also appeared in *Theatre Journal*, *Journal of American Drama and Theater*, and *Samuel Beckett Today/Aujourd'hui*. Forthcoming publications include chapters in *Analysing Gender in Performance*, *American Theatre Ensembles*, and *The Great North American Stage Directors*.

CHASE BRINGARDNER is Professor and Chairperson in the Department of Theatre at Auburn University. He specializes in the study of popular entertainments; regional identity construction; and intersections of race, gender, and class in popular performance forms. His publications include chapters in *The Oxford Companion to the Musical*; *Performing the Family Dream House: Space, Ritual, and Images of Home*; and *Performance and the Disney Theme Park*. He has published in a variety of journals, including *Theatre Topics*, *Theatre Journal*, *Studies in Musical Theatre*, *Performing Arts Resources*, and *Theatre Symposium*.

FAEDRA CHATARD CARPENTER is Associate Professor in the Department of Performing Arts at American University. She is a freelance dramaturg, theatre scholar, and cultural critic. As a professional dramaturg, Dr. Carpenter has worked with Mosaic Theater Company, Baltimore Center Stage, The John F. Kennedy Center for the Performing Arts, and Arena Stage. She is the author of *Coloring Whiteness: Acts of Critique in Black Performance*, and her scholarly articles have been published in *Theatre Topics*; *The Cambridge Companion to African American Theatre*; *Women & Performance*; *Callaloo: A Journal of African Diaspora Arts and Letters*; and *The Routledge Companion to Dramaturgy*, among others.

DAVID A. CRESPY is Professor of Playwriting, Acting, and Dramatic Literature at the University of Missouri and the founding Artistic Director of MU's Missouri Playwrights Workshop. Crespy codirects MU's award-winning Writing for Performance Program and is the founding president of the Edward Albee Society. Books include *The Off-Off Broadway Explosion* (2003); *Richard Barr: The Playwrights' Producer* (2013); *Lanford Wilson: Early Stories, Sketches, and Poems* (2017); and *Edward Albee as Theatrical and Dramatic Innovator,* co-edited with Lincoln Konkle (2019).

LAURA MACDONALD is Assistant Professor in the Residential College in the Arts and Humanities at Michigan State University. With William A. Everett, she edited *The Palgrave Handbook of Musical Theatre Producers* (2017). Together with Ryan Donovan, she is editing *The Routledge Companion to Musical Theatre*. Her articles and reviews have appeared in *Studies in Musical Theatre, Performance Research, The Journal of American Drama and Theatre, New England Theatre Journal, Theatre Research International, Theatre Journal,* and *Theatre Survey.* Her book project explores long-running Broadway musicals, marketing, and audiences.

ELIZABETH A. OSBORNE is Associate Professor in Theatre Studies at Florida State University, where she teaches courses in theatre history and historiography, dramaturgy, and contemporary theatre. Her work has appeared in *Theatre Survey, Theatre Topics,* and *Theatre History Studies.* She is author of *Staging the People: Community and Identity in the Federal Theatre Project,* coauthor of Revel for *Explore Theatre* (2nd edition) with Michael O'Hara and Judith Sebesta, and coeditor of *Working in the Wings: New*

Perspectives on Theatre History and Labor with Christine Woodworth. She is an editorial board member for the *Journal of American Theatre and Drama* and Immediate-Past-President of the Mid-America Theatre Conference.

CINDY ROSENTHAL is Professor of Drama and Dance at Hofstra University and a scholar, performer, and director. She coedited *Restaging the Sixties: Radical Theatres and Their Legacies*, *The Rise of Performance Studies: Rethinking Richard Schechner's Broad Spectrum*, and *The Sixties, Center Stage* with James Harding. With Julia Listengarten, she coedited *Modern American Drama: Playwriting 2000–2009*. She has written on political theatre, the avant-garde, ensembles, and contemporary playwrights and directors in the *New York Times*, *Performance Research*, *Women: A Cultural Review*, *Theatre Survey*, and *TDR*. Her monograph *Ellen Stewart Presents: Fifty Years of La Mama Experimental Theatre* won the 2017 George Freedley Prize.

TIMOTHY YOUKER is an independent theatre scholar. He has taught theatre and drama at Columbia University's Graduate School of the Arts, the Tisch School of the Arts at NYU, and the University of Toronto. His book *Documentary Vanguards in Modern Theatre* was published in 2018.

Acknowledgments

This book would not have been possible without the generous support and guidance of many people. We are grateful to Cambridge University Press publishers Kate Brett, who first invited us to spearhead this project, and Emily Hockley, who guided us through the process. Our contributors' firm commitment to the project from its inception to completion is appreciated, and we are greatly indebted to them for their willingness to participate in the book and share their scholarship and critical perspectives. Our graduate students Johann Robert Wood and Sage Tokach offered invaluable research assistance, and we thank them for their insight and dedication.

We also thank our academic institutions – University of Central Florida and Michigan State University – for providing resources that allowed us to complete the book. We acknowledge the role of ATHE and ASTR in shaping ideas that foregrounded this project; the conversations we had with our colleagues and students at conferences and in class discussions about the necessity to reexamine American theatre profoundly informed the direction of this undertaking.

And last, we express our gratitude to our families for their encouragement and patience. This book is dedicated to them.

Introduction

Julia Listengarten and Stephen Di Benedetto

Representing a vast array of voices and practices that developed in American theatre over the past seventy-five years is almost an impossible task. As we embarked on the journey of creating this companion, our goal was to consider key social and political touchpoints of each era, while staying conscious of changing contemporary perspectives that define the ways in which we revisit past theatre developments. Furthermore, in assembling ten original contributions, we felt an urgency to disrupt traditional historiography that perpetuates hierarchies of power and privileges overwhelmingly white male voices in post-1945 American theatre.

This volume discusses transformative artistic practices across racial and gender representation, which often resulted from rising social and political consciousness, and highlights multiple dialogues and disparate voices woven into the complex tapestry of American theatre. We craft our companion not around individual playwrights and influential theatre makers such as directors, actors, or designers; instead, we focus on collective practices and collaborative models in different artistic communities. The collaborative effort has become progressively more visible in American theatre of the last decades, and scholars and practitioners have begun to develop a vocabulary for describing how artistic teams operate, what choices have worked, and how they have transformed theatre. Discussing how these models work in a variety of markets and communities, the contributions provide a framework to reflect the multivocal and collaborative nature of theatre production and put into context the works of the renowned artists of the time.

In a volume that covers such a long period, there is always a question of what voices to include and how to best represent intersecting trends, overlapping narratives, and artistic dialogues across mainstream, regional, and experimental theatre. Examining voices and practices that were left outside standard theatre historiography, we are challenged to decenter what has been held up as seminal work. Our contributors recognize the significance of iconic plays of Eugene O'Neill, Arthur Miller, and Tennessee Williams and acknowledge the groundbreaking contributions of artistic visionaries such as Elia Kazan and Jo Mielziner. Rather than survey the best-known luminaries, though, the contributors select artists whose work exemplifies changes that have led to contemporary production and collaboration standards. The examples they consider often complement the better-known histories and give voice to the figures who have been largely neglected. Thus the volume focuses on the increasing presence of women and artists of color in theatre and drama since the mid-twentieth century, pointing to a paradigm shift toward diversity that has brought about a richly textured theatrical landscape in the twenty-first century. As the contributing writers engage with the historiographic task to reassess and reframe past theatre's legacy and its influence on contemporary theatrical developments, the volume considers the ways in which this growing diversity in theatre practice has inspired changing dramaturgical expressions and theatrical idioms.

In the seventy-five years after World War II, American theatre transformed significantly. Besides major shifts in Broadway and Off-Broadway theatres, Broadway itself progressively decentralized, and powerful movements such as Off-Off-Broadway and regional theatre emerged, giving voice to playwrights of color and experimenting with forms. Experimental theatre companies such as the Caffé Cino, the Living Theatre, the Open Theater, the San Francisco Mime Troupe, and La MaMa fostered diverse communities of theatre artists dedicated to debunking the aesthetic and political status quo. Fringe festivals, found spaces, and interdisciplinary performance events proliferated, often combining theatre innovation with popular entertainment. New technologies influenced theatre in unexpected ways, creating new possibilities for playwrights, directors, designers, and actors to tell stories, and transforming performance experiences for the audience. Driven by financial availability, technological innovation in design often took place in popular entertainments – concerts and Las Vegas extravaganzas – and, once popularized, influenced theatrical production. Grand lightshows and projected imagery led the way in touring mega-concerts, then slowly worked their way onto Broadway stages and regional and university theatres.

We organize our discussion of post-1945 theatre by employing three categories: commercial/mainstream theatre, regional theatre, and experimental theatre and other forms of entertainment. This structure anchors contributors' critical engagement with each category and gives them an opportunity to resist fixed categorization, defy binary framing, and explore practices at the intersections of the mainstream and the experimental. In recent scholarship, efforts to legitimatize community theatres, street performances, and popular touring theatrics have coincided with a stronger recognition of mutual influences between the popular and Broadway or the mainstream and experimental. This volume explores the ways in which different artistic trajectories intersect, blurring the borders that separate commercial enterprises from noncommercial theatre practices.

In conceiving this volume, we consulted with previously published companions on American theatre. Gerald Bordman and Thomas Hischak's *The Oxford Companion to American Theatre*[1] and Don B. Wilmeth's *Cambridge Guide to American Theatre*[2] provide a detailed discussion of theatre terms, plays, playwrights, and practitioners. Wilmeth and Christopher Bigsby's *Cambridge History of American Theatre: Volume III*[3] offers an insightful analysis of theatrical contexts from the end of World War II through the 1990s. Theresa Saxon's *American Theatre: History, Context, Form*[4] broadly addresses developments from the eighteenth through the twentieth centuries, offering a series of snapshots of a diverse American theatre. A more focused overview of the twentieth-century American drama, David Krasner's *A Companion to Twentieth-Century American Drama*,[5] looks at the development of literary themes in relation to major political underpinnings and theatrical contexts.

Our approach to this companion, however, has been closely guided by recent publications on American theatre that radically rethink the significance of collective creation, erase dichotomies of periphery and center, and reveal how theatres often maintain as well as challenge systems of power. Although not looking exclusively at American theatre, the trilogy on collective creation by Kathryn Mederos Syssoyeva and Scott Proudfit (*A History of Collective Creation*; *Collective Creation in Contemporary Performance*; and *Women, Collective Creation, and Devised Performance*)[6] affirms the central role of collective theatre practices and traces the journey of ensemble creation from margin to center. Mike Vanden Heuvel's two volumes on American ensemble theatres[7] reassess theatre process as a collaborative creation, challenging the notion of ensemble theatre as a linearly developed, somewhat homogenous practice, and disrupt the delineation between radical, politically driven collectives and "apolitical" ensembles. James Harding and Cindy Rosenthal, considering a transformative era in *The Sixties, Center Stage*, offer compelling case studies that demonstrate how "experimentation and anticonsumerism moved throughout [the decade] with great fluidity, traveling back and forth between the margins and mainstream."[8] Through her nuanced examination of the Arena Stage, a prominent regional theatre, Donatella Galella in *America in the Round: Capital, Race, and Nation at Washington DC's Arena Stage*[9] inspires a rigorous reevaluation of the regional theatre movement, particularly its engagement with both political forces and economic structures. Seminal histories of the avant-garde in America such as Theodore Shank's *Beyond the Boundaries: American Alternative Theatre*[10] and histories contextualizing American practice in relation to international practice such as Steve Dixon's *Digital Performance: A History of New Media in Theater, Dance, Performance Art, and Installation*[11] lay a foundation for analyzing avant-garde experimentation, its relationship to commercial theatre practice, and its influence on contemporary markets. Like this recent scholarship, our companion challenges the long-established binaries that separate center from periphery, popular from experimental, political from apolitical, and profit from nonprofit.

In Part I, "Commercial and Mainstream Theatre," this companion outlines developments in Broadway and Off-Broadway theatre markets and observes how shifts in economics, politics, and demographics have influenced changes in aesthetics and collaborative methods. The four chapters describe how varied collaborative models fostered more inclusive theatrical practices and more diverse dramaturgies and theatrical style, representing the voices and histories of various American communities at the intersections of mainstream and experimental theatre. Placing theatre in dialogue with social movements, this section depicts a wealth of mainstream American theatre over the seventy-five years when Broadway maintained its vital role by continuing to redefine itself. As Broadway was compelled to respond to a shifting national narrative and socioeconomic pressures, it often found itself engaging innovative artistic voices, diversifying its repertoire, and expanding its audience to include multigenerational and racially diverse patrons. The four scholars in this section identify pivotal moments in the trajectories of Broadway and Off-Broadway that defined key developments in mainstream theatre. They describe troubling labor practices and point to the increasing role of corporations in economic and artistic decisions in mainstream theatre. Also, they provide multiple perspectives on theatrical expressions, organizational and artistic hierarchies, and collaborative methodologies, revealing a complicated history in which commercial and innovative patterns frequently converge on Broadway and Off-Broadway.

As Susan C. W. Abbotson argues in "Broadway Post-1945 to 1960: Shifting Perspectives," the period can be characterized as a Golden Age for American theatre, when Broadway emerged as a major force in developing themes and theatrical styles that explored what it meant to be distinctly American, but also challenged American exceptionalism and rising xenophobia. Her chapter establishes a historical framework for post-1945 developments in theatre and drama, offers an overview of theatrical and dramaturgical innovations amid social and economic anxieties, and highlights Broadway's expansion of topics and styles. The chapter strikes a delicate balance between paying tribute to mid-century figures such as Williams, Miller, and William Inge and revising the canon to include women and artists of color. Arguing that Williams, Miller, and Inge "collectively created a distinctively American theatre that traversed and reflected the entire nation," Abbotson demonstrates how these playwrights offered ways to rethink the genre of family drama and address the themes of individual conscience and collective responsibility during the McCarthy era. But she also directs attention to the rise of women's voices in American playwriting. Lillian Hellman's progressive politics pushed the boundaries of American narrative to address homophobia, greed, and inequality. Black playwrights Alice Childress and Lorraine Hansberry exposed the country's systemic racism, shattered racial stereotypes that dominated mainstream American culture, and paved the ground for many playwrights of color to define a multivocal theatre.

Abbotson identifies significant moments in the development of musical and nonmusical theatre on Broadway, underscoring the powerful contributions of women artists who worked alongside their male counterparts to experiment with new artistic techniques and methodologies. The list of legendary theatre innovators and collaborative teams of the period often includes Kazan, designers Mielziner and Boris Aronson, and visionary musical theatre producers, directors, and choreographers such as George Abbott, Hal Prince, and Bob Fosse. The chapter examines their contributions but also emphasizes the compelling legacies of Cheryl Crawford, Margaret Webster, Mary Hunter, and Dorothy Fields, among others, in reinventing American theatre.

The dialogue between mainstream and experimental stages is at the heart of Cindy Rosenthal's "Bridging the Gap: Broadway and the Experimental from the 1960s to 2020," in which she identifies key theatre developments in each decade and positions them in relation to social and economic characteristics. Her chapter engages with the critical term "the mainstream experimental" that she and Harding introduced in *The Sixties, Center Stage* to demonstrate how in the 1960s "Broadway musicals, mainstream dramas, and experimental performances all participated in a complex dialogue about politics, society, and culture."[12] In this chapter,

Rosenthal extends this reexamination of a complicated dynamic between commercial and noncommercial theatre beyond the decade of the 1960s into the present time. She traces the dynamic to the artistically and commercially successful rock musical *Hair*. First produced at the Public Theater in 1967 and moved to Broadway in 1968, *Hair* triggered the transfer of productions from the Public Theater to Broadway, under the leadership of Joseph Papp and, later, George C. Wolfe and Oskar Eustis, who championed artistic innovation and pushed for bold, uncompromising representations of diverse voices. As Rosenthal examines major transfers from nonmainstream stages to Broadway, she reflects on how socially minded and artistically innovative musicals and plays such as *Bring in 'da Noise, Bring in 'da Funk*; *Angels in America*; *Topdog/Underdog*; *Caroline, or Change*; *Hamilton*; *Fun Home*; and *Eclipsed* "moved identity politics and the energies and explorations of diverse makers center-stage on Broadway, and into the mainstream."

The chapter traces how theatre has responded to the pivotal moments in post-1960 American history: the 1960s civil rights protests, the impact of the AIDS epidemic, the rise of Third Wave feminism, the terrorist attacks of 9/11, and the recent Black Lives Matter and LGBTQ+ movements. Rosenthal pays particular attention to Black and LGBTQ+ theatre artists – Ntozake Shange, August Wilson, George C. Wolfe, Anna Deavere Smith, Danai Gurira, Jeremy O. Harris, Larry Kramer, Tony Kushner, and Lisa Kron – whose work exemplifies productive crossovers between innovative theatre practices and commercial theatre developments. A long-standing commitment by innovative theatre makers and activists to diversify the Broadway audience has led to many bold artistic and financial decisions to strengthen multiracial and multigenerational audience engagement. Rosenthal contemplates the shifting demographics of the mainstream theatre audience and describes the Broadway productions of *Bring in 'da Noise* (1996) and *Rent* (1996) as the "mainstream experimental" examples of the 1990s theatre, signaling "a new wave of 'street' musicals that spoke to and of the energies, spirit, passions, and desires of Generation X." The Broadway productions of *Hamilton* (2015), *Eclipsed* (2016), and *Slave Play* (2019), which deeply engaged with issues of racial and gender inequality, are more recent attempts to confront Broadway's economic stratification and reach out to young people and communities of color who otherwise would not afford the prohibitive cost of tickets. Arguing that "mainstream/ commercial theatre today continues to push the culture forward as it did in the 1960s, often in ways that sometimes the experimental realm cannot," Rosenthal remarks that in the case of *Slave Play*, "more folks had a voice in the conversation, and . . . a wider and more diverse and younger-skewing demographic took a seat at the discussion table."

The development of artistic practices in post-1945 American theatre is directly connected to the changing principles of creative collaboration informed by theatrical innovations, economic considerations, and social contexts. How do new theatrical forms and funding structures inform collaboration in theatre? How do unique collaborative models foster and activate different kinds of socially relevant theatrical practices? These questions figure prominently in the chapters by Laura MacDonald and Jessica Silsby Brater, who examine how various collaborative relationships reflected major shifts in developing theatrical material. MacDonald's "What's Inside? Collaborative Relationships at the Heart of the American Musical" looks at the evolution of American musical theatre through transforming creative collaboration. Beginning with *Oklahoma!* (1943), "a watershed in musical theatre history," and ending with the groundbreaking *Hamilton*, MacDonald illustrates how "practitioners assembled creative teams in response to shifting economics, audience demographics, and the rise of mediated popular culture on television and the internet." Hierarchies shifted to favor musical theatre directors and choreographers such as Prince and Jerome Robbins; to include performers' voices, stories, and perspectives during the developmental workshop phases of *A Chorus Line* (1975) or *Hamilton* (2015) at the Public Theater; and to diversify themes, styles, and demographics through women directors (Julie Taymor and Diane Paulus, to name two) and artists of color, such as Lin-Manuel Miranda. Broadway musical theatre investors and producers, however, often usurp power over directors and choreographers, and Disney and other international corporations play an increasingly bigger role in musical theatre development.

MacDonald also draws attention to inequitable labor practices that continue to affect musical theatre creation, as they did when Agnes de Mille, the first woman choreographer on Broadway, worked on the original production of *Oklahoma!* "Conscious of innovators such as de Mille being undervalued and underrecognized as the legacy of their musicals extended," MacDonald writes, "their successors would become more mindful of contracts, royalties, and billing." Disputes over appropriate financial remuneration still pervade complicated contract negotiations when musicals transfer from Off-Broadway or regional theatres to Broadway stages. Drawing parallels between *A Chorus Line* and *Hamilton*, MacDonald shows how original performers who developed these productions felt neglected and underpaid when the shows moved uptown and became commercial hits. For *Hamilton*, though, an agreement was reached to grant actors and stage managers in the Public Theater run "a retroactive share of 1 percent of net profits" from the Broadway production and a smaller share of future shows.

Brater, in "Shaping Broadway and Off-Broadway Plays through Collaborations: Playwrights, Directors, Designers, and Companies," focuses on diverse dramaturgical voices and styles that arose after 1960 from playwrights' interactions with other theatre makers and organizations. She investigates six collaborative models that reveal multiple negotiations, disruptions, and tensions that permeate creative process but also offer ways to consider the relationship between artistic practices and new work. Putting the playwright at center of the creative process, Brater investigates how this center continues to shift, enforcing or eroding traditional hierarchies. Examples range from more conventional collaborative practices, which maintain the boundaries of the playwright-director-designer involvement, to collectively conceived and guided creative interactions in which the roles of theatre makers intersect and the boundaries blur. The relationship among playwright Edward Albee, director Alan Schneider, and set designer William Ritman, who worked on Broadway and Off-Broadway on a handful of Albee's plays, including *The American Dream* and *Who's Afraid of Virginia Woolf?*, represents a more traditional artistic hierarchy, maintaining the primacy of the dramatic text and supporting the playwright's vision. A decade-long collaboration between playwright Sam Shepard and director Robert Woodruff at the Magic Theatre in San Francisco and the Public Theater in New York in the 1970s and 1980s advanced a workshop setting in regional and Off-Broadway theatres, in which work was conceived and fostered under less stringent pressures for commercial success. The collaboration of August Wilson and Lloyd Richards at the Eugene O'Neill Theater Center in Waterford, Connecticut, inspired the tremendous growth of African American theatre. Wilson's early writing – his work on *Ma Rainey's Black Bottom* and *Fences* – is closely connected to the O'Neill Center, where Richards served as artistic director from 1968 to 1999 and cultivated many playwrights.

Moving chronologically and across commercial and experimental venues, Brater's discussion of artistic practices shifts to examination of collaborative dynamics between women artists. A leading voice in experimental theatre and a revered mentor of Latinx playwrights, dramatist, director, and visual artist Maria Irene Fornes disrupted traditional hierarchies by blurring the director-playwright distinction and elevating the role of theatre designers in play/production development; she encouraged them to "shape the space and the language of her plays." Rooted in a more traditional practice in which the director sees herself "outside of the writing process," an enduring partnership between playwright Suzan-Lori Parks and director Liz Diamond at the Yale Repertory Theatre and Public Theater led to innovations in playwriting and staging, largely driven by Parks's commitment to explore Black history and reexamine Black identity through nonlinear storytelling and poetic language. The Yale Repertory productions of *The Death of the Last Black Man in the Whole Entire World* (1992) and *The America Play* (1994) are among their works that created transformative experiences for the audience and laid the groundwork for experimentation across race and gender. Playwright Paula Vogel and director Rebecca Taichman brought to Broadway an acclaimed production, *Indecent* (2017), a riveting love story between two women. The product of five years of "workshopping and collaboration," their work is a compelling example of "a highly inclusive development process."

Part II, "Regional Theatre Movement," examines the pivotal role of regional theatres in supporting playwrights' development of work that serves diverse audiences in local regions, considers the impact of economic, social, and artistic factors on regional theatre, and questions the narrative that characterizes regional theatres in opposition to commercial Broadway. Offering a nuanced reading of the regional theatre movement, the three chapters in this section highlight the centrality of regional theatres in American theatre history, reveal challenges and tensions that have accompanied their development, and envision ways to strengthen their place in local and national theatre communities.

Elizabeth A. Osborne's "Money Matters: Dismantling the Narrative of the Rise of Regional Theatre" challenges the view that regional companies are "financially stable sellouts or artistically brilliant destitutes." Through case studies of Theatre '47 in Dallas, the Alley Theatre in Houston, Arena Stage in Washington, DC, and the Guthrie Theatre in Minneapolis, Osborne shows how these regional theatres navigated various artistic and economic circumstances, "offer[ing] different financial approaches and structures, based on leadership styles, ideological goals, and community needs." Drawing on the contributions of Margo Jones, Nina Vance, Zelda Fichandler, and Tyrone Guthrie, artistic directors who led the development of regional theatres in the mid-twentieth century, Osborne illustrates how the movement played a major role in decentering Broadway, engaging with local communities, and cementing the core of American national theatre. She argues, however, that these artists created regional theatre companies not solely because of a desire to break from commercially driven theatre to produce socially minded work or experiment with new forms. Their motives ranged from a commitment to foster a network of regional theatres, to respond to community needs, and to build a highly professional nonprofit theatre. While leading regional theatre companies, these directors often continued to stay in dialogue with Broadway, directing Broadway shows, hiring company members from Broadway, or transferring their productions to Broadway stages. As Osborne considers how regional theatres constantly negotiate between the creative and the economic, she builds on the concept of the "mainstream experimental," showing how artistic practices that produced pioneering work often converged with the companies' goals of commercial success.

Major national foundations, such as Ford, Rockefeller, and Mellon, and local funders have always played a key role in supporting regional theatre. But "lack of control over the markets and culture wars that decimate public funding" imperil regional theatres, especially as funding structures often privilege rich companies that produce work for white upper-middle-class audiences over "community-centered, culturally specific groups [which] remain chronically underfunded," Osborne observes. As theatres nationwide closed in March 2020 because of the COVID-19 pandemic, more questions emerged about regional theatres' sustainability and the necessity to reimagine their funding models in a postpandemic landscape.

Diverse voices – Black, Latinx, Asian American, LGBTQ+ among them – proliferated in post-1960 American theatre, primarily in regional communities. Responding to the rise of social consciousness and engaging with social activism and political unrest in the 1960s and beyond, playwrights such as August Wilson, Parks, Kushner, Wendy Wasserstein, Henry David Hwang, and José Rivera, whose work often originated in regional theatres, grappled with racism, colonialism, homophobia, religious intolerance, and gender discrimination. Faedra Chatard Carpenter's "When and Where They Enter: Black and Brown Voices in American Theatre" highlights regional theatres' promotion of diverse representations of American cultures and identities. Positioning Amiri Baraka and Luis Valdez at the forefront of Black and Chicano theatre movements, she notes the invaluable contributions of women of color who "have tilled, labored, and harvested just like their male counterparts, thereby creating further avenues for those – of various identificatory categories – to follow." But Carpenter, cautioning against the oversimplification of diversity and inclusion, and the assertion of "monolithic paradigms of identity," encourages discussion of race, ethnicity, gender, sexuality, class, disability, religion, and age, "among the many identificatory categories that need to be considered when honoring the politics and experiences of difference." As she reminds us, "documenting the story of diverse voices in American Theatre is, like all historical narratives, a challenge that is inescapably compromised by archival gaps and silences." Analyzing plays by Fornes, Adrienne Kennedy, Lynn Nottage, and Quiara Alegría Hudes, Carpenter demonstrates how their work defies easy classification in identity politics and racial representation. They reveal nuances, tensions, and contradictions in their communities to "counter qualitative judgments related to 'whiteness' or 'blackness' or 'brownness' … [and] challenge previously held definitions of what constitutes a culturally specific play."

In the larger context of the regional theatre movement, play development has become entrenched in companies' economic, social, and artistic structures. David A. Crespy closely examines a complex system of commissions, grant-writing, and collaborative practices in developing new work in regional theatres. "El Jardín Mágico: Commissions, Collaboration, and New Play Development in American Regional Theatre" describes the arduous process that playwrights are compelled to endure to get their work commissioned, developed, and produced, often by different theatres in succession. Crespy offers snapshots of play development by experimental director-playwrights Carey Perloff and JoAnne Akalaitis, and the frequently produced regional theatre playwright Lauren Gunderson. He directs careful attention to Latinx playwright Elaine Romero, whose work has been tied to regional companies including the Arizona Theatre Company, Chicago's Goodman Theatre, Houston's Alley Theatre, and most recently the O'Neill Center. A recipient of multiple grants and fellowships, Romero exemplifies the high-producing mid-career playwright who has effectively navigated the complicated network of play development over the past twenty years. Crespy offers a detailed account of Romero's achievements, illustrating American regional theatre as fertile ground for new and exciting work, but he also raises difficult questions about economics and artistic growth.

Part III, "Experimental Theatre and Other Forms of Entertainment," considers the shifting practices of avant-garde performance, ranging from happenings, street theatre, underground theatre, and theatre for social change since 1945. Experimental theatre practices from one generation often become mainstream practices in the next. From Cirque du Soleil's touring circus tents and Blue Man Group's storefront performances in Manhattan to purpose-built stages in Las Vegas and giant exhibitions at Universal Studios in Orlando, Florida, experimental forms have instigated novel relationships between performance and audience that continue to push other forms of theatre in new directions. The three contributions in this section of the companion explore how techniques developed outside conventional commercial venues have led to innovation at the center, replicating a pattern where the periphery breeds innovation that is absorbed into the mainstream.

Timothy Youker's "Experimental Collectives of the 1960s and Their Legacies" charts the development of work that serves as a foundation for the post-avant-garde and digital experimentation. Experimental ensembles worked "against the rigid, homogenizing structures of the corporation, the nuclear family, and the military" to explore "alternative modes of community and nonhierarchical approaches to making plays." Models for ensemble creation by the Living Theatre, The Performance Group, the Open Theater, and the San Francisco Mime Troupe influenced creation and playwriting in companies such as Spiderwoman, the Wooster Group, SITI, Pig Iron, and the Tectonic Theater Project. Community building and experimental innovation, not financial success, drove production for experimental companies that were able to sustain themselves largely because of Ford Foundation philanthropy. With boundary-breaking attention to the elements of production, in which text, speech, movement, scenography, and theme became a *gesamtkunstwerk*, these theatres challenged the divisions between actors and audience. Theatres' found space aesthetic, in which environments were adapted for performance, disregarding conventional illusionistic scenographic expectations, determined Off-Off-Broadway's relationship to space.

More recent work since the 1990s demonstrates that collective creation is central to contemporary practice, and that contemporary ensembles' varying systems, methods, and multidisciplinary approaches to composition are a legacy of 1960s artistic and political rebellion. Youker identifies the common characteristics of recent ensemble-based companies that include "striving for an egalitarian rehearsal space, equalizing the expressive elements of theatre, seeking a dramatic structure that fits the thematic and aesthetic goals of a specific piece instead of defaulting to a linear dramatic plot, and . . . treating audience and space as components of a performance rather than external to it."

Further exploring collective creation, Arnold Aronson's "Post-Avant-Garde Theatre" examines the ways in which theatre and performance experiment with visual and digital technology, making possible new dramaturgical modes, fragmented narrative, and the means of affecting audience responses to the world. Tracing the transformation of avant-garde practice away from its traditional goals into the post-avant-garde mode influenced by mass media, he defines the post-avant-garde as an extension of "experimentation, innovation, the search for new forms of expression, or attempts to alter our perception of the world." Development of the American post-avant-garde is rooted within the practices of the Ontological-Hysteric Theatre and the Wooster Group. Richard Foreman's and Elizabeth LeCompte's companies nurtured subsequent generations through internships and financial support that enabled experimentation. Rather than argue that avant-garde is "dead," Aronson shows that recent experimental theatres foster a framework that incorporates "electronic and digital media into live performance often co-equal with or dominant over the human actors."

Recent experimental companies mined "ideas and practices derived from the visual arts, performance art, American avant-garde cinema, video art, modern philosophy, popular culture, contemporary psychology (notably Lacan) . . . to create work that was essentially unlike anything that came before and that rejected the highly physical, ensemble-based theatre that had dominated the experimental theatre world of the 1960s." Collectives such as Collapsable Giraffe, The Builders Association, Big Art Group, and theatre, performance, and visual artists such as Jay Scheib, Laurie Anderson, Andrew Schneider, Hsin-Chien Huang, Annie Dorsen, and Richard Maxwell stretched notions of dramaturgy and audience experience. Performances based in the technological and the physical "aimed to disrupt the conventional relationship of spectator to performance," and, as Aronson argues, the introduction of "the digital to the theatre allowed for the disintegration of temporal and visual continuity and coherence – all of which constituted a crucial aspect of the post-avant-garde." These experiences at the periphery of audience consumption continue to find their way into mainstream performance, particularly in popular entertainments.

As experimental theatre practices influenced generations of artists, popular entertainments engage with contemporary media to craft spectacles and immersive experiences that transform our perception of twenty-first-century America. Chase Bringardner's "Populist Provocations and Commercial Cavalcades: Popular Entertainments and the Rise of Mass Mediated Performance" considers how forms such as the circus, Las Vegas spectacles, the modern pop/rock concert, living history museums, and theme parks helped reshape forms and methodologies of theatrical engagement by exploring novel uses of technology, narrative, authenticity, and audience engagement.

"Popular entertainments … engage in a critical conversation … [about] the relationship between the human and technology … [and] stage interactions between technologies and humans, re/performing history, challenging the limits of the body, and re/defining and re/creating spectacle," Bringardner writes. The financially successful extravaganzas of the Ringling Brothers and Barnum and Bailey Circus and Cirque du Soleil prompted investment in technological innovations later adopted in mainstream theatre. Creative teams incorporated design and technology from lucrative Las Vegas shows in the 1980s and 1990s into concerts by artists such as Madonna, U2, and Taylor Swift, paving the way for theatre's technological advancements: "The hazer that emits atmospheric fog as Beyoncé appears on an arena stage also helps create the ice effect as Elsa builds her ice castle in the *Frozen* musical."

The contributors to our companion examine social and economic contexts, themes, demographics, and collaborative teams to navigate the landscape of post-1945 American theatre. What, they ask, does that history look like alongside the resurgence of women in the workplace and the rise of civil rights? How does the representation of multiple narratives in theatre make visible diverse communities and blur the line between popular performance and legitimate drama? Excavating past practices in mainstream, regional, experimental, and popular forms that serve as models for present theatre developments, they reveal overlooked artistic contributions pivotal to shaping the trajectory of theatre – for example, women artists, whose uncredited or overshadowed labor built some of the most influential regional and experimental theatres, and playwrights whose portrayals of their communities have become key to contemporary explorations of race, gender, and sexuality.

The story of American theatre, our chapters demonstrate, is not just a story of Broadway. It is a story of artists and communities that speak in many voices, present various perspectives, and intersect the traditional with the experimental – all to model collaborative practices, create spaces, produce theatre to meet the needs of their audiences, and find ways to sustain their art. They face a future that, as we write in mid-2020, is clouded because of COVID-19. With the closure of theatres and the disappearance of funding, artists and companies have had to find other avenues to stay active and keep themselves afloat. Our story of how past generations transformed theatre amid political and economic challenges, however, gives us reason for optimism about the theatre that will emerge from the crisis.

Notes

1. G. Bordman and T. S. Hischak, *The Oxford Companion to American Theatre* (Oxford University Press, 2004).
2. D. B. Wilmeth (ed.), *The Cambridge Guide to American Theatre*, 2nd ed. (Cambridge University Press, 2007).
3. D. B. Wilmeth and C. Bigsby (eds.), *Cambridge History of American Theatre: Volume 3; Post World War II to the 1990s* (Cambridge University Press, 2006).
4. T. Saxon, *American Theatre: History, Context, Form* (Edinburgh University Press, 2011).
5. D. Krasner (ed.), *A Companion to Twentieth-Century American Drama* (Blackwell, 2005).
6. K. M. Syssoyeva and S. Proudfit (eds.), *A History of Collective Creation* (Palgrave Macmillan, 2013); *Collective Creation in Contemporary Performance* (Palgrave Macmillan, 2013); and *Women, Collective Creation, and Devised Performance* (Palgrave Macmillan, 2015).
7. M. Vanden Heuvel (ed.), *American Ensemble Theatres*, 2 vols. (Methuen Drama, forthcoming).
8. J. M. Harding and C. Rosenthal (eds.), *The Sixties, Center Stage: Mainstream and Popular Performances in a Turbulent Decade* (University of Michigan Press, 2017), p. 7.
9. D. Galella, *America in the Round: Capital, Race, and Nation at Washington DC's Arena Stage* (University of Iowa Press, 2019).
10. T. Shank, *Beyond the Boundaries: American Alternative Theatre* (University of Michigan Press, 2002).
11. S. Dixon, *Digital Performance: A History of New Media in Theater, Dance, Performance Art, and Installation* (MIT Press, 2007).
12. Harding and Rosenthal, *The Sixties, Center Stage*, p. 13.

PART I

Commercial and Mainstream Theatre

CHAPTER I

Broadway Post-1945 to 1960
Shifting Perspectives

Susan C. W. Abbotson

Despite global recognition of American drama afforded by Eugene O'Neill's 1936 Nobel Prize, it would not be until after World War II that American theatre took flight, came into its own, and developed its own distinctive identity. These postwar years through to 1960 can be viewed as a Golden Age for American drama as new plays, new staging, and new acting styles emerged that could be viewed as distinctly American and would become increasingly influential worldwide. Though developed through the exigencies of this particular period, what audiences witnessed would provide benchmarks for future American theatrical productions in every decade to follow.

Although the Federal Theater Project had been shut down in 1939 and Group Theatre had disbanded in 1941, these theatrical pioneers had offered productive training and proving grounds, as well as excellent sounding boards for ideas and talent that would continue to grow as America began to prosper financially and become able and willing to support a more specialized theatre. Also, the Theatre Guild, established in 1918, encouraged theatrical excellence into the 1970s and sponsored many burgeoning playwrights. When coupled with the tremendous optimism of an age in which the United States had emerged as a world superpower – concerned with establishing its own cultural exceptionalism and validating its sociopolitical beliefs – we witness American artists of the period determined to create both drama and musical theatre that were uniquely their own.

Changing social and political forces in the nation inspired dramatists to rewrite what was possible on an American stage, and plays of the time expanded on themes, styles, and character types previously witnessed as they began to explore the varied mosaic of American types and concerns and eschew mere entertainment for personal and national scrutiny and contemplation. Edward Albee defines this collective aim in his description of how Arthur Miller's plays "hold a mirror up to us, saying, 'This is who you are. If you don't like what you see don't look away. Change!'"[1] These playwrights were assisted by the introduction of new techniques that brought greater realism and depth to how actors performed, as well as innovations in directing and stage design. The American musical was wholly reinvented, with the "book" becoming a virtual necessity to craft strong narrative arcs over previously episodic sketches and adding an additional voice into the teams that conceived these productions. Musicals of this period experimented with darker material and more advanced choreography and composition, melding together story, character, lyric, music, and dance to form a perfectly integrated whole that would inspire all musicals to come.

Many of the period's theatrical successes and innovations were fueled by groups of creative artists – enthused by those earlier theatrical pioneers – whose collective vision helped bring these new scripts, scores, and aesthetics to the stage. Though white males continued to dominate the theatrical field, and equal rights still seemed distant, women and minoritized groups began to make strides in writing, directing, and producing drama in mainstream theatres. It was becoming clear that women had a place in every aspect of mounting a play, and the work of several African Americans led the way for Lorraine Hansberry's *A Raisin in the Sun* to become the first play written by a Black woman and directed by a Black director, Lloyd Richards – who also helped advance other Black playwrights – to become a Broadway smash in 1959 and point to the need for greater diversity in theatre. Sadly, Asian Americans and Latin Americans had yet to make such inroads as their stage representations over this period were created by nonethnic writers, who, despite becoming more sympathetic, had the tendency to create fetishized stereotypes. Nevertheless, the period began the move toward a fuller exploration of American multiculturalism.

Despite a contraction of venues and productions from earlier in the century – many of which had been focused on entertainment rather than "art" – the period saw Broadway establishing its primacy in both musical and nonmusical theatre, remaining strong against the inroads of movies and television. Due to rising costs and changing tastes, Broadway's audiences were becoming increasingly elite, and thus economic changes and artistic aspiration also eventually fueled the growth of Off-Broadway, Off-Off-Broadway, and a future growth of regional theatre to help create an even more vibrant national theatre for the future. Many of these regional companies would entertain resident artists and produce new plays alongside classics and other contemporary works and so ensure that people need not travel to New York to see a decent play.

Economic, Social, and Political Challenges

After World War II, America had become a leading world superpower with economic and population booms to support this new identity. Unemployment stood around 4.6 percent, with continued military spending from both the Cold and Korean Wars to keep the economy buoyant. The democratic American image of freedom and prosperity was spread globally, enhanced by media that depicted an opulent suburban American lifestyle, glossing over the inequities of continued segregation. Society was vastly altered by this postwar prosperity and the surface conformism of a growing middle class determined to grasp a bright new American future. This was modeled around the perfect nuclear family, while holding at bay the demons of communism, the atom bomb, and juvenile delinquency. These common fears were fed by radio and television programs, films, magazines, and newspapers, all eager to cash in on being able to grab the nation's attention, and to that end would often oversensationalize their stories. Not surprisingly, there was a corresponding growth in psychoanalysis and tranquilizers as people tried to deal with the stress of living in a growingly materialistic society in which postwar xenophobia encouraged everyone to "buy American." As corporate profits tripled and American per capita income more than doubled, many could afford to do this, though not all shared in the general prosperity, and discrimination remained evident regardless of a rise in education and literacy.

Despite prosperity, these were mentally uncomfortable times; brutalities uncovered during the war had sorely tested people's trust in humanity, and rampant consumerism caused new jealousies and social divides. Alan Petigny suggests that while publicly, many conformed to conservative middle-class ideals and quietly lived in suburbs with their large families, attending church and avoiding radical politics, conservatism was losing ground and, privately, attitudes toward sex, parenting, and religion were moving away from a traditional conservative framework.[2] However, when Alfred Kinsey's *Sexual Behavior in the Human Male* appeared in 1947, people were shocked by his exposure of the gap between actual sexual practices and what people wanted to believe. His 1953 sequel, *Sexual Behavior in the Human Female*, which dared to suggest that premarital sex led to more successful marriages, was met with furious disagreement, and he lost his funding; but even Kinsey could not bring himself to normalize homosexuality. People wanted to be titillated, possibly fueling the growing popularity of playwrights such as Tennessee Williams, but they were not yet ready to openly discuss sexual issues; that would not occur for at least another decade.

In the 1940s, many women had moved into the workplace to help with the war effort, but with the return of the men, who were fearful of being replaced, there was retrenchment; women were once more relegated to home and family. Even while nearly 50 percent of wives worked for at least some period during their marriage (no doubt to afford those extra luxuries), gender roles remained pretty rigid – underscored by toys, cookbooks, magazines, and the rest of consumer culture – and only heterosexual relationships had societal approval; little did drama of the period directly challenge any of this. Again, it would not be until after the upheavals of the civil rights era that these issues could be more openly explored.

Referring to the practice of making accusations of subversion or treason without real evidence, the term "McCarthyism" is possibly Senator Joseph McCarthy's biggest legacy. His grandstanding demands to investigate people he suspected of communism, coupled with hearings called by Congress's House Un-American Activities Committee (HUAC), became a polarizing feature of American history. Hounding people for their past connections to the Communist Party, and forcing many to give the names of friends to save their own careers, HUAC fed a political and social paranoia that distorted American freedoms throughout the 1950s. The harsh treatment of the group of producers, directors, and screenwriters who became known as the Hollywood Ten – who were refused the protection of the First Amendment regarding the right to free speech when called to testify before HUAC and who were sent to jail for up to a year – scared many into going along with whatever the Committee asked. During this time, the entertainment industry became fiercely divided between those who gave names and those who refused. More than 300 actors, writers, and directors were denied work in America through the informal blacklist that evolved. Some left the country to find opportunities, while others wrote under pseudonyms or the names of colleagues: Dalton Trumbo was unable to claim the Oscars for his screenplays *Roman Holiday* (1953) and *The Brave One* (1956) because he had been forced to use another name.

The theatre was less targeted by HUAC – whose energies focused on those involved in film and television – and blacklisting never became official on Broadway as it had in Hollywood, but as Brenda Murphy insists, "the show business investigations had a tremendous effect on American drama and theatre between 1947 and 1960," becoming a "persistent subtext" in many plays of the period.[3] Arthur Miller bravely addressed what he saw as the dangers of mob rule and an overly conservative governance through dramas that include his translation of Henrik Ibsen's *An Enemy of the People* (1950) and *The Crucible* (1953), but his was not a solitary voice. Even light comedy, such as John Van Druten's *Bell, Book and Candle* (1950), contains commentary on the ridiculousness of the HUAC activities with its references to hexes and witch hunts, and Jerome Lawrence and Robert E. Lee provided several popular works that centered on people taking a stance against limiting individual freedom, satirizing self-serving authoritarians. American drama was not afraid to critique its own culture and, given a constitutional right to freedom of speech, could not be silenced. The issue of American freedom was also growing among the country's varied ethnic groups.

In the first half of the century, the Jewish population of America had quintupled, and by 1950, it was 5 million, which constituted almost half of the world's Jewry after the atrocities of the Holocaust. Anti-Semitism was on the decline but still evident, and so many Jews became more "secular" or fully assimilated, an option not available for those of color still dealing with Jim Crow laws in the South. Incidents of racial violence were common throughout the era, including the awful lynching of Emmett Till, and membership in the Ku Klux Klan was on the rise. However, there was also Rosa Parks's refusal to leave her seat that led to the Montgomery bus boycott and the desegregation of public transport, the government-enforced desegregation of schools in Little Rock, and the welcome rise of Martin Luther King Jr. While the major social changes of the civil rights era would not be enacted until the 1960s, much of the groundwork was being laid, both in the real world and on the American stage.

Play Production and Demographics

At the turn of the century, many cities had resident theatre companies, with more than 2,000 professional establishments across the country. New plays could spring up anywhere, although the majority were entertaining escapism rather than the explorations of humanity and ideas that would become common after World War II and put American theatre on the map. However, the growing importance of New York City as a producing center, coupled with the lower costs of touring and a desire to see longer runs of a single production, led to a small section of Manhattan that came to be known as Broadway becoming the center of American theatre, to which most talent was drawn. At this time, many regional theatres closed as people just wanted to see the latest Broadway hit; the few that remained were predominantly amateur, summer stock, or used for Broadway tryouts.

By the 1920s, Broadway consisted of 70 to 80 theatres that produced more than 250 plays a season, many imported from abroad, and often with huge casts. Fifteen daily papers meant that most productions could win one critic's support to help keep them running, but as Brooks Atkinson points out, "when Broadway was at its best, the awful plays were still in the majority."[4] After the war, rising property costs made theatres expensive real estate, and many were converted into more lucrative properties. Changing postwar finances also drove up the cost of producing a play to ten times that of prewar rates; it now cost $60,000 to mount a straight play, while a musical cost $250,000. The break-even point had risen to around 200 performances for a play and 300 for a musical. Producers were gamblers, but while a hit play could return the initial investment fourfold, only 20 percent recouped their initial investment. Broadway suffered a severe contraction despite the population of New York City more than doubling in the first half of the century, and by 1950–51, around thirty theatres were left, and new productions had dwindled to an annual total of eighty-seven.[5] While the number of theatres would rise, the number of new productions would halve by the close of the century, and Broadway theatre would become a venue predominantly for out-of-towners.

In 1948, state law was changed to make Sunday performances legal to try to increase the profit line. Only seven daily papers remained, which made it more imperative to win critical approval as, given the increased running costs, shows needed to make a profit swiftly to stay open, and this would only worsen by the century's end. By the close of the 1940s, one-third of attendees had become out-of-town visitors who might see as many as five shows during their stay. Some cities organized "show trains" that combined travel and tickets into one easy package. Broadway was becoming a more upper-middle-class venue, with less than 10 percent of attendees identifying themselves as "working class" and ticket prices averaging eight times those of movie attendance. People also no longer dressed for the theatre, and dramatic tastes had changed.

Theatre box offices reflected a growing lack of enthusiasm for foreign plays, with Agatha Christie's suspenseful courtroom drama *Witness for the Prosecution* (1954) being one of the few imported successes. American audiences wanted to see American plays that were not escapist but dealt with current American issues. Responding to the uncertainties of the times, even comedies and musicals began to demand a more serious edge. Atkinson suggests that "during the war, the public mood had changed.

Plays in styles that had been acceptable before the war no longer interested the public."[6] He illustrates his point by noting how *Life with Mother* (1948), the sequel to the runaway smash comedy of 1939 *Life with Father*, despite having the same writers and lead actors, was a flop.

The biggest-selling productions of this period were musicals. However, some comedies could still run for more than 1,000 performances. Mostly designed to seem outrageous to titillate the audience, they retained reassuring conclusions to satisfy the nation's conservatism. Good examples of this are George Axelrod's *The Seven Year Itch* (1952), which allows a man to explore his sexual fantasies while bringing him back to the fold, and John Patrick's *Teahouse of the August Moon* (1953), in which Captain Fisby tries to impose American values on the residents of a Japanese island but gets seduced by the natives, who end up keeping their traditions. Other, more serious plays also proved box-office gold, including Miller's *Death of a Salesman* (1949), about the implosion of the American Dream; Lawrence and Lee's *Inherit the Wind* (1955), about issues of free speech as a schoolteacher is tried for teaching evolution in the Bible Belt; *Two for the Seesaw* (1958), about a damaged couple attempting to connect in the big city; and *The Miracle Worker* (1959), depicting the relationship of teacher Anne Sullivan and her deaf and dumb student Helen Keller, both by William Gibson.

Numerous alienated figures can be found in plays of the period: individuals cut off from the larger society by unpopular politics, morality, or mere appearance. An insistence on paying attention to those deemed lesser in society, and concern for the effects of such uneven hierarchies in a supposedly democratic society, encouraged a future proliferation of plays from Tony Kushner's two-part *Angels in America* (1991–93), with its exploration of AIDS and homosexuality, to any of Lynn Nottage's or Suzan-Lori Parks's plays about those marginalized by class and/or race. Such works emulate Tennessee Williams's evident desire to depict the lives of those deemed social outcasts in order to engage for them a greater empathy in the wider community, as well as his dedication to experimentation in how that might be accomplished.

Bruce McConachie suggests that the 1940s reliance on radio and telephone for communication provoked a move toward greater abstraction and allegory in 1950s theatre as playwrights moved away from realism and audiences were more willing to accept such innovation, just as the onset of television would change the writing styles of the following decade.[7] The introduction into stage drama of the flashbacks and stream-of-consciousness often utilized in radio drama certainly gave playwrights more options. Writers drew on different theatrical styles and ideas from home and abroad to create a variety of engaging theatrical hybrids. This cross-cultural pollination has only increased over the years to produce such blockbusters as Lin-Manuel Miranda's *Hamilton* (2015), with its mélange of musical styles, blatant color-blind casting, and scenery and dance that underscore and advance the narrative rather than simply embellish it.

Many writers of the 1940s and 1950s had developed their craft during the Great Depression and leaned toward socialist agendas with an interest in those on the margins; they were happy to expose inequities that lay beneath the country's prosperous veneer. In some, a darker understanding emerged that everyone is capable of evil, that unselfish goodness is a rare commodity, and that we are often our own worst enemies. Under the social and political persecution of McCarthyism and continued intolerance, partly because it was not as dependent on finance as the films, theatre provided a safer refuge for dissenters and original thinkers – a tendency that would not change.

Emerging Dramatists

Eugene O'Neill and Thornton Wilder had shown the world that American dramatists were capable of more than copying their European forebears, but Tennessee Williams, Arthur Miller, and William Inge collectively created a distinctively American theatre that traversed and reflected the entire nation and fully realized new dramatic forms and theatrical characters. Miller explored the lives of those living in the North both past and present; Williams explored the complexities of the South; and Inge brought audiences previously overlooked images of the small-town Midwest that were less than the expected ideal, filled with dissatisfaction, frustration, and desire. The three played with realism and expressionism to produce engaging productions that spoke to the inner lives of their characters and presented tragedies and comedies of everyday Americans. Their audacity would lead American playwrights who were writing in the 1970s and 1980s to further explore and expand on what it means to be both American and human, from Sam Shepard looking out West to Lanford Wilson or Larry Kramer, among many others, exploring what it means to be gay.

Critics tend to view Miller as a predominantly political commentator on America, exploring moral and social concerns through the lives of ordinary people, while Williams is more poetically engaged with the psychological and emotional problems of society's outcasts. However, Gerald

Berkowitz's all-too-common description of them as "the pamphleteer of social issues and the poet of loneliness and fear" being "poles of a continuum on which most other dramatists of the late 1940s lay"[8] is somewhat of an oversimplification. Even while their tone and philosophy may differ, both playwrights focused on social, political, psychological, and emotional issues in their work; both were wary of American idealism; and both were identical in their strong work ethic, embrace, and innovation of new theatrical aesthetics and their mutual goal to change America and American theatre. This courage and commitment would inspire subsequent playwrights, such as Edward Albee, who came to notice in the 1960s, David Rabe in the 1970s, and David Mamet in the 1980s, who each acknowledged this influence to successfully push theatre to even newer boundaries.

Williams's semiautobiographical *The Glass Menagerie* (1945) explores the tortured existence of the Wingfield family, trapped in unfulfilled lives and unable to extricate themselves from their psychological burdens. Miller's *All My Sons* (1947) passes comment on the moral injustices of an acquisitive capitalist system that causes the deaths of innocent pilots fighting for their country. That Miller beat O'Neill and *The Iceman Cometh* for the Tony Award that year underlines the extent to which the theatrical world was welcoming this new talent. Though critical of their nation, both Miller and Williams remained highly successful, and their next plays would set the bar even higher.

David Halberstam insists that *A Streetcar Named Desire* (1947) "was not just a play – it was an event. Its frank treatment of sophisticated sexual themes marked it as a part of a powerful new current in American society and cultural life" that would shatter "the pleasant conventions of American life."[9] Its depiction of a tragic, deluded Southern Belle was as evocative of southern decay as *Death of a Salesman* (1949) and Miller's portrayal of washed-up salesman Willy Loman would be of the dehumanizing capitalism of the North. As Atkinson opined, "nobody had written about the dark side of the American fantasy with the sympathy and knowledge Mr. Miller brought to it."[10] Both plays became seminal within American theatre for their subject matter and creative design, and for their extension of the possibilities of sympathetic characterization and how modern tragedy could be defined.

Miller followed this with what has become his most produced play, *The Crucible* (1953), comparing the show trials of HUAC to the witch trials of Salem, to expose the savagery of McCarthyism and the self-serving hypocrisy on which it rested. Williams was no less political in a play he produced that same year, *Camino Real,* in which a naive American wanderer, Kilroy, gets caught up in a nightmare town filled with tyranny and corruption. Having the central character run around the auditorium was also highly inventive for the time, though nowadays it is almost commonplace. Williams further cemented his reputation with *The Rose Tattoo* (1951), *Cat on a Hot Tin Roof* (1955), *Suddenly Last Summer* (1958), and *Sweet Bird of Youth* (1959), which collectively offer celebration and warning of the sexual life and commentary on the callousness, cruelty, and mendacities of modern life. His plays would grow increasingly shocking, as if to challenge the conformity of the times, with references to abortion, castration, and cannibalism, and they were also swiftly made into popular movies. Less prolific, partly due to his dalliance with Marilyn Monroe, whom he would marry in 1956, Miller produced *A View from the Bridge* (1956), the story of a troubled longshoreman caught between morality and desire, in which he sought to further assert his view of the "tragedy of the common man." The frequency with which both playwrights continue to be revived is further testament to the strength and continuing influence of their work.

Inge was less technically innovative than Miller and Williams, but despite their stature, his impact was hardly lesser in terms of showing Americans the darker truths about their often-stunted lives that people preferred to avoid. His hits of the 1950s – *Come Back, Little Sheba* (1950), *Picnic* (1953), *Bus Stop* (1955), and *The Dark at the Top of the Stairs* (1957) – sold more tickets than the plays of either Miller or Williams over the same period (a fact about which Williams was terminally jealous, especially since he had encouraged Inge to write). Thomas Adler correctly views Inge as "the most significant dramatizer of the Midwest."[11] Despite surface comedy, which possibly made them more palatable to the masses, Inge's plays are filled with the same nonjudgmental depictions of outcasts and damaged characters as are Miller's and Williams's, and the works of all three playwrights expose inequities of gender and class and the problems of a society that may seem prosperous on the surface, yet is filled with people unable to attain this prosperity and longing for something better.

Inspired by these three, other playwrights expanded on dramatic topics, characters, and styles throughout the era, presenting psychologically troubled individuals in a variety of mainstream plays, such as Carson McCullers's *Member of the Wedding* (1950), about adolescence and race, or Robert Anderson's *Tea and Sympathy* (1953), about sexual orientation and related prejudice. Theatre paid attention to those marginalized, giving a venue for the growing liberal voices of the nation to air concern and express belief in the more positive values of American democracy they saw endangered. Even a popular comedy like Garson Kanin's *Born Yesterday* (1946) highlights the dangers of corruption with its characterization of Harry Brock, who made a fortune selling junk to war industries and believes anyone can be bought. For Atkinson, through Kanin's exposure and denigration of the potential corruption against which the nation should be aware, *Born Yesterday* "demonstrates a belief in the American democratic system that service in the war induced in many men. Fascism lurks in the back of its mind as a pitfall into which democracy might easily fall."[12] Many plays of the period featured individuals taking an ethical stance as warning against the loss of personal freedom in an overly conformist society, setting a clear standard for future works to remain vigilant in maintaining the freedoms offered the nation by its Constitution. Their work would be assisted by profound changes during this period in how plays could be presented on the stage.

Collaborative Models: Direction, Staging, and Methodology

Though the short-lived Group Theatre, with its mission to present naturalistic, socially relevant, and highly disciplined theatre to the American public, had closed its doors in 1941, its influence persisted. Its artists, whose vision helped bring new scripts, scores, and aesthetics to the American stage continued to work together. Formed in 1931 by Cheryl Crawford, Harold Clurman, and Lee Strasberg, the Group had embraced the theories of Konstantin Stanislavsky, by which actors learned their characters from the inside out by tapping into their inner emotions to create an authentic performance. Referred to as the Method, it became the preferred style of performance on stage and film, much changing how plays were performed, though it continues to be interpreted differently by different people.

Formed in 1947, Strasberg took over direction of the Actors Studio from Cheryl Crawford, Elia Kazan, and Robert Lewis in 1951 and expanded it from a free workshop for gifted stage performers into an influential, though controversial, acting school. Strasberg added his own psychoanalytical ideas to Stanislavsky's teachings; instead of asking actors to search their memories for clues as to how to respond in an acting situation, he wanted them to reconstruct a character's life from childhood. Strasberg asked actors to delve into their own, often darker subconscious – not to *think* but to *feel* the part. Some saw this approach as abusive, but actors such as James Dean, Geraldine Page, Al Pacino, and even Marilyn Monroe deeply admired his techniques, and his influence continues today through acting schools on both coasts.

Stella Adler joined the Group Theatre at its inception, but after spending time with Stanislavsky, she grew resistant to Strasberg's use of affective memory, realizing an actor could use imagination supplemented by research to forge a character rather than personal experience, and with less danger to the psyche. She established the Stella Adler Acting Studio in 1949, with a curriculum that went beyond just speech, voice production, and make-up to include script analysis, characterization and acting styles, and improvisation. She taught actors like Marlon Brando, Eddie Albert, Warren Beatty, and Elaine Stritch to build characters more pragmatically from material within the text and the play's historical context, and her techniques also continue to be taught across America. Another Group alumnus, Sanford Meisner, followed Adler's lead and split off to develop a behavioral method that relied more on instinct, focusing on other actors rather than the self, and many current figures have trained in his methods, from Jeff Goldblum and Tom Cruise to Amy Schumer and Stephen Colbert.

Creating a landmark play had become more than writing a great script; it also depended on finding the right production team. This period began to acknowledge this by often placing the names of directors or actors above that of the playwright in theatrical advertising – a practice still common. Dynamic and innovative directors such as Josh Logan and Elia Kazan were much sought, despite the demands they made on writer, cast, and crew. As a skilled theatrical craftsman, who directed with great emotional force, Logan was able to create hits out of comedy (*Mister Roberts* [1948], which he also co-wrote), drama (*Picnic* [1953], *Middle of the Night* [1956], and *The World of Suzie Wong* [1958]), and musicals (*Annie Get Your Gun* [1946] and *South Pacific* [1949], also co-written). He frequently assisted with writing and production on the material he directed, and his contributions in this period are considered his best. Less provocative than Kazan, he knew how to please an audience and worked predominantly with expert stage and lighting designer Jo Mielziner.

Kazan was possibly the best-known and most influential director of the era, and that influence would only grow. After his death in 2003, Mervyn Rothstein would refer to him as "one of the most honored and influential directors in Broadway and Hollywood history."[13] Having honed his craft while acting and directing for the Group, he continued to produce with fellow alumnus Clurman. A solid but less forceful director than Kazan, who tended to let the actors find their way in a role rather than impose readings, Clurman often championed new plays and playwrights, being a co-producer of *All My Sons*. He was best directing subtle dramas, such as

Member of the Wedding, Bus Stop, and Lillian Hellman's *The Autumn Garden* (1951). Clurman's biggest impact in this period, however, was through his work as a drama critic for *The New Republic* (1948–52) and *The Nation* from 1953.

Using the Method, Kazan worked closely with actors. Skilled at drawing out intensely realistic and edgy performances, he helped create many new stars such as Marlon Brando, Rod Steiger, James Dean, Julie Harris, and Natalie Wood. He energized productions with lots of stage business, creating countless mini-climaxes to engage audiences and maintain a constant sense of onstage movement. Tending toward the new and the provocative, he had little interest in musicals or classics. Without him directing their plays, it is likely neither Miller nor Williams would have been as successful as they became; he also directed the movie version of *A Streetcar Named Desire.* Both Logan and Kazan balanced their talents between stage and screen, and it may have been partly their familiarity with cinematic techniques that led them to try different things on stage. Like Logan, Kazan often worked with Mielziner as his stage and lighting designer, but he also collaborated with Boris Aronson and other designers.

Acknowledging the importance of their contribution, especially as scenic design moved away from single-room sets to offer a variety of inventive designs, Tony Awards for scenic designers were offered from the awards' start in 1947, and designers were often nominated for more than one show in the same year. The use of representational scenery, scrims, transparencies, and the forestage allowed playwrights far greater scope in how they could present place, time, and even state of mind. Two of the best at this were Aronson, who designed thirty-six shows during this period, of which thirteen were nominated for a Tony, although he only won once, and Mielziner, who designed an amazing seventy-eight shows during this same time, of which seventeen were nominated for a Tony; he won three times.

Mielziner was a master of understatement; influenced by Robert Edmond Jones, who preferred delicate designs, Mielziner used subtle nuances of light and shade to create an aesthetic unity. His lighting often used windows to illuminate actors, and he utilized a variety of scrims and effects to accomplish swift scene or mood changes. His designs evoke a cinematic sensibility, and his sets were famed for their flexibility, ingenuity, and ability to create a sense of fluidity in time and space. He had won the Tony Award in 1949, not only for *Death of a Salesman,* but also for *South Pacific, Anne of the Thousand Days, Summer and Smoke,* and *Sleepy Hollow,* showing his ability to work on any kind of production. His frequently abstract, skeletal, and minimalistic scenography had moved stage design away from the detailed minutiae of realism that had previously dominated, yet got closer to each work's emotional and psychological truth. His design for *Salesman* became so iconic that many subsequent productions would emulate it, including the 2012 Broadway revival.

Bolder than Mielziner, Aronson preferred epic dramas requiring complex and often asymmetrical staging filled with obstacles and odd angles to better challenge an audience; avoiding flat painted scenery, he preferred a three-dimensional approach that offered actors a greater range of movement. Using a "constructivist" style, he interpreted rather than copied real life to bring out a work's inner essence. He designed such plays as *The Crucible*, *A View from the Bridge*, and *A Memory of Two Mondays*, *Bus Stop*, *J.B.*, and his biggest commercial success, *The Diary of Anne Frank*, for which he created a cross-section of the building, filled with small compartments, each with its own representational clutter to convey character, in which small details were changed to show the passage of time and keep the production fluid.

It had become clear that it took a full team to create a hit, for without the collaboration of Kazan, Aronson, and ANTA Playhouse on Archibald MacLeish's chilling *J.B.* (1958), it seems doubtful that a verse drama based on psychiatry, theology, and Marxism, featuring an updated version of the biblical Job, would have had such a lengthy run and won the Pulitzer Prize. Frank Rich spoke of Aronson's circus tent design as "the most significant achievement in American theatre design since the Mielziner sets for *Death of a Salesman* and *Streetcar Named Desire* a decade earlier."[14] Another major advance during this period assisted by such collaborations was in the realm of musical theatre, which, by the 1960s, had worked its way into dominating how musicals were written and produced worldwide.

Musical Theatre

After the breakthrough hit of *Oklahoma!* in 1943, in which the farmers and cowboys ended as friends, despite some dark moments surrounding the rivalry of Curly and Jud, Richard Rodgers and Oscar Hammerstein had discovered a formula that would flourish on Broadway and change the face of how musicals were created. They offered well-developed characters, strong narratives full of romance and humor, though not without a dark tinge, and song and dance that built character and advanced the storyline. They had created what came to be known as the "integrated" musical, in which all the elements of the show align into a combined whole.

Rodgers and Hammerstein's other successes include *Carousel* (1945), with its tragic antihero carnival roustabout, and *South Pacific* (1949), about the tribulations of forces overseas fraught by racist attitudes. *South Pacific* was the second musical to ever win the Pulitzer Prize for Drama. The first had been 1932's *Of Thee I Sing*, and the award had left out the composer, George Gershwin; by including Richard Rodgers in the award for *South Pacific*, the Pulitzer Prize committee was acknowledging that the music was an integral part of the show. The team continued with *The King and I* (1951), relating the friendship between a British lady and the King of Siam, and *The Sound of Music* (1959), based on the singing von Trapp family and their escape from the Nazis. Their locations were often exotic, and the plots frequently sentimental, but in all their musicals there is also an undercurrent of violence created through inequity that spoke to the sociopolitical concerns of the time. This political edge would inspire future artists to do more than just offer an engaging story. Acknowledging their continuing influence on current musicals to address important social concerns rather than just entertain, Lin-Manuel Miranda explains how *The Sound of Music* "isn't just about climbing mountains and fording streams. Look beyond the adorable von Trapp children: It's about the looming existential threat of Nazism."[15]

Rodgers and Hammerstein had a string of successes that cemented their approach and solidified their influence. Frederick Loewe, along with Alan Jay Lerner, successfully used their formula in *Brigadoon* (1947), about a mystical Scottish village, and *Paint Your Wagon* (1951), about people in a Gold Rush mining camp. Then, they adapted George Bernard Shaw's *Pygmalion* (1913), which relates a romance between a confirmed bachelor and the young cockney girl he trains to pass as a lady, into *My Fair Lady* (1956) and broke records, clocking up 2,717 performances to become the third longest running Broadway production at that time. Many consider this to be the perfect musical with its flawless story-song integration that allows the lyrics to convey the plot, such as "The Rain in Spain," which relates the first breakthrough in Eliza's development into a lady, and Higgins's "I've Grown Accustomed to Her Face," which conveys his understanding of his true feelings for Eliza. Other successful creations of the period that followed a similar design, but with new twists, were Richard Adler and Jerry Ross's hits, *Pajama Game* (1954) and *Damn Yankees* (1955). These were additionally energized by the innovative and sensual choreography of Bob Fosse and the adept comic direction of George Abbott, further promoting the idea that the best musicals were created by teams, and not just writers.

Known for his deft hand with comedy and musicals, George Abbott was revered for his ability to craft hit shows out of even moderate material, with swift pacing and solid construction. Hal Prince, especially, would follow his guide into the 1980s, and many current directors continue to follow this style. During this period, Abbott directed twenty-five shows, eighteen of them musicals, including *Wonderful Town* (1953), *The Pajama Game* (with Jerome Robbins), *Damn Yankees*, and *Fiorello!* (1959), many for which he also wrote the book. Perhaps key to Abbott's success was his ability to recognize and nurture up-and-coming talent, including Jerome Robbins and Bob Fosse, both of whom would have a profound effect on how musicals were presented.

Robbins had mostly worked as a choreographer in the 1940s, and first directed in 1945, helping both Abbott and Logan on various shows. Trained in ballet, he brought elements of this to the musicals he directed such as *The King and I*, Mary Martin's *Peter Pan* (1954), and *West Side Story* (1957). He created the narrative dance and oriental styling of "Small House of Uncle Thomas Ballet" for *The King and I*, as well as the memorable "March of the Siamese Children" and "Shall We Dance." His balletic choreography, alongside the Latin moves he created for *West Side Story*, so match the characters that it is almost impossible to think of the musical without their recall, and this matching of choreography to character and situation has only grown more central in today's musicals.

Coming from a jazz background, Bob Fosse's alternate but equally distinctive style of dance includes the use of turned-in knees and the "Fosse Amoeba" made up of sideways shuffling, rolled shoulders, and jazz hands.[16] Fosse also commonly used props, especially hats, canes, and chairs. He would win three Tony Awards for Choreography in the 1950s alone – for *The Pajama Game*, *Damn Yankees*, and *Redhead* (1959) – the same as Michael Kidd who won for *Guys and Dolls* (1951), *Can-Can* (1954), and *Li'l Abner* (1956). Like Robbins, Kidd had an interest in ballet but believed that dance should be derived from ordinary everyday movements in life. He would take these and enlarge upon them to create a dance form that organically related to the character's behavior and personality – the perfect approach for the integrated musicals of the day, and the future. This period not only expanded on how dance was used in musicals, but also the types of music composed.

As a serious musician, Leonard Bernstein created some of the most ambitious musical theatre scores of the period, blending classical, jazz, and pop into distinctive productions, and elevating the complex musical possibilities of the form. His score for *Wonderful Town* (1953) included an aria, a comic duet, innovative jazz, and a wild conga. *West Side Story* had the pure operatic strains of "Maria" and "Somewhere," alongside the vaudeville of "Gee Officer Krupke," the Latin sound of "America," the hit ballad "Tonight," and several jazz compositions, and has become his most memorable. It presents an amalgam of high and low culture; Arthur Laurents's book based on Shakespeare's *Romeo and Juliet*, updated to depict street gangs in a modern city, coupled with libretto written by the up-and-coming Stephen Sondheim, heralded the development of another new kind of American musical. In *West Side Story*, violence spirals and the young hero lies dead, reflecting a more pessimistic and deterministic worldview than most preceding musicals. Though it may have lost out to Meredith Willson's more conventional *The Music Man* (1957) for the Tony that year, it would be revived countless times and become one of the most celebrated Broadway musicals. Also, its lyricist, Sondheim, would change the Broadway stage forever through his creation of the "concept musical" that is built around an idea rather than a traditional narrative, and presents even deeper psychological characterizations, shunning sentimental romance or complacent reassurances, to address more complex social issues.

The musicals of this period established how musicals would develop into the future, with their creative commitment to exploring techniques in writing, including strong narrative arcs and topics with an often-serious agenda, as well as their innovations in composing, directing, and choreography. This period also saw some major advances in women's theatrical involvement.

Women in the Theatre

Throughout the nineteenth century, outside of acting, few women had influence or authority in the theatre. The number of women writing for the stage could be improved only when women began to take a larger role as producers and directors. In 1910, women directed less than 5 percent of Broadway shows, and most of those were only given this opportunity because they had written the play. However, in 1935, it was a woman – the dynamic and charismatic Hallie Flanagan – who was chosen to head the Federal Theatre. Although Congress closed this down in 1939 for fear of its integrationist policies and socialist sympathies, Flanagan had done an amazing job. After the war, the number of female directors initially rose to 11.6 percent as more women challenged the odds, forcing their way into directing, and also into staging and producing. The number involved in these fields would plummet to 2 percent during the 1950s, most likely due to a conservative backlash against female advancement, but it would eventually improve. The pioneering and innovative women who broke through at this difficult time helped pave the way for future female artists by reminding everyone of what was possible.[17]

To show that women could direct, they needed to be seen at the helm of serious drama, and not just "women's plays," and they needed to show that they could innovate as well as their male counterparts, and be equally successful. Margaret Webster arrived from England in 1937 to direct Shakespeare with actor Maurice Evans. George Jean Nathan declared she was "the best director of the plays of Shakespeare that we have."[18] Committed to integrated casts, she pioneered the first Black Othello on an American stage, directing Paul Robeson with Uta Hagen and José Ferrer in *Othello* in 1943, and at 296 performances, this remains the longest run of any Shakespeare play on Broadway. Her 1945 *The Tempest* also broke records and featured African American actor Canada Lee in the role of Caliban. In a relationship with Eva Le Gallienne since 1938, having met during a production of *Hamlet*, Webster jumped at the chance to help form American Repertory Theatre in 1946 (not to be confused with Robert Brustein's later manifestation) with Le Gallienne and Cheryl Crawford.

A leading proponent of repertory theatre, Le Gallienne had run the Civic Repertory Theatre from 1926 to 1934, mounting classic European plays, including several of Ibsen's that she herself translated, and staging worthy American plays, especially those by women, such as Susan Glaspell's *Inheritors* (1927) and *Alison's House* (1930). Though only running from 1946 to 1948 due to finance, the American Repertory Theatre followed the same program as Le Gallienne's previous Rep and won critical acclaim in its short tenure, again proving that women were capable of producing effective drama. After it closed, Webster's relationship with Le Gallienne ended, and she formed the Margaret Webster Shakespeare Company to tour the country, an experience she personally credits as being "the most valuable contribution I ever made to theatre in America."[19] However, in 1950 she also became the first woman to direct Metropolitan Opera and once again was able to effect change as, under her guidance, the Met's operatic productions became more theatrical. She also staged operas for New York City Opera and thus made her mark in yet another field.

Where Webster had proven women could direct Shakespeare and opera, Mary Hunter was a pioneer in directing musical theatre. The huge budgets and large casts of musical theatre had mostly male producers thinking female directors would be unreliable. When Hunter was hired to direct *High Button Shoes* in 1947, she was replaced two weeks before rehearsals began by George Abbott, explaining they needed a bigger name. Supported by fellow theatricals she brought a grievance; Mielziner testified: she was "one of three or four people in the profession who understood all the elements that go into a musical show."[20] New York Supreme Court awarded her an unprecedented $40,000, agreeing it had been sexism that had resulted in her firing. Her innovative combination of folklore and Americana with musical theatre, through such pieces as *Ballet Ballads* (1948) and her touring production *Musical Americana* (1953–55), suggested new ways to integrate song and dance. Robbins hired her as assistant director for *Peter Pan* (1954), but the following year, she retired to marry and start a family.

Cheryl Crawford, however, was dedicated to the theatre throughout her life. Possibly the most influential female producer on Broadway to this day, she produced over 100 plays, helped create one of America's most influential acting schools, and helped the careers of many well-known actors. She was a graduate of the Theatre Guild's school, whose co-founder, producer Theresa Helburn, was the impetus behind getting *Oklahoma!*, *Carousel*, and several of Inge's dramas to the stage. Fascinated by theatre, but not wanting to act, Crawford took various administrative positions within the Guild until joining fellow employees Clurman and Strasberg to form the Group. She also helped found the American Repertory Theatre and the Actors Studio. In addition, she became an important independent producer, with such successes as *Brigadoon* (1947), *The Rose Tattoo* (1951), *Paint Your Wagon* (1951), and *Sweet Bird of Youth* (1959). In 1979, both she and Margaret Webster were inducted into the Theater Hall of Fame, Crawford being, at the time, possibly the first nonacting female to gain that honor (inductees need twenty-five years of distinguished service in American theatre and at least five major production credits on Broadway). Women such as Crawford and Helburn proved that one need not be male to become a successful producer, fully involved in the life of the theatre, and both blazed an inspirational trail for future women wanting to follow in their capable footsteps.

Though likewise in a minority, women writers also proved their worth during this period. Librettist and lyricist Dorothy Fields, with her brother Herbert Fields, wrote books and/or lyrics for several musicals including *Up in Central Park* (1945) that investigated crooked politics and proved women need not be restricted to safe topics, as well as *By the Beautiful Sea* (1954), *Redhead* (1959), *Annie Get Your Gun* (1949), and *A Tree Grows in*

Brooklyn (1951), all of which feature strong female protagonists. Working with Adolph Green, Betty Comden also thrived, writing books and lyrics for such rollicking hits as *On the Town* (1944), *Wonderful Town* (1953), and *Bells Are Ringing* (1956). These may not have privileged female characters, but they proved women could write successful musicals, albeit with a male partner. Bella Spewack also worked with her husband Samuel to produce the book for *Kiss Me Kate* (1948), a hugely successful musical adaptation of Shakespeare's *Taming of the Shrew*.

Women were also making progress in regular drama with Mary Chase becoming the fourth woman to get a Pulitzer Prize for *Harvey* (1944), an imaginative tale about a man guided by a "pooka" in the form of an invisible giant rabbit, which was directed by Antoinette Perry and has spawned several revivals and filmed versions. In 1952, Chase had further success with *Bernardine*, another original offering about a group of teen-agers, and *Mrs. McThing*, the first children's play to be produced on Broadway. Ketti Frings also gained a Pulitzer in 1958 for her adaptation of Thomas Wolfe's bildungsroman novel, *Look Homeward, Angel* (1929). None, however, engendered more acclaim than Lillian Hellman, who can be viewed as America's first successful female playwright, viewed as equal to the men of her time, and thus a normalizing inspiration for future female dramatists.

Having come to prominence before the war, Hellman continued to produce strident drama that critiqued American complacency as much as that of Miller. Her insistence on living life on her own terms caused several scandals – over her sexual exploits and dismissive treatment of HUAC – but also placed her firmly in the spotlight. In 1952, concern with the sociopolitical atmosphere led her to revive her 1934 play *Children's Hour* about how malicious gossip ruins lives. She also adapted Jean Anouilh's *The Lark* (1955), viewing the trial of Joan of Arc as a fitting emblem of victimized innocence, and Voltaire's *Candide* (1956), in which the titular character and others are sentenced to die on spurious evidence. Other less political plays included a sequel to *The Little Foxes, Another Part of the Forest* (1946), which showed how the awful Hubbard family had evolved, *The Autumn Garden*, about the difficulties of middle age, and *Toys in the Attic* (1960), about sisters who sacrifice their lives for their wayward brother. Plays written by women in the 1950s were as successful as those by men, but they overall penned less than 20 percent of the plays produced on Broadway, and it would be several decades before that improved.

On an interesting note, the Tony Awards for drama began in 1947, named after a woman, Antoinette Perry – actress, director, and co-founder of the American Theatre Wing. Outside of the awards for actresses, up until 1960, Fields and Spewack won awards for their books, Fields and Comden won for their lyrics, Frances Goodrich won best play for *The Diary of Anne Frank*, Agnes de Mille and Helen Tamiris each won for choreography, and Lucinda Ballard, Mary Percy Schenck, Aline Bernstein, and Irene Sharaff won for costume design. No women were even nominated for any music award, director, or stage design. There was clearly still much to do, but ground had been broken. A similar story can be told of the growth of African American theatre.

Minoritized Inroads

The Harlem Renaissance (1918–37) gave African American writers a voice, but aside from a few outliers, these voices were not often heard in the theatre until after World War II when we witness a growing African American presence both on and Off-Broadway. A committee was formed to try and increase African American employment in Broadway shows, combat racial stereotyping in the theatre, and encourage upcoming African American writers. Many African American soldiers had fought against fascism, only to find themselves despised on their return in a supposedly democratic country. African American plays of the period offered positive identities for Black people to counter offensive mainstream stereotypes and bring the plight of people of color to the nation's attention.

Owen Brady points out how Theodore Ward used "history to shed light on the problem of racial justice in 1940 America"[21] in his challenging play, *Our Lan'* (1947). It addressed the Reconstruction period in the South and even had a short Broadway run, though white producers did not present it as effectively as its initial production, adding music and lessening its impact. Off-Broadway, William Branch had success with *A Medal for Willie* (1951), about the way African American servicemen were treated, and *In Splendid Error* (1954), which depicts a meeting between Frederick Douglass and John Brown in which they discuss the efficacy of rebellion. Taking another approach, Louis Peterson's *Take a Giant Step* (1953) depicts a young Black man growing up in a predominantly white middle-class neighborhood to explore the pressures of assimilation and its attending self-hatred, and Loften Mitchell wrote *A Land Beyond the River* (1957), about a Black couple joining the legal fight against school segregation. All effectively reflected the psychology of being segregated and constantly treated as second-class citizens, but they were also predominantly written from a male perspective.

By the close of the 1950s, Lorraine Hansberry's *A Raisin in the Sun* (1959) would show the nation what an African American woman writer could achieve, but it was prior work of Alice Childress – as actress, activist, director, and playwright – that did much to make Hansberry's success possible. Addressing Black and gender concerns, and having characters confront white antagonists on stage to encourage interracial casts, Childress began writing plays to create decent roles for Black actresses. Despite a veneer of comedy, such plays as *Florence* (1949), *Just a Little Simple* (1950), *Gold Through the Trees* (1952) – the first play written by a Black woman professionally produced with Equity actors on a New York stage – and *Trouble in Mind* (1955), she encouraged protest and political commitment, presenting authentic representations of Black life on the stage. While writing a column for Paul Robeson's newspaper *Freedom*, Childress met, inspired, and encouraged Lorraine Hansberry.

Rather than strike audiences as combative, as much drama from 1960s African American playwrights appeared, *A Raisin in the Sun* spoke as much to white audiences as Black, for as McConachie suggests, "Hansberry used the specific language, cultural habits, and social situations of a particular ethnic group to suggest the dilemma of many groups at a similar stage of history." Thus, "the African American experience of the Younger family could be both particular and universal."[22] The Younger family wants to live in a nicer area, but a representative from a white neighborhood organization tries to bribe them not to move. Rediscovering his self-hood, the family's son refuses the offer, and the story ends as they leave for their new home. The play offered challenges to American racism and sexism and won an African American woman the New York Drama Critics' Circle Award, as well as becoming the longest running play on Broadway by a Black writer for a quarter of a century. Its success partly depended on a continuing growing openness in American theatre at that time for new ideas, new writers, and new ways to present. As the 1950s drew to a close, it was becoming increasingly evident that Broadway alone did not represent all that was happening on stage.

Experimental Theatre

For theatre to remain vital, it must have the opportunity to continuously experiment. Despite, or possibly because of the commercial restraints on mainstream drama, since the Provincetown Players of the 1920s, American theatre had struggled to maintain that prerogative. During this period, the success of Broadway indirectly generated the development of

Off-Broadway, and, by the close of the 1950s, Off-Off-Broadway allowed resourceful practitioners to continue to explore new possibilities for the public that would also keep the mainstream invigorated.

The best examples of this would be Julian Beck and Judith Malina, who founded Living Theatre in 1947 to create a venue that offered intense experience beyond simple realism. They adopted Antonin Artaud's theory on "Theatre of Cruelty" that demanded an audience feel plays intimately, breaking down the separation of actors from audience, to create organic productions of communal expression. Experimenting with avant-garde pieces by Pablo Picasso, William Carlos Williams, and Gertrude Stein, they moved around a variety of small nontraditional performance spaces, which were frequently closed due to finance or conflict with city authorities. Jack Gelber's largely improvised play about drug addiction, *The Connection*, was produced by them in 1959 to disturbing effect. Their dedication to create a noncommercial alternative to Broadway that freed people to experiment was a clarion call.

In 1949, the newly formed Off-Broadway Theatre League negotiated a contract with Actors' Equity to allow Equity actors to perform at token salaries, which gave theatre practitioners opportunity to try new ideas without going bust, while allowing them to maintain a high professionalism. As well as providing opportunities for more talented actors and directors to come to the nation's attention, Off-Broadway influenced Broadway and the growing regional American theatres that were springing up in a variety of ways. The use of different theatrical spaces and their effects on staging, the passion and determination to produce ideas beyond the mainstream as well as forgotten classics, and the pioneering of color-blind casting, were all largely led by the Off-Broadway theatres.

Several theatres contributed to the growth of the movement, but Circle in the Square, established in 1951 by director José Quintero and others, is often credited as leading the way. Using an old nightclub with an arena stage configuration, they produced a mix of American and European plays, but their successful 1952 revival of Williams's *Summer and Smoke* (which fared better than the 1948 Broadway production) proved it was possible to have a hit play Off-Broadway and made the careers of Quintero and leading actress Geraldine Page. Quintero was far less analytical and doctrinaire than Kazan, and not as technically savvy as Abbott, but he was an instinctual director with a strong emotional commitment, who allowed his actors to find their own way into a role. He also understood the different blocking and staging demands of the arena configuration. His revival of O'Neill's *The Iceman Cometh* in 1956, not only made Jason Robards a star, but also helped rejuvenate the playwright's reputation and led to O'Neill's widow giving him *A Long Day's Journey into Night* (1956) to direct on Broadway, years ahead of O'Neill's intent – a play many now consider O'Neill finest work.

Success also came for Marc Blitzstein's adaptation of Kurt Weill and Bertolt Brecht's *The Threepenny Opera* in 1954 at Theatre de Lys. Blitzstein softened the anger of Brecht's vision, which made it more engaging, and although an incoming booking initially forced the play to close, it reopened the following year and broke all records by running for more than six years. It proved that shows did not need the opulence and glitz of a Broadway production to succeed and presaged the success of Tom Jones and Harvey Schmidt's low-budget *The Fantasticks* (1960) that ran for an incredible forty-two years.

Mention should also be made of Joseph Papp, who founded the New York Shakespeare Workshop in 1954 "so that poetic plays can be done on the stage in a highly realistic way without sacrificing the poetry and the style"[23] with the aim of making Shakespeare more accessible to the masses. His first "free" Shakespeare in the Park was in 1956, and by the next decade, Papp had created the Public Theater to nurture new artists and audiences, operating from five stages.

It became clear that to keep American theatre vibrant, alternate venues to Broadway needed to be maintained. "Between 1950 and 1962 Off-Broadway theatres presented close to one thousand productions, of which a third were new American plays."[24] In 1956, the Obie Awards were created by *Village Voice* to bring attention to their efforts, promoting up-and-coming playwrights, such as Horton Foote and Edward Albee, whose work would gain wider acceptance in the 1960s. Complaints that Off-Broadway was starting to mirror Broadway, rather than offer an alternative, led to the opening of Joseph Cino's Caffé Cino in 1958, and the Off-Off-Broadway movement began. The next decade would see the establishment of many more groups – such as La MaMa, Judson Poet's Theater, and Theatre Genesis – to ensure experimentation in American drama would continue to flower. In 1964, their productions would become eligible for Obie Awards, and they would bring writers such as Sam Shepard, Adrienne Kennedy, and Harvey Fierstein to the nation's attention.

Conclusion

Without the energy and creativity of the post-1945 to 1960 period, American theatre would not be what it is today in terms of its content, staging and acting, and attraction toward innovation. This "Golden Age" took Broadway beyond simple realism and allegiance to European theatre to develop its own unique style and voice that has now been globally recognized. The works of Arthur Miller alone have been translated into multiple languages and are regularly performed around the world. American theatre has become as complex as the nation itself in its variety and continued commitment to the exploration of what it means to be an American. It is perhaps this endeavor, begun in earnest during a period of tremendous optimism, that allowed the national drama to sustain an ongoing celebration and critique of the "American experiment" rather than embrace the cynical absurdism coming out of Europe in the 1960s. Instead, Americans continued to insist on meaning, even while acknowledging their own divisions and inequities. Demands to be heard and recognized by the country's ethnic, sexual, and gender identities would soon become more strident, but within the light of a humanistic belief that the country could be made better, containing a bedrock belief that drama could make a difference in that endeavor.

Notes

1. E. Albee, *Remembering Arthur Miller*, ed. C. Bigsby (Methuen, 2005), p. 14.
2. A. Petigny, *The Permissive Society: America, 1941–1965* (Cambridge University Press, 2009), p. 255.
3. B. Murphy, *Congressional Theatre: Dramatizing McCarthyism on Stage, Film, and Television* (Cambridge University Press, 1999), pp. 2–3.
4. B. Atkinson, *Broadway* (MacMillan, 1970), p. 249.
5. Ibid., p. 418.
6. Ibid., p. 394.
7. B. McConachie, *American Theater in the Culture of the Cold War: Producing and Contesting Containment 1947–1962* (University of Iowa Press, 2003), p. xi.
8. G. M. Berkowitz, *New Broadways: Theatre across America 1950–1980* (Rowman and Littlefield, 1982), p. 9.
9. D. Halberstam, *The Fifties* (Random House, 1993), p. 256.
10. B. Atkinson and A. Hirschfeld, *The Lively Years* (Association Press, 1973), p. 206.
11. T. P. Adler, *American Drama, 1940–1960: A Critical History* (Twayne, 1994), p. 85.
12. Atkinson and Hirschfeld, *The Lively Years*, p. 178.
13. M. Rothstein, "Elia Kazan, Influential Director, Dies at 94," *New York Times*, September 28, 2003, A1.
14. F. Rich, *The Theatre Art of Boris Aronson* (Knopf, 1987), p. 129.
15. L.-M. Miranda, "What Art Can Do," *The Atlantic*, 324 (December 2019), p. 113.

16. J. Cutcher, *Bob Fosse* (Rosen, 2006), pp. 21, 27.
17. H. M. Housely, "The Female Director's Odyssey: The Broadway Sisterhood," in *Women and Society* (Marist College, 1993), pp. 107, 112.
18. "Margaret Webster Dies at 67; Stage Director and Ex-Actress," *New York Times*, November 14, 1972, p. 33.
19. M. Webster, *Don't Put Your Daughter on the Stage* (Knopf, 1972), p. 173.
20. P. Moor, "Lady on Her Way," *Theatre Arts*, 33 (January 1949), p. 54.
21. O. E. Brady, "Theodore Ward's *Our Lan'*: From the Slavery of Melodrama to the Freedom of Tragedy," *Callaloo* 21 (1984), p. 41.
22. McConachie, *American Theater*, p. 190.
23. J. Papp, quoted in "Brooklyn's Gift to the Bard," *Theatre Arts*, 342 (January 1958), p. 11.
24. Berkowitz, *New Broadways*, p. 48.

Select Bibliography

Abbotson, S. C. W. *Modern American Drama: Playwriting in the 1950s, Voices, Documents, New Interpretations*. Bloomsbury Methuen, 2018.

Adler, T. P. *American Drama, 1940–1960: A Critical History*. Twayne, 1994.

Albee, E. *Remembering Arthur Miller*, C. Bigsby (ed.). Methuen, 2005.

Berkowitz, G. M. *New Broadways: Theatre across America 1950–1980*. Rowman and Littlefield, 1982.

Bigsby, C. *Modern American Drama: 1945–2000*. Cambridge University Press, 2000.

Halberstam, D. *The Fifties*. Random House, 1993.

Krasner, D. *American Drama 1945–2000*. Blackwell, 2006.

McConachie, B. *American Theater in the Culture of the Cold War: Producing and Contesting Containment 1947–1962*. University of Iowa Press, 2003.

Murphy, B. *Congressional Theatre: Dramatizing McCarthyism on Stage, Film, and Television*. Cambridge University Press, 1999.

Petigny, A. *The Permissive Society: America, 1941–1965*. Cambridge University Press, 2009.

CHAPTER 2

Bridging the Gap
Broadway and the Experimental from the 1960s to 2020

Cindy Rosenthal

This chapter launches with "the movement" of the 1960s. The notion of a movement – forged by individuals who join together to make change – is often associated with "underground" efforts or "outsider" status, and connected to avant-garde impulses. I argue here that powerful agendas, made manifest via a groundswell of creative innovations, can transcend barriers and shake foundations. Indeed, "established" culture centers undergo transformations and reshape society profoundly. Broadway and mainstream theatre – as was true of most manifestations of the human spirit, of culture, of the intellect, of collaborative efforts to make change, to make "something new" – underwent multiple and significant transformations during the 1960s and in the decades that followed.

The 1960s and the "Mainstream Experimental"

The 1960s were characterized by mass protests beginning with struggles for civil rights and Black Power, with antiwar demonstrations, with actions for gay rights, women's rights, and Indigenous peoples' rights, and by a sweeping generational divide. In *The Sixties, Center Stage*, James Harding and I argue, along with our contributors, that innovative performance aesthetics were not exclusively the domain of experimental theatres (Off and Off-Off-Broadway), but rather that mainstream and popular performances of the period also demonstrated a movement toward the politically progressive and toward making radical choices in aesthetics, style, and content. Arguing against a binary opposition, Harding and I coined a phrase to capture this phenomenon: "the mainstream experimental."[1] An illustrious and key example of "the mainstream experimental" was director Peter Brook's Royal Shakespeare Company production of *Marat/Sade*, which arrived from London, opening to acclaim on Broadway in December 1965.

In addition to the commercial and critical success of lauded foreign imports like *Marat/Sade*, shifts in the style(s) and content of US mainstream theatre were driven in part by the fact that theatre artists frequently worked both uptown and downtown during this period. Playwright Edward Albee, director/choreographer Jerome Robbins, performer Zero Mostel, designers Boris Aronson and Patricia Zipprodt, and director/composer Tom O'Horgan are significant examples.

Regional and Off-Broadway theatres, known for producing original works and plays of emerging writers, also became collaborators with mainstream commercial theatre producers. One example of a successful regional to Broadway transfer was Washington DC's Arena Stage's move of Howard Sackler's *The Great White Hope* (1967–68) to Broadway. The Public Theater, under the leadership of Joseph Papp, helped a trio of early ground-breakers – *Hair*, *A Chorus Line*, and *for colored girls* – become Broadway hits. The Public is an especially important downtown, Off-Broadway institution that continues to play a crucial role in moving Broadway/mainstream theatre forward. In the decades that followed the 1960s, other pathbreaking Public Theater shows including *The Normal Heart, Bring in 'da Noise, Bring in 'da Funk, Topdog/Underdog, Caroline, or Change, Hamilton, Fun Home,* and *Eclipsed* moved identity politics and the energies and explorations of diverse makers center-stage on Broadway, and into the mainstream. Joseph Papp chose *Hair*, in its first iteration, to officially open the Public Theater in the fall of 1967.

The Movement: From Ensemble to Tribe

Hair opened at the Biltmore Theater on Broadway on April 29, 1968, and in scholar Elizabeth Wollman's words "served as a linchpin that harnessed the commercial potential of the theatrical mainstream to the experimentalism of Off-Off Broadway."[2] The 1967–68 Broadway season proved to be a financial highpoint for the decade; annual grosses on Broadway reached $59 million and ticket sales $9.5 million. And *Hair* soared to the height of commercial success. Thanks to never-before-seen coverage in print, radio, and television media and a phenomenally successful cast album, *Hair*'s message (and commercial appeal) rapidly spread internationally. Laura MacDonald's notion of *Hair* as a "global commodity" was born in the heyday following its opening, at the end of the 1967–68 Broadway season.[3]

Hair was collaborative on multiple levels – first of all, it joined the efforts of radical ensemble Open Theater members Gerome Ragni and James

Rado, who created the book and lyrics and would play leading roles in the musical with the contributions of another "downtown" artist, La MaMa Experimental Theatre Troupe director, Tom O'Horgan. The centrality of collaboration was also key to an emphasis on the creative work of the ensemble and the notion that a cast could be conceived as a tribe instead of as a hierarchically structured entity where celebrity actors' names were situated above the title. Indeed, the importance of the ensemble was a crucial element in experimental performance in the 1960s and 1970s, but it also became a powerful through-line that connected the work of "downtown" artists and their performances with "uptown" artists and their theatre work.

Iconic of the sexual revolution of the 1960s, *Hair* famously broke ground in its inclusion of full-frontal nudity in its final Act 1 scene, again, shattering barriers between practices of and expectations for experimental, downtown theatre and commercial, uptown theatres. [In fact, the actor playing Marat, in *Marat/Sade*, Ian Richardson, had already revealed his naked rear end on a Broadway stage three years earlier.] Although nudity on stage might seem to be an emblem of freedom more aligned with the downtown, experimental scene, the Off-Broadway productions of *Hair* at the Public and at the Cheetah that preceded the Broadway run did not include the removal of clothing at the end of Act 1. Whether the gesture was spontaneous or planned (this remains a controversial point), the first occurrence of a nude scene in *Hair* took place on its Broadway opening night. Although some spectators and critics hailed this choice as an aesthetic and political milestone, others decried it as "commercialism."

Hair also broke ground in its nonlinear, fragmented structure and its foregrounding of characters that directly connect with issues that were central to "the movement" of the 1960s. Claude, a central figure in the show, is a lost and untethered soul who personifies the hope and heartbreak of the 1960s generation. Claude's death, as a casualty of the Vietnam War, is *Hair's* final and devastating image. Scholar Sarah Browne emphasizes *Hair's* resonances with the civil rights movement in her close reading of "Colored Spade," sung by Hud, a character who is African American. She argues that although the song plays on stereotypical representations of Black males, Hud and the ensemble bring to the stage a powerful and effective reappropriation of Blackness in this number.[4]

Holding a Mirror up to America

Interrogating the half-century of Broadway theatre that began in the 1960s without highlighting the vision, power, and prowess of Harold Prince is unimaginable. Prince, who died at age ninety-one in July 2019 after a sixty-year career, produced thirty-three Broadway shows and directed twenty. He, more than any other director, is attributed with creating "the concept musical," although it was critic Martin Gottfried who first referenced the term extensively. *Fiddler on the Roof* (1964) and *Cabaret* (1966) were both produced by Prince, who also directed *Cabaret* and many other break-out Broadway musicals of magnitude including Stephen Sondheim's *Company* (1970) and *Follies* (1971).

Fiddler and *Cabaret* emerged out of growing interest in looking "back to one's roots" for Jewish Americans.[5] *Fiddler* was thought of as the last "golden age" musical while *Cabaret* was regarded as the first "concept musical," a term that refers to works that explore a theme, rather than accentuate a conflict-driven plot and often eschew a traditional happy ending. Both shows center on crises in Jewish history brought about by anti-Semitism and are radical/experimental in numerous ways. Gender bias and discrimination based on sexual preferences were also part of the story *Cabaret* was telling, and the push for women's rights was integral to the father–daughter struggles at the heart of *Fiddler*. In Stacy Wolf's view, "*Fiddler* navigates the politics of gender as much as ethnicity."[6] Wolf points to the significance of the publication of Betty Friedan's 1963 *The Feminine Mystique* as a significant backdrop for the opening of *Fiddler* — with Tevye's daughters' striving for independence as a reflection of the second wave feminist movement that surged forward in the 1960s and 1970s.

In *Changed for Good: A Feminist History of the Broadway Musical*, Wolf analyzes Harold Prince's staging of musical numbers in *Cabaret*'s Kit Kat Club, illuminating how these scenes comment on the preceding scenes and interrupt the flow of the plot in a Brechtian way. Prince positioned the audience as the Club's spectators and implicated them as witnesses of the "decadent" performances staged in this highly charged milieu. Further supported by Boris Aronson's set design, which included a large mirror that reflected the audience, Wolf stated, "*Cabaret* is as much about mid-1960s America as it is about pre-Nazi Germany."[7]

It is worth noting that *Hair, Fiddler, Cabaret*, and *The Boys in the Band*, a landmark work in gay theatre that premiered Off-Broadway in 1968, were each holding a mirror up to mid-late 1960s America. With themes that spotlighted racism, feminism, pacifism, anti-Semitism, antiauthoritarianism, and homophobia, expressed via innovations in style and aesthetics, these works sharpened spectators' awareness of societal issues and especially identity politics during a tumultuous time.

The Stonewall riots in Greenwich Village, June 1969, were a watershed moment in gay rights activism and had a sizable impact on the broad spectrum of theatre and performance work that reflected LGBTQ+ consciousness-raising, community building, and the fight for equality and freedom in the decades that followed. Opening a year before Stonewall (April 15, 1968), and produced midtown at Theatre Four, *The Boys in the Band*, about a group of male gay friends at a birthday party, was a commercial hit and a controversial representation of male gay urban life. A number of gay artists and activists pushed back against the defeatism of the characters, while others saw a stark but utterly recognizable way of life on the stage – and pointed out that in Mart Crowley's play at least there were no suicides, deaths, or heterosexual marriages to tie things up neatly.

The 1970s: Expanding Ensemble Work on Broadway

In the 1970s, two other transfers Papp orchestrated from the Public Theater to Broadway were quintessential ensemble pieces, albeit works that couldn't be more different in style, agenda, and production values – *A Chorus Line* (1975) and *for colored girls who have considered suicide/ when the rainbow is enuf* (1976). *Company* (1970) and *Godspell*, which opened Off-Broadway in 1971 and on Broadway in 1976, were two other very different ensemble-based pieces. *Godspell*'s origins trace back to Off-Off-Broadway and La MaMa Experimental Theatre. La MaMa, the downtown home of Tom O'Horgan and countless other artists, is an East Village theatre founded by pioneering producing director Ellen Stewart (aka "MaMa") in 1961. Stewart was especially receptive to producing the work of young, not-yet-established playwrights, and *Godspell*'s writer, John-Michael Tebelak, a graduate student at Carnegie Mellon University, fit that bill. *Godspell* ran for two weeks at La MaMa before producers Edgar Lansbury and Joseph Beruh moved it, with a score by Stephen Schwartz, to two Off-Broadway theatres before transferring the already very successful show to Broadway.

Although Stewart was renowned for making a home for her theatre artists/"babies" even in the worst of times and circumstances, New York City in the 1970s was a "forbidding" place in the words of theatre critic Brooks Atkinson.[8] New York suffered in myriad ways from the impact of a severe economic downturn – a perfect storm of financial issues – including a stock market decline and the cost of municipal services skyrocketing in the 1960s. There were lay-offs and there were strikes (police, teachers, and sanitation workers) that contributed to a debilitating downward spiral in the quality of life day to day in New York City. A visceral phrase that captured the city's decay described one of its five boroughs – "the Bronx is burning" – but, indeed, the city as a whole experienced a significant upsurge in crime and a concomitant shrinking of industry and population.

Elizabeth Wollman describes *Company* as a post-Stonewall musical that had a seismic impact on gay theatre. She points out that the indecisive, possibly bisexual central character of Bobby and the heterosexual couples that are his friends were resonant with the "uncertainty and the emotional malaise of [the time] period" and made contemporary audiences uncomfortable. Wollman draws a connection between Claude in *Hair* and Bobby – neither could make a commitment to another human and the worlds they inhabited are fragmentary, and very loosely strung together.[9]

In describing the phenomenal success of *A Chorus Line*, scholar Eric Grode states that the show proved to be "even more popular than *Hair*," ultimately "generating approximately $40 million for the New York Shakespeare Festival."[10] Philip J. Smith spoke of the direct and seismic impact *A Chorus Line* had on the Shubert Organization. Smith had served as President and Chairman of the legendary company/theatre owner that co-produced the show: "Before *A Chorus Line* there was no money. After *A Chorus Line* there was nothing but money."[11]

A Chorus Line, which opened at the Shubert Theatre on Broadway July 25, 1975, turned a dazzling spotlight on the lives of Broadway dancers who were typically viewed only as the attractive background/ support team for stars in musical theatre. Instead, in *A Chorus Line*, the specifics of the tough, sweaty, dramatic, and sometimes hilarious stories of individual Broadway "gypsies" took center stage. Theatre artists, critics, and "lay" spectators were bowled over by the show's penetrating and poignant score and book, which were based on director/choreographer Michael Bennett's tape-recorded, late-night, wine-infused talk sessions with Broadway dancers he knew. *A Chorus Line*'s show-within-a-show conceit left audiences with the "singular sensation" of a showbiz fairy tale come true for the dancers who shared their hopes, fears, and dreams on the stage. This was not the whole story, nor how the story played out for cast members of *A Chorus Line*, splendidly bedecked, as they were, in the final number's iconic white top-hats and tails. Much as members of the *Hair* cast, such as Lorrie Davis, reported on their experiences,[12] *A Chorus Line* performers' substantial sharing of personal information and artistic processes, which were the creative building blocks of these projects, were never appropriately acknowledged nor were the performers properly remunerated as contributors. Although huge profits landed in Michael Bennett's, the Public Theater's, and the Shubert Organization's pockets, performers were left woefully under or uncompensated. Decades later law suits provided long overdue financial compensation to many of the dancers that had gifted Bennett their stories. With greater union [Actors Equity Association] oversight and specific legislation in place, safeguards are now in place that prevent the sidelining of performers/co-devisers. Excluding performers from the economic windfalls experienced by Broadway mega-hit producers and directors was an unfortunate outcome of meshing experimental (ensemble) work with the realm of the mainstream/commercial (especially in the 1960s and 1970s).

Significantly, *A Chorus Line* and Ntozake Shange's *for colored girls* share a through-line, an important trope and activist strategy that was born out of the second wave women's movement – the consciousness-raising group – or CR group. As Stacy Wolf points out, the origins of *A Chorus Line* (Bennett's late-night gatherings where dancers shared their stories) and the opening sections of the musical itself (Zach, the character of the director, asks the dancers to talk about themselves) closely mirror consciousness-raising group practices. Wolf defines these as "the activity of gathering to share stories for personal affirmation as well as impetus for larger political action."[13] But, unlike feminist practices, the gathering and sharing in *A Chorus Line* is not connected to any larger political action; although personal affirmation and community building were outcomes, art-making was the immediate goal for Bennett (and for Zach).

Bennett's agenda was to build a show that derived from dancers' stories. Once Bennett conceived the idea, he paid dancers who participated in workshops for the show $100 for their efforts. As noted above, a positive change in the form of more appropriate financial remuneration for performers was not achieved until decades later.

However, the "personal is political" agenda at the core of Shange's *for colored girls* was vibrantly clear from the start – making Black women's stories accessible, audible, and visible. As critic Jack Kroll notes, "These poems are political in the deepest sense, but there's no dogma, no sentimentality no grinding of mythic axes."[14] Ntozake Shange began performing her poetry about Black women's experiences in the San Francisco Bay area in the early 1970s, first collaborating with dancer/choreographer Paula Moss on stringing together Shange's poems as a performance piece. Shange and Moss came east and performed in bars in Manhattan's East Village where they came to the attention of Oz Scott, then a New York Public Theater stage manager (now a highly celebrated stage, film, and television director, writer, and producer), who became the director of the piece. Scott invited five other Black women performers to collaborate with him, Shange, and Moss on creating a unique ensemble work Shange described as a choreopoem.

Character identities in *for colored girls* and in *A Chorus Line* are both distinguished and circumscribed by their relationship to the ensemble, albeit with important distinctions. Shange named her ensemble for the colors of the rainbow: Lady in Brown, Lady in Yellow, Lady in Red, Lady in Green, Lady in Purple, Lady in Blue, and Lady in Orange. At the end of *A Chorus Line's* Act I, Zach identifies the ensemble (except for his former partner, Cassie) by their assigned "audition" numbers only. The rainbow constituted by the ensemble members in *for colored girls* speaks to the creation of an organic, shimmering, powerful community, stronger in its unity than in its separate parts – a goal of the consciousness-raising group. When Zach uses their numbers to identify members of the chorus line at the end of Act I, each is separated from the other – some dancers will be chosen, and others will be rejected in his cut. At this crucial juncture, the *Chorus Line* ensemble loses power, voice, and agency because the power/authority in *A Chorus Line* is located not in the group but in the director/choreographer/decider, Zach, who is in charge of who remains in the ensemble.

At its openings Off-Broadway and on, *for colored girls* spoke to and of an underrepresented community in experimental and mainstream theatre. In cultural critic Michele Wallace's view, *for colored girls'* audiences in the Anspacher Theater were not typical of Public Theater spectators because one-third to two-thirds were Black. Wallace declared, "As a black feminist I usually feel cheated by black theatre, but this is the night I'll make up for all those other nights."[15] When *for colored girls* moved to Broadway (opening September 15, 1976), Joe Papp (co-producing with Woodie King, Jr. of the Henry Street Settlement's New Federal Theatre, who first presented the show downtown) was mindful of the breakthroughs this piece was making in a mainstream, commercial venue. Seven performers – all Black women – made up the cast of an original show comprised of poetry and movement by two newcomers, a Black playwright and a Black director. In Papp's view, *for colored girls* "upgrades the entire standard of Broadway. . . . We've introduced the first work of a writer, also the first work of a director. And, for some of the women in it, this is the first time they've played roles of this magnitude and received recognition for it."[16]

The 1980s: Identity Politics amid the Rise of Consumerism on Broadway

If the 1970s had made it possible for some of the ideals and goals of feminism(s) to be illuminated on "mainstream experimental" stages, the 1980s seemed like a step backward, as Stacy Wolf notes, with fewer central roles and breakthroughs for women.[17] And although the economy surged and expanded in the 1980s, gaps between the haves and the have-nots widened. The conservative, capitalism-focused administrations of Ronald Reagan in the United States and Margaret Thatcher in Great Britain marked a decisive shift away from the progressive politics of the 1960s and 1970s. And yet, the 1980s also made room for new voices and American stories that were crafted with the grit of realism and with lyricism. The plays in the following sections connect Broadway audiences to a fresh perspective on and experience of American identities and journeys through a re-visioning of character, language, and imagery for the contemporary stage, a far cry from the commercial spectacle of mega-musicals.

CATS *Conquers Broadway*

Along with the flash of new consumerism came an appetite for the mega-musical hits that were proliferating on London's West End stages – *CATS* in 1982 was the first of these to make a splash in the United States. The epitome of "the British Invasion," *CATS* was a commercial triumph for the triumvirate of Cameron Mackintosh (producer), Andrew Lloyd Webber (music and lyrics), and Trevor Nunn (director). The eye-popping spectacle created for *CATS* required a complete overhaul of Broadway's Winter Garden Theater. Although full of technical feats, the show was structured as a revue and based on a collection of cat poems published by T. S. Eliot in 1939. This too, like *Company* and *A Chorus Line,* was an ensemble-based show, and much as *A Chorus Line* was built on the stories of dancers, *CATS* was built on the stories of particular cats (!), but dancers embodied each of these cat personalities. Hence, like *A Chorus Line, CATS* was predominatcly a dance show. In 1997, it surpassed *A Chorus Line* as the longest running musical on Broadway and at its closing in 2000, "it had grossed 380 million on Broadway (and nearly $3 billion world-wide)."[18] Instead of skewing the musical theatre experience toward "high" culture, *CATS* took spectators on a deep dive into mass culture, not unlike "a theme park ride," as critic Larry Stempel describes it.[19] The lure of *CATS* and its family-friendly appeal live on. A musical feature film version of *CATS* produced by Universal Pictures with a celebrity in each cat role landed in movie theatres during the 2019 holiday season to unanimously poor notices but fast became a cult classic.

Wilson's American Century Cycle

Playwright August Wilson whose work first came to Broadway in the 1980s was a path-breaker in myriad ways – no playwright besides Neil Simon has had more work produced on Broadway. Wilson's mission and vision were unique – he tasked himself with telling the story of African American generations dealing with the legacy of slavery – the boisterous beauty, profound poetry, and turbulent tragedy of African American experience in the twentieth century. His project consisted of writing ten plays, one to represent each decade of the century. Blues was an ongoing motif and inspiration in his writing, as was collage, influenced as Wilson was by visual artist Romare Bearden. Wilson's ten-play series was sometimes called *The Pittsburgh Cycle*, sometimes *The American Century Cycle*. *Ma Rainey's Black Bottom* (1984) was the first of his plays to be produced on Broadway. Director Lloyd Richards of the National Playwrights Conference at the O'Neill Theater Center and the Yale Repertory Theatre was a comrade and collaborator of Wilson's and a nurturer and director of his work. In *Ma Rainey's Black Bottom*, directed by Richards on Broadway, Wilson turned a spotlight on the 1920s rhythm and blues singer, Gertrude (Ma) Rainey, who achieved early "cross-over" success when her recordings were sought after by whites as well as Blacks. Her indomitable personal power and the deep pain she and her band members struggle with in the face of racial discrimination and brutality drive the play. Even as Rainey holds onto her truth and independence (for now) in dealing with the white men who run the recording studio, in the play's final scene, trauma, loss, and violence crush the life out of the Black male musicians she works with. Frank Rich writes in his review of the Broadway opening, "This play is a searing inside account of what white racism does to its victims and it floats on the same authentic artistry as the blues music it celebrates."[20] *Ma Rainey* earned three Tony nominations. *Fences*, a family drama that explodes the American Dream, is set in the 1950s. *Fences* opened on Broadway in 1987 and won the Tony and the Pulitzer Prize. Wilson won a second Pulitzer Prize for *The Piano Lesson* (set in the 1930s, premiered 1987, on Broadway, 1990). The first play Wilson wrote for the cycle, *Jitney* (1982), set in the 1970s, was the last of his works to make it to Broadway (2017). Although roles like Ma Rainey and Troy in *Fences* were substantial and often drew well-known actors (Whoopi Goldberg in the 2003 revival of *Ma Rainey*, James Earl Jones in *Fences'* Broadway premiere in 1987, and Denzel Washington in its 2010 revival), Wilson's plays were built on strong ensemble casts. Wilson died of cancer at the age of sixty in 2005; he was the first African American to have a Broadway theatre named after him.

The Impact of AIDS

The AIDS epidemic decimated artistic communities throughout the United States. Some of the most profound and sharply crafted plays of the mid/late 1980s were created in response to the fury, terror, and tragic losses caused by this scourge. These works originated both Off-Broadway and in theatres outside New York City before moving to Broadway. Gay rights activist Larry Kramer's *The Normal Heart* opened to rousing acclaim at the Public Theater in 1985. His autobiographical and documentary-style play tracked the early history of the Gay Men's Health Crisis organization and was a call to arms, forecasting the full extent of the catastrophe and blasting some in the gay community and outside of it for not heeding the lethal outcomes of homophobia.

A quarter of a century later, in 2011, *The Normal Heart* was finally produced on Broadway with an all-star cast in a devastating production that raised the magnitude of the work to that of a modern Greek tragedy, garnering the Tony Award for Best Revival of a Play. As spectators left the theatre (this writer included), they came face to face with Kramer, then seventy-five, handing out flyers in front of the marquis. A practice more typical of the downtown scene, surely – but Kramer, with his characteristic passion and rage, wanted to meet theatregoers head-on and impress them directly with the urgent need to continue the fight against homophobia and the spread of AIDS. This work, in its breathtaking twenty-first-century production, was a revelation, especially for the twenty and thirty-somethings, gay and straight, who had never witnessed this level of intensity in arts-activism before. This uniquely powerful and polemical theatre experience that "changed the lives" of those who saw it when AIDS was entering full crisis in 1985 did not take place on the fringes or in the experimental realm in 2011, but on a Broadway stage. This time, it shook mainstream, commercial audiences – many with little or no awareness of the history and ferocity of AIDS – to their core.

However, a realistic drama about the impact of the AIDS crisis did open on Broadway in 1985. William Hoffman's *As Is* had none of *The Normal Heart's* anger or manifesto-spirit, but it made the fear, struggles, and grief of gay men, their families, friends, and health care workers visible and palpable to mainstream audiences for the first time. Critics and spectators found the play's sensitive, elegiac quality intensely moving. After a brief run downtown at the Circle Repertory Company, *As Is* transferred to Broadway where it won the Drama Desk Award for Outstanding New Play and was nominated for a Tony Award.

Feminisms?

One of the few plays that made it to Broadway in the 1980s written by a feminist playwright was Wendy Wasserstein's *The Heidi Chronicles* (1989), a lively dramatic comedy in the style of realism about a feminist art historian, who, after a series of unsuccessful love affairs, finally finds happiness in motherhood. *The Heidi Chronicles* premiered Off-Broadway at Playwrights Horizons in 1988 where its instant success resulted in a speedy move uptown. On Broadway, Wasserstein's play won the Tony Award in 1989 and the Pulitzer Prize for Drama but was lambasted by some feminist critics at the time (and again in 2015 when the show had a Broadway revival) for Wasserstein's depiction of Heidi. Some critics saw the piece as "anti-feminist" and pushed back against Heidi's trajectory – the serio-comic coming of age story of a highly educated career woman who tries "to have it all" and fails – only finding fulfillment after she adopts a child. Wasserstein made her mark on Broadway with two other realistic, comic/dramatic works, which also chronicle contemporary women striving to balance work, love and family – the semiautobiographical *The Sisters Rosensweig* (1993) and *An American Daughter* (1997). Wasserstein's last play, *Third*, opened at Lincoln Center (Off-Broadway) in 2005. In his *Times* review, Ben Brantley observes with prescience (no one besides Wasserstein's closest friends knew she was terminally ill at the time), "*Third* exhales a gentle breath of autumn, a rueful awareness of death and of seasons past, that makes it impossible to dismiss it as a quick-sketch comedy of political manners."[21] Wasserstein died of lymphoma, at the age of fifty-five, in January 2006.

Wasserstein's plays owe a substantial debt to the legacy of Friedan's *The Feminine Mystique* and its impact on second wave feminism and the many achievements of the 1960s–1980s women's movement. There were – shockingly – no other plays in evidence on Broadway during the 1980s that paid a similar debt to Freidan or reflected emerging and shifting feminist perspectives, beyond the second wave. As Stacy Wolf points out, feminists in the 1990s and beyond took steps to make art that in terms of style and content was a corrective to the second wave, and this movement, originally put forward by women of color, sought "to incorporate race and ethnic consciousness into a gendered critique." Wolf adds that this third wave also takes on "trans, queer and shifting affiliations" and that the numerous stylistic and aesthetic expressions of third wave feminisms are as diverse as the specific individuals who take on this praxis,[22] which we shall see in the next section, which explores mainstream theatre in the 1990s.

The 1990s: Corporate Partners, Disneyfication, and Reaching Generation X with New Forms of Theatre

Corporatization of musicals in the United States became the norm in the 1990s and 2000s. As Wolf points out, multimedia star Oprah Winfrey's production of *The Color Purple* (2005), an adaptation of Alice Walker's Pulitzer Prize–winning novel with an African American central character in a lesbian relationship (indeed, a third wave-influenced production), also remarkably fit and thrived on this new model.[23] The change to corporate control of Broadway began with the "Disneyfication" of the Times Square neighborhood in the mid-1990s, led by then Mayor Rudolph Giuliani and Governor George Pataki, with the goal of attracting tourist dollars back into the city by cleaning up porn shops and restoring deteriorated and abandoned theatres. Even before *Beauty and the Beast* opened at the Palace Theatre (April 18, 1994), the Disney organization had begun to investigate how to acquire a Broadway theatre of its own; indeed, Disney Theatrical Productions was founded in 1993 with this goal in mind. On July 20, 1995, Giuliani and Pataki announced that Disney would take a forty-nine-year lease from the city on the New Amsterdam Theatre, which Disney would renovate with a substantial loan from New York State.[24] Soon after, AMC, the movie chain, and Madame Tussauds also joined forces, as Disney had, with the 42nd Street Development Project, and established locations on the once honky-tonk stretch of 42nd Street between Broadway and Eighth Avenues.[25] And thus, the rebirth of Times Square and its environs was under way.

Kushner's (First) Great Work on Broadway

The winner of the Pulitzer Prize (*Millennium Approaches*, 1993) and the Drama Desk Award for Outstanding Play and the Tony Award for Best Play (*Millennium Approaches, 1993* and *Perestroika, 1994*), *Angels in America: A Gay Fantasia on National Themes* premiered at the Eureka

Theatre in San Francisco in 1991. This two-part epic work focused on Tony Kushner's critical and fantastical interrogation of the impact of the AIDS crisis in the United States. With numerous productions throughout the United States and the globe, the kudos Kushner received established him as one of the great playwrights of the century.

Directed on Broadway by George C. Wolfe, *Angels* was a monumental and transformative political theatre event in the mainstream, commercial realm. The two parts of the epic play were presented in repertory on Broadway in November 1993, following *Millennium's* opening in May. Oskar Eustis and Tony Taccone of the Eureka Theatre had originally commissioned the work in 1990; David Esbjornson directed the play's first iteration at the Eureka. As per Kushner's notes, the performance style was meant to be minimalist and actor-driven and the actors were double or triple cross-gender cast, which highlighted the gender, class, sexuality, and age critiques integral to his work. A fan of Brecht's episodic, epic theatre, Kushner was interested in the visibility of theatre apparatus throughout – allowing spectators to be fully conscious of and even participatory in the theatre event. Frank Rich wrote of the London production, which preceded the Broadway opening, "that even as the AIDS body count continues to rise, this tragedy has pushed some creative minds, many of them in the theatre, to new and daring heights of imaginative expression."[26] As theatre critic Chris Jones writes, "Roy Cohn or no Roy Cohn, [Kushner had] made the point that Broadway could and must be about a lot more than snagging tickets to *Cats* . . . and with apologies to Prior's final lines in one of the most important plays of its century – the Great Work had begun."[27]

Bridging the Downtown–Uptown Divide as the Millennium Approaches

Making Great Work happen on a Broadway stage – especially if one defines Great Work as being politically efficacious, theatrically innovative, and powerfully of the moment (as Kushner understood it) – was challenging and Kushner's work was pathbreaking. But, following Kushner's triumph, Broadway ground was broken again when Anna Deavere Smith's solo show, *Twilight: Los Angeles, 1992,* moved uptown from the Public Theater in 1994 (again, directed by George C. Wolfe). Her "meticulous," "panoramic," and "transformative" work was nominated for two Tony Awards. In his *New York Times* review of the Public Theater production David Richards writes, "she does people's souls. She is so good at the task that to describe *Twilight: Los Angeles, 1992* as a one-woman show is patently ridiculous."[28] Smith fluidly and precisely embodied and voiced the hundreds of individuals she interviewed – African Americans, Korean Americans, and whites in LA who were caught up in the violence that followed the savage beating by Los Angeles police of Rodney King (a "pre"-Black Lives Matter atrocity that went viral via a video recording). The miracle and wonder of Smith's performance technique is her creation of *communitas* – the shared sense of unity and connection with the Other – among her spectators. She performs her subjects' exact words, intonations, and movements in order "to become them" – in this way, performing her own take on "the personal is political." Anna Deavere Smith, a light-skinned woman of color "becomes the Other" – in fact, many others, who speak through her bodily presence and voice on the stage. Her work in the mainstream/ commercial realm reminds us of Stacy Wolf's claim for the emergence of third wave feminist experimentation in 1990s theatre. *Twilight: Los Angeles* deploys fruitful and challenging gender, race, class, and age critiques via Smith's multilayered Brechtian-inspired acting technique.

She first presented her original performance method and practice in New York to standing ovations at the Public Theater in 1992. Her *Fires in the Mirror: Crown Heights, Brooklyn and Other Identities* explores the violent conflicts between Jews and Blacks in Crown Heights, August 1991, when riots erupted following the death of a Caribbean American boy and led to the death of a young Orthodox Jewish scholar. *Fires* was nominated for the Pulitzer Prize. Smith's solo performances are in the style of documentary or verbatim theatre, a form that is usually associated with the downtown, avant-garde scene, not produced on mainstream/commercial stages. A recipient of a MacArthur "genius" grant and the National Humanities Medal, Smith's one-person plays – each based on dozens and sometimes hundreds of interviews that focus on individuals and communities challenged by social issues – have been widely produced and several have been turned into films, including *Fires* and *Twilight*. Whether produced with the playwright as the central performer, with other performers, or with large casts, Smith's plays continue to achieve critical and financial success at regional theatres and in New York City, where Second Stage and the Signature Theatre have produced her work Off-Broadway in midtown spaces. Her work provides vivid evidence of the positive reception an experimental maker can receive uptown and how feminist playwriting techniques have shifted beyond the second wave.

Spalding Gray's monologue-based performances also originated downtown; and he too developed a unique method for creating and performing his original work, which had a distinctive impact on spectators. Like Smith, he generated a new form of theatre that played with and exploded notions of character and identity. Both artists first presented their monologue performances on Broadway in the early/mid-1990s, irrevocably shifting mainstream/commercial theatre spectators' expectations for and understanding of solo work from that time forward. Gray, like Smith, moved his performances to a Broadway-size house (in his case, Lincoln Center) after first presenting them in Off- or Off-Off-Broadway spaces. Gray's works are not documentary in style, however; they are entirely – if fantastically – autobiographical. *Monster in a Box* was the first monologue Gray performed on Broadway (1991, made into a film in 1992), and *Morning, Noon and Night* was the last of his monologues to play on Broadway (1999). In *Monster in a Box*, Gray directly addressed his audience, seated at a desk with his open journal/script before him, telling the "truth" (which was always in question) about his struggles with the Hollywood film industry and his attempts to publish a "monster" novel, probing the devastating impact his mother's suicide had on him.

The first of Gray's monologues that brought him mainstream, commercial attention was *Swimming to Cambodia*, which premiered Off-Broadway (1986) and was made into a film (1987). *Swimming to Cambodia* detailed his harrowing, disturbing, and sometimes hilarious experiences working on the film *The Killing Fields*, about the Cambodian genocide, shot in Thailand. All of Gray's monologue accounts were compellingly self-deprecatory and careened from zany to lyrical to tragic on a dime. Gray spent the majority of his life in the theatre creating experimental work with celebrated downtown avant-garde ensembles: The Performance Group, with director Richard Schechner, and the Wooster Group, under the direction of Elizabeth LeCompte. Gray committed suicide in 2004 at age sixty-two.

In her detailed account of the collaborations that culminated in *Bring in 'da Noise, Bring in 'da Funk*, another dance-based show that galvanized the "dying" Broadway theatre (in her view, much as *A Chorus Line* had done twenty years before), Elizabeth Kendall describes George C. Wolfe (his tenure as the Public Theater's artistic director was from 1993 to 2004) as a kind of ring master/school teacher. Wolfe sent disparate artists (choreographer/dancer Savion Glover, composer/singer Ann Duquesnay, poet-performer Reg E. Gaines, and street "bucket" drummers Jared Crawford and Raymond King) into different rehearsal studios at the Public Theater downtown to experiment and create. On the first day of rehearsal, August 17, 1995, there was no script. The artists' connective tissues met in a mess of index cards on a rolling bulletin board that Wolfe supervised. Slightly later in the process, set designer Riccardo Hernández joined the "class"; he threw away his original elaborate designs and listened to and watched rehearsals, creating new sketches. Similarly, Wolfe asked lighting designers Jules Fisher and Peggy Eisenhauer to use light in contrasting ways – "sometimes to set the scene, sometimes to visually express the music." Eisenhauer commented on the rarity of working without a script and declared, "we were in heaven." The projection artist Robin Silvestri and her team dove into extensive archival research, excavating previously buried images (some were of lynchings) from Black American history. Duquesnay described the working process as a "symphony of ideas."[29]

Wolfe first directed Glover as the young Jelly Roll Morton in *Jelly's Last Jam* (1992) for a production in Los Angeles that moved to Broadway; Glover's explosive tap virtuosity opened Wolfe's mind to the possibility of telling a story with a different stage-language. In poet Gaines's view, "we're telling the story of racism through tap. It's not didactic and preachy. The text is secondary to the tap." Glover and Gaines talked about a new truth that was being communicated through this collaborative work on the stage. In Glover's words, it was "thanks to George Wolfe. Before, I was happy if people came up to me after a performance and said 'You were good.' . . . Now I hope they say 'I understand you.'"[30]

Bring in 'da Noise and the New York Theatre Workshop's *Rent* moved almost simultaneously from downtown to Broadway, signifying a new wave of "street" musicals that spoke to and of the energies, spirit, passions, and desires of Generation X – somewhat loosely defined as the generation born between 1965 and 1980. According to Glover, "a lot of younger people, we want to express ourselves on a broader level, showing, groovin.' We want to be seen and be heard."[31] Critic Peter Marks reported that "crowds of teenagers gather at the Ambassador [Theatre's] stage door for the show's young tap stars to emerge."[32] The show was speaking to a young community of theatregoers who saw themselves reflected in the energy, athleticism, and power of the mostly teenage cast of *Bring in 'da Noise*. Born out of Glover's distinctive tap style, "the beat" was the metaphor that cracked open and drove home the history of young Black men in the United States – thrust on to slave ships, pushed up on auction blocks, framed on the "silver screen," hung by lynch mobs, and (still) not being able to hail a cab in front of the theatre. But the show was also expanding notions of what Broadway musical theatre could or should be. There was controversy leading up to the Tony Awards ceremony (is this really a musical if it doesn't have a "book"?), but *Bring in 'da Noise* tapped away with four awards – for Wolfe's direction, for Glover's choreography, for Fisher and Eisenhauer's lighting, and for featured actress in a musical (Duquesnay).

Broadway ticket prices continued to rise, with a dramatic increase in the mid-1970s and further increases each decade (top ticket prices went from $17.50 in 1975 to $30.00 in 1980). The top ticket price for *Rent* in 1996 was $70. But from its April 29, 1996, Broadway opening and throughout its twelve-year run, *Rent* took a stand, at least in a small way, against the elitism and bourgeois tendencies of Broadway ticket pricing by offering $20 tickets for the first two rows on performance day to the first in line. The lucky ones with those tickets – mostly young people who slept overnight on the street to achieve their goal – looked a lot like the young performers onstage in the raucous ensemble number "La Vie Bohème," bonding over and celebrating their struggles and hoping to survive the multiple odds against them.

Rent opened in 1995 at the New York Theatre Workshop in Manhattan's East Village where the world of the play inside the theatre felt and looked like the world outside the theatre – abandoned buildings and empty lots teetering on the brink of gentrification. The seedier side of Hell's Kitchen (West Forty-First Street, where *Rent* opened on Broadway at the resuscitated Nederlander Theater) looked and felt like a similar milieu. The response to *Rent* pre-Broadway was hailed in a *New York Times* headline as "The Birth of a Theatrical Comet." The show's little-known composer and book writer, Jonathan Larson, who died suddenly before the show's first preview downtown, had tapped into the moment as no one else had.

Rent transformed Broadway terrain in specific ways that spoke volumes to its young fan-base. It was one of the first Broadway musicals to feature numerous and diverse gay characters and a lesbian relationship (*Falsettos*, in 1992, another transfer from downtown, featured the first lesbian couple in a Broadway show). *Rent* was also the first Broadway musical where half of its named characters were living with AIDS.

Around the corner, but miles away in style and spectacle, *The Lion King* landed with tremendous fanfare on the shiny, new Forty-Second Street (thanks to Disneyfication) in the impressively renovated New Amsterdam Theatre in fall 1997. The Off-Broadway artist and MacArthur Grant winner Julie Taymor was Disney's choice to re-vision and direct a new version of the animated film. Taymor's production exploded with ingenious theatricality, thrillingly melding the experimental with the mainstream. In the musical's heart-stopping opening sequence, "Circle of Life," Taymor drew on her knowledge of indigenous African rituals, craft, and performance techniques to create the sensation of many animals surging together, alongside and among spectators in the auditorium. Performers playing animals in masks and headdresses were visibly, splendidly human and yet were simultaneously transformed into magnificent nonhumans before mesmerized spectators of all ages. This multigenerational appeal is, in fact, crucial; from the opening number, parents as well as children signed on, transfixed by the glorious, moving spectacle. Taymor's skills in non-Western performance modes honed internationally and Off-Off-Broadway (especially Indonesian puppetry) proved to be foundational to Disney's first Broadway success story. As Taymor declared: "*The Lion King* is a very commercial work, but what they've let me do is very experimental. I was totally delighted and surprised."[33] And as Chris Jones observes, "such a hit being almost impossible to replicate ... function[s] as a pinnacle – both financial and aesthetic – for every Broadway show that would follow."[34]

The 2000s: Post 9/11 and Beyond

> Sometimes I think the bad years happen when playwrights, actors, and directors are as appalled as everyone else by the world and the misbehavior of our leaders, and dumbstruck, exasperated, flabbergasted. Speechlessness is unavoidable. But we recover, and rage is a good engine for the stage.
>
> Tony Kushner[35]

Kushner's statement above resounds even more loudly as I write this chapter in the pandemic spring of 2020. His words followed soon upon the shocking, tragic event of the 9/11 terrorist attacks. The impact of 9/11 was felt immediately and globally, but the trauma sustained by residents of New York City was of an intensity never experienced before. The social fabric of the city was sharply torn and urban institutions stalled, until society and culture embarked on a painful period of adjustment. Post 9/11, arts and artists, especially New York City's theatre communities, played a key role in bringing people together and shining light through the darkness.

With the mission of staving off an economic crisis as well as recharging New Yorkers and tourists with creative, community energy, Mayor Rudolph Giuliani and New York's Cultural Affairs Commissioner Schuyler G. Chapin asked Jed Bernstein of the Broadway League to open theatres as soon as possible. And although all lights on Broadway were out September 11 and 12, 2001, on September 13, twenty-three Broadway theatres opened their doors and were back in business.

There was no easy road back for many performers and spectators, but the Broadway houses on September 13 were at least a half or even three-quarters full.[36] A few productions that opened months and even years later struck particularly deep chords with New Yorkers, resonating in profound ways with the shattered calm and the indelible film of sadness and grief that permeated the city. Mary Zimmerman, a MacArthur Award–winning theatre maker from Chicago, created *Metamorphoses*, which opened at Second Stage's midtown space Off-Broadway a month after the attacks. Based on stories by classical Roman poet Ovid, Zimmerman's ravishing, epic work, made in collaboration with her experimental ensemble, The Lookingglass Company, generated an acute emotional response from spectators and critics. The sold-out production's gut-thrust impact was evoked in part by the presence of a huge pool on stage through which performers emerged and moved. The metamorphosis of characters in the work inspired a kind of group hope and healing in the immediate aftermath of September 11, much as Anna Deavere Smith's work had done in a different way for New York audiences a decade earlier, following the 1991 violence in Crown Heights, Brooklyn. In Chris Jones's words, "here was a show that was explicitly designed to help its audience better deal with loss and suffering, which was pervasive."[37] Unlike the intentionality of Smith's work, however, the timing of *Metamorphoses* was not designed by Zimmerman – how could it be? In spring 2002, the production moved to Broadway, where it ran for a year with the original Chicago cast at the Circle in the Square Theatre. Zimmerman won a Tony Award for Best Director.

Over the next two decades, very different plays and performances on and Off-Broadway reverberated with New Yorkers' abiding sense of loss and the psychic scars that remained after 9/11. Sarah Ruhl's *Eurydice*, a wildly imagistic, melancholic, and playful re-visioning of the Greek myth about Orpheus and Eurydice explores love, longing, and loss and thrusts Eurydice into the center, a more active player in the story than in other versions of the tale. Although Ruhl describes this play as a personal journey, a chance for her to have another conversation with her deceased, beloved father, when *Eurydice* was first produced in New York at Second Stage's midtown Off-Broadway space in 2003, "audiences and critics alike [experienced it] as an opportunity for both personal and collective mourning," scholar Wendy Arons observes.[38] There was a delicate and searing connection between Orpheus's heartbreaking inability to read Eurydice's last letter in the play and the terminal isolation and hopelessness that mourners feel in their separation from lost loved ones. In describing her reaction to the last scene, Anita Gates in the *New York Times* states "the tears came with the suddenness of grief."[39] Both Gates and *Times* critic Charles Isherwood describe how Ruhl's play served contemporary New York audiences, who had been admonished to move on quickly after the terrorist attacks as patriotic citizens should. The crucial thing in a healing process may be instead to (re)experience the loss and come to terms with what Arons describes as a mourner's "yearning to communicate" with the lost loved one. Spectators' responses to Ruhl's play seemed especially generative of this kind of collective healing.[40]

A Charge to Shift Broadway's Demographic

Suzan-Lori Parks's *Topdog/Underdog* opened Off-Broadway at the Public Theater in July 2001 and closed at the Public a few days before September 11. In the audience at both the downtown production and on Broadway, where the play premiered at the Ambassador Theatre on March 12, 2002, the proportion of African Americans was significantly higher than what was typical for the Public or for Broadway. When the show transferred, actor Don Cheadle, known for solidly successful, varied film work, was replaced by rap artist Mos Def in his Broadway debut. Def's performance not only created a sizable buzz in the uptown, commercial realm, but also attracted a younger demographic to the theatre. Critic Linda Winer credits George C. Wolfe, director, for the accolades that accompanied the splashy Broadway opening but also for selecting Def to replace Cheadle in the virtuosic role of Booth, one of two brothers (the other, named Lincoln, plays Abraham Lincoln in whiteface) who compete in a three-card monte "duel" that ultimately turns deadly. Winer compares Def's star power to Glover's in *Bring in 'da Noise* and asserts that the electric charge of these performances helped shift the composition of Broadway audiences and generate mega-excitement among young people at stage doors.[41] Parks's play won the Pulitzer Prize in 2002, receiving a strong vote of confidence from the established theatre elite as well. According to *Variety's* account, producers of *Topdog/Underdog* broke even on their investment in the Broadway show.[42]

Tony Kushner, with director George C. Wolfe once again at the helm, was committed to reaching a wider and more diverse audience for *Caroline, or Change*, his first musical collaboration with composer Jeanine Tesori, which received mixed notices when it opened at the

Public Theater, November 30, 2003. About the civil rights–era musical that focused on the interactions between a white Jewish family in the South and the family of the African American maid who works for them, Kushner said, "we've worked hard to create something that honors a certain aspect of black experience. I want black people to come. I want young people to come. I want everyone to come. I believe in it."[43] Enthusiasts, like critic Peter Marks in *The Washington Post,* shared Kushner's perspective on the play's importance and timeliness in content and message and its usefulness for a wider audience.[44] But some critics, like Michael Sommers, whose review was mostly favorable, did not: "*Caroline, or Change* is not a Broadway-bound crowd pleaser. Instead it ponders changing times with imaginative artistry."[45] Kushner, understanding that *Caroline* was not an easy sell because it was "a new kind of thing" – not just in terms of its content but because the musical was sung-through, with minimal spoken text – got on the phone to persuade producers (many of whom had supported *Angels in America* a decade earlier) to bring *Caroline, or Change* to Broadway.[46] Ultimately, a team of twenty producers was assembled – some with what the *Times* described as the "deepest pockets" – like Rocco Landesman, Scott Rudin, Daryl Roth, and Carole Shorenstein Hays (all of the producers were white). At Kushner's urging, producers sought audiences from communities based around historically Black churches and schools. According to the Marketing Group's Carol Chiavetta, "student discounts were more than half off [and] over six hundred clergymen have been invited to spread the word."[47] An orchestra seat for Kushner's semiautobiographical musical cost $101.

The move to Broadway became fraught with controversy when Tonya Pinkins, the acclaimed actor playing the maid at the Public Theater, demanded a salary commensurate with other leading Broadway musical performers – which was over five times the salary she was originally offered. Pinkins, described as "extraordinary," "nothing short of magnificent," and "soon to be legendary" by Adam Feldman in *TimeOut,*[48] held on for a higher salary and a compromise was reached. Most of the seventeen-member cast earned Broadway minimum ($1,354 with additional benefits), while Pinkins's salary was $2,500 a week with benefits that included a per diem, a stipend for housing, and a sum to cover child care costs. Feldman's review shouts out to the show's producers, who he acknowledged had to be prepared to lose money, and to the "courageous" audiences too. *Caroline, or Change* earned back about half of its initial investment after four months on Broadway, losing $5 million according to the *Times.*[49] Pinkins received her third Tony Award nomination for her performance (she had won for Featured Actress in *Jelly's Last Jam* in 1992).

Who's Afraid of Edward Albee? (Not Broadway Producers)

Triple Pulitzer Prize–winning playwright Edward Albee had always been a key bridge builder between the experimental and the mainstream – beginning in the late 1950s and through the 1960s when his short plays, such as the *The Zoo Story* drew crowds downtown in Off-Off-Broadway theatres while his full-length, explosive *Who's Afraid of Virginia Woolf?* rocked Broadway audiences uptown. Significantly, after a read-through of his new play *The Goat, or Who Is Sylvia?* in late summer 2001, Broadway producers Elizabeth Ireland McCann, Daryl Roth, and Terry Allen Kramer chose to open this provocative work on Broadway instead of testing audience response first in an Off-Off or Off-Broadway theatre. Albee's play concerns the passionate love affair a "happily" married and prize-winning architect has with a goat (Sylvia). Television and film stars Bill Pullman and Mercedes Ruehl were husband and wife in the original cast; ticket sales soared when Sally Field and Bill Irwin took over as the replacement cast. Thirty-nine years after receiving his first Tony Award for *Virginia Woolf*, Albee received a second Tony in 2002 for *Sylvia*. The play shared a Drama Desk Award for best play with *Metamorphoses*. According to *Variety*, *The Goat, or Who Is Sylvia?* only "returned about a third of its original investment."[50] Although few critics made note of this at the time, Albee was not the first to explore bestiality as a subject for the stage; Rochelle Owens had done that over three decades earlier in *Futz!*, her 1968 hit play about a man's love for a pig, which first opened downtown at La MaMa, then toured internationally, and was ultimately made into a film, all directed by Tom O'Horgan, another mainstream/commercial bridge builder.

Although powerful playwrights who have strong ties to specific producers, as Albee had with McCann, Roth, and Carole Shorenstein Hays and Kushner had with Rocco Landesman, Scott Rudin, Roth, and Hays is one model for moving "harder sell" works to Broadway, the importance of the mentoring and support of powerful, well-connected artistic directors, such as the Public Theater's Papp, Wolfe, and Eustis cannot be underestimated.

From the Public to Broadway

Let me be blunt. It is pretty freaking amazing to have a major musical production about a lesbian, and a butch lesbian to boot. "Did I really

just see a butch lesbian on the stage of the Public Theater? Did I just
watch a 100-minute adaptation of one of the most brilliant lesbian
texts in the theater?" . . . Finally our story.

Marcie Bianco[51]

The Public Theater production of *Fun Home* that critic Marcie Bianco
so enthusiastically describes in her production review opened in 2013.
When Public Theater artistic director Eustis transferred *Fun Home* to
Broadway in 2015, it earned twelve Tony Award nominations – more
than any other musical that year (it tied with *An American in Paris*).
What better evidence for encapsulating the pinnacle of the "mainstream
experimental"? This unlikely mega-hit that centered on "a butch lesbian"
and her difficult relationship with her closeted father who killed himself
soon after she came out to her parents was the outcome of another mighty
feat of collaboration. No one was more surprised than graphic novelist
Alison Bechdel, who stated she had no idea how her memoir (published in
2006) could be transformed into a musical. Lisa Kron (book/lyrics),
Jeanine Tesori (music), and Sam Gold (director) worked theatre magic –
as did the ensemble of performers with whom they collaborated, especially
the three actors playing Alison at different ages – spotlighting the coming
of age of a gay woman – and "giving voice to a group surprisingly
underrepresented in musical theater," wrote critic David Gordon of the
Public Theater production.[52]

Eustis describes this creative process as being "in a class by itself." The
show went through "more iterations and more drafts than I think I've ever
seen a musical go through."[53] Originally, Bechdel's drawings were a crucial
framework that the show was built upon – and the set took on the look of
Bechdel's studio. But in director Gold's words, because the creators' job
was to "tell the story through theater" they had to let that go. The show is
not about Bechdel "making the book – the show is our version of the
book."[54]

The artistic team describes a process that resembles the index cards on
the rolling bulletin board that was the genesis of *Bring in 'da Noise* – they
stuck index cards, charts, and maps on a wall, Tesori remembers. Judy
Kuhn, who played Alison's mother from the early reading for backers and
on through the Broadway production, recalls that "the structure was very
hard to get . . . it has an emotional chronology that's different from the
time chronology."[55] Critic Ben Brantley singled out the expressive range
and shifts in Tesori's music,[56] and Gordon and other critics highlight
Michael Cerveris's deeply nuanced performance in building the necessary

complexity and vulnerability of the character of Alison's father as essential to the show's success.

Fun Home was a finalist for the Pulitzer Prize – indeed, a testament to the powers of collaboration. It was also a solid affirmation of the Public Theater's artistic directors' ongoing mission to nurture, support, and propel the work of new, edgy artists forward – a practice that continues to forge a vital, undeniable connection between the experimental and the mainstream.

Eustis's fostering of and support for Lin-Manuel Miranda's *Hamilton* is legendary – although space will not permit a thorough exploration of the collaborative, creative processes that culminated in the *Hamilton* success story on Broadway here (opening night, August 6, 2015). Many, many critics have acknowledged the artistic interventions that *Hamilton*'s creative team made in the production's opening moments – thrilling and unexpected choices in every aspect of the work's style and content. There was excitement generated by the stunningly diverse cast representing iconic figures in US history (Hamilton, Thomas Jefferson, George Washington, James Madison, Aaron Burr are but a few of the famous white men played by actors of color). The pared-down-to-the-wood stage and turntable pulsed with the exhilarating power of rap. Dialogue, scenes, and sharply penned song lyrics were directly and astutely inspired by Ron Chernow's 2005 best-selling and much-lauded biography of Alexander Hamilton. But perhaps most crucial and immediately apparent was the phenomenon of *Hamilton*'s universal appeal and its euphoric, unanimous critical reception. Indeed, unlike previous post-1960 musicals that tapped into the zeitgeist and prodigiously broke Broadway ground (*Hair* and *Rent*), *Hamilton* does not speak exclusively or even predominately to a younger demographic. *Hamilton*'s appeal and acclaim were instantly and fully multigenerational. Hence, why shouldn't the Richard Rodgers Broadway theatre be four times the size of the Newman Theatre at the Public, where the show premiered in February 2015?

Hamilton won eleven Tony Awards (two went to Miranda), a Grammy, an Olivier, Kennedy Center Honors, and the Pulitzer Prize. The show has been a game-changer in social media promotion, in part due to Miranda's insistence and innovative strategies – the #Ham4Ham ticket lottery is a case in point. But *Hamilton*'s artistic team and producers have also made reaching out to educators and students a big part of the show's mission, providing ample discounts and field trips to students, and talkbacks and course materials for multiple grade levels.

In a similar way, the artistic team and producers for *Eclipsed*, which opened on Broadway at the Golden Theatre on March 6, 2016, after a sold-out run at the Public Theater, constructed their own campaign to reach students and educators, targeting young women and girls of color specifically. Zimbabwean-American actor-playwright Danai Gurira's work captures the lives of five women caught in the maelstrom of the Liberian Civil War, where they alternately support and challenge each other in a desperate struggle to survive the relentless violence and sexual abuse, day to day. Academy Award winner Lupita Nyong'o was an original cast member and champion of the ensemble work; she had played the role of "the Girl" (the Commanding Officer's "Wife #4") from the production's inception at the Yale Rep, while she was still a student at the Yale Drama School. *Eclipsed* was her New York stage debut. A key feature of the marketing campaign for Gurira's *Eclipsed*, which Liesl Tommy directed, was the composition of its company of artists – it was the first play to boast an all-Black and female cast and creative team on Broadway. Reviews were strong, but not as uniformly stellar as for Lynn Nottage's *Ruined*, which was also centered on women as the weapons of an African intranational war and won the Pulitzer Prize in 2009. As of this writing, *Ruined* has not been produced on Broadway.

At the *Eclipsed* opening, first-time Broadway producer La La Anthony, along with Stephen C. Byrd and Alia Jones-Harvey, announced that the show would launch the "10,000 Girls Campaign," with the goal of bringing 10,000 girls (ages sixteen to twenty-four) to the show who would not otherwise have the opportunity to see it. Gurira, a spokesperson for the initiative stated: "I wrote this play and gave it the title *Eclipsed* for young girls and women to be celebrated. ... Ten Thousand Girls pursues that vision by exposing ... them to women performers who look like them, shining onstage. I hope and believe this initiative will spark a mind, an imagination, and awaken the many giants within these young women."[57] Hence, with *Eclipsed*, spectators who would not have access to or could not afford to attend a Broadway show were specifically targeted and invited by the producers and by the creative team; this younger, female, and diverse demographic composed a significant majority of the spectators at each performance.

Before Everything Stopped: Rocking the 2019–2020 Season

In much the same spirit and with a parallel agenda as the *Eclipsed* team, *Slave Play*'s playwright, Jeremy O. Harris reached out via social media and word of mouth to students and young people of color when his play premiered Off-Broadway at the New York Theatre Workshop. The run at NYTW received explosive responses from critics and spectators, ranging from extreme outrage to jubilant cheers. Indeed, the play's speedy move to Broadway in fall 2019 was a watershed moment for mainstream/commercial theatre. Perceived by some as a high-risk endeavor, *Slave Play* raised acutely uncomfortable questions about theatre's intersection with culture, economics, and politics. *Slave Play*'s subject was the graphic and often horrifying, occasionally hilarious sex-therapy training/techniques and role-playing that three interracial couples engage in at an antebellum plantation – complete with corsets, high leather boots, whips, and a pair of supervising therapists. The play sequences one potentially traumatic and triggering scenario after another that feature sustained, sexual encounters circling around debasement and rape.

Slave Play "did not recoup its $3.9 million capitalization, so it was technically not a hit,"[58] but very few plays actually recoup their costs on Broadway. Over 100,000 spectators saw the play at the Golden Theatre. Because of the media buzz, film, TV, and music celebrities flocked to the show. But just as the playwrights and producers of *Caroline, or Change* and *Eclipsed* had especially targeted young people and communities of color, playwright Harris and *Slave Play*'s producers were committed to bringing a particular demographic to *Slave Play*. In an interview for the *New York Times*, Greg Nobile, producer, explains that over 30 percent of the audience were first-time ticket buyers, which he claims is "an incredible number … especially for plays."[59] Playwright Harris noted that the majority of Black and Brown and young people were seated in the mezzanine – hence, his goal was to make sure their experience of the play was just as powerful as the experience of spectators in the orchestra. Actor Ato Blankson-Wood attributes the numbers of people of color and "queer folks" in the audience directly to "the initiatives that Jeremy O. Harris spearheaded."[60] As Charles McNulty writes in an article he subtitles "Broadway may never be the same," Harris "knows that being young, gifted, opinionated and black is in itself disruptive to the white mainstream." McNulty states that the following Harris quote "could serve as an epigraph for his young body of work": "History is written on our skins the moment we are born." In McNulty's view, "the theater is where he [Harris], a gay black man carrying the scalpel of an elite education, performs surgery on his psyche." At thirty, Harris is also the youngest Black male playwright to be produced on Broadway.[61]

Additionally, *Slave Play* spearheaded #Blackout performances (Harris's label) where all 804 seats in the theatre were filled with people of color. In director Robert O'Hara's words, "It felt more like church." Actor Joaquina Kalukango said, "I felt like the weight of racial trauma was carried in a room full of 800 people. I didn't have to carry it myself, and it was one of the lightest feelings I've ever had."[62]

There is little doubt that the visceral, spiritual, and emotional impact of the performances and the highly charged debates generated by *Slave Play* will be integral to the complicated legacy of the 2019–20 Broadway season. Mainstream/commercial theatre today continues to push the culture forward as it did in the 1960s, often in ways that sometimes the experimental realm cannot. From director O'Hara's point of view, moving *Slave Play* uptown gave the artistic team "control of the narrative," which they did not have downtown. In the commercial Broadway arena, they took "control of the images we gave out to the press and the story we were telling." Producer Nobile added, "A lot more people had the opportunity to see the play. . . . People got to see the work and the work won."[63] More spectators were brought into "the room where it happens," more folks had a voice in the conversation, and certainly, in the case of *Slave Play*, a wider and more diverse and younger-skewing demographic took a seat at the discussion table.

A COVID Coda

As I pen the final words of this chapter, the future of live theatre and performance is entirely unknown. On May 13, 2020, the *New York Times* headline declares "Broadway Extends Hiatus to Labor Day." On May 24, 2020, the *Times* forecasts that mainstream theatre will not return until sometime in 2021. The live arts and entertainment industries are in an economic freefall.[64] There is no clear sense of a time and place where we will once again be together "in the room where [live theatre] happens."[65]

Yet, a silver lining may exist. This strikes me as I sit home alone and participate in or witness Zoom Room performances, where some very unusual and imaginative work is happening. A kind of democracy is modeled here in the straightforward arrangement of tiles that illuminate the diverse human faces before me.

When we resurrect our life *in* the theatre, there must be a fundamental restructuring; we must discover or develop a way to make the spaces more open to all, to accommodate all the visions, and hear all the voices. This will only happen when we bridge the gaps and break apart and heal the divide. With that deep core impulse and with widely collaborative efforts we can – and we will – move forward.

Notes

1. J. M. Harding and C. Rosenthal (eds.), *The Sixties Center Stage: Mainstream and Popular Performances in a Turbulent Decade* (University of Michigan Press, 2017), p. 7.
2. E. Wollman, *Hard Times: The Adult Musical in 1970s New York City* (Oxford University Press, 2012), p. 11.
3. L. MacDonald, "'Where Do I Go?' The Commercial Renewal of the American Musical," *New England Theatre Journal*, 21 (2010), pp. 71–94.
4. S. Browne, "'Dedicated to the Proposition …' Raising Cultural Consciousness in the Musical *Hair*," in S. Whitfield (ed.), *Reframing the Musical: Race, Culture and Identity* (Red Globe Press, 2019), pp. 167–83.
5. A. Solomon, "Boris Aronson, the Jewish Avant-Garde and the Transition to Broadway," in J. M. Harding and C. Rosenthal (eds.), *The Sixties Center Stage*, pp. 97–116.
6. S. Wolf, "*The Feminine Mystique* Goes to Broadway: Housewives in 1960s Musical Theater," in Harding and Rosenthal (eds.), *The Sixties Center Stage*, pp. 27–51.
7. S. Wolf, *Changed for Good: A Feminist History of the American Musical* (Oxford University Press, 2011), p. 68.
8. Wollman, *Hard Times*, p. 193.
9. Ibid., pp. 45–46.
10. E. Grode, *Hair: The Story of the Show That Defined a Generation* (Running Press Books, 2010), p. 45.
11. M. Riedel, *Razzle Dazzle: The Battle for Broadway* (Simon and Schuster, 2015), p. 158.
12. L. Davis, *Letting Down My Hair* (Arthur Fields Books, 1973), pp. 109–10.
13. Wolf, *Changed for Good*, pp. 118–19.
14. J. Kroll, "*For Colored Girls*," *Newsweek*, June 14, 1976, n.p.
15. M. Wallace, "*For Colored Girls*," *Village Voice*, August 16, 1976, p. 108.
16. H. Epstein, *Joe Papp: An American Life* (Little, Brown, 1994), p. 341.
17. Wolf, *Changed for Good*, pp. 130–132.
18. Ibid., p. 135.
19. L. Stempel, *Showtime: A History of the Broadway Musical Theater* (W. W. Norton, 2010), p. 620.
20. F. Rich, "Theater: Wilson's *Ma Rainey* opens," *New York Times*, October 12, 1984, p. C1.
21. B. Brantley, "As Feminism Ages, Uncertainty Still Wins," *New York Times*, October 25, 2005, n.p.
22. Wolf, *Changed for Good*, p. 161.
23. Ibid., pp. 161–63.

24. Riedel, *Razzle Dazzle*, p. 389.

25. Ibid., p. 390.

26. F. Rich, "The Reaganite Ethos, with Roy Cohn as a Dark Metaphor," *New York Times*, March 5, 1992, p. C15.

27. C. Jones, *Rise Up! Broadway and American Society from "Angels in America" to "Hamilton"* (Bloomsbury Methuen, 2018), p. 21.

28. D. Richards, "*Twilight, Los Angeles, 1992*; A One-Woman Riot Conjures Character Amid the Chaos," *New York Times*, March 24, 1994, p. C13.

29. E. Kendall, "*Bring in 'da Noise* Steps Uptown, Feet First," *New York Times*, April 21, 1996, p. 7.

30. S. Horwitz, "Of Noise and Funk," *Theater Week*, November 13–19, 1985, p. 24.

31. T. Vellela, "Street Musicals Infuse Theatre with Energy of Improvisation," *Christian Science Monitor*, April 1, 1996, p. 10.

32. P. Marks, "On Stage and Off," *New York Times*, May 3, 1996, p. C2.

33. J. Taymor, in R. Zoglin, "*The Lion King*: A Different Breed of *Cats*," *Time*, 150: 4 (July 28, 1997).

34. Jones, *Rise Up!*, p. 68.

35. T. Kushner in A. Abramovich, "Hurricane Kushner Hits the Heartland," *New York Times*, November 30, 2003, p. 5.

36. Jones, *Rise Up!*, p. 84.

37. Ibid., pp. 89–90.

38. W. Arons, "Sarah Ruhl," in J. Listengarten and C. Rosenthal (eds.), *Modern American Drama: Playwriting 2000–2009, Voices, Documents, New Interpretations* (Bloomsbury Methuen, 2018), p. 166.

39. A. Gates, "Critic's Notebook: Love and Loss, in This Life and the Next," *New York Times*, October 8, 2006.

40. Arons, "Sarah Ruhl," p. 169.

41. L. Winer, "An Unqualified Champ in *Topdog/Underdog*," *Los Angeles Times*, April 9, 2002, n.p.

42. R. Hofler, "Off B'way Seeks a Surge," *Variety*, December 8, 2002, p. 66.

43. T. Kushner in J. Dziemianowicz, "Maid for Broadway," *Daily News*, April 25, 2004, p. 15.

44. P. Marks, "Caroline: A Pocket of Hate," *Washington Post*, January 4, 2004, n.p.

45. M. Sommers, "*Caroline, or Change*," *New Jersey Star Ledger*, December 1, 2003, n.p.

46. T. Kushner in J. McKinley, "A Matter of No Small Change: *Caroline's* Broadway Angels," *New York Times*, February 22, 2004, p. 8.

47. R. Hofler, "Crix Nixed in *Caroline* Pitch," *Variety*, April 12, 2004, p. 48.

48. A. Feldman, "Change Is Good. But Is *Caroline, or Change* Too Good for Broadway?," *TimeOut*, May 6–13, 2004, n.p.

49. J. McKinley, "Let's Put on a Loser," *New York Times*, January 3, 2005, and "Picking Up a Broadway Tab," *New York Times*, February 27, 2005, p. 2:6.

50. R. Hofler, "Off B'way Seeks a Surge," *Variety*, December 8, 2002, p. 66.
51. M. Bianco, "Translating Fun Home," www.lamdaliterary.org, November 1, 2013.
52. D. Gordon, "Fun Home," *Theatermania.com*, October 22, 2013.
53. O. Eustis in R. Pogrebin, "Memoir to Musical: Five Year Journey," *New York Times*, November 20, 2013, p. C1.
54. S. Gold in ibid., p. C4.
55. J. Kuhn in ibid.
56. B. Brantley, "Searching a Father's Past and Her," *New York Times*, April 20, 2015, p. C2.
57. W. McBride, "*Eclipsed* Team Launches Their 10,000 Girls Campaign!," broadwayworld.com, February 11, 2016.
58. E. Harris and R. Ugwu, "Was Broadway Ready for *Slave Play*?," *New York Times*, January 27, 2020.
59. G. Nobile quoted in ibid.
60. All quotes in ibid.
61. C. McNulty, "*Slave Play* Writer Jeremy O. Harris Has Arrived. Broadway May Never Be the Same," *Los Angeles Times*, November 29, 2019.
62. Harris and Ugwu, "Was Broadway Ready for *Slave Play*?"
63. All quotes in ibid.
64. M. Paulson, "Broadway Extends Hiatus to Labor Day," *New York Times*, May 13, 2020, p. C3, and M. Paulson, J. Barone, B. Sisario, and Z. Woolfe, "The Fall of Autumn: Live Performance Producers Are Giving Up on 2020," *New York Times*, May 24, 2020.
65. Author's riff on Lin-Manuel Miranda's song lyrics for "The Room Where It Happens" from Act 2 of *Hamilton*.

Select Bibliography

Arons, W. "Sarah Ruhl." In J. Listengarten and C. Rosenthal (eds.), *Modern American Drama: Playwriting 2000–2009, Voices, Documents, New Interpretations*. Bloomsbury Methuen, 2018.

Black, C., and S. Friedman. *Modern American Drama: Playwriting in the 1990s, Voices, Documents, New Interpretations*. Bloomsbury Methuen, 2018.

Grode, E. *Hair: The Story of the Show That Defined a Generation*. Running Press Books, 2010.

Harding, J. M., and C. Rosenthal (eds.). *The Sixties Center Stage: Mainstream and Popular Performances in a Turbulent Decade*. University of Michigan Press, 2017.

Jones, C. *Rise Up! Broadway and American Society from "Angels in America" to "Hamilton."* Bloomsbury Methuen, 2018.

Riedel, M. *Razzle Dazzle: The Battle for Broadway*. Simon and Schuster, 2015.

Sell, M. *Modern American Drama: Playwriting in the 1960s, Voices, Documents, New Interpretations*. Bloomsbury Methuen, 2018.

Stempel, L. *Showtime: A History of the Broadway Musical Theater.* W. W. Norton, 2010.
Wolf, S. *Changed for Good: A Feminist History of the American Musical.* Oxford University Press, 2011.
Wollman, E. *Hard Times: The Adult Musical in 1970s New York City.* Oxford University Press, 2012.

CHAPTER 3

What's Inside?
Collaborative Relationships at the Heart of the American Musical

Laura MacDonald

In the 2016 Broadway musical *Waitress*, the baker and diner waitress Jenna sings, "What's inside? Everyone wants to know what's inside?" She is referring to the pies she bakes, but musical theatre creators are similarly questioned by spectators and journalists about what goes into the musicals they write. *Waitress* is a collaboration between librettist Jessie Nelson, songwriter Sara Bareilles, director Diane Paulus, and choreographer Lorin Latarro. Breaking ground on Broadway with an all-female creative team, *Waitress* was developed out of town at the American Repertory Theater, a regional theatre on the campus of Harvard University. It opened on Broadway in the same season as *Hamilton*, a musical developed by writer-composer Lin-Manuel Miranda in collaboration with director Thomas Kail, choreographer Andy Blankenbuehler, and music director Alex Lacamoire, through workshops and an Off-Broadway production at the not-for-profit Public Theater. They call themselves the Cabinet, in a nod to George Washington's cabinet depicted in the musical, but also in recognition of their strong collaborative relationship. Together, *Hamilton* and *Waitress* illustrate the vastly different creative collaborations made possible by the infrastructure of regional and not-for-profit theatres. The funding and venues supporting the creation of American musicals have shifted since 1945, as have the techniques and technologies employed in creating musicals, ultimately changing how musicals are made and what stories they might tell.

Whether motivated by potential profit, formal innovation, and/or social relevance, what's inside a musical has *not* changed, to the extent that it is still the result of creative collaboration. "The writing of a good musical is one of the most complex undertakings ever conceived by man," composer and conductor Lehman Engel writes. "It is a many-sided collaboration, and each person working on it must be talented, knowledgeable, experienced, and the possessor of such selflessness that he can know when he is proceeding in the wrong direction or can coolly evaluate criticism from his co-workers which might wisely lead to his removing the poorer material he has fallen in love with."[1] More than persevering despite egos and hierarchies of power measured by Tony Award wins and box-office grosses, collaboration in musical theatre writing and production is at its best when creative members respect one another's skill and expertise, and value an interdisciplinary creative process over any individual glory.

Oklahoma! (1943), a watershed in musical theatre history for its innovations in integrating music and dance to tell a story, was the result of collaboration between lyricist Oscar Hammerstein II, composer Richard Rodgers, choreographer Agnes de Mille, and the Theatre Guild. Though Rodgers and Hammerstein controlled that collaboration, in the decades that followed, the creative impulse for new musicals increasingly came from producer-directors like Harold Prince and director-choreographers like Bob Fosse and Michael Bennett. The power dynamics of collaborative relationships in musical theatre reveal the developments in the form, as songwriting was displaced in guiding a musical's creation by conceptual, cinematic staging conceived by directors and director-choreographers. Examining these musical theatre icons and their major collaborations, this chapter chronicles the evolution of the American musical, as practitioners assembled creative teams in response to shifting economics, audience demographics, and the rise of mediated popular culture on television and the internet.

Such developments have contributed to convergence whereby film studios and corporations such as Disney now develop and produce their own musicals, bringing new resources and structures that both support and expand the collaborative creation of musical theatre. At the same time, regional theatres and not-for-profit venues developed new models of their own for participating in musical theatre collaboration. Whether conceived in consultation with a corporate producer, or tested through a low-budget laboratory process, creative, collaborative relationships are still what's inside twenty-first-century American musicals.

The Collaborative Creative Teams Behind Rodgers and Hammerstein's Broadway Hits

The collaborative creation of American musicals was well established prior to World War II, and the art form's early milestones were successful, thanks to their creative teams working collaboratively.

Some early examples of collaboration usefully demonstrate shifting hierarchies and different motivations driving musical theatre creation. When a fire at the Academy of Music in 1866 left producers Henry C. Jarrett and Harry Palmer with a ballet troupe and stage machinery, imported from Europe, but no venue, they collaborated with fellow producer William Wheatley and playwright Charles Barras whose melodrama *The Black Crook* could accommodate a ballet. "Into this fairly boilerplate melodrama Wheatley shoehorned Jarrett and Palmer's distinguished company of European ballerinas,"[2] Bradley Rogers writes, reinforcing the producers' willingness to collaborate in order to profit from the spectacle of interdisciplinary elements conveniently contained by a melodrama.

Decades later, an NAACP fundraiser in Philadelphia in 1920 introduced vaudeville performers Flournoy E. Miller and Aubrey Lyles to jazz songwriters Noble Sissle and Eubie Blake. Together, they expanded a Miller and Lyles comic sketch to create an entertaining show for weary post–World War I audiences. Brian Valencia calls *Shuffle Along* "a scrappy little hodgepodge,"[3] of variety, revue, operetta, and musical comedy. Combining Miller and Lyles's comic take on southern plantation culture, a traditional musical comedy love story but between an African American couple, and the novelty of Sissle and Blake's modern, jazz score, the show was a hit with Black and white theatregoers when it opened in 1921. Nearly a century later, Sissle, Blake, Miller, and Lyles's remarkable collaboration was depicted onstage when writer-director George C. Wolfe adapted the musical as *Shuffle Along, Or The Making of the Musical Sensation of 1921 and All That Followed* (2016).

Another significant musical theatre collaboration prior to World War II also engaged with southern culture and racial politics in the United States. Upon reading Edna Ferber's novel *Show Boat* in 1926, composer Jerome Kern immediately bought the theatrical rights and recruited Oscar Hammerstein II to write the book and lyrics. Taking almost a year to adapt Ferber's novel (an unprecedented development period for a musical), they created a musical with songs that carry the action of the play and represent the characters who sing them, and dances, crowd scenes, and instrumental music arising directly from the plot. *Show Boat* chronicles fifty years in the life of a show business family but also deals with racism, alcoholism, and spousal abandonment. It was critically acclaimed when opened in 1927. Along with *The Black Crook* and *Shuffle Along*, *Show Boat* helped establish the standards musical theatre collaborators would seek to achieve decades later: commercial success, innovation in style and form, and social engagement through themes and topics relevant to theatregoers' own lives.

While the 1940s introduced other well-crafted musicals exploring how songs can develop serious plots and characters in musicals, such as *Pal Joey* (1940) with songs by Richard Rodgers and Lorenz Hart and *Lady in the Dark* (1941) with songs by Kurt Weill and Ira Gershwin – it would be Rodgers' first collaboration with Hammerstein that would have the greater commercial success and more lasting influence on musical theatre. When *Variety* reviewed the 1943 New Haven out-of-town tryout of these song-writers' new musical about romance blossoming in turn-of-the-century Oklahoma, the critic's description focused on the interdisciplinary creative team's collaborative work: "They've jigsawed Lynn Riggs' 'Green Grow the Lilacs' and re-assembled it as 'Away We Go!' a tune-dance concoction whose title is indicative of the show's potential marathon."[4] The combination of dance with music was called "a pretty-ditty, fancy-prancing combo" that "lacks only editing to weld it into a first-class tuneshow."[5] While the trade publication was directed at industry readers keen to know the prospects of a new musical heading to New York City, Bone's repeated attempts to capture multiple elements in a phrase evidence his awareness that the musical he attended was the product of a range of artists with different skills, and that their successful collaboration was likely to yield a profitable long run. "They've" worked collaboratively to adapt Riggs's play, and calling the new musical both a concoction, a tuneshow, and a combo emphasizes that it has been created by a team, from multiple ingredients. *Oklahoma!*, as *Away We Go* was retitled, was not the first musical to experiment with how different elements of the form can work in collaboration to develop character and progress a narrative, but its success and popularity have made it a definitive example for professionals, theatregoers, and scholars.

As Claudia Wilsch Case explains, the Theatre Guild's executive director Theresa Helburn had both commercial and artistic success in mind when she began assembling a team to adapt Riggs's play. She struggled to find investors to support the wholesome musical theatre adaptation, "and soon the project became known throughout New York's theatre circles as 'Helburn's Folly.'"[6] Helburn and Guild founder Lawrence Langner nevertheless recruited Richard Rodgers and Hammerstein to collaborate for the first time, and the songs they wrote "emerge effortlessly from the book, explore the play's characters and themes, and propel the action forward."[7] Director Rouben Mamoulian was tasked with achieving coherence between all of the musical's elements, and designers Lemuel Ayers and

Miles White had the challenge of creating sets and costumes, respectively, with a limited budget and resources given the Unites States' involvement in World War II.

In 1942, choreographer Agnes de Mille had written to Helburn, urging her to bring Rodgers and Hammerstein to the premiere of de Mille's new ballet *Rodeo*, an exploration of American folk culture through dance, with a score by Aaron Copland. De Mille writes, "I had heard they were contemplating a play on Western cowboy life and I thought I could do good dances for them."[8] With a background in ballet, de Mille's first musical theatre experience was choreographing and performing in a revival of *The Black Crook* in New Jersey in 1929. By 1933, she was collaborating with composer Cole Porter, choreographing the premiere of his musical *Nymph Errant* in London. It would be a decade before her Broadway debut as a choreographer, and despite the success of *Rodeo*, Rodgers insisted on supervising the first woman to choreograph a Broadway musical for the first few days of rehearsals, before accepting de Mille as a collaborator.

A musical achieving a long run, high grosses, and wide circulation like *Oklahoma!* is not always the result of a happy or easy collaboration. "Director Rouben Mamoulian and de Mille clashed as Mamoulian wanted chorus girls chosen for their looks, while de Mille insisted on her trained dancers,"[9] musicologist Susan C. Cook points out. The director and choreographer's disagreement over the musical's aesthetics illustrates how undefined a musical might still be throughout its development. The lack of consensus suggests that the hierarchy of priorities was in flux, and the skillful execution of innovative, new choreography won out over the potential pleasure of visually appealing women onstage. De Mille's *Oklahoma!* choreography replaced dialogue at multiple points, including the Dream Ballet at the end of Act One, where the heroine Laurey drinks an elixir to help her make up her mind between Curly and Jud Fry.

Kara Anne Gardner chronicles de Mille's Broadway work and explains how the choreographer "read the draft librettos she received from her collaborators and then devised her own scenarios for the dances."[10] De Mille wrote sketches, but also made notes regarding the plot, costumes, sets, and music. Working with de Mille, Rodgers was not as agreeable a collaborator as were composers Aaron Copland and Cole Porter, who had composed dance scoring after close consultation with the choreographer.[11] After a few days of surveillance by Rodgers, and no piano score forthcoming, "de Mille was ultimately given free rein and claimed that she and her rehearsal pianist created the musical accompaniment for 'the Dream Ballet' drawing on the songs from the first act."[12]

The show was a hit when it opened on Broadway in 1943 and stayed there for five years. Andrea Most suggests that the show's energy "celebrates a wartime utopia. Differences meld into a unified loving American community. Access to this community is determined not by character but by function: anyone willing and able to perform the songs and dances can join."[13] This optimistic, patriotic musical entertained countless American servicemen on leave in New York City during World War II, enjoyed national and international tours, and returned to Broadway in multiple revivals. Like the milestone musicals introduced earlier, *Oklahoma!* was a commercial success, innovative in its style and form, and engaged themes and topics relevant to Americans' own lives in the early 1940s. Helburn may have initiated the production as a producer, but as composer and writer, Rodgers and Hammerstein were ultimately at the top of the collaboration's hierarchy.

Despite the collaborative friction the team experienced on *Oklahoma!*, Rodgers, Hammerstein, Mamoulian, and de Mille reunited to collaborate on another adaptation produced by the Theatre Guild, *Carousel* (1945). Charting the doomed romance between a carousel barker and a mill worker in turn-of-the-century New England, Gardner calls the musical "the pinnacle of de Mille's work with Rodgers and Hammerstein and one of the most significant productions of her career."[14] She contributed choreography for "June is Bustin' Out All Over," a Hornpipe for "Blow High, Blow Low," and a second act ballet on the beach where Billy first sees his daughter Louise, happy and dancing, then witnesses her distress when the Snow family passes by, and ignores her. Billy recognizes he is to blame for Louise's ostracization, and de Mille's richly detailed ballet drives the second act forward.

While George Balanchine had created ballet choreography in 1936 for *On Your Toes*, Anthea Kraut notes that de Mille's *Oklahoma!* choreography "is generally regarded as launching the ascendance of ballet on Broadway and the increased centrality of dance within the musical."[15] Reflecting on the impact of de Mille's detailed, characterful choreography, Hammerstein observed, "Here indeed the choreographer becomes the collaborator of the author and composer, not merely for the enhancement of one or two moments in the play but in helping to build the very bone and muscle of the story."[16] Separating the authorship of a new musical from its first production can be difficult, the inevitable consequence of an interdisciplinary, collaborative effort. Mamoulian and other directors, as well as designers, also made key contributions as creative team members who shaped the creation of these musicals. Gardner points out that "Without [de Mille's] dances, the shows might still have power and impact, but they become different works of art."[17]

Rodgers and Hammerstein's musicals have remained in regular circulation since their Broadway premieres, and as composer, lyricist, and librettist, their authorship has been rewarded with royalties from all subsequent productions. As Kraut explores, while de Mille "benefitted enormously from the unprecedented success of *Oklahoma!*, the terms of her contract left her with a profound sense of injustice."[18] De Mille was awarded $50, then $75 a week once the musical opened and was a hit, in addition to $2,000 in fees, though Rodgers and Hammerstein and source material author Riggs were receiving thousands of dollars a week in royalties as the Broadway production's $7 million grosses accumulated. "[I]t took years of bitter arguments for the Guild to finally agree in 1947–48 to give de Mille a .5% percentage of the royalties."[19] She then campaigned for choreographers to obtain copyright protection for their work and also contributed to the formation of the Society of Stage Directors and Choreographers in 1959.[20] The collaborations de Mille participated in may have produced pioneering musical theatre, but power relations and profits also set important precedents. Conscious of innovators such as de Mille being undervalued and underrecognized as the legacy of their musicals extended, their successors would become more mindful of contracts, royalties, and billing, to resist being positioned at the bottom of collaboration hierarchies.

Jerome Robbins's and Harold Prince's Productive Collaborative Relationships

The integration of songs and dance to advance a musical's narrative became a standard approach to the craft of American musical theatre through the 1950s and 1960s, requiring creative teams to work collaboratively and negotiate to define individual contributions. The hierarchies of musical theatre collaboration began to shift, as Broadway's songwriters heard their songs covered by popular singers and broadcast on the radio with less frequency. Songs' commercial potential could no longer be used as justification for composers' or lyricists' greater power in decision-making processes. Instead, directors, and director-choreographers, conceived of new musicals and took the helm of collaboration hierarchies, gathering collaborators to serve an overall concept.

West Side Story began life in 1949 with high aesthetic aspirations, as *East Side Story*, when choreographer Jerome Robbins approached composer Leonard Bernstein and playwright Arthur Laurents about writing a contemporary musical version of *Romeo and Juliet*, with star-crossed Catholic and Jewish lovers on the Lower East Side during Easter-Passover. Laurents quickly bowed out, citing similarities to the 1920s blockbuster comedy *Abie's Irish Rose*. The *Romeo* project gained momentum again in 1955 when Bernstein and Laurents were in Los Angeles and discussed headlines reporting on Mexican and Anglo gangs of juvenile delinquents. Bernstein suggested an LA setting, but Chicanos were foreign to the Brooklyn-born Laurents. The writer instead proposed Puerto Ricans and Blacks in New York, and producer Cheryl Crawford urged Laurents to document the socioeconomic history of the musical's Upper West Side setting.

Carefully chosen language from Laurents and lyricist Stephen Sondheim, evocative urban sounds from Bernstein, and angry, passionate movement from Robbins (who also directed) melded to create a contemporary American world. Invented words such as "frabbajabba" in combination with new implied meanings for words such as "cool" suggested the modern rhythms of the lives of the characters who spoke them, further developed by Bernstein's sound and Robbins's dance vocabularies. To supplement Robbins's ballet background, choreographer Peter Gennaro was hired to co-choreograph, bringing Latino and Afro-Cuban dance vocabularies that informed his choreography of "America" as well as elements of the Prologue and "Dance at the Gym."[21]

Beyond their engagement with ethnic tensions in contemporary Manhattan, the creative team had grand aspirations to elevate musical theatre with their innovations. Laurents notes how without knowing what they might achieve, he and his collaborators settled on the label "lyric theatre" for their work on *West Side Story*.[22] Their work began with Laurents's outline, but it was Robbins who suggested short, introductory scenes be written for Tony and Maria before they meet. Laurents privileges Robbins's choreography, insisting "his staging of the meeting did more than any words could."[23] *New York Times* theatre critic Brooks Atkinson concurred and reported on how, "Everything in 'West Side Story' is of a piece. Everything contributes to the total impression of wildness, ecstasy and anguish … The ballets convey the things that Mr. Laurents is inhibited from saying because the characters are so inarticulate."[24] Laurents wrote a speech for Maria in the musical's final scene, dummy lyrics to hold a place for an aria Bernstein never managed to write music for, leaving Laurents's words to conclude the musical.

The ideas Tony, Maria, Anita, Bernardo, and their gang members expressed in *West Side Story* illustrated the concerns of a new generation of Americans. The gang relations depict the brutal realities of immigrant life in mid-century America, while the ideas the Puerto Rican women express may also anticipate the nascent women's movement. The contemporaneity of *West Side Story*'s interethnic romance distinguished it, however, as did the urban setting of the ethnic conflict it staged, conflict familiar to Americans across the country, not only in New York City. The musical was ready to try out in 1956, but producer Cheryl Crawford had backed out, putting the production at risk and making her eventual replacements, producers Robert E. Griffith, Hal Prince, and Roger L. Stevens, much valued collaborators. *West Side Story* opened in 1957 and ran for 732 performances on Broadway, with a return engagement of 249 performances following a national tour, an international tour, and film adaptation in 1961. All of the collaborators are credited in every edition of the published script except Gennaro, who granted Robbins an exclusive copyright for all choreographic material.[25] Robbins receives double billing in any edition of the script, credited with the musical's conception, and with having directed and choreographed the entire original production, ensuring his perpetual position at the top of the *West Side Story* collaboration.

Robbins's style and approach to creating musical theatre as a director-choreographer generated so many iconic musicals that these were excerpted in 1989, in a compilation musical, *Jerome Robbins' Broadway*. His staging and choreography for musicals including *West Side Story, Gypsy* (1959), and *Fiddler on the Roof* (1964) were revived, providing a survey of the many writers and composers he had collaborated with, such as Stephen Sondheim, Leonard Bernstein, Arthur Laurents, and Jule Styne. The revue was also an opportunity for Robbins to claim some of his uncredited work – his contributions as a show doctor helping struggling creative teams develop new musicals out of town. In 1962, Robbins famously advised director George Abbott and composer Stephen Sondheim that a new opening number explaining the story to follow was needed for their new musical, *A Funny Thing Happened on the Way to the Forum*, based on Roman playwright Plautus's comedies. "Comedy Tonight" was the result and became iconic enough as a humorous ensemble number that it was included decades later in *Jerome Robbins' Broadway*.

The revue show's title reinforced Robbins's position at the top of collaborative hierarchies and was a suitable extravagance to cap off the gilded 1980s. The distillation of his oeuvre required a cast of more than sixty performers, and so great was Robbins's stature, even decades after leaving Broadway to focus on ballet choreography, that he could command the budget needed to hire such a large cast. In 2017, Robbins's sometime producer, Harold Prince, was also celebrated with a revue show, *Prince of Broadway*, similarly excerpting the musicals he had produced and directed, including Robbins's *West Side Story* and *Fiddler*. Both of these musical theatre history pageants privileged men who regularly had good ideas for musicals, however Robbins's choreography, in concentrated form given the revue format, preserved him as a visionary, above his collaborators. By contrast, while Prince was present via a voiceover narration, performers speaking his words and wearing his iconic glasses, *Prince of Broadway* lacked coherence. The director-producer had consistently created musicals radically different from one another, shepherding different combinations of collaborators to create new work. Collaborating designers' names were included within the re-creation of their sets to celebrate their contributions, but a production honoring a powerful white man was unlikely to succeed in 2017 when the #MeToo movement gained greater traction and the public vilification of white men's abuses of power intensified.

Toronto's *Globe and Mail* theatre critic, Herbert Whittaker, reviewed *West Side Story* in 1957, noting how "it sets out to achieve a blend of singing, dancing and acting, of costumes and scenery, that will serve that story to best effect. These component parts are first of all at the service of the play's idea, secondarily for the exhibition of individual talent."[26] Where Robbins facilitated such blending, and showcased his talent, Prince often sought to make the boundaries between a musical's elements transparent. Showing audiences how a musical was assembled was Prince's way of challenging spectators to actively engage with a given musical's strategies and thereby engage with the bigger ideas behind them, whether about history, society, or identity. Robbins's choreography persisted in countless subsequent productions, as if it were a glue that a musical required to hold itself together, while Prince's musicals invited wider reinterpretation.

Initially mentored by legendary writer, director, and producer George Abbott, Prince went on to collaborate with, and in some cases mentor, writers, composers, and choreographers such as John Kander and Fred Ebb, Michael Bennett, and Stephen Sondheim. A producer of multiple musicals before he finally directed one, Prince preferred musicals that were both commercially viable and socially relevant. Without his achievement with *Cabaret* in 1966, balancing serious politics with seemingly diverting song and dance (*seemingly* diverting because Kander and Ebb's songs fully and consistently support and develop Prince's concept, catchy and clever though they may be), subsequent serious, conceptual musicals might not have enjoyed the enthusiastic reception they did from ticket buyers. Prince had contemporary American politics in mind when he decided to produce and direct a musical adaptation of the John van Druten play *I Am a Camera*, itself a dramatization of Christopher Isherwood's 1930s Sally Bowles story. Prince explains what his goals with *Cabaret* were: "The question the play asks is, 'What would you do?' This is a show about survival and about how most people unheroically look the other way in order to survive."[27] Rather than simply staging a narrative about specific characters, Prince's concept for the show was to explore the issues of survival and civil rights in 1960s America. At the first rehearsal, Prince showed his cast a 1966 *Life* magazine photo of young people in Chicago protesting against integration, establishing a clear parallel and visual association with the Nazis' rise to power in the 1930s.

To help raise questions, the musical's master of ceremonies character exists in a limbo world of a cabaret, performing numbers but more importantly observing and questioning the lives and actions of the other characters, thereby encouraging the audience to do the same. While serving in Germany during the Korean War, Prince had spent his evenings at Maxim's, a sleazy nightclub. "There was a dwarf MC, hair parted in the middle and lacquered down with brilliantine, his mouth made into a bright-red cupid's bow, who wore heavy false eyelashes and sang, danced, goosed, tickled, and pawed four lumpen Valkyres waving diaphanous butterfly wings,"[28] Prince recalls in his memoir. His personal reaction to the German MC resonated with him strongly enough that he wanted to see that character again. He eventually conceived of an androgynous master of ceremonies character for *Cabaret*, initially a bad-taste entertainer who became a Nazi and performed a song in which he imitated famous Weimar entertainers. In rehearsal, Joel Grey, cast to originate the role, "was unhappy because he felt that his role had nothing to do with the book and because he hadn't seen much of Prince,"[29] *Cabaret* historian Keith Garebian writes. Choreographer Ron Field assuaged Grey's concerns, recognizing the role's potential should Prince's concept for the musical succeed.

Librettist Joe Masteroff described all the collaborators, but Prince especially, as being turned on by the material, while Fred Ebb recalled the director-producer's passion.[30] To emphasize the parallel between contemporary American civil rights issues and German history, and reinforce

Prince's caution that the same atrocities can happen in the United States, designer Boris Aronson hung a tilted mirror above the stage. Offering a distorted reflection of the audience back at itself before the musical began was a provocation for theatregoers to begin asking questions. The American writer abroad, Cliff Bradshaw, is in some ways a traditional integrated musical leading man, but also functions as a cipher and thus as another aid for the audience. Kander and Ebb wrote Cliff a song, "Why Should I Wake Up?" in which he embraces the hedonism of his new, Berlin-lifestyle. Later, when Cliff questions an older couple's decision to break off their engagement because of the changes taking place in German society, the Gentile woman, Fraulein Schneider, no longer engaged to a Jewish man, asks Cliff, "What Would You Do?" These questions, as songs, reinforced the provocation provided by Aronson's tilted mirror and offered audiences a way to consider a range of responses to political change and civil rights abuses, from indifference to outrage. The MC, as written by Masteroff and staged by Prince and Fields, almost constantly offered his own responses through one-liners, animated facial expressions, and gestures; and his hovering presence encouraged audiences to raise their own questions, thereby fulfilling Prince's concept.

"Tomorrow Belongs to Me," a beautiful melody with lyrics envisioning an idealized future, is first sung by the cabaret waiters who act as observers on a staircase in the limbo area. It is reprised in the real world of the musical by a guest at the older couple's engagement party. Party guests join in, including Cliff and Sally's friend Ernst Ludwig, a late arrival to the celebration, who comes directly from a Nazi party meeting, wearing a swastika armband. As the song ends, no longer an innocent hymn, the set disappears and the characters freeze in a tableau. The MC appears on the stairs, commenting once more, with a shrug and a smile at the audience before exiting. Prince's staging provided a more complex frame for Kander and Ebb's song, and, together, they efficiently and skillfully progressed the musical's civil rights and survival mandate.

Fields, the choreographer, was not initially feeling as involved in the collaborative process as he might have liked, assigned to rehearse dancers in a hotel ballroom twelve blocks away from Prince's rehearsals. Hired after the script and score were completed, Fields discussed *Cabaret* intermittently with Prince, "but the idea of the cabaret as the central metaphor was Prince's, just as the cabaret music and lyrics were other artists' material he had to enhance."[31] Fields became aware of the volume of songs Kander and Ebb were churning out, excited to be invited to work with Prince again despite their first collaboration, *Flora, the Red Menace*, flopping a year earlier. Sensing his fellow creative team members were underselling themselves, the choreographer helped advocate for what became the title song, "Cabaret," a song Prince initially rejected. As musical theatre historian Stephen Citron writes, "Prince had always said that exchanging ideas is one of the most important things collaborators can do while creating a musical."[32] At one point, the title song was shifted much earlier in the show to make room for "I Don't Care Much" in the second act, the latter written when the songwriters wanted to show off to friends at dinner and write a song in fifteen minutes. The shuffled order was not successful, and "Cabaret" was returned to the eleven o'clock position in the second act while "I Don't Care Much" went into Kander and Ebb's trunk of discarded songs.[33]

Fields worried he might lose dance numbers after Prince invited Jerome Robbins to watch a run-through and share his comments before the out-of-town tryout premiere in Boston. Robbins proposed cutting all the choreography that was not performed in the club's acts, which included the "Telephone Song," a creative ensemble number for Kit Kat Club patrons, and Lotte Lenya's dance with sailors at her character's engagement party. Prince chose not to take that particular note from Robbins, preserving the range of choreography Fields had created for the musical.[34] Having established a strong, collaborative relationship developing *Cabaret*, Fields, Prince, Kander, Ebb, Aronson, along with music director Harold Hastings, orchestrator Don Walker, and costume designer Patricia Zipprodt, reconvened two years later for *Zorba*, a more modest success.

Prince then moved on to collaborate more closely with Stephen Sondheim, who had contributed lyrics to the Prince-produced *West Side Story*. When Sondheim solicited Prince's opinion on his friend George Furth's series of plays examining marriage, the characters' unmusical nature and nonsingability proved an irresistible challenge for the director and the songwriter who collaborated with Furth to create *Company* (1970). Though inexperienced in drafting musical libretti, Furth's background as an actor on the West Coast served him well in crafting the brash, sophisticated New Yorkers who perform the socially prescribed roles of wife, husband, or lover. Bobby, *Company's* central character, is described by some as a blank, undefined character, a cipher (more developed than *Cabaret's* Cliff) against whom the musical's other characters define themselves. *Company's* exploration of marriage and singledom, in primarily private spaces, in many ways anticipated the major shifts American society would experience through the 1970s: divorce rates rose, the feminist movement splintered, and a host of crises prompted Americans to withdraw into their private lives and away from the public sphere.

Five married couples sing about Bobby's life meeting theirs, as "parallel lines who meet, side by side."[35] Sondheim's polyphonic music provides additional parallel lines, as did Aronson's set design for a high-rise apartment building, its elevator moving Bobby parallel to each couple in their apartments. Furth's script served as the grid upon which music, design, and staging could rest, presenting a blueprint for such a grid in the opening birthday party scene and in subsequent scenes, framing each couple. *New York Daily Mail* critic Douglas Watt suggested Furth provided "song situations" for Sondheim to approach.[36] These are not the book scenes of the traditional integrated musical but an expansion and complication of how they might function as expressors of Furth and Prince's concept.

Sondheim has admitted he is an imitator, and as theatre historian Foster Hirsch observes, one who took his cues from "Furth's 'bright, sharp, no-nonsense dialogue.'"[37] While the song "The Little Things You Do Together" does not flow logically out of the couple Harry and Sarah's dialogue in their domestic vignette (as a song in an integrated book musical might), it mirrors the content and structure Furth's libretto establishes. After the demonstration of Sarah's hobby with her husband in the book scene, Joanne comments on their relationship, singing "It's not so hard to be married/As two maneuver as one," the couple still actually maneuvering together. Additionally, though Joanne sings a solo at first, her melody and lyric lines listing "the little things" follow the structure of a couple's conversation as demonstrated in the scene, one partner finishing the other's sentences, an increasingly rushed volley of one-liners.[38] With characters singing and simultaneously existing in multiple frames, Furth, Sondheim, and Prince explore the concept of marriage rather than developing a narrative.

"In a good musical, the book and the songs are one piece and in *Company* we wanted a total texture," Sondheim explains, and happily acknowledges how Furth's sharp, rhythmic dialogue inspired musical ideas: "My music and lyrics grew out of the way we commented about the characters in conferences; before I began to write I absorbed the play's ambience and atmosphere, its style of speech."[39] Musicologist Geoffrey Block and others have suggested that Bobby, who learns about compromises in his friends' marriages, and later Sondheim characters are pressured to compromise and that this pattern is autobiographical for the composer. Block even titles a section of a chapter on Sondheim "The Art of

Compromise." The negative connotations of compromise imply that in writing musical theatre songs Sondheim may not be fully realizing his artistic goals and potential, reluctantly moving side by side with writers, directors, and designers. Though mentored by Hammerstein, who consistently asserted his status with Rodgers at the top of creative teams, Sondheim has been quicker to acknowledge and celebrate his collaborators.

While compromise is inherent in collaboration, the relationships that generated *Company* suggest that the give and take between all collaborators is a positive aspect of the creation process, making the musical itself deeper and stronger as a work and ultimately more satisfying for its audience. The increasingly complex collaborative process whereby a composer-lyricist such as Sondheim worked with a director-producer such as Prince, or librettist-director such as James Lapine, helped musicals transcend the form's conventions and engage audiences more deeply. Michael Bennett contributed musical staging to *Company*, then collaborated with Prince again, a year later, as co-director and choreographer on *Follies*. Having toured Europe in Robbins's *West Side Story* early in his career, and then collaborated with Prince, Bennett had tremendous insight into commercially and artistically successful collaborations. As a director-choreographer, he was soon at the top of the hierarchy, conceiving his own new musical, which would bring major innovations to the creation and production of musical theatre.

A Choral Collaboration Off-Broadway

Disheartened by the unfolding of the Watergate scandal and politicians' dishonesty, Michael Bennett gathered the most honest people he knew – a group of dancers (some coming after performing in Broadway shows) – to dance and talk late one Saturday night in January 1974. Bennett tape-recorded what ended up being a twelve-hour exploration session. The dancers answered biographical questions and discussed their dance training, as well as their experiences in the industry in New York City. Bennett bought their stories, for $1 each. In his previous work, Bennett had always tried to feature chorus dancers and develop individual characters with them, and this new project was his effort to shine a spotlight on the dancers in the chorus. He organized a second session to include more dancers and collect more material, before striking a deal with Joseph Papp to pay dancers and a creative team $100 a week each to help Bennett develop the material at Papp's Public Theater. The Off-Broadway venue had already developed the musical *Hair* in 1967, but *A Chorus Line* enjoyed a more extended development period. On and off over the course of nine months, Bennett worked with dancers, as well as his associate Bob Avian, composer Marvin Hamlisch, lyricist Edward Kleban, and librettist Nicholas Dante. Bennett changed the musical theatre industry forever, establishing the workshop process that would become Broadway's new normal for developing musicals.

The dancers were given transcriptions of the tape-recorded sessions to work with, and Bennett and the songwriters gradually identified the moments they would expand as songs. Hamlisch and Kleban interviewed the dancers further, writing multiple versions of songs that would be performed along with monologues. Beyond editing dancers' stories, Hamlisch and Kleban remained mindful of the musical's focus on dance and the range of vocal abilities, crafting songs that the dancers would be able to perform alongside Bennett's demanding choreography. The first part of the process generated four hours of material, and before the workshop continued, Bennett recruited the more experienced writer James Kirkwood to collaborate with Dante, a dancer and novice writer. The material was reworked several times until Bennett was ready for previews in April 1975. In keeping with the project's new approach to musical theatre creation, lighting designer Tharon Musser requested a $160,000 computerized lighting board to replace traditional lighting operators and allow her to design with more subtlety and detail. It would be the first such technology used for a Broadway musical. Critics immediately and unanimously recognized what Bennett had achieved, and by July, *A Chorus Line* had moved uptown to the Shubert Theatre, where it would stay for nearly fifteen years.

After the musical swept all the major awards including the Pulitzer Prize for Drama, Bennett masterminded the casting, rehearsal, and touring of multiple replica companies. The original cast soon felt neglected, continuing to perform but no longer recognized for their contributions to the musical's development. Bennett had his lawyers draft an agreement for sharing half a percent of grosses and some income from subsidiary rights. The agreement divided thirty-seven dancers and actors involved with the creation of the musical into three groups based on the degree of their participation.[40] "This kind of agreement was new because the extensive workshop process was new," Campbell Robertson reported in the *New York Times*. "[A] similar, but less generous agreement that was hammered out for Mr. Bennett's next musical, 'Ballroom,' has become standard on Broadway."[41] Performers who were previously not accounted for as collaborators were now recognized in the hierarchy of collaboration, fulfilling Bennett's original goal to celebrate dancers' labor, though at a higher rate of remuneration than he intended.

In their performances, the original dancers and their successors shared the loving community of the late-night tape sessions and the characters who made it onto the line but offstage the collaborative experience had soured. Wayne Cilento, who originated the role of Mike and became a successful choreographer of musicals such as *Wicked*, laments, "We were the authors of the show, and we should have been paid accordingly."[42] The Public Theater paid $250,000 by the end of the workshop, much less than the million-dollar budget common in the mid-1970s for opening a new musical on Broadway using the traditional out-of-town tryout process. The savings in development costs were very attractive to commercial producers of musicals written by a traditional creative team, but not-for-profit and regional theatres also recognized they were well placed to host such development.

Ken Harper and Michael Eisner Produce Corporate Collaborations

While the Public Theater established a new model for musical theatre development through collaboration in workshop settings, corporate collaborations also suggested a new model for musical theatre development and thereby introduced new collaborators to the creative team's hierarchy. African American producer Ken Harper was working in radio in the 1970s when he decided that he had to produce an all-Black musical theatre adaptation of the much-loved novel and film *The Wizard of Oz*. Theatre historian Allen Woll explains, "The formula for *The Wiz* involved placing Dorothy and company in a different context. The music, the choreography, the sets, and the costumes would all reflect contemporary Black life rather than the mythical Kansas barnyard on MGM's back lot."[43] Harper recruited Charlie Smalls to contribute music and lyrics, with a book by William F. Brown.

Baltimore critic Carl A. Schoettler pointed out in his review that Brown was white and had written a respectful adaptation of Baum's fairytale. He called Smalls's score, "a virtual anthology of contemporary black popular music"[44] that challenged the Arlen and Harburg songs from the film musical. The multitalented Trinidadian Geoffrey Holder remembers first listening to Smalls's songs on a cassette early in the musical's development process: "I saw the whole thing, just how everyone should act and move and I put it all into 40 drawings in about two hours."[45] Holder was ready to direct, choreograph, and play the Wiz, in addition to designing costumes, but although Harper used Holder's designs to secure $1.2 million from 20th Century Fox to produce the musical, Holder was initially only contracted as a designer. "My costume drawings determined the choreography and the choreography was the show,"[46] he recalls. Harper chose Gilbert Moses to direct and Moses hired George Faison to choreograph.

The Wiz struggled out of town in Baltimore, and calls were made to Patricia Birch, Donald McKayle, and Harold Prince who turned down invitations to be show doctors. Holder eventually took over as director during the Philadelphia and Detroit tryouts. "[H]e gave the show a coherent vision,"[47] Woll notes. Holder switched Stephanie Mills's Dorothy costume from pants to the now iconic fluffy white dress; Hinton Battle was promoted from the chorus to play Scarecrow; and Faison's previously cut Tornado Ballet was restored. Philadelphia critic Howard A. Coffin was not impressed, lamenting, "It is an ill-fated marriage of separately marvellous parts."[48] He suggested the set and costumes were what you might expect from a show backed by 20th Century Fox, noting the dazzling effect of corporate backing that decades later continues to support lavishly produced musicals such as *Anastasia, Charlie and the Chocolate Factory*, and *Beetlejuice*.

When mixed reviews in New York threatened to close the Broadway production of *The Wiz* (1975), the film studio provided additional funding for advertising. A lively television commercial saved the musical, while a campaign by the Black community challenging white critics' unenthusiastic responses helped establish that the musical offered Black audiences an experience that white critics could not evaluate. La Donna Forsgren considers how the musical's use of a codified Blackness helped ensure its success: "The song lyrics walk a fine line between catering to the sensibilities of white and black audiences by, for example, using symbols and metaphors that reference slavery, emancipation, the Great Migration (1916–70), the dangers of urban living, domestic servitude, the black church, and law enforcement's untenable relationship to the black community." Holder's "vibrant, futuristic sets and costumes helped disconnect the day-to-day struggles of the average black American from this fantastic world." Forsgren goes further to note that, "while the book itself alludes to black political struggle, the modes of production also establish *The Wiz* as a consumable product for a broad (meaning white) audience."[49]

Decades later, Disney Theatrical Productions advanced the corporate collaborator's Broadway potential. "Hoping to elevate Disney's sagging image from a company solely interested in making money into a company respected for fueling the performing arts, Disney CEO Michael Eisner struck a deal with the city of New York in 1994,"[50] Elizabeth L. Wollman explains. Disney committed to renovating the New Amsterdam Theatre, where it has presented musicals since 1997. Disney benefited from low interest loans from the city and the state, "in return for 2 percent of all ticket receipts from shows staged at the theater."[51] The same year Disney struck its deal with the city, it opened a stage adaptation of the hit animated musical *Beauty and the Beast.* Despite critics' unenthusiastic response to what they perceived as theme park aesthetics, the musical thrived on Broadway for thirteen years, becoming the tenth longest running musical. Even more care was taken to assemble a team of theatre artists to adapt *The Lion King* (1997). Helmed by director and costume designer Julie Taymor (who collaborated with Michael Curry to create masks and puppetry elements), the musical's creative team benefited from its corporate producer's unparalleled resources. As a highly respected theatre artist willing to collaborate with a corporation such as Disney, Taymor offered an important model for future collaborations between musical theatre creators and corporate producers.

Twentieth-First-Century Musical Theatre Collaborations

From the late 1980s onward, regional theatres such as California's La Jolla Playhouse found regular success developing new musicals prior to Broadway premieres. Creative teams from New York traveled further afield than traditional tryout cities such as Boston or Chicago, collaborating with a show's producer and their regional hosts. Seattle's Fifth Avenue Theatre hosted *Hairspray*'s creative team and the musical's world premiere in 2002, and its songwriters, Marc Shaiman and Scott Wittman, returned with director Jack O'Brien in 2009 to develop *Catch Me If You Can* prior to a 2011 Broadway premiere. Regional theatres such as Fifth Avenue use the presence of Broadway creative teams and the chance to preview a future Broadway show to appeal to their subscribers, and also earn their own Broadway credits as associates of any future Broadway premiere. New musicals with Broadway in their sights can take advantage of regional theatres' resources and guaranteed audiences, expanding how we might understand the collaborative process. Particular regional partners and cities have sustained relationships with certain creative teams and/or producers. Disney Theatrical tried out *The Little Mermaid* and *Frozen* in Denver, and also tests material at Utah's Tuacahn Center for the Arts, capitalizing on readily available and enthusiastic family audiences. Fans of *Frozen* who attended the Denver performances expressed their dismay on social media over Elsa's appearance in a flimsy white dress. By the time she arrived on Broadway, she was not only singing a new song, but did so while wearing newly designed pants. The pants' designer, Christopher Oram, is a veteran who has designed for plays and musicals in London and New York, but working for a corporate producer such as Disney requires collaboration with the beloved brand and its devoted consumers.

The world premiere of *Waitress*, a musical theatre adaptation of the 2007 film about Jenna, an unhappily pregnant diner waitress and baker of pies, was not on Broadway but was part of the American Repertory Theater's 2015–16 season. Broadway producers Barry and Fran Weissler were involved from the outset, having secured the rights for an adaptation almost as soon as the film opened. It would take nine years and $12 million before that adaptation opened on Broadway, and after false starts with two different creative teams, the project allowed the Weisslers to continue a relationship they had begun with ART and director Diane Paulus on a revival of *Pippin*.[52] Her first choice for the musical's score was Sara Bareilles.

Though well versed in musical theatre from childhood, for a singer-songwriter like Bareilles, "pivoting from the familiar world of composing pop songs to the collaborative craziness of the Broadway musical can induce a sort of cultural whiplash."[53] Paulus saw potential in Bareilles's well-crafted songs, but the songwriter admits she is very protective of her work "until it's completely finished, fleshed out, until I'm ready and willing to go to battle for it. . . . That is less helpful in this process, because this show depends on the music serving the book, the book serving the music, the music serving the actors. Everything has its mirror image."[54] Screenwriter and director Jessie Nelson was hired to write the libretto. Bareilles installed herself in Cambridge, Massachusetts, for the musical's ART run, claiming, "I'm also a control freak, so there was no way this production was going to get up on its feet without me watchdogging every move."[55] While Bareilles added just one new song to the score between Boston and New York, the libretto was much revised, and a new choreographer, Lorin Latarro, contributed new movement "to unlock the fantasy life of Jenna during her pie-making études and to turn a static show into one where the ingredients (the ensemble and band, in particular) literally swirl on stage."[56] The ingredients successfully swirled on stage for a nearly four-year run on Broadway. Bareilles contributed a song to another Broadway musical, *SpongeBob Squarepants: The Broadway Musical*, the following season, while Paulus moved on to collaborate with another singer-songwriter, Alanis Morissette. Directing the new jukebox musical *Jagged Little Pill* first at ART in 2018, Paulus has established a productive home for musical theatre collaborators and a successful axis in the Broadway musical's regional network.

A much shorter axis stretches from the Public Theater at Astor Place uptown to Broadway. The Public has been an important room where musical theatre collaboration happens since Joe Papp first invited James Rado and Gerome Ragni to develop their musical *Hair* there in 1967. Papp's successors have each continued to welcome musical theatre collaborators, and when the most successful projects transfer to Broadway, the share of profits the Public receives helps to sustain the Off-Broadway venue and develop more new work. *Hamilton*'s origin story is now legend, wherein rising musical theatre writer and performer Lin-Manuel Miranda took Ron Chernow's *Alexander Hamilton* biography with him on vacation in 2008 and reveled at how similar the founding fathers' swagger and wordplay were to contemporary hip hop. He began work on a mixtape to combine history with hip hop and consulted with Chernow, with whom he shared the first song he wrote. Chernow recalls, "He had packed the first 40 pages of my book into this 4.5-minute song and had done so very accurately. Then he spent a year on the second song. I think that those were the two breakthrough songs that convinced him and certainly convinced me he would be able to do it."[57] At a White House evening of performance in 2009, Miranda performed the same song in public for the first time: the rap song sung by Aaron Burr that would eventually open the musical. Oskar Eustis, artistic director of the Public, saw a video and decided he needed to bring it to his theatre.

Continuing to consult with Chernow, and with an assignment from friend and director Thomas Kail to generate two songs a month, the show grew. Miranda says, "There are things that don't exist, and that are not going to exist, until we have actors in the room, and I go, 'Oh!'"[58] Chernow attended one of the first rehearsals of material with actors and was taken aback at the African American and Latinx performers standing behind music stands before recognizing the casting as revolutionary. Miranda and future *Hamilton* cast members including Christopher Jackson and James Monroe Iglehart performed *The Hamilton Mixtape* at Lincoln Center's American Songbook series in 2012, and Eustis invited Miranda to the Public again, but he demurred, claiming his work was an album.

A workshop was then held at Vassar College and New York Stage and Film's Powerhouse Season in 2013, directed by Thomas Kail. Chernow remained involved throughout the musical's development, attending rehearsals and workshops every few months. "And then … when it was still at the Public Theater, I was seeing the show about every third or fourth night because Lin was still making changes."[59] After seeing each new version of the show, Chernow spent hours at a time giving Miranda notes. Miranda previously collaborated with playwright Quiara Alegría Hudes on *In the Heights* (2008) but worked with no writing partner on *Hamilton*, serving as composer-lyricist-librettist-actor thereby making Chernow an invaluable interlocutor. The musical's progress nevertheless depended on collaboration, among "the Cabinet" – Miranda, Kail, music director Alex Lacamoire, and choreographer Andy Blankenbuehler.

"Lin is really open to suggestions," Lacamoire notes. "When he brings in a piece of music, he really gives me the freedom to explore stuff. He really allows me to put a stamp on it. I really get to play and suggest."[60] Thomas Jefferson opens Act 2 with "What'd I Miss?," a song Lacamoire and Miranda worked on closely together. The composer sometimes provided just a chord sheet for the music director to work with, and other times a fully formed demo. Miranda delights in such collaboration and explains: "We're all pretty good editors of each other's work. I bring a song in to them, and it's like a pit crew with a car. The song's going to come out leaner and faster as a result."[61] Miranda chronicled his writing process via social media, including an excursion to Weehawken, New Jersey, with Kail to visit the site of Hamilton and Burr's 1804 duel.

The musical previewed at the Public in January 2015 and its run there was extended before the show finally opened on Broadway that August. Not unlike the frenzy around *A Chorus Line* and Michael Bennett, Miranda was celebrated for the multiple revolutions his new musical was staging. As with *A Chorus Line*, the performers who had consistently contributed to the musical's development felt overlooked. Those actors had signed a developmental lab contract in the early stages of the musical's creation, rather than an Equity workshop contract that guarantees royalty participation for eighteen years.[62] The month they opened on Broadway, twenty-two cast members signed a letter to the musical's producer, Jeffrey Seller, acknowledging their love for the show and recognizing Miranda's genius, but noting, "There was a collective genius in the *approach* to the material. That is what we brought."[63] Seller responded quickly with an offer of lump sum checks based on the difference between what performers were earning on Broadway and what they had been paid at the Public. Leslie Odom Jr. who originated the role of Burr encouraged his fellow cast members to not accept the checks, and their deliberations continued over e-mail. An agreement was finally announced in April 2016, granting a group of thirty-eight people, including stage managers involved in the Off-Broadway run, a retroactive share of 1 percent of net profits from New York, and a smaller share of some future productions.[64] The announcement prompted the Public to delay development of a new musical because an agreement could not be reached with cast members, and many actors began wondering about whether they were owed royalties from other shows they helped develop.

Conclusion: Some Things Never Change

The $12 million the Weisslers spent on developing *Waitress's* and *Hamilton's* difficult negotiations with cast members suggest that investment and potential return are as important an element of musical theatre collaboration as they were in the late nineteenth century when Barras, Jarrett, Palmer, and Wheatley joined forces to create *The Black Crook*. The funding to facilitate and sustain collaboration in musical theatre has come from individuals, theatre companies, and corporations in New York City and further afield. Where that funding comes from increasingly informs the collaboration that unfolds, suggesting perhaps that musical theatre investors and producers may be usurping director-choreographers as the captains of musical theatre creation. Commercial theatre producers frequently provide enhancement money to regional theatres developing new musicals, thereby claiming the right to develop the show for Broadway. *Big River* premiered at the American Repertory Theater in 1984 and was further developed later that year at the La Jolla Playhouse, thanks to enhancement money provided by Dodger Productions, who would be one of the lead producers when the musical journeyed to Broadway in 1985 and won the Best Musical Tony Award. Winning the Tony has motivated investors to contribute funding to Broadway-bound musicals. In the past, they might have been better known as angels or investors, but more and more funders who do not actually contribute to the creative process now receive credit as producers, enabling them to claim a greater collaborative role than they may have actually performed.

Other collaborators increasingly earning Broadway credits with limited or no musical theatre pedigree include pop songwriters. Tina Turner, The Temptations, Gloria and Emilio Estefan, Jimmy Buffett, Carole King, and Cher are just some of the many songwriters whose music and often biography formed the basis of new Broadway musicals in the 2010s alone. Jukebox musicals based on existing popular music have been on Broadway since the 1970s, with more and more assembled each decade. The celebrity songwriters and performers who are still living typically participate in aspects of the musical creation process and are often visible in the marketing and promotion of the musicals created from their song catalogs. Regional theatres already committed to developing new musicals, such as the American Repertory Theater and La Jolla Playhouse, have been especially active in collaborating with popular music artists or their catalogs, such as Sara Bareilles, Alanis Morissette, the Four Seasons, and Donna Summer. Where Rodgers and Hammerstein or Michael Bennett once helmed new musical collaborations, now existing songs created for albums, concerts, or music videos establish or suggest what scripts, choreography, and direction might contribute to a musical.

Whether working on a revue, integrated musical, concept musical, or hip hop bio-musical, each creative team must negotiate a hierarchy within their collaboration. The ideas for new musicals can come from a producer, a director, a director-choreographer, writer-composer-actor, or, more recently, a song catalog and compelling biography. Whether the motivation driving a new musical collaboration is social relevance, financial profit, or creative innovation, collaborators' best work emerges when ideas can be freely exchanged and where musical theatre craft has time and space to flourish.

Notes

1. L. Engel, *Words with Music: Creating the Broadway Musical Libretto* (Schirmer Books, 1972), p. 221.
2. B. Rogers, "Redressing the Black Crook: The Dancing Tableau of Melodrama," *Modern Drama*, 55:4 (2012), p. 478.
3. B. Valencia, "Musical of the Month: Shuffle Along," New York Public Library, www.nypl.org/blog/2012/02/10/musical-month-shuffle-along.
4. Bone, "Legitimate: Play Out of Town – AWAY WE GO!," *Variety*, March 17, 1943.
5. Ibid.
6. C. W. Case, "Inventing the Heartland: The Theatre Guild, Oklahoma! And World War II," *Theatre Symposium*, 14 (2006), p. 36.
7. Ibid., p. 37.
8. A. de Mille, *Dance to the Piper* (Columbus Books, 1951), p. 302.
9. S. C. Cook, "Pretty Like the Girl: Gender, Race and 'Oklahoma!,'" *Contemporary Theatre Review*, 19:1 (2009), p. 44.
10. K. A. Gardner, *Agnes de Mille: Telling Stories in Broadway Dance* (Oxford University Press, 2016), p. xvii.
11. Ibid., p. 25.

12. Cook, "Pretty Like the Girl," p. 44.

13. A. Most, *Making Americans: Jews and the Broadway Musical* (Harvard University Press, 2004), p. 104.

14. Gardner, *Agnes de Mille*, p. 89.

15. A. Kraut, *Choreographing Copyright: Race, Gender, and Intellectual Property Rights in American Dance* (Oxford University Press, 2015), p. 167.

16. Qtd. in T. S. Purdum, *Something Wonderful*, Reprint ed. (Picador Paper, 2019), p. 85.

17. Gardner, *Agnes de Mille*, p. xvii.

18. Kraut, *Choreographing Copyright*, p. 199.

19. Ibid., p. 200.

20. Ibid., pp. 201–3.

21. "Peter Gennaro: The West Side Story You Haven't Heard – The New York Public Library for the Performing Arts," in Google Arts & Culture, http:// artsandculture.google.com/exhibit/peter-gennaro-the-west-side-story-you-ha ven-t-heard/KQKyTxP-6nqAKQ.

22. A. Laurents, *Original Story By: A Memoir of Broadway and Hollywood* (Knopf, 2000), p. 330.

23. Ibid., p. 348.

24. B. Atkinson, "Theatre: The Jungles of the City," *New York Times*, September 27, 1957, sec. Archives, www.nytimes.com/1957/09/27/archives/t heatre-the-jungles-of-the-city-west-side-story-is-at-winter-garden.html.

25. "Peter Gennaro."

26. H. Whittaker, "Exciting, Dazzling, Electrifying, Energetic West Side Story Advances Art of Musical," *Globe and Mail*, November 16, 1957.

27. Qtd. in F. Hirsch, *Harold Prince and the American Musical Theatre* (Cambridge University Press, 1989), p. 42.

28. H. Prince, *Contradictions: Notes on Twenty-Six Years in the Theatre* (Dodd, Mead, 1974), p. 126.

29. K. Garebian, *The Making of Cabaret* (Mosaic Press, 1999), p. 109.

30. "Landmark Symposium: Cabaret," *The Dramatists Guild Quarterly*, 19: 2 (1982), p. 21.

31. Garebian, *Cabaret*, 109.

32. S. Citron, *Sondheim and Lloyd-Webber: The New Musical* (Oxford University Press, 2001), p. 247.

33. Garebian, *Cabaret*, pp. 110–11.

34. Ibid., p. 111.

35. G. Furth and S. Sondheim, "Company," in Stanley Richards (ed.), *Great Musicals of the American Theatre*, vol. 1 (Chilton, 1973), pp. 513–72.

36. D. Watt, "'Company' Has Brilliant Fun with Couples in Manhattan," *New York Daily News*, April 27, 1970.

37. Hirsch, *Harold Prince*, p. 72.

38. Furth and Sondheim, "Company."

39. Qtd. in Hirsch, *Harold Prince*, pp. 85–86.

40. C. Robertson, "'Chorus Line' Returns, as Do Regrets over Life Stories Signed Away," *New York Times*, October 1, 2006, sec. NY/Region, www.nytimes.com/2006/10/01/theater/chorus-line-returns-as-do-regrets-over-life-stories-signed-away.html.

41. Robertson, "'Chorus Line' Returns."

42. Qtd. in ibid.

43. A. Woll, *Black Musical Theatre* (Da Capo Press, 1991), p. 263.

44. C. A. Schoettler, "'Wizard of Oz' Reborn in Mechanic Premiere," *Baltimore Evening Sun*, October 22, 1974, sec. B.

45. Qtd. in E. Lester, "Geoffrey Holder – The Whiz Who Rescued 'The Wiz,'" *New York Times*, May 25, 1975, sec. Archives, www.nytimes.com/1975/05/25/archives/geoffrey-holderthe-whiz-who-rescued-the-wiz-hes-the-whiz-who.html.

46. Qtd. in ibid.

47. Woll, *Black Musical Theatre*, p. 263.

48. H. A. Coffin, "'Wiz' Gets Lost in Splendor," *Philadelphia Inquirer*, December 13, 1974, the Wiz clippings file, Billy Rose Theatre Collection, New York Public Library for the Performing Arts.

49. L.-D. L. Forsgren, "The Wiz Redux; or, Why Queer Black Feminist Spectatorship and Politically Engaged Popular Entertainment Continue to Matter," *Theatre Survey*, 60:3 (2019), p. 331.

50. E. L. Wollman, "The Economic Development of the 'New' Times Square and Its Impact on the Broadway Musical," *American Music*, 20:4 (2002), p. 447.

51. Ibid., p. 447.

52. L. Manly, "Sara Bareilles Takes Her Slice of Broadway with 'Waitress,'" *New York Times*, March 17, 2016, sec. Theater, www.nytimes.com/2016/03/20/theater/sara-bareilles-takes-her-slice-of-broadway-with-waitress.html.

53. Ibid.

54. Qtd. in ibid.

55. Qtd. in L. Manly, "'Waitress' Musical Sets the Table for Broadway," *New York Times*, August 13, 2015, *ArtsBeat* blog, http://artsbeat.blogs.nytimes.com/2015/08/13/waitress-musical-sets-the-table-for-broadway/.

56. Manly, "Sara Bareilles."

57. Qtd. in T. Baker, "Meet the Biographer Who Inspired Broadway's 'Hamilton,'" *Newsweek*, 26 (September 2016), www.newsweek.com/hamilton-biographer-ron-chernow-502295.

58. Qtd. in R. Mead, "A Hip-Hop Interpretation of the Founding Fathers," *New Yorker*, February 2, 2015, www.newyorker.com/magazine/2015/02/09/hamiltons.

59. Qtd. in J. C. Simpson, "The Man Who First Brought Us Hamilton – Ron Chernow on Serving as Lin-Manuel Miranda's 'Right Hand Man,'" *Playbill*, January 12, 2016, www.playbill.com/article/the-man-who-first-brought-us-hamilton-u2014-ron-chernow-on-serving-as-lin-manuel-mirandas-right-hand-man.

60. Qtd. in S. Evans, "The Cabinet behind Lin-Manuel Miranda's 'Hamilton,'" *American Theatre*, August 6, 2015, www.americantheatre.org/2015/08/06/the-cabinet-behind-lin-manuel-mirandas-hamilton/.
61. Qtd. in ibid.
62. M. Paulson, "'Hamilton' Producers and Actors Reach Deal on Sharing," *New York Times*, April 15, 2016, sec. Theater, www.nytimes.com/2016/04/16/theater/hamilton-producers-and-actors-reach-deal-on-sharing-profits.html.
63. Qtd. in R. Morgan, "How the "'Hamilton' Cast Got Broadway's Best Deal," *Bloomberg*, September 28, 2016, www.bloomberg.com/features/2016-hamilton-broadway-profit/.
64. Ibid.

Select Bibliography

Citron, S. *Sondheim and Lloyd-Webber: The New Musical.* Oxford University Press, 2001.

Gardner, K. A. *Agnes de Mille: Telling Stories in Broadway Dance.* Oxford University Press, 2016.

Hirsch, F. *Harold Prince and the American Musical Theatre.* Cambridge University Press, 1989.

Kraut, A. *Choreographing Copyright: Race, Gender, and Intellectual Property Rights in American Dance.* Oxford University Press, 2015.

Laurents, A. *Original Story By: A Memoir of Broadway and Hollywood.* Knopf, 2000.

Woll, A. *Black Musical Theatre.* Da Capo Press, 1991.

CHAPTER 4

Shaping Broadway and Off-Broadway Plays through Collaborations
Playwrights, Directors, Designers, and Companies

Jessica Silsby Brater

Theatrical processes and performances on US stages in the second half of the twentieth century and the dawn of the twenty-first century reflect the turbulence of American political and social life during this period, revealing a variety of approaches to playwriting and new play production. The rise of smaller, independent theatres across the country – pioneered in the 1950s by venues such as the San Francisco Actors' Workshop and the Living Theatre in New York – helped to foster an organic, process-oriented approach to the development of new plays. This decentralization of power in new play development reflects the rebellion and unrest that swept American society in the 1960s and 1970s. Tumultuous social and political events and movements during this period such as free love, the civil rights movement, the Vietnam War and accompanying protests, and the assassinations of Martin Luther King Jr. and John F. Kennedy resulted in an upheaval of US dramaturgy as the theatre began to reflect a diversity of voices from a wider range of racial and cultural backgrounds, genders, and sexual orientations.

New voices need new modes of expression and invention. In some cases, we see a shift from playwright-centered development to a more porous, inclusive process. In other cases, playwrights opted for script-based dramaturgical revolutions while embracing more traditional modes of production that maintained the autonomy of writers and directors. The wide range of dramaturgical styles and development processes itself unveils newfound freedom and inclusivity in who makes American theatre, how it ends up on stage, and what it looks and sounds like when it gets there. As playwright Suzan-Lori Parks writes of the non-Aristotelian dramaturgical structure and subjects of her plays, "It's like this: I am an African American woman – this is the form I take, my content predicates the form, and this form is inseparable from my content."[1] The increasingly diverse array of artists who populate the second half of the twentieth century have felt free to colonize conventional ways of working, to seek new forms, or to operate in a hybrid world of old and new.

Despite the variety of dramaturgies and production processes, one aspect has been consistent: collaboration has remained constant at the heart of new play development. The significant American plays emerging between the 1960s and the present result from fruitful and dynamic artistic relationships among playwrights, directors, and designers. One post-1960 inheritor of this meaningful collaboration is Edward Albee's work with director Alan Schneider and designer William Ritman, who worked on premieres of his plays, including the Tony Award–winning *Who's Afraid of Virginia Woolf?* Another crucial director-playwright relationship existed between August Wilson and Lloyd Richards; many of Wilson's *American Century Cycle* plays were developed under the auspices of the Eugene O'Neill Theater Center, where Richards served as chair of the Playwrights Conference. Following workshop development at the O'Neill, these productions moved to regional houses and later to New York for Off-Broadway or Broadway productions. Designers have often served as equally important collaborators in the process of staging new dramatic texts; Maria Irene Fornes, who frequently directed her own plays, was deeply invested in long-term collaborations with set designer Donald Eastman, lighting designer Anne Militello, and costume designer Gabriel Berry.

The plays resulting from these collaborations and the others discussed here unearth and confront uncomfortable American histories or grapple with an increasingly diverse fabric of family and society. Several are also stylistically ambitious. As Parks suggests above, for some playwrights, content has regularly dictated form. But for other artists, such as playwright Paula Vogel and director Rebecca Taichman, changing collaborative and inclusive processes have fostered the development of plays that engage with difficult subjects. The nuances of the collaborative relationships and processes that moved new plays from page to stage in post-1960 America are as varied as the diverse backgrounds of the artists themselves. This chapter will draw upon some of these artistic interactions to explore the development of dramaturgical expressions in plays produced on and Off-Broadway post-1960.

Edward Albee, Alan Schneider, and William Ritman

The best-known collaboration between Alan Schneider and Pulitzer Prize–winning playwright Edward Albee was their momentous 1962 production of *Who's Afraid of Virginia Woolf?* Albee, who guarded his plays closely, responded to Schneider's keen instincts and dedication to the text. In his preface to Schneider's memoir, *Entrances*, Albee writes, "Alan understood that the director (indeed the entire production – actors, sets, costumes, all) is at the service of a worthwhile play. Alan was meticulous, detailed and exhaustive in his examination of a text, and woe to an author who could not answer the hundreds of textual questions thrown at him."[2] Albee, supported by Schneider and frequent collaborator William Ritman, brought a distinctly American version of European theatre of the absurd to US stages. His collaboration with Schneider is characterized by a traditional hierarchy that privileged the text, and therefore the playwright.

The team's first collaboration was the premiere of *The American Dream* (1961). Albee was finding critical and professional acclaim, in part because of a scholarly association between his work and that of Beckett's and Ionesco's, which critic Martin Esslin characterized as the theatre of the absurd. Meanwhile, Schneider was finding a home Off-Broadway. "I liked working in this less frenzied, more intellectually and emotionally stimulating, and at the same time more intimate theater. I had not felt at home on Broadway," he explains.[3] Appropriately, Albee and Schneider's first collaboration took place Off-Broadway on *The American Dream* at the York Theatre on a double bill with Albee's adaptation of Herman Melville's *Bartleby the Scrivener*, directed by William Penn. *The American Dream* was the first production to bring together collaborators that would become Albee's most trusted team: Schneider as director and Richard Barr and Clinton Wilder as producers. It also featured Ritman, whose designs were to have a crucial role in *Who's Afraid of Virginia Woolf?*, among others of Albee's plays.

The relationship between Albee and Schneider was both complicated and productive, as evidenced by their collaboration on *Who's Afraid of Virginia Woolf?* Schneider was contracted for a production at the San Francisco Actors' Workshop (one of the first theatres in the United States to bring the European avant-garde plays that influenced Albee to American audiences) and was not present at the first read-through of the play. In an early sign of trust between the director and Albee, Schneider sent instructions to Albee about managing rehearsal in his absence. Schneider's letter provides guidance on opening lines of communication with the cast. "I think it is valuable for you to tell them anything you want about the play's nature or meaning for you," Schneider suggested to Albee.[4] Schneider also recommends that Albee confer with Ritman on the scenic design, underscoring the director's ease in deferring to the playwright. Though Schneider liked and respected the play, he did not find it without fault. He lauded the structure and its incisiveness in "detailing the decay of American virtues and values, and amazingly prophetic in certain of its insights." But he critiqued Albee's "inability to blend the more somber stylization of the Young Man with the other highly colored comic-strip characters," suggesting, however, that it would have violated the boundaries of the director-playwright relationship to articulate these concerns to Albee.[5] This implies Schneider's respect for Albee as a writer but also indicates that their communication was not entirely transparent.

While Schneider identifies the emerging writer's struggle for proficiency with what was to become American absurdism, he also recognizes a theme in Albee's work – the deterioration of the American nuclear family – that proved to be one of the playwright's most crucial contributions to an American theatre of the absurd. As an adopted child and a gay writer, Albee was in a singular position to reveal the fault lines in heteronormative and patriarchal familial ideals, and though the collaborative arrangement with Schneider was a traditional one, the American families Albee wrote about were anything but. Schneider's comments also reveal a delicate directorial approach to developing new plays and a hierarchical relationship between the playwright and the director, one that emphasizes Albee's authority over the process. In the case of Albee and Schneider, the playwright and director opted for a conventional model to support the vision of a playwright whose dramaturgy was aimed at disrupting notions of the traditional American family.

Who's Afraid of Virginia Woolf? opened on Broadway at the Billy Rose Theatre the next year. Schneider remembers pressure to cast stars – precisely the sort of burden he could avoid in an Off-Broadway setting more conducive to the incubation of new work. Schneider had good reason to be concerned. Albee's play was, at four hours in length, unwieldy for the typical Broadway schedule. The production team responded creatively to the challenge of staging the lengthy play in a three-week rehearsal period, short even for a Broadway production because of other cast commitments. In an arrangement highly unusual on Broadway – "unheard of" in Schneider's words – the director, Ritman, and producers planned for the company to rehearse on stage at the theatre on the full set with props from nearly the beginning of the rehearsal period.[6] According to Mel Gussow, the set was up at the Billy Rose approximately ten days after rehearsals began.

This expanded rehearsal period on set was not the only way in which the collaboration on *Who's Afraid of Virginia Woolf?* disrupted conventional collaborative practices. Uta Hagen, who played Martha, was uncomfortable with what she perceived as an unorthodox approach to scenic design. She complained that Albee, Schneider, and the producers, rather than the designer, were making choices about the set, singling out an episode in which the group discussed upholstery. She was furthermore distressed that she, a performer, was invited into the decision-making process about scenic design by Schneider; it is unusual to actively involve actors in the design process in commercial productions. "Alan said to me," she remembered, "'Which do you like?' I said I'm not a designer. Where the fuck is the designer? I said you're playing games up there decorating living rooms without a designer."[7] Despite Hagen's irritation, the scene she describes indicates a surprisingly fluid relationship among playwright, director, designer, and producers, especially given Albee's reluctance to cede control of his vision. Hagen's alarm at the process she observed is unsurprising, however, in the context of a Broadway production, suggesting once again why Schneider felt such an affinity for the intimacy of Off-Broadway.

Schneider directed significant productions of nine of Albee's plays between 1961 and 1980. After 1980, Albee began to direct his own work, and Schneider ceased to be a collaborator. Ritman designed the original set for most of Albee's premieres, developing a reputation for "detailed theatrical versions of apartments and houses" such as "the mansion-within-a-mansion"[8] in Albee's *Tiny Alice,* which Gussow described as "monumental."[9] In a significant loss to Albee, both Schneider and Ritman died in 1984.

Although the best-known Albee–Schneider–Ritman production premiered on Broadway, many of the trio's collaborations were originally presented at regional theatres such as the Studio Arena Theater in Buffalo, where Albee's *Box-Mao-Box* premiered in 1968. The most significant legacy of this collaboration was an unflinching examination of American family life through a stylistically adventurous lens. Through a collaborative process that replicated a traditional, text-first hierarchy, Albee's unconventional subjects and style staged by Schneider and Ritman helped pave the way for a greater diversity of voices and approaches on American stages as the century progressed.

Sam Shepard, Robert Woodruff, and the Magic Theatre

The partnership between Sam Shepard and Robert Woodruff included work at various venues such as the Magic Theatre in San Francisco and Public Theater in New York. The playwright/director team collaborated for ten years, most centrally at the Magic Theatre, and as they worked together, they refined their process, revealing where their collaborations were most successful. This symbiosis between playwright and director was made possible by the Magic Theatre's emphasis on incubating new plays and emerging artists. By the 1970s, a number of smaller independent theatres had set up shop around the country to develop the sort of boundary-pushing new plays Albee was known for. San Francisco, where Shepard met Woodruff in 1974, was a hub of these independent, experimental environments. Shepard was playwright-in-residence at the Magic from the mid-1970s to early 1980s. The Magic, founded in 1967, featured a small house with a proscenium stage, an inviting environment for the development of Shepard's intimate and mysterious theatrical worlds. Shepard's first production there was the West Coast premiere of *La Turista* in 1971. Not all moves from independent theatres such as the Magic transfer successfully to more prominent venues, and collaborations between Woodruff and Shepard were at their strongest in this small theatre in San Francisco.

The 1960s saw a rise of smaller, independent theatres that offered an alternative to commercially driven (Broadway) venues. These independent theatres, such as the Magic, brought with them new ways of developing plays. Because of the financial pressures on Broadway productions, rehearsal periods have traditionally been limited: scripts are complete except for the most minor changes before actors and directors arrive in the rehearsal room, and design decisions have been finalized before rehearsals begin. Independent theatres such as the Magic allowed artistic collaborators to work outside of these restrictions. For example, playwrights could experiment with dialogue and stage directions with actors in the room, making changes to text organically. The Magic Theatre allowed Shepard to engage in this kind of workshopping process, testing out new material in a supportive setting, often surrounded by handpicked collaborators (such as Woodruff) and without the pressure of commercial producers. Additionally, audiences at independent theatres were more intimate than those at commercial houses, creating a sympathetic environment in which to present new works in production. Independent theatres and workshops gave Shepard (and other emerging playwrights) the opportunity to make bold choices and subsequently adjust them before new plays moved on to larger, economically driven regional theatres or New York venues. This way of working has persisted, most notably for American avant-garde companies such as Mabou Mines and the Wooster Group, but it has also had a lasting impact on venues that feature more conventional dramaturgies. One twenty-first-century example is Paula Vogel's *Indecent*, discussed below, which benefited from the kind of progressive development process pioneered by theatres such as the Magic.

Shepard and Woodruff's collaboration was characterized by an aesthetic affinity. "I think we both share a desire for anarchy," the director has said of his connection with Shepard.[10] The turmoil and rebellion Woodruff describes are indeed a hallmark of Shepard's texts, which the offbeat nature of the workshopping process at the Magic allowed Shepard to cultivate. Where Albee capitalized on the influence of European avant-garde writers, Shepard drew on American popular culture and a mythology of the American West to reveal a sinister underside of nuclear family relationships and traditional masculinity, to which Woodruff responded keenly. Stephen Bottoms notes that where some critics looked down upon Shepard's reliance on melodrama, Woodruff embraced these elements. Of his approach to *Buried Child*, Woodruff explained, "The form of it is, of course, The Great American Melodrama. I got the deed! No you don't! I got the money! Here come the cops! And the guy with the black moustache comes on at the end twirling it. The problem was basically seeing how far you could stretch the distance between these people and the audience and still have the play work."[11] Woodruff's sensitivity to Shepard's form and style on *Buried Child* provides an example of his artistic affinity with the playwright that extends beyond anarchy.

Aside from the artistic connection between Woodruff and Shepard, the pair also exhibited complimentary approaches in the rehearsal room, although they worked on separate tracks on their initial production together. For their inaugural collaboration, Woodruff asked Shepard if he had any unproduced material. Shepard gave him *The Sad Lament of Pecos Bill on the Eve of Killing His Wife*, a half hour long musical. Woodruff directed the play for the Bay Area Playwrights Festival, which he had recently founded. Shepard didn't see the 1976 production but, according to Woodruff, liked what he heard. This led to a collaboration on *Suicide in B Flat* at the Magic in 1978 (the second production of the new play first produced at the Yale Repertory Theatre), in which Shepard, a drummer, would occasionally play percussion. The independent nature of the Magic meant that artists had more opportunity to select collaborators than they might in a commercial setting and that there was a greater possibility for fluidity in roles, allowing Shepard to serve irregularly as a percussionist in the performance. The company's dexterity in accommodating Shepard as a sometime percussionist was aided by the playwright's frequent presence in the rehearsal room; Ellen Oumano describes Shepard as "actively present at the Magic Theatre" with Woodruff.[12] Harry Mann, who performed as an actor and musician in Shepard plays including *Suicide in B Flat*, described a working relationship between Shepard and Woodruff in which the playwright would often defer to the director's choices in rehearsal even as the playwright maintained open lines of communication with the actors. "He would never trespass on the director," Mann explained.[13] Woodruff recalls that he and Shepard found performers who had collaborated previously and that the music was improvised at every performance; there was a "fine sense of listening to make that improvisational element work. Some nights it wasn't there; other nights it soared."[14] Woodruff's comments reveal the director and playwright's willingness to risk consistency for a daring and original live dramaturgy of American popular culture and the company's practiced pliability in allowing for these shifts in performance.

Shepard and Woodruff also collaborated on the New York premiere of *Curse of the Starving Class* at the New York Shakespeare Festival/Public Theater in 1978 (the play had premiered in London in 1977). *Curse of the Starving Class* is the first play in Shepard's family trilogy; Woodruff would go on to direct the others, *Buried Child* and *True West*, as well. Among Shepard's oeuvre, these plays most directly take up Albee's legacy of unmasking the falsehoods of patriarchal family values. Woodruff recalls that Shepard suggested the director to founding artistic director Joseph Papp for *Curse of the Starving Class*, and, though Shepard did not see this production either, he was evidently pleased enough with the results to team up with Woodruff for the premiere of *Buried Child* at the Magic Theatre in 1978. This time, the collaborators were in rehearsal together. Shepard revised the play as the company rehearsed. "He was . . . shaping the play around the actors," Woodruff recalled, describing how the playwright manipulated the flexibility of the Magic's artistic independence to shape an original vision of American family relationships.[15]

For critic Don Shewey, Woodruff's work on Shepard's plays, though only a decade of the director's lengthy career, proved seminal, characterizing him "as a low-key director skilled at removing from the stage environment – and from the actors' performances – anything that might jeopardize the humor, mystery, and explosive theatricality of Shepard's word-music." Shewey's description of *Buried Child* unearths the evocative imagery of Shepard's plays as staged by Woodruff; the critic "can hear Mary McDonnell's hysterical laughter as the intruder-girlfriend Shelley, . . . can feel the shock of Christopher McCann smashing beer bottle after beer bottle against the back of the porch-wall set, . . . can see eerie Tom Noonan coming in from the backyard with his increasingly dreadful bundles."[16] Shewey's review reveals a director and playwright well matched in their ability to elicit an ominous association between images of American popular culture and the deterioration of intimate American relationships. This description also provides a sense of the accumulation of objects crucial to visualizing the emptiness of American capitalism on the Shepard stage. In this production of *Buried Child*, beer bottles and bundles cluttered the stage. In *Curse of the Starving Class*, the refrigerator overflowed with artichokes. *True West* would bring an excess of toasters. The production Shewey describes garnered several Obie Awards, and *Buried Child* won the 1979 Pulitzer Prize, cementing Shepard as a significant voice in American theatre.

Though the development and premiere of *True West* at the Magic Theatre in 1980 was a success for the collaborators, the production did not fare as well when it moved to New York. Shepard was once again in rehearsal at the Magic with Woodruff. The director remembers, "it was great to have his voice there. He and I would be in the audience and the actors would talk, he would talk, I would talk – it was a really great open dialogue." Woodruff recalls that Shepard "wanted to give" actors "room to explore. And he wasn't in a hurry about that. He was always very generous with time."[17] For his part, Woodruff used personal experiences with Shepard in the rehearsal room. The pair attended a Sugar Ray Leonard-Roberto Duran fight; at rehearsal the following day, the director drew inspiration from this distinctly American experience of popular culture in staging the physical altercation between brothers Lee and Austin. Shepard was apparently pleased with the production: "this is the first one of my plays I've been able to sit through night after night and not have my stomach ball up in embarrassment," he said.[18]

But the production at the Public Theater in New York was "a rough moment," Woodruff reports.[19] The director resigned. Rather than using their San Francisco cast, Woodruff remembers that they were pressured by Papp to take on movie stars Tommy Lee Jones and Peter Boyle for their commercial potential. The strain Woodruff experienced here was not unique; the economic burden of commercial theatre ventures often disrupts collaborative processes, particularly ones that have been developed in noncommercial, independent contexts such as the Magic. The resulting production was widely panned by critics. Shepard, who was away filming *The Raggedy Man*, called Michael Feingold at the *Village Voice* to disavow it, though he allowed the run to continue.

Despite this blemish, Woodruff describes an easy going, if sometimes enigmatic communication with Shepard in rehearsal. This opacity, however, may ultimately have ended the collaboration. At Shepard's request, Woodruff provided an outside eye during previews for a production of *A Lie of the Mind* at the Promenade Theatre in New York in 1985 that the playwright was directing. Woodruff weighed in on revisions. Later, for a production of the play in Los Angeles, the director reinserted some of the scenes that had been cut, discovering retroactively that Shepard was dissatisfied with this decision. "But I didn't know it until years later," Woodruff explained, "because he was never precious." Because, as Mann described, Shepard regularly acceded to the director in rehearsal, Woodruff assumed he was at liberty with decisions about the text. "So we had a kind of parting of the ways on that," according to Woodruff, "but I didn't know we were having a parting of the ways. I just thought we had run our race – and that we'd had a great run."[20] By the mid-1980s, Shepard began to direct his own plays with regularity.

The Magic Theatre was not only a successful ground for collaboration between Woodruff and Shepard but also played a formative role in shaping and supporting Shepard's playwriting and career, producing eighteen of his forty plays in twenty-six productions between 1971 and 2015. After his death in 2017, artistic director Larry Eilenberg linked Shepard's ties to the Magic Theatre to "Chekhov and the Moscow Art Theater, O'Neill and the Provincetown Players, and Odets and the Group Theatre," and suggested that the Magic Theatre was Shepard's "home stage."[21] This intimate, independent theatre proved formative in the style and structure of Shepard's plays, providing the playwright with an incubator for much of his most important new work before it moved to New York. The collaboration between Shepard and Woodruff at the Magic helped to establish a precedent for the importance of a supportive and flexible incubation process for bringing new plays to the stage, one that is carried on in the contemporary theatre with institutions such as the Lark, Playwrights Horizons, and the Magic Theatre itself.

August Wilson, Lloyd Richards, Constanza Romero, and the O'Neill Theater Center

Where Shepard drew upon the mystique of the cowboy in examining white masculinity, August Wilson created a mythic cycle of African American family life, largely from a male perspective. Director Lloyd Richards was indispensable in securing a legacy for Wilson's *American Century Cycle*.

Critic John Lahr has suggested that the director-playwright partnership between Richards and Wilson "is, along with [Elia] Kazan's with Tennessee [Williams], the great collaboration of the twentieth century."[22] Richards, the first Black director of a Broadway play (Lorraine Hansbury's *A Raisin in the Sun*), was significant for the development of Wilson's plays and career at the National Playwrights Conference at the Eugene O'Neill Theater Center in Waterford, Connecticut, where Richards served as head from 1968 until 1999. He "discovered" Wilson with *Ma Rainey's Black Bottom* in 1981, selecting it for development at the O'Neill with the help of a committee from approximately 1,400 submissions. The O'Neill Theater Center, founded in 1964, almost immediately became a central institution for play development, and it was crucial to Wilson's emergence as a major US playwright. The new play festival's emphasis on incubating new work in a supportive workshop setting became foundational to Wilson and Richards's mode of collaboration. Wilson submitted several plays to the festival, starting in 1979 with *Jitney*, but *Ma Rainey* was the first to gain traction. "There were characters [in the play] that were well delineated," Richards says. "And the things they were talking about, I believed. So the playwright, in a sense, was speaking for me as well as to me."[23] Richards and Wilson were deeply impacted by urban African American oral history. As Wilson puts it, "I was trying to answer James Baldwin's call for a profound articulation of the black experience, which he defined as that field of manners and ritual of intercourse that will sustain a man once he has left his father's house."[24] The O'Neill's Playwrights Conference, like the Magic, has a strong ethos that places workshopping at the center of the development process, and has played a unique role in nurturing – especially under Richards's leadership – a diverse range of emerging playwrights such as Wilson, Wendy Wasserstein, and David Henry Hwang as they found their voices. At the O'Neill, Richards helped Wilson to find dramaturgical expression for his ideas. O'Neill resident designer Skip Mercier, who worked on a number of Wilson's plays in development at the Playwrights Conference, observed "August was a kind of offbeat poet who wrote character studies that went all over the map. Lloyd basically taught August what a playwright is."[25] Richards supported Wilson in creating a revolution in the American theatre, one that reshaped the notion of who constitutes an American family.

Ma Rainey was directed by William Partlan at the O'Neill's Barn in 1982. *New York Times* critic Frank Rich was in the audience for the second performance and had strong praise for the emerging playwright in his article "Where Writers Mold the Future of Theater."[26] Richards then invited Wilson to bring the play to the Yale Repertory Theatre (Yale Rep) under his direction, where Richards served as artistic director from 1979 to 1991 – the first Black dean of an Ivy League university. In 1984, *Ma Rainey* opened on Broadway and won the New York Drama Critics' Circle Award.

Next, Wilson brought *Fences* to the O'Neill (1983). In a description that provides a window into the intense impression O'Neill collaborators left on Wilson's plays, Mercier recalls that Wilson's first draft of *Fences* took place in a number of different rooms in the Maxson family house. Mercier began to ask the playwright how he envisioned each of these spaces. Wilson described "Pittsburgh and the Hill District and the yard and the tree," but no particular vision for the rooms of the house. Mercier recalls, "I said, 'Why are we going there?' And the next morning, he grabbed me and he said, 'Do you think this can all happen in the back yard?' I said, 'That's your play. It's a boxing ring between a father and a son around that tree you can see.'"[27] Indeed, the setting for the play Wilson would eventually publish calls for "a yard which fronts the only entrance" to the Maxson family's "two-story brick house" and "a tree from which hangs a ball made of rags. A baseball bat leans against the tree."[28] Although Mercier did not design the Broadway premiere, his comments, paired with Wilson's stage directions, suggest the strong influence designers and the O'Neill's work-shopping process had on Wilson's visual storytelling. The bat and the ball of rags at the tree suggest both possibilities and limitations; Troy is a talented baseball player but America's systemic racism will not allow him to fulfill his potential. As Act II opens, Cory is seen "at the tree hitting the ball with the bat" in an attempt to "mimic Troy," who we have seen engage earlier in this action, "but his swing is awkward, less sure."[29] Here the tree becomes a visual anchor for the generational struggle between father and son – root and branch.

The O'Neill Theater Center collaborators, including Richards and Mercier, recall that the first drafts of Wilson's plays were always lengthy. Richards remembered a revision process reminiscent of peeling an onion. "It was a lot of wonderful material, and hidden in it was a story," he explained. The job of Wilson's collaborators, according to Richards, was "searching for that line and putting that line through the material and lifting it up and seeing what hung on it, what belonged there, what was essential, what was necessary, and finding the core of the life of that man."[30] Wilson was willing to make cuts, but Partlan, who also directed *Fences* at the O'Neill, recalls that in both cases the playwright wanted to hear the play aloud in front of an audience first. The Playwrights Conference, designed as an incubator for new plays, cultivated this organic development process.

Wilson's plays also benefited from development in regional theatres, which have often served as a testing ground for new work that might make its way to higher profile commercial productions in New York. *Fences* provides an excellent example of how plays are often developed regionally before coming to Broadway. Following its workshop production at the O'Neill, *Fences* was produced at the Yale Rep under Richards's direction, and then moved on to Chicago's Goodman Theatre so that Richards and Wilson could continue to develop the play. Producer Carole Shorenstein Hays optioned the production, bringing it to San Francisco and finally to Broadway at the Forty-Sixth Street Theatre in 1987. But the process was not without controversy; in San Francisco, Shorenstein was at odds with Wilson and Richards about the play's ending. Shorenstein insisted that Cory, the protagonist Troy's son, should sing a song to Troy at the play's conclusion, while Wilson maintained that it should end with Troy's brother Gabriel blowing his horn. Richards supported the playwright and, echoing Woodruff's response to Papp, briefly resigned from the production. But in this case, the playwright was on-site. Wilson developed a compromise and the show went on with Gabe blowing his brother Troy into heaven at the play's conclusion. This conflict elucidates some of the challenges of moving new plays to progressively larger venues – in this case, from the O'Neill to regional theatres, and finally to Broadway. The increasingly high commercial stakes in moving from the O'Neill to a regional venue and then on to Broadway mean that there are more producers involved at each stage, many of whom have the authority to provide artistic feedback, whether or not it is desired by the playwright or director. In this case, Wilson gracefully navigated the various pressures that can sometimes conspire to derail artistic decision-making.

Wilson won a Pulitzer Prize and received the Tony Award for best new play for *Fences*, and Richards received the Tony for best director. Subsequently, Ben Mordecai, Yale Rep's managing director and later Broadway producer, became the lead producer of Wilson's new plays as they continued to follow the pattern of early development at the O'Neill, a production at Yale Rep, and an eventual Broadway premiere. Over a span of more than twenty years, Richards directed five seminal premieres of plays from Wilson's *Century Cycle*. Six were presented at the Yale Rep before making their way to Broadway: *Ma Rainey's Black Bottom* (1984), *Fences* (1985), *Joe Turner's Come and Gone* (1986), *The Piano Lesson* (1984),

Two Trains Running (1990), and *Radio Golf* (2005). All of Wilson's plays went to Broadway during his lifetime except for *Jitney*, which was produced there posthumously. His collaboration with Richards is one of the most enduring and best known among writers and directors in the second half of the twentieth century. The pair was united in their commitment to bringing plays about the African American experience into the US canon, and Richards was deeply invested in utilizing his experience as an artistic director to support and promote Wilson's development as a writer.

Wilson's relationship with the Yale Rep brought him another crucial collaborator – his costume designer Constanza Romero. They met there when Romero designed the world premiere of *The Piano Lesson* in 1987. The couple married in 1994. "There was immediate connection as artists, but our friendship grew from there," Romero explains.[31] Romero also designed costumes for *Seven Guitars*. Their collaboration on that play was integral to Wilson's writing process. As Romero sketched, Wilson often revised his play. Romero recalls "a couple of times he saw my sketches, and he looked at them really closely and he would say, 'Huh, I'm going to go downstairs and write the character to fit more like the sketch.'"[32] Romero recalls Wilson's eagerness to embrace Mercier's visual ideas as he developed *Fences*, an early signal of what would emerge as Wilson's strong focus on visuality in his plays.

Clothing – and dresses in particular – provide subtle clues to character relationships in *Seven Guitars*. In the beginning of Act II, close friends Louise and Vera discuss an attractive red hand-me-down dress. It is too small for Louise, and she suggests Vera try it on. Vera insists it will be too small for her as well.[33] When Floyd returns at the end of Act II after disappearing for two days, he brings, along with his guitar, a new dress for Vera. Floyd, who is trying to make up for his past indiscretions, is at pains to demonstrate the thought he put into this peace offering. "Size nine," he says as he presents the dress, "That's your size." Vera responds, "Floyd it's beautiful. I don't believe it. I ain't never had nothing like this."[34] Floyd's gesture is meaningful and Vera seems to agree to reconciliation. Here, with Wilson's attention to the theatricality of visuality, the dress becomes a metaphor for a new beginning between Floyd and Vera.

Romero read every draft of *Seven Guitars*. Though some of the characters who appeared in earlier versions had disappeared in the final version, Romero explains how her proximity to the play in development impacted her design process: "I had these personal histories in my mind, I was able to have a much richer sense about who these people were. ... To live with August was almost like living with a family of many interesting, complex characters."[35] Considering Wilson's reliance on visual symbolism in his play texts, it is unsurprising that he found a long-term collaborator as well as a life partner in a costume designer. Certainly, the luxury of having a designer present in his home from the earliest stages of writing would have had a significant influence on pictorial development in his plays.

While Romero and Wilson shared a marital bond, the relationship between Richards and Wilson paralleled a familial relationship. In a 1989 interview with *Vanity Fair*, Wilson described this relationship as father and son. Their connection changed as Wilson grew into a mature artist and began to seek out other directors such as Walter Dallas, who took over *Seven Guitars* after Richards had to step down due to health reasons. This truncated collaboration was to be the last between Wilson and Richards. Romero suggests that the evolution of the relationship was natural: "when you gain your wings, you have to try out how you're going to be going on your own. August felt he needed to experience the work more on his own."[36] Wilson and Mordecai then formed a new production company, and other directors staged the last three plays he wrote. After Wilson's death, the Virginia Theater on Broadway was named in his honor. Richards died in 2006, eight months after Wilson. Richards's influence on Wilson's plays through his work at the O'Neill and the Yale Rep remains integral. "What makes my work with August possible," Richards said in 1995, "is that there is a level on which we meet that is also a part of my background, and my sense of being. Those things are understood between us. There's not a lot of questions that I have to ask him."[37] The collaboration between Richards and Wilson altered the face of the American family drama by making space for the African American experience. Using traditional Aristotelian dramaturgy, Wilson's plays theatricalize what it means to be an African American family in the twentieth century.

Maria Irene Fornes and the Design Triumvirate

Maria Irene Fornes may be the best-known American playwright never to appear on Broadway. Where Wilson began as a poet, Fornes was a painter before she became a writer. Among the major American playwrights examined in this chapter, Fornes is the only to have been born outside of the United States, emigrating at age fifteen from her native Cuba. Fornes is also unusual in the profound connection between her writing and her directing. "I am a single creator," she said.[38] Her most significant collaborators were designers Donald Eastman (sets), Anne Militello (lights), and

Gabriel Berry (costumes). Perhaps the deep connections she found with designers stem from her own background as a visual artist. Fornes's writing is unconventional in style, structure, and in her characters. While Shepard and Wilson examine American men, Fornes's plays, particularly *Fefu and Her Friends*, have entered the canon of feminist dramaturgy. As both a playwright and director, she worked closely with designers to revise her plays, both textually and visually, as rehearsals unfolded, creating a nontraditional theatricality of female spaces (Fornes's plays frequently take place in a domestic setting belonging to a woman), characters, and ideas. Despite the potential for friction between a visual artist-turned-director and her designers, the evidence suggests that Fornes's collaborations with her design team were harmonious and productive. Fornes eschewed popular success. She never wrote a standard two-hour play, which perhaps explains the absence of such a highly regarded writer from Broadway stages. "I belong to the Off-Off-Broadway movement," Fornes declared, "which was the idea of doing art. And doing something that we loved doing."[39] Fornes was responsible for directing more than 300 iterations of her own plays. "When you love someone, don't you want to see them again?" she asked, insisting that she did not know a play as a director until she staged it for the third time.[40] Fornes, who died in 2018, was the recipient of nine Obie Awards and the subject of the documentary film "The Rest I Make Up." She was highly regarded by contemporaries such as Sam Shepard and Tony Kushner. Fornes was also a teacher, best known for her influence as INTAR Hispanic Playwrights in Residence Lab's "La Maestra."

Fornes credits the directors who worked on her early texts, such as Larry Kornfeld, who directed Promenade at Judson Church in 1965, for teaching her how to direct. Still, her impulse to stage her own plays stemmed from her frustration with the choices other directors made. "I didn't know I had to direct my own work right away," she said, but "I did find out immediately that the position of the playwright is unbearable," citing an excruciating process of surrendering her play to the director. In traditional settings, directors work more closely with actors than playwrights do, so it is telling that Fornes always felt an affinity for actors "because lines have to go *through* the actor." While directors regularly made what to Fornes seemed like "wrong choices," she argues that "often the actors begin, instinctually, to say things as I thought I had written them."[41] Deeply impressed by her observations of Joe Chaikin's nonnaturalistic Open Theater, she taught herself to direct and began to direct her own plays by the late 1960s. She objected to the notion that playwrights could not be objective in staging their own work, noting that directors, too, have biases.[42] Fornes is unique among the playwright/directors discussed here because, although Albee and Shepard eventually turned to directing their own work, Fornes made this shift early in her career and was more committed to consistently staging her own writing.

Maria Delgado describes Fornes's plays as "pictorial."[43] In this sense, her playwriting is an organic outgrowth of her background as a painter. Fornes's inclination to direct her own plays allowed her to capitalize on her visual instincts in working with designers to simultaneously shape the space and the language of her plays. The first production of *Fefu and Her Friends*, written in 1977, was presented site-specifically in a furnished loft space with a living room, kitchen, bedroom, and lawn – all settings in the play. Fornes chose the performance location before she finished writing the play and completed it, inspired by what she had seen there. Though she moved away from creating site-specific work in subsequent plays, Fornes was acutely inspired by the theatre spaces she used, explaining that she liked to conceptualize the scenic design only after seeing the performance space. "I find that the theatre space has a spirit and that that spirit begins to suggest the way the play should be done in that space. I don't mean to be done on a bare stage but what structure should the set have in that space," she said.[44] It is unsurprising, then, that Fornes, who found the spirit of her plays in theatre spaces, gravitated naturally to design collaborators, who could most readily help install the world she imagined there.

As Alice Reagan points out, Fornes's productions in the 1980s to mid-1990s were characterized in part by her collaborations with Eastman, Militello, and Berry. Eastman and Berry first designed for Fornes's *Evelyn Brown (A Diary)* in 1980 Off-Off-Broadway at Theater for the New City. All three designers were in the early stages of their careers and had previously collaborated in 1981–82 on LaMama's twentieth anniversary season. Berry's first design in New York was for another downtown stalwart – Charles Ludlam (*The Enchanted Pig*, 1979). Militello had previously worked at the Magic Theatre with Sam Shepard, who had pointed the New York-bound designer to Ellen Stewart (LaMama) as well as Fornes. The backgrounds of these designers suggested a readiness to embark in unconventional and deeply collaborative work with Fornes. Likewise, for a playwright who felt most at home in the downtown New York theatre scene, the Off-Off-Broadway pedigree of these designers made them ideal matches. According to Reagan, Fornes's plays from this period, which include *The Conduct of Life* (1985) and *Enter the Night* (1993), span time and place and "almost all feature a young woman looking outside herself and her station for something better. Most do not end happily. The beauty in these plays resides in Fornes's poetic language and in the stage architecture she created."[45] Fornes's unconventional women and nontraditional stories needed original language and space, which the playwright and director established collaboratively as she rehearsed with Eastman, Berry, and Militello. Her collaborative relationships were equally nontraditional. Fornes's way of working disrupts traditional collaborative hierarchies in several ways. First, she amalgamated the roles of playwright and director in a manner that became central to the development of her new plays. Second, she elevated a group of designers to primary artistic positions in the development of her new plays. While Wilson's design collaborators left deep impressions on the visual world of his plays, his emphasis on visuality never coalesced around a single set of designers. Finally, Fornes was inclined to edit her plays in the rehearsal room as she and her designers worked together to shape the physical world on stage, unusual both in the context of the playwrights discussed here and in twentieth-century practice.

By 1984, for *The Danube* at the American Place Theater, Fornes's design triumvirate was in place. Reagan suggests that Fornes's move away from site-specificity in her writing was inspired in part by her success in sculpting her plays in rehearsal with this design team. "Once she found her family team, which was us," says Miletello, "she knew she could trust us, that our intentions were to learn from her and to work with her and help. She liked our ideas too."[46] Eastman remembers that the design process would often begin before the script was complete, though Berry recalls a more script-oriented process. Both remember an emphasis on characters. Eastman also describes a focus on research. "Every time I design a set with Irene," he says, "is an opportunity to design a heaven room. . . . When I say heaven, I'm speaking of a purity. It's all based on reality and research, but captured in a golden moment. There is a purity and honesty of materials."[47] Fornes occasionally collaborated with two of the three designers when a third was not available; in 1987 Eastman and Militello brought Fornes's Obie-winning *Abingdon Square* to the stage at the Women's Project under founder Julia Miles's artistic directorship, this time with costumes by Sam Fleming.

Fornes always wanted to rehearse her plays in the theatre on set. While this is unusual in commercial theatre, it allowed her to edit the physical world of the play in real time with her designers in the room. It also gave actors the opportunity to physically interact with the objects and furniture they would use in performance, thereby developing a more intimate relationship with the physical world of the performance early on. Echoing the unconventionality of Albee and Schneider rehearsing *Who's Afraid of Virginia Woolf?* on their set, Militello explained that even in the Off and Off-Off-Broadway context "we have had to defend ourselves to several production managers, to convince them why we need another day of tech time in the beginning of rehearsals."[48] Just as Fornes revised her scripts in rehearsal, so she worked with Eastman to revise the set design. Fornes moved objects and furniture around the stage in rehearsal, actively participating in the design process. As Militello puts it, "Irene Fornes is one of the greatest visual artists in the theater today, as well as being one of the greatest playwrights. She is an expert on visual language. She knows exactly how to integrate all the design elements so that her plays can exist in a perfect space."[49] Fornes sculpted actors and light as well as space. Militello describes this process: "When she directs, she choreographs every movement of the actors and the light together with focused precision. Somehow, she gets the actors to respond to the movement of light, and every night, they remember and use it for great effect."[50] Fornes was even present at fittings for actors, attending to the smallest details of fabric. "What I got from her," says Berry, "which is something that I'd like to think is a hallmark of my work now, is that you want to spend time with every person onstage."[51] Fornes's influence extends beyond this trio of designers and is especially evident in the coterie of writers she nurtured in her well-known writing workshops at INTAR. There, she fostered a sense of togetherness and collectivity in what can often be a solitary, isolated process. She also infused her teaching with the same sense of spontaneity and reliance on intuition that Berry, Militello, and Eastman describe in her rehearsals.

Fornes also directed plays by other writers, including Henrik Ibsen's *Hedda Gabler* at the Milwaukee Repertory Theater and Anton Chekhov's *Uncle Vanya* at New York's Classic Stage company, both in 1987 and both designed by Eastman. In *Vanya*, the four settings of the play (Vanya's study, the sitting room, the dining room, and the garden) are seen by the audience throughout the performance, emphasizing Fornes's painterly interest in what Scott Cummings describes as "domestic interior" spaces.[52] Fornes's collaboration with Eastman on a play by another writer indicates that her reliance on her design team in building an aesthetic was central to her approach as a director even when the play was not her own.

Fornes's plays are, by and large, about women. They explore female psychology and experiences. Her resistance to conventional, commercial structure and style is, in and of itself, a feminist dramaturgical expression that meets the subjects of her plays on their own terms. Fornes's plays, emerging alongside second wave feminism, bring the concerns of that movement to the stage. Her theatrical revolt against predictable measures of success required an equally imaginative approach to development, rehearsal, and staging, which is exactly what she created with her design collaborators. Her focus on theatricalizing a female experience necessitated a different collaborative approach, so she invented one that worked for her as both a writer and a director. The legacy of her work is most obvious in the contemporary plays of Latinx writers she mentored at INTAR, such as Migdalia Cruz and Eduardo Machado, but is also seen in the explosion of feminist dramaturgy on American stages ranging from Annie Baker to Lynn Nottage, and in downtown New York theatre's sustained emphasis on visually based theatrical development, evident in the work of artists as varied as Basil Twist and the dance-theatre troupe Advanced Beginner Group who rely on the same sort of immersive, unconventional collaborations characteristic of Fornes's process.

Parks and the Public Theater

Among the playwrights addressed here, Suzan-Lori Parks's stylistic innovations have been the most radical. Similarly to Wilson, Parks was keenly inspired by James Baldwin, whose writing course she took at Hampshire College when she was an undergraduate at Mount Holyoke. Bolstered by Wilson and Lorraine Hansberry, whose plays first featured African American families as imagined by African American writers on Broadway stages, Parks's dramaturgy seeks new forms beyond realism: "I don't explode the form because I find traditional plays 'boring' . . . It's just that those structures never could accommodate the figures which take up residence inside me."[53] Parks's dramaturgical revolution was supported by long-term collaborations with director Liz Diamond and the Public Theater. Though her plays are characterized by an upheaval of Aristotelian conventions, her collaborative processes in production followed a more traditional path, akin to the siloed approach favored by Albee and Schneider and less similar to Fornes's porous collaborations.

Parks's first productions were in New York in 1987. By 1989, Diamond was directing Parks's plays, beginning with *Imperceptible Mutabilities in the Third Kingdom* at BACA Downtown in Brooklyn. She also directed *Betting on the Dust Commander* at the Working Theater, and *The Death of the Last Black Man in the Whole Entire World*, a commission by the Humana Festival staged at the Yale Rep in 1992. Diamond is a faculty member in the Yale School of Drama and produced several of Park's plays there. With each play, Parks explains, "I got a little more adventurous" in the formal utilization of the style she calls "Rep & Rev." Here, Parks refers intentionally to repetition and revision, musical rephrasing foundational to jazz. Parks describes Rep & Rev as "a central element in my work; through its use I'm working to create a dramatic text that departs from the traditional linear narrative style to look and sound more like a musical score."[54] Parks has also cited the formal innovations of Adrienne Kennedy and Gertrude Stein among her stylistic influences.

Parks's relationship with the Public Theater began when artistic director George C. Wolfe, who was at the Public's helm from 1993 to 2004, produced *The America Play* there in 1994. Echoing the journeys made by a number of plays by Shepard and Wilson, *The America Play* was commissioned by New York's Theatre for a New Audience, developed by the Arena Stage in Washington, DC, and the Dallas Theatre Center, and presented at the Yale Rep before moving to the Public Theater. In *The America Play*, as in much of her work, Parks uses Rep & Rev as dramaturgical historiography, unearthing and rehashing the past, in this case featuring a Black Abraham Lincoln impersonator known as the Foundling Father. Distinct from Fornes's relationship with her designers, Diamond described herself as "outside of the writing process" during most of Parks's writing process for *The America Play*. The director details an exchange with the playwright in which, at more final stages of the writing, "we'll begin to do readings together and sometimes Suzan-Lori will read it out loud for me and I'll ask questions." Diamond notes that these exchanges are crucial to the production: "preliminary production ideas really take off from those first encounters, with the text in front of us, together." She also suggests that Parks has a similar respect for Diamond's autonomy as director once rehearsals begin, similar to the leeway Shepard allowed Woodruff. "Suzan-Lori will leave me alone as much as I need to be left alone," she says.[55]

Diamond's description of her process with Parks comes after several years of sustained collaboration, and she also notes a shorthand ease in her communications with Parks while in rehearsal. As was the case with Shepard and Woodruff, Diamond and Parks were free to develop, adapt, and eventually establish a working rhythm that suited their partnership outside of the pressures of an economically driven commercial theatre schedule. In this case, however, Parks and Diamond consistently worked more independently than Woodruff and Shepard sometimes did. Parks, who resists the notion of one specific interpretation in her texts, describes her work with Diamond as "together, giving meanings."[56] Building on the inventiveness and ingenuity of Parks's texts, Diamond's staging asks spectators to look at Parks's plays in new ways. She encourages audiences to trust their instincts and rely on stage pictures, where they will find visual versions of Rep & Rev. Parks's dense and imaginative stage directions demand an equally inventive visuality of directors and designers. Of her production of *The America Play*, Diamond says, "you can look at that glistening black coal dust on the floor and look at those old columns all smeared with filth ... and look at Lucy wandering around and listening, listening, listening for echoes of her husband and ... trust that the ideas that come up in you about those images are valid."[57] Diamond's comments echo Parks's statements about the reception of her writing throughout her career; her plays invite both her collaborators and audiences to participate in an active process of reception, asking audiences to turn over both sonic and visual variations in their minds after the lights have come down: in the case of *The America Play*, the Foundling Father's Black body as Abraham Lincoln, his trope of digging, and Lucy's "listening, listening, listening," in Diamond's words.

Although Diamond was Parks's most consistent collaborator in the late 1980s and early 1990s, the playwright continued to work with other directors. In 1996, downtown avant-garde director Richard Foreman directed and designed scenery for the premiere of *Venus* at the Yale Rep. The production was co-commissioned by New York City's Women's Project and San Francisco's Life on the Water and produced by the Public Theater, where it made its New York premiere. In 2001, artistic director Wolfe directed Parks's story of card shark brothers, *Topdog/Underdog*, at the Public Theater himself. This production moved to the Ambassador Theatre on Broadway in 2002. Ben Brantley described the Broadway production, featuring Jeffrey Wright and Don Cheadle, in glowing terms for the *New York Times*, calling it "the most exciting new home-grown play to hit Broadway since Mr. Wolfe's production of Tony Kushner's 'Angels in America.' And it's blowing through the dusty, dim corridors of a lackluster theater season like the breeze of a long-delayed spring."[58] Brantley also alludes to improvements in the play that are the result of the gradual development process that brought *Topdog/Underdog* from the Public to Broadway.

Topdog/Underdog won the Pulitzer Prize in 2002. The same year, Parks also made the decision to write one play a day for 365 days. The resulting body of playlets was collected into *365 Days/365 Plays* and produced by the Public and other theatres and universities across the country over the course of 2006, including at Chicago's Steppenwolf and Goodman and by smaller outlets such as a San Antonio company of Latinx artists, La Colectiva. As productions unfolded, Parks established "Watch Me Work," in which writers and audiences were invited to join her in the lobby of the Public as she wrote to observe or to write themselves. Parks has periodically returned to the Public for this event and has replicated her meta-performance of the creative process throughout the United States, inviting audiences into the same sort of collaborative making of meanings that characterizes her work with Diamond. The Public has continued to program Parks's plays under the artistic director Oskar Eustis, who succeeded Wolfe, with productions such as *White Noise*, which was directed there by Eustis in 2019, underscoring the importance of her relationship with the company. Parks found an artistic home at the Public, echoing Shepard's relationship with the Magic and Wilson's with the O'Neill and Yale Rep. In each case, these partnerships were a result of specific artistic practices developed in the context of institutional environments that supported aesthetic independence in order to nurture emerging writers.

Paula Vogel and Rebecca Taichman

Playwrights and creative teams' commitment to expanding the kinds of people represented on American stages and how they are presented when they get there has paved the way for more inclusive performances, some that have reverberated with Broadway history. Such is the case with the unusual evolution of Paula Vogel and Rebecca Taichman's *Indecent*, based on the true story of Yiddish playwright Sholem Asch's Broadway debut in 1923 of *God of Vengeance*, originally written in 1907. Asch's play occupies a controversial position in Jewish cultural history, in part because it dealt with the hypocrisy of pious Jews at a time of rising anti-Semitism. It also featured the first lesbian kiss on Broadway. Vogel is best known for her 1998 Pulitzer Prize–winning play *How I Learned to Drive*. Her plays, which also include *The Long Christmas Ride Home*, *The Mineola Twins*, and *Desdemona*, have been regularly staged at independent and adventurous New York and regional theatres such as New York Theatre Workshop, the Vineyard, Circle Repertory Company, the Woolly Mammoth, the Magic Theatre, the Goodman, and American Repertory Theater. She is also a distinguished teacher of playwriting and has held positions at Brown and Yale. Vogel's plays are characterized by an investigation into previously uncharted places in women's experiences. As does Vogel, Taichman has extensive experience in highly regarded venues in New York and in regional theatres such as Playwrights Horizons, MCC, Lincoln Center, the Old Globe, La Jolla, and the Yale Rep. Taichman may be best known as a frequent director of plays by the daring playwright Sarah Ruhl. In another parallel to Vogel, Taichman is also a teacher with affiliations at institutions including New York University and the O'Neill National Theater Institute. A former artistic director of the Woolly Mammoth suggests that Taichman's "visual imagination for … elements of design is what many people consider her greatest strength."[59]

The uniqueness of the partnership between Vogel and Taichman lies in the impetus for their collaboration on *Indecent* and their intensely collaborative method of developing the piece. Vogel and Taichman both had first encounters with *God of Vengeance* as graduate students. Taichman's 2000 MFA thesis at Yale incorporated Asch's play and transcripts of the obscenity trial against the play that took place in 1923. Years later Taichman called Vogel to ask if she would collaborate on a new version based on the same idea. "It was very clear to me that there was an important story to tell about what happened to this play in New York in 1923 and how it was an extraordinary window into political history, Jewish history, gay history. But I did not have the capacity to tell that story myself," Taichman explains.[60] Vogel, who had seen Taichman's thesis and remembers it as "fascinating," says it took her "thirty seconds" to say yes.[61] Taichman's flexibility in pivoting to a playwright other than herself to actualize the creative idea she had initiated is bold and unusual.

In a highly inclusive development process, the playwright-director team co-created the production over a five-year period of workshopping and collaboration. It was first produced by Oregon Shakespeare Festival in the American Revolutions project. After workshops at Sundance, it was co-produced by Yale Rep and La Jolla Playhouse in 2015, then moved Off-Broadway to the Vineyard Theater in 2016. The Broadway premiere of *Indecent* (2017) took place at the Cort Theatre, only a few blocks from the theatre where *God of Vengeance* had been presented. Though the development process followed a traditional regional theatre to Broadway route, it was also characterized by an unusually significant interchange of ideas between Vogel and Taichman. Vogel reports that she wrote forty-two drafts of the play and discussed "every word" with Taichman. While workshopping the play, Vogel would often write late into the night, returning with new pages, which Taichman would enthusiastically suggest trying out. Similarly, Vogel explains that Taichman "was very open in terms of her process. I was in the room all the time. She would say, 'What do you think about that?' And I'd say, 'Oh, that was interesting. I'm wondering if we might want to try . . .' So there was a back and forth."[62] As with Wilson and Richards, the shared cultural background between Vogel and Taichman – both artists come from Jewish backgrounds – helped to foster creative fluency and a unified sense of the importance of the story they told, which follows the *God of Vengeance* company from Broadway to concentration camps.

The generous collaboration between Taichman and Vogel extended to the design team, who worked closely with the director and playwright to find expressive and sensitive ways to communicate the near-cultural extinction caused by the Holocaust. Taichman describes one of Vogel's original stage directions, in which Yiddish writing is wiped off of a wall by rain. Video artist Tal Yarden "turned it into these disappearing letters," Taichman says. "That became to me, and I think Paula, a very profound and important way to talk about what happened, which was the attempt to murder an entire language, not just a people (not that there's a 'just'), and how do you embody that?"[63]

Taichman emphasizes that the design team worked in tandem to find a visual vocabulary rooted in Vogel's text. Though she had worked closely with set designer Riccardo Hernández on a number of occasions, Taichman describes the entire creative team as a "family," pointing out a meta-theatrical connection to the original Yiddish company. "I feel the process is not just Jewish," she explains, "it was 19th century" because they "became a repertory troupe," workshopping, rehearsing, touring, and performing together. "We developed a shorthand the way the Yiddish troupes did as they traveled through Europe. We thought about that a lot when we tried to set up a process and get theatres to co-produce together," Taichman says.[64] While she describes a process indebted to the tradition of family troupes, the highly collaborative process was also influenced by more recent trends in collective creation and devising in American theatre. The 1960s and 1970s saw a rise of theatre collectives such as the Living Theatre, Mabou Mines, and the Wooster Group that captured the period's spirit of collectivity by often working as a group to devise plays without a single author. These works include the Living Theatre's *Paradise Now* (1968) and Mabou Mines's *Dead End Kids* (1980). The impact of collective creation has been particularly influential on alternative American theatre in the twenty-first century; the tradition is continued by companies including Elevator Repair Service, the Civilians, and Tectonic Theater Project.

The intimate and generous collaboration Taichman and Vogel elucidate resulted in a number of awards for the company. Taichman was the seventh woman to receive the Tony Award for Best Director (2017). She also received a 2017 Obie Award for best direction at a ceremony in which Vogel was honored with a lifetime achievement award. Though Vogel won a 1998 Pulitzer Prize for *How I Learned to Drive*, she made her Broadway debut with *Indecent* at age sixty-five.

Recent productions such as *Indecent* demonstrate expanding boundaries of how plays make their way to Broadway. Its reliance on the controversial history of *God of Vengeance*, for example, reveals starkly expanded possibilities for daring dramaturgy on major American stages. Contemporary theatre makers follow in the footsteps of the other pioneering creative teams and companies examined here. The plays that have resulted from those collaborations have relied on carefully cultivated gestation, typically in intimate venues, to introduce increasingly diverse and inclusive dramaturgies to US audiences.

Perhaps the most significant legacy of the new plays and collaborative relationships examined here is the modeling of teams made up of artists from a wide range of backgrounds in terms of race, culture, and sexual orientation. These theatrical teams were a better facsimile of the American population than ever before seen in US theatre history and brought with them a more comprehensive compendium of American characters, stories, and ideas to refashion US stages into more accurate mirrors of society. In mounting a cultural revolution that insisted upon inclusivity on the basis of race, gender, and sexual orientation in the theatre, these artists departed from the past by refusing to conform to a single way of working. Parks, whose inventive dramaturgy intentionally subverted patriarchal structures, opted for traditional collaborative relationships inherited from a model passed down by Albee and Schneider. Shepard and Woodruff, alongside Wilson and Richards, helped to bring workshopping into the foreground of new play development. Designers too have played a pivotal role in shaping new dramaturgies, seen most obviously with Fornes, who worked with Eastman, Militello, and Berry to build visual worlds in the theatre that proved just as important to the dramaturgy of her plays as spoken dialogue. Among these varied approaches, however, one theme emerges: post-1960 collaborative teams have demanded their own ways of working. This insistence on artistic independence has established an American theatrical legacy of inclusive performance, from process to product.

Notes

1. S.-L. Parks, "Elements of Style," in *The America Play and Other Works* (Theatre Communications Group, 1995), p. 8.

2. A. Schneider, *Entrances: An American Director's Journey* (Viking Penguin, 1986), p. ix.
3. M. Esslin, *The Theatre of the Absurd* (Anchor Books, 1969), p. 278.
4. M. Gussow, *Edward Albee: A Singular Journey* (Simon and Schuster, 1999), p. 142.
5. Schneider, *Entrances*, p. 289.
6. Ibid., p. 322.
7. Gussow, *Edward Albee,* p. 175.
8. Gussow, "William Ritman, Designer, Dies," *New York Times*, May 8, 1984, p. B6, www.nytimes.com/1984/05/08/obituaries/william-ritman-designer-dies.html.
9. Gussow, *Edward Albee,* p. 220.
10. R. Coe, "Interview with Robert Woodruff," in Bonnie Marranca (ed.), *American Dreams: The Imagination of Sam Shepard* (Performing Arts Journal Publications, 1981), p. 152.
11. Ibid., p. 153.
12. E. Oumano, *Sam Shepard: The Life and Work of an American Dreamer* (St. Martin's Press, 1986), p. 105.
13. Ibid., p. 121.
14. Coe, "Interview," p. 157.
15. Ibid.
16. D. Shewey, "Robert Woodruff: A Boot in Two Camps," *American Theatre*, October 1986, www.donshewey.com/theater_articles/robert_woodruff.html.
17. S. Holdren, "Director Robert Woodruff Remembers Sam Shepard," *Vulture*, August 1, 2017, www.vulture.com/2017/08/director-robert-woodruff-remembers-sam-shepard.html.
18. Oumano, *Sam Shepard*, p. 138.
19. Holdren, "Woodruff Remembers."
20. Ibid.
21. Magic Theatre San Francisco, "Magic Remembers Sam Shepard," http://magictheatre.org/sam-shepard.
22. J. Sweet, *The O'Neill: The Transformation of Modern American Theater* (Yale University Press, 2014), p. 147.
23. A. Austin, "Lloyd Richards and August Wilson: A Winning Partnership Plays On," *Christian Science Monitor*, September 18, 1995, www.csmonitor.com/1995/0918/18132.html.
24. A. Winkler (host), "What It Takes: August Wilson, Lloyd Richards," *Voice of America* podcast, June 1, 2018, http://learningenglish.voanews.com/a/what-it-takes-august-wilson-lloyd-richards/4414089.html.
25. Sweet, *The O'Neill*, p. 155.
26. F. Rich, "Stage View, Where Writers Mold the Future of Theater," *New York Times*, August 1, 1982, 2:1, www.nytimes.com/1982/08/01/theater/stage-view-where-writers-mold-the-future-of-theater.html.
27. Sweet, *The O'Neill*, pp. 155–56.
28. Wilson, *Fences* (Penguin, 1986), p. xv.

29. Ibid.
30. Winkler, "What It Takes."
31. B. Minamore, "Pittsburgh State of Mind: How August Wilson's Flame Burns On," *Guardian*, May 20, 2019, www.theguardian.com/stage/2019/may/20/august-wilson-playwright-black-america-constanza-romero-interview-king-hedley-ii.
32. Minamore, "Pittsburg State of Mind."
33. Wilson, *Seven Guitars* (Samuel French, 1996), p. 77.
34. Ibid., p. 96.
35. M. Lurie, "Constanza Romero on Costume Design and Her Relationship with August Wilson," *August Wilson Red Door Project*, October 16, 2012, http://reddoorproject.org/787-exclusive-constanza-romero-interview.
36. Sweet, *The O'Neill*, p. 166.
37. Austin, "Lloyd Richards and August Wilson."
38. A. Fliostos and W. Vierow, *American Women Stage Directors of the Twentieth Century* (University of Illinois Press, 2008), p. 180.
39. Ibid, p. 181.
40. M. Delgado and C. Svich (eds.), *Conducting a Life: Reflections on the Theatre of Maria Irene Fornes* (Smith and Kraus, 1999), p. 265.
41. Fliostos and Vierow, *American Women Stage Directors,* p. 180.
42. Ibid.
43. Delgado and Svich, *Conducting a Life,* p. 261.
44. Ibid.
45. A. Reagan, "Maria Irene Fornes, World Builder," *American Theatre*, July 7, 2017, www.americantheatre.org/2017/07/05/maria-irene-fornes-world-builder.
46. Ibid.
47. Delgado and Svich, *Conducting a Life,* p. 105.
48. Ibid., p.106.
49. Ibid.
50. Ibid.
51. Reagan, "Maria Irene Fornes, World Builder."
52. S. Cummings, "'The Poetry of Space in a Box': Scenography in the Work of Maria Irene Fornes," in M. Robinson (ed.), *The Theater of Maria Irene Fornes* (Johns Hopkins University Press, 1999), pp. 175–76.
53. Parks, "Elements of Style," p. 8.
54. Ibid., pp. 8–9.
55. S. Drukman, "Doo-a-diddly-dit-dit," *TDR*, 39:3 (Autumn, 1995), pp. 57–59.
56. Ibid., p. 59.
57. Ibid., pp. 65–67.
58. B. Brantley, "Theater Review, Not to Worry, Mr. Lincoln, It's Just a Con Game," *New York Times*, April 8, 2002, p. E1, www.nytimes.com/2002/04/08/theater/theater-review-not-to-worry-mr-lincoln-it-s-just-a-con-game.html.

59. N. Pressley, "Rebecca Taichman Gets a Big Palette to Fill Directing 'Twelfth Night,'" *Washington Post*, December 8, 2008, www.washingtonpost.com/wp-dyn/content/article/2008/12/07/AR2008120702551.html.
60. V. Myers, "An Interview with Rebecca Taichman," *The Interval*, June 20, 2017, www.theintervalny.com/interviews/2017/06/an-interview-with-rebecca-taichman.
61. Vineyard Theatre, "An Interview with the Playwright: Paula Vogel on *Indecent*," Vineyard Theatre website, www.vineyardtheatre.org/interview-playwright-paula-vogel-indecent.
62. V. Myers, "An Interview with Paula Vogel," *The Interval*, April 18, 2017, www.theintervalny.com/interviews/2017/04/an-interview-with-paula-vogel.
63. Myers, "An Interview with Rebecca Taichman."
64. Myers, "An Interview with Paula Vogel."

Select Bibliography

Delgado, M., and C. Svich (eds.). *Conducting a Life: Reflections on the Theatre of Maria Irene Fornes*. Smith and Kraus, 1999.

Fliostos, A., and W. Vierow. *American Women Stage Directors of the Twentieth Century*. University of Illinois Press, 2008.

Oumano, E. *Sam Shepard: The Life and Work of an American Dreamer*. St. Martin's Press, 1986.

Parks, S.-L. "From Elements of Style." In *The America Play and Other Works*. Theatre Communications Group, 1995.

Robinson, M. (ed.). *The Theater of Maria Irene Fornes*. Johns Hopkins University Press, 1999.

Schneider, A. *Entrances: An American Director's Journey*. Viking Penguin, 1986.

Shannon, S. G. *Modern American Drama: Playwriting in the 1980s, Voices, Documents, New Interpretations*. Bloomsbury Methuen, 2018.

Sweet, J. *The O'Neill: The Transformation of Modern American Theater*. Yale University Press, 2014.

Vanden Heuvel, M. *Modern American Drama: Playwriting in the 1970s, Voices, Documents, New Interpretations*. Bloomsbury Methuen, 2018.

Young, H. (ed.). *The Cambridge Companion to African American Theatre*. Cambridge University Press, 2012.

PART II

Regional Theatre Movement

CHAPTER 5

Money Matters
Dismantling the Narrative of the Rise of Regional Theatre
Elizabeth A. Osborne

In 2015, Jim O'Quinn, founding editor and editor-in-chief of *American Theatre* magazine from 1984 to 2015, pointed to the outstanding success of regional theatres. He described the regional theatre as the "creative crucible" of the nation's theatre, and the "commercial sector" as

> dependent upon its sprawling not-for-profit counterpart for virtually every aspect of its well-being. Broadway is still the place where talents are validated and economic prospects escalated, but it is no longer the singular, or even the primary, font of the nation's theatrical creativity. ... That distinction belongs to the array of not-for-profit professional theatres that has blossomed into being over the past 45 years in every nook and cranny of this country: the diverse, still-evolving network that must be acknowledged for what it is – America's national theatre.[1]

Whether because Broadway lacks the ability to generate new work in a way that appeals to the nation as a whole or because of its geographic or economic inaccessibility, O'Quinn makes a compelling case for the essential role of the regional theatre in contemporary US theatre. Regional theatres serve as vital homes for nourishing playwrights and new work. From Sarah Ruhl to Lynn Nottage, August Wilson to Lauren Yee – major and emerging voices have found critical support in regional theatres through commissions, residencies, fellowships, readings, workshops, premieres, and subsequent productions. Some, like the incredibly prolific Lauren Gunderson – the most produced playwright in the country in the 2019–20 season – have made successful careers in the regional theatre without ever appearing on Broadway.[2] While Gunderson's success has been extraordinary, it is not an isolated case. As of 2019, thirty-five of the past thirty-eight Pulitzer Prize–winning plays premiered in regional theatres.[3] Clearly, the evidence supports O'Quinn's assertion. The regional theatre has collectively become "America's national theatre."

At the same time, there is a glaring problem in the system. Theatre Communications Group (TCG) has studied the economic realities of regional theatres for more than forty years. By focusing on multiyear trends for a select group of "trend theatres" and expanding their numbers to include the larger study size of nearly 2,000 member theatres, TCG has accumulated a vast array of data points on capital gains, expenses, royalties, subscriptions, the impact of inflation, and more, all of which is published annually in *Theatre Facts*. During the same period in which O'Quinn was writing, when thirty-five of the thirty-eight Pulitzer Prize–winning plays premiered at regional theatres and regional theatres had become "America's national theatre," approximately 60 percent of the nation's regional theatres had negative working capital. This suggests that many theatres are "borrowing funds internally or externally to meet [their] daily operating needs[, and] may face serious financial trouble."[4] It would seem that roughly half of the nation's major regional theatres live hand-to-mouth even as they provide the artistic "meat" of the nation's theatre. This systemic problem leaves theatres disturbingly vulnerable and, since over half of the average regional theatre's operating budget is dedicated to salaries, this leaves the field as a whole in an extraordinarily precarious economic position.

This disconnect between artistic worth and economic viability did not always exist. So, what factors led to this rift, and how has it contributed to the ongoing, foundational deficiencies highlighted by economic crisis? This chapter examines the rise of the regional theatre movement historiographically. In particular, it focuses on dismantling what revisionist theatre historian Vincent Landro describes as the "standard narrative" of the rise of regional theatre, and argues that the addition of an economic lens will reveal some of the reasons for the ongoing financial struggle that we see in the regional theatre. As Tracy Davis argues in *The Economics of the British Stage,* "If culture's historians ignore business, they overlook the resources that make or break an artist's choice."[5] In this case, the standard narrative of regional theatre history flattens the goals, methods, and challenges of all of the individual theatres into a single, polarizing story that targets either artistic or commercial success, but not both. Excellent scholars have recently begun the undertaking of deepening the literature, but much work remains. Historiographically, this has meant that the existing narrative has gone largely uninterrogated for too long.

Moreover, if regional theatres are serving as the centers that nurture emerging playwrights and produce new plays, this contemporary "national theatre" is clearly in need of scholarly attention that works to dismantle the standard narrative and employs an economically centered historiographical approach. With this in mind, I first examine the traditional narrative of the rise of regional theatre, considering how this particular story came to be, how it has taken hold, and how it has influenced the ways that scholars have interpreted the regional theatre movement. Then, recognizing the lack of recent scholarship that brings together the regional theatre movement as a whole, I focus on four primary case studies that disrupt this narrative in various ways: Margo Jones's Theatre '47, Nina Vance's Alley Theatre, and Zelda Fichandler's Arena Stage laid the early foundations for the movement, and Tyrone Guthrie's Guthrie Theatre provided a model for high-profile regional theatres entering the field after the nonprofit, grant-making structure had been established. These early regional theatres offer different financial approaches and structures, based on leadership styles, ideological goals, and community needs. Finally, I look at social and cultural forces that impact regional theatre funding and suggest that an economically centered analysis exposes structural problems within the regional theatre system that have serious implications for the future viability of "America's national theatre."

The Rise of the Regional Theatre Narrative: A History

For regional theatres, artistic idealism and economic stability seem to be opposite ends of a binary – a catch-22 that could never be achieved simultaneously. Yet when founders conceived of regional theatres in the late 1940s and early 1950s, most did so in anticipation of becoming self-supporting artistic centers of their communities. The Ford Foundation injected funds in the early 1960s based on the premise that a relatively small infusion of capital could help a few theatres to establish resident companies and gain local support, thus changing the face of the movement permanently.[6] Then William J. Baumol and William G. Bowen's groundbreaking *Performing Arts: The Economic Dilemma* (1966) soberly announced that the performing arts would never be self-supporting, and that the ongoing economic problems faced by the industry were systemic rather than transient. The regional theatre movement, it seemed, was doomed to be perpetually dependent on a complex combination of outside funds from foundations, private donors, and municipal, state, and federal organizations.

Early chroniclers of the rise of the regional theatre such as Martin Gottfried and Joseph Zeigler saw this dependence on foundations and fundraising as failure. Regional theatres that depended on others for funds were, by definition, sellouts. For Gottfried, the regional theatre movement was under siege. Foundations – which saw themselves as "cultural heroes" leaping in to save the anticommercial theatre – became extraordinarily powerful in shaping the regional theatre as a whole. Gottfried concluded that theatre leaders changed their actions to cater to foundation desires, thus leading to a gradual institutionalization of regional theatres, loss of individual vision, and diminished artistic worth.[7] Zeigler envisioned the regional theatre movement as both a wider decentralization of theatre and an anti-Establishment "revolution" that disintegrated as regional theatres matured from their shoestring budgets and battles for artistic legitimacy to major regional centers that vied for major foundation funds. As they grew more financially stable and solidified their places in their communities, regional theatres gradually shifted closer to the very Establishment that Zeiegler identified them as against, and thus he, too, declared the regional theatre movement as a whole compromised.

As Landro argues, this narrative "portrays the evolution of nonprofit regional theatre in America as having its origins in the pioneering work of like-minded visionaries through the 1940s and 1950s whose dream was to fill a national cultural vacuum by bringing the world's great stage works to communities outside New York City."[8] This oversimplifies a complex web of artistic goals, economic and administrative structures, and relationships with local communities.[9] While some artists did rebel against the strictures of Broadway or set out to create spaces for independent, avant-garde, anticommercial art, others hoped to decenter the theatre geographically, or find a place to create a different kind of new work. Such work would likely require different models to function in smaller communities, but though the theatres were not necessarily intended to be anticommercial or avant-garde, the *narrative* was polarizing. While founders and their theatres may have walked a middle ground, the narrative portrayed them at one extreme or the other – financially stable sellouts or artistically brilliant destitutes.

The initial history of the regional theatre was written during the late 1960s, an era of widespread social upheaval and revolution. Within regional theatre historiography, this narrative created untenable expectations. James Harding and Cindy Rosenthal trace this phenomenon in *The Sixties, Center Stage*, showing a scholarly tradition that privileges the avant-garde – and with it, values of experimentation, anticonsumerism, and counterculturalism – while rejecting the commercial theatre.[10] They look to Richard Schechner's polarizing comments in *The Tulane Drama Review* in 1963 for the origins of this trend: "You choose Broadway and I'll choose an experimental theatre. There are many roads to truth. But neither of us can choose *both* Broadway and an experimental theatre. That's a contradiction in intention."[11] With this comment, Schechner places Broadway and its tendency toward commodification in opposition to experimentation, leaving regional theatre in a yet-to-be-determined limbo that "could earn (or lose) national respect," depending on its ability to stay true to its identity, attract and keep high-caliber talents, and engage in experimental work.[12] As Harding and Rosenthal argue, Schechner's declaration "signaled a very clear course for the journal," and his influence as a long-time editor of a major journal cannot be dismissed.[13] *The Tulane Drama Review* published a number of articles on the regional theatre under Schechner's editorship in the 1960s, critiquing regional theatres' lack of ideological framework, the corrupting influence of foundation dollars, and the predominantly middle-class (rather than poor or working-class) audiences.[14] These essays shaped the narrative that would polarize the discussion around regional theatre, and they quickly showed a preference for theatres that prioritized edgy, avant-garde work over commercial appeal. This critical bias privileged some regional theatres over others, often relegating those that attained financial stability to a lesser status.

Yet even a passing exploration demonstrates that there is more to the story. Whether founders were focused on creating great theatre, nurturing new work, making a living as an artist, decentering US theatre, developing a long-term relationship with a community, becoming part of a resident company, or something else altogether, the economic reality required them to survive first. Moreover, as Donatella Galella argues in her excellent book on Arena Stage, "institutionalizing, professionalizing, and maintaining a balanced budget did not necessarily mean reducing artistic standards and experiments."[15] Clearly, it is time to reimagine the narrative.

The Regional Theatre Movement Begins

Much of the extant regional theatre history focuses on a few case studies, and it is rarely critical, contextualized in historical or sociological data, or theorized. While there are certainly some notable exceptions, many of the major sources either perpetuate the standard narrative or are created by the theatres themselves in an effort to write their own origin stories. Here, I gather three of the first regional theatres together to explore their historiographical connection to the narrative that has been perpetuated so as to highlight their differences rather than elide them. While there was also a fourth regional theatre that is considered one of the initial companies – Herbert Blau and Jules Irving's Actors' Workshop

(San Francisco, California) – I have chosen to amplify the work of early women theatre makers. As Helen Krich Chinoy argues, the association between women and "regional, institutional, little, art and alternative theatres is striking," and that is certainly the case with the rise of the regional theatre in the United States. Without Margo Jones's advocacy for the decentralization of the US theatre, Nina Vance's founding of Houston's Alley Theatre, and Zelda Fichandler's work at the Arena Stage, the regional theatre movement might never have begun.[16]

In 1947, Margo Jones founded Theatre '47 in Dallas, Texas. Dubbed the "Texas Tornado" by Tennessee Williams, Jones has widely been considered one of the pioneers of the regional theatre movement.[17] A member of the American National Theatre and Academy's (ANTA) board of directors, Jones worked for the Federal Theatre Project in Houston, directed the Houston Community Players, received a grant from the Rockefeller Foundation to study professional nonprofit theatre in the United States in 1944, and built a reputation as a director in New York. She was an outspoken advocate for a decentralized national theatre and argued that the people of the United States deserved access to high-quality entertainments regardless of where they happened to live. As she announced at an ANTA dinner in 1946, "a nation's drama will shrivel and die from too intensive centralization. Good theatre entertainment must be made available to people outside the narrow confines of Broadway."[18] Theatre '47 opened the following June. It would serve as a conceptual and economic model for many of the regional theatres to come with its clear intent and diverse array of professionally produced new and classic plays.

Jones documented her process in *Theatre-in-the-Round,* an eminently practical volume in which she expands a vision that differs markedly from the standard narrative. Her first sentence lays out her approach: "The dream of all serious theatre people in the United States in the middle of our twentieth century is the establishment of a national theatre, in which playwrights, actors, directors, designers, technicians and business managers can find an expression for their art and craft as well as earn a livelihood, and which will provide audiences with beautiful plays."[19] For Jones, "serious theatre people" wanted to create a high-quality, decentralized national theatre that valued artists and their art, led to the creation of great theatre, and served the audience. The challenge was the execution: economics, buildings, and limited opportunities for emerging artists. In concert with her sweeping ideas for reform, Jones focused on practicalities. Actors required living wages. Directors and designers were deprived of sufficient opportunities for professionalization. Emerging playwrights were leaving the field because few new plays were being produced. Regional theatres like Theatre '47 provided solutions.

Nor did Jones reject her connection to Broadway; she leveraged it to give Theatre '47 credibility with Houston donors. Having established her reputation as a director in New York and on Broadway with productions like *The Glass Menagerie* (1945) and *Joan of Lorraine* (1946), she continued to work there after she founded Theatre '47 with *Summer and Smoke* (1948), *Southern Exposure* (1950), and *Inherit the Wind* (1955). As Boone Hopkins has argued, Jones capitalized on her burgeoning celebrity to build her theatre: "the surety for investors was Jones's attachment to each project."[20] To build donor trust, she enlisted Manning Gurian, a Broadway company manager, to ensure that the nonprofit company ran "in as businesslike a fashion as a department store."[21] Focused on creating the highest-quality theatre, she hired a small company of New York actors with an eye toward flexibility and range and brought them to Texas for her first season.[22] Jones produced both classical works and new plays, and Theatre '47's first season attracted theatre luminaries from all over the country.[23] *New York Times* reviewer Brooks Atkinson "dropped in" for *How Now, Hecate*, which featured prominently in the story he wrote on Jones and Theatre '47.[24] He lists others in attendance as well: ANTA president Vinton Freedley; Mr. and Mrs. Sherman Ewing, Broadway producers; and scenic designer Jo Mielziner. Contrary to the standard narrative of the rise of regional theatre, Jones fought to provide Houston with high-quality theatre works – both new and classical – while also building a financially sustainable organization that provided employees with viable, living wages and built on her own connections to Broadway. Though Theatre '47 would close its doors in 1959, four years after Jones's untimely death, Jones would prove to be an extraordinarily influential figure and her dream of a regional theatre would spread.

The same year that Jones founded Theatre '47, Nina Vance established the Alley Theatre in Houston. Nina Vance had been well known in Houston for her work with Margo Jones's Houston Community Players, the Houston Little Theatre, and the Jewish Community Center Player's Guild, as well as her teaching and directing at area high schools. She was a founding member of the Theatre Communications Group (1961), invited to serve on President John F. Kennedy's advisory council for the proposed National Culture Center, and appointed to the US Advisory Commission of International Education and Cultural Affairs.[25] Vance's choice to found the Alley was motivated by the Houston arts community, many of whom felt that something important had been missing since the closing of Jones's

Players. Thus, she brought a desire to create theatre in and for Houston rather than a rejection of Broadway's commercialism or a need to decenter US theatre as a whole.[26]

The Alley was initially an amateur endeavor. It began with the money Vance had in her pocket – $2.14 – which purchased 214 penny postcards which she mailed to community members interested in starting a theatre.[27] As part of an amateur organization, the Alley performers were unpaid volunteers, the cast often doubled as production staff, and the performances and rehearsals took place in a donated space. That space had a "day job" as a dance studio, so all vestiges of rehearsal and performance had to be struck every night by the cast; they moved a piano, rugs, furniture, seats, and more.[28] In those early years, Vance relied on ticket sales for the majority of the budget, moving to patron donations only when absolutely necessary to make up the difference.[29] However, it soon became clear that Vance's vision for the Alley required the time, training, and commitment that only paid collaborators could offer.

Reimagining the Alley as a semiprofessional or professional organization required a fundamental restructuring. Unlike Jones's Theatre '47, the Alley was founded on a democratic model with members who contributed $0.10 for voting rights on theatre policies. Rather than a board, the Alley relied on the generosity of patrons, who donated a minimum of $25 and received "nothing except knowledge that they were helping to launch an exciting theatre venture."[30] It is noteworthy that Vance had explicitly rejected a model with ten patrons donating $50 each because she felt those ten people would "want to run the theatre"; this decentralized leadership model offered Vance the artistic authority and funding she required.[31] However, a more nimble form of decision-making soon developed through a de facto board consisting of six individuals elected by the voting members and five permanent staff members appointed by Vance, that formed to handle emergencies.[32] Over the next six years, the Alley transformed into a professional theatre. In 1948, it became a nonprofit. In 1951, it nearly closed due to competition from the neighboring Equity Playhouse, a well-funded entity with a strikingly similar approach to work, taste, and style, and with the backing of a number of Houston scions; Vance engaged in emergency fundraising and a battle with the Board of Trustees, but emerged firmly established as artistic and administrative leader of the theatre.[33] The Alley had been semiprofessional, offering salaries to select actors, but it began a process of hiring out-of-town talent to generate box-office success and in 1954 became an Equity theatre.[34]

Like Jones, Vance had a penchant for a blend of contemporary and classic theatre. Far from rejecting Broadway, Vance preferred to gather the latest plays from the Great White Way. Under Vance's leadership, the Alley specialized in what she described as "Broadway flops – that is, plays that were critically successful in New York but not commercially so."[35] She traveled to New York – on annual, self-funded journeys – and hobnobbed with agents and writers when she was not seeing work in the theatre. The Alley's first play, Harry Brown's *A Sound of Hunting*, premiered on Broadway to critical praise and poor box-office receipts, but did reasonably well in Houston.[36] Plays by Arthur Miller, Tennessee Williams, Eugene O'Neill, and Jean Giraudoux appeared frequently in Alley seasons, but comedies consistently drew the steadiest audiences, and Vance faced criticism regarding the lack of "sophistication" of these more popular works.[37] Though this may seem to reflect Landro's standard narrative, for Vance, choosing a play was about communicating ideas and connecting to her community rather than setting up a binary between artistry and financial success.

While Jones and Vance both chose a nonprofit model for their theatres from the beginning, Zelda Fichandler and Edward Mangum also broke away from the standard narrative when they cofounded Arena Stage in Washington, DC, in 1950. They also wanted to create high-quality, professional work outside of New York, but they founded Arena Stage as a for-profit venture. As Mangum explained, few people wanted to contribute to a "shaky . . . non-profit enterprise," but some "were willing to gamble on my making a success of a new kind of theatre."[38] Thus, having accumulated $15,000 from forty stockholders, Mangum and Fichandler hired a small company of young professionals and set out to produce their first season – largely classics. By the second year, Arena gained Equity status and Mangum resigned to pursue other opportunities. Within five years, the company's corporate worth had nearly doubled.[39]

Under Fichandler's careful stewardship, Arena seemed to demonstrate that the regional theatre could successfully create professional theatre on a for-profit model, and she regularly paid out at least some stockholder dividends. At the same time, she also worked toward larger goals of a permanent resident company, playwright residencies, and long-term community outreach initiatives. However, prosperity was temporary, lasting only as long as production and administrative costs lagged behind ticket sale revenues. As Fichandler explained, Arena changed locations because "we weren't taking enough in to do what we wanted to do, and we were selling out. It was success that turned us into non-profit."[40] At the same time, Arena was relying on unpaid and underpaid labor in order to make ends meet, whether it was early-career actors, Fichandler, or her husband (the company's unpaid business manager). As Thomas Fichandler noted, "we were subsidized indirectly by people working for very low salaries or none at all."[41]

When Fichandler reincorporated the Arena as nonprofit in 1959, it established a stable home, enlarged the theatre to 800 seats (thus increasing ticket revenue), and made the theatre eligible for grants, tax breaks, and donations. Fichandler quickly became an expert at attaining foundation support and procured a grant from the Ford Foundation that covered the majority of the debts the theatre had accrued in building their new theatre (mortgage, land acquisition, bonds, etc.) while leaving $150,000 for operating costs.[42] She went on to obtain foundation funding to increase actor wages with the goal of building a resident company, creating educational outreach programs, and producing challenging new work, thus employing foundation funds to further the theatre's mission.

Arena Stage's production of Howard Sackler's *The Great White Hope* is often marked as a turning point because it showed that regional theatres could create work that would gain national recognition. *The Great White Hope* also catalyzed a legal argument about the legitimation and rights of regional theatre. *The Great White Hope* was Arena's first breakaway hit. It opened on Broadway in 1968, ran for 556 performances, won the Tony Award and Pulitzer Prize for Drama, and "proved the national power of new plays."[43] *The Great White Hope* depicts the life of a young African American boxer in blank verse and requires a large cast, nearly two dozen scene changes, and 250 costumes. Fichandler worked closely with Sackler on play revisions and secured Ford Foundation and NEA grants that made the Arena production possible: $25,000 for production costs; $7,000 for playwright commission (a figure just above the average annual salary in 1968); and a $1,000 weekly stipend for Sackler during the six-week run of the show at Arena.[44] Sackler then sold the film rights to 20th Century Fox for $550,000 without informing Arena management. He used those funds to secure a Broadway producer and invested a quarter million dollars in a Broadway transfer that used most of the Arena cast, design, and production team, but without a contract that would give Arena credit or royalties. Sackler earned $7,000 a week while *The Great White Hope* ran on Broadway; he offered Arena 5 percent of the profits up to a maximum of $50,000. After a protracted public battle for credit and 10 percent of the profits, Arena lost many of its company members and Broadway billing, and failed to recoup the $50,000 debt the show had incurred in DC.

Following this hard lesson, the League of Resident Theatres (LORT) negotiated a model contract for regional theatres that developed new work that later transferred to Broadway.[45] This contract would prove to be vital for regional theatres in their role as "creative crucibles" of contemporary US theatre. It also reinforces the strong creative and economic connection between regional theatres and Broadway, further complicating the historiographical narrative of the rise of regional theatre.

Margo Jones's Theatre '47, Nina Vance's Alley Theatre, and Zelda Fichandler's Arena Stage were three of the first regional theatres founded in the United States. As demonstrated above, all brought varying motivations, strategies, and practices to a discussion of the rise of regional theatre. All of the founders decentered theatre in some way by moving it out of New York City and into new locations, but their motivations differed; Jones was animated by creating a network of regional theatres, while Vance wanted to meet community needs in Houston. Similarly, the standard narrative puts regional theatre founders actively in opposition to the commercialism of Broadway and in search of a home for new or experimental work. While these founders sought opportunities for a range of new work and ways of working, they did not actively reject Broadway. Jones continued directing on Broadway, transferring productions to Broadway, and hiring actors and other workers from Broadway. Vance sought out Broadway plays that "flopped" for the Alley. One of Fichandler's great successes was *The Great White Hope*, the Pulitzer Prize– and Tony Award–winning production that demonstrated that regional theatres could create great artistic works, even if it did so at a great cost to Arena.

A New Nonprofit Model

The story does not end with that initial flush of regional theatres, nor does the narrative stagnate. Jones and Vance founded the first regional theatres in 1947. In 1960, only ten regional theatres existed nationwide, half of which had formed since 1955. By 1965, that number had jumped to thirty-two.[46] TCG included 147 theatres in its 1980 *Theatre Facts* analysis. By 1991, TCG listed 229 theatres in *Theatre Profiles,* and the 2000 issue of *Theatre Facts* included 262 theatres. In their 2018 *Theatre Facts* report, TCG included 1,855 member and not-for-profit theatres.[47] According to Actors' Equity, as of 2017, LORT theatres were the second largest source of employment nationwide and the largest source of employment in the central and western regions. In 2018, Equity issued its first *Regional*

Theatre Report, which showed that fully 40 percent of all Equity work weeks for the 2016–17 season took place in regional theatres.[48]

Clearly regional theatres – and their influence – have become widespread even if the scholarship on their enormous breadth of work is only beginning to catch up. It is hard to believe that such a proliferation could occur if it were motivated by a simple rejection of Broadway's commercialism or a desire for decentralization, and contemporary scholars like Donatella Galella (Arena Stage), Macelle Mahala (Penumbra Theatre), and Susannah Engstrom (Guthrie Theatre) suggest much more complexity.[49] I shift now to the social and economic forces that made this explosion of regional theatres possible. The Guthrie Theatre serves as a case study for a prominent, highly professional, nonprofit approach that would prove to be a model for future regional theatres.

In 1959, the Ford Foundation designated approximately $559,000 to help establish resident acting companies with salaries of at least $200 a week at New York's Phoenix Theatre, the Alley, the Arena, and Actors' Workshop, beginning a long-term relationship between foundations and nonprofit theatres.[50] Within a few years, Ford Foundation funding had grown to $6.1 million,[51] and national foundations like the Rockefeller, Mellon, and Kresge joined a vast array of local organizations like the Lilly (Indiana) and William Penn Foundations (Pennsylvania). Municipal and state funding joined the mix and, with the establishment of the National Endowment for the Arts (NEA) in 1965, federal funding became a possibility as well. Agencies funded many different activities: playwright residencies, actor training programs, resident acting companies, operating expenses, theatre fellowships, salaries, debt repayment, capital campaign start-up, theatre buildings, equipment acquisition, education programs, professionalization, and more.[52] They funded specific activities, sometimes fully, sometimes requiring matching funds. Savvy theatres hired grant writers who could shape existing activities into fundable proposals or leverage foundation support to work toward long-term strategic goals. However, as more funding became available, regional theatres became more dependent on it. Thus, this external funding made regional theatre possible even as it changed the way that those theatres functioned.

In 1963, more than fifteen years after the initial rush of regional theatres, actor/director Tyrone Guthrie, producer Oliver Rea, and production manager Peter Zeisler established the Minnesota Theatre Company, which would eventually become the Guthrie Theatre. The Guthrie is a useful case study because it became the model for a new kind of top-down, high-profile regional theatre. It was the first such theatre to launch with the majority of the nonprofit framework, foundation funding, and local support already in place, and thus came with enormous resources, high expectations, and little room for error. The Guthrie was the brainchild of three established artists who had become weary of Broadway and wanted to bring professional classical and new work to new audiences. They "shopped" for a home city by convincing Brooks Atkinson to describe their idea on the drama page of the *New York Times*; seven cities responded.[53] They ultimately selected Minneapolis/St. Paul, Minnesota, having obtained the backing of city scions who donated land, raised more than $2.25 million for a custom-built theatre, and marshaled widespread foundation and community support.[54] The Twin Cities also offered access to the University of Minnesota, an educated population, and increasing interest in growing the city's cultural climate.[55] When the Guthrie opened its doors for its glamorous first production, a four-hour *Hamlet* featuring stars like Hume Cronyn, Jessica Tandy, and George Grizzard, it was supported by a full professional staff with specialists in marketing, publicity, audience development, business management, public relations, and fundraising.[56]

Guthrie, Rea, and Zeisler intended for the Guthrie to be self-supporting, but they created it as a nonprofit. For the first three seasons the Guthrie nearly met this goal, which Rea calculated would occur if the theatre reached 75 percent capacity. With the help of Ford Foundation grants, the Guthrie ended each year in the black. However, after Tyrone Guthrie's retirement in 1965, followed by Rea's, the theatre that *Life* magazine had called the "miracle in Minneapolis" only two years earlier began to fall into decline.[57] Attendance dwindled and, by 1967, earned income and the anticipated NEA grant covered only 74 percent of projected expenses. The following year, the Ford Foundation notified the Guthrie that it would no longer support theatre operating expenses, spurring a critical moment in the theatre's development. The Guthrie's leadership would struggle to find a balance between economic survival, audience appeal, and artistic worth as national foundation funding lessened and the need for local fundraising intensified.

Susannah Engstrom argues that the problem the Guthrie faced was due to its identity as a "professional" theatre. This required the Guthrie to *begin* as a fully formed, paying entity that hired only the most highly qualified actors, designers, directors, and staff. Since it opened with major foundation funding and the nonprofit framework established, supporters expected professional handing at the administrative level. But the work of administering the growing number of grants, researching and writing more grants to support the upcoming season, developing the audience, and producing highly organized budget materials required an ever-growing, already-proficient staff.[58] As Jack Poggi argues, "The larger and more complex the operation, the more likely a theatre is to shift its major emphasis from putting on plays to insuring its growth and survival as an institution."[59] The Guthrie was not able to make this shift because it was already effectively at this point when it began – investing in administrative staff that catered to funding needs, sometimes at the cost of production work. Even so, other theatre leaders watched the Guthrie carefully. Both the successes and challenges became an important part of the high-profile, nonprofit theatre model for future companies that employed similar strategies.

Funding Culture

The timing of the regional theatre explosion coincided with a boom in foundation giving, but it also came on the cusp of a national cultural shift. President Kennedy's election ushered in a period of cultural awareness and engagement, while First Lady Jackie Kennedy was an icon of elegance and patron of the arts. Poetry, music, art, and theatre flourished nationwide by virtue their support. Kennedy's administration saw the establishment of the President's Advisory Council on the Arts (the predecessor of the National Council of the Arts), the beginnings of the Kennedy Center in Washington, DC, the National Endowment for the Humanities (NEH), and the NEA.[60] However, it was not just the Kennedys that made culture chic in the 1960s. In the midst of the Cold War, the quality of a nation's arts became a way to measure cultural superiority, and *funding* the arts demonstrated the nation's civilization. It is not surprising that senators' speeches surrounding the founding of the NEA and NEH look outward to the world and often reference fear, hopelessness, and bombs before recall-ing the importance of the arts to a civilized society.[61] Culture became one antidote to the Cold War, and Americans' interest in cultural expression expanded accordingly.

Since then, interest in the arts has ebbed and flowed and, with it, so has foundation and public funding. This economic instability is especially challenging in the nonprofit performing arts because of basic funding structures. First, as Princeton economists W. J. Baumol and W. G. Bowen explain, nonprofits, by definition, earn no return on invested capital and fulfill some social purpose: the "objectives of the typical nonprofit organiza-tion are by their very nature designed to keep it constantly on the brink of financial catastrophe."[62] Second, according to roughly thirty years of TCG's *Theatre Facts* reports, most regional theatres spend between 52 and 60 percent of their annual budgets on salaries. Third, as TCG Executive Director Ben Cameron notes, few regional theatres have endowments that meet the National Arts Stabilization Fund standard of at least 200–500 percent of its annual operating expenses. When Cameron was writing in 1999, only three met that standard and 54 percent had no endowment at all.[63] While these numbers have improved since then, theatres have also weathered significant economic downturns with the "dot.com" bubble in 2001, 9/11, and the subprime mortgage crisis from 2007 to 2009. This combination of factors – little in the way of savings or an endowment, annual budgeting that directs the majority of their funds toward salaries, and a nonprofit philosophy that normalizes operating "on the brink of financial catastrophe" – leaves regional theatres terribly vulnerable. The standard narrative that creates a binary between great art and economic success has contributed to this problem, which is one reason that it is so necessary to dismantle it.

Clearly, a major challenge for regional theatre leaders is their lack of control over the markets and culture wars that decimate public funding. Foundation funds may seem predictable in comparison, but the Ford Foundation was one of the largest donors to regional theatre for decades, and while it made many things possible, its annual contributions varied considerably. When grants were a critical slice of the budget, theatres could only plan so far ahead in hiring, outreach plans, or even the season itself. Paul DiMaggio's 1986 study of philanthropic giving described certain patterns: the vast majority of foundation support was distributed locally, and "most local support [was] concentrated on the largest, most prestigious, and most artistically conventional institutions." Few foundation funds supported experimental work, community-oriented organizations, or those serving BIPOC or LGBTQ+ populations.[64]

Thirty years later, Helicon's 2017 study documents similar trends. The majority of arts funding continues to go to the largest organizations, with budgets in excess of $5 million and predominantly white and upper-class audiences. Even in cities like Los Angeles – where the population is 72 percent BIPOC – only 8 percent of available funding went to organizations focused on BIPOC, low-income, or LGBTQ+ populations while three times that many arts organizations (24 percent) self-identified as working directly with these groups.[65] This systemic inequity compounds over time as the most affluent theatres gain more and more support while community-centered, culturally specific groups remain chronically underfunded.

Chronically underfunded organizations have more trouble paying a living wage; recall that more than half of most theatres' budgets go toward salaries. They are more limited in their ability to support artists and new work. They struggle to reserve funds for an endowment or to hire additional staff to run a capital campaign, thus destabilizing long-term financial planning. And cataclysmic events like the COVID-19 pandemic reveal systemic ruptures. Even theatres that are on solid economic ground cancel contracts, cut benefits and salaries, and furlough staff in order to survive. Theatres in more tenuous economic positions must take more drastic steps, including firing employees, closing for the season, or closing permanently.

At the 2020 TCG Conference, actress/writer Nikkole Salter offered a call to action in response to the Black Lives Matter protests: "the story of a person or organization's values lies in its budget. How you spend your money and your time tells a story of what means the most to you, tells the prophecy of what you will become. I want our budgets to reflect the truth of nature."[66] Salter's call is a reminder that budgets reveal values and goals at a fundamental level. From the beginning, regional theatre has been shaped by visionary leaders who attended to both artistic goals and practicalities. Whether they worked toward building a repertory company, boosting actor salaries, building the company, or creating a national model for nonprofit theatres, they continued this work while commissioning new plays, reimagining the classics, decentering the nation's theatre, and building bridges between regional theatres and Broadway. Contemporary regional theatres that launch capital campaigns dedicated to increasing actor salaries or improving artist housing, like Center Stage (Baltimore, Maryland), Round House Theatre (Silver Spring, Maryland), and Writers Theatre (Glencoe, Illinois), demonstrate a similar commitment to both the vision and the reality.[67]

As I write this, regional theatre stands at a crossroads. Numerous theatres, including the Alley, saw leadership changes in 2017–18 in response to allegations of sexual misconduct and the #MeToo movement.[68] In 2020, theatres nationwide are closed due to the pandemic, waiting to see whether they will open again and, if they are able to do so, what form that reopening will take. Economics and art clash again. How will theatres produce their work safely within the confines of social distancing: reducing their ticket sales by as much as two-thirds; distributing masks to audience members for every performance; administering COVID-19 tests to cast and crew regularly, if not daily; and convincing audiences that it is safe to return to the theatre for performances? All of this requires theatres – and artists – to survive until reopening. They will need additional funds before ticket sales come in, suggesting that those theatres most likely to succeed are those with deep donor pockets, especially sound prepandemic financial management, and/or supportive communities. Theatres that rely on community support are likely to be more diverse, but history shows that external funding is likely to favor high-profile, wealthy theatres that cater to primarily white audiences.

As a reimagined regional theatre emerges, how will leaders and communities apportion the budgets that are available? What will those budgets reveal about their values as artists and humans who make up a field? What stories will they tell? Whose voices will emerge?

Notes

1. J. O'Quinn, "Going National: How America's Regional Theatre Movement Changed the Game," June 16, 2015, www.americantheatre.org /2015/06/16/going-national-how-americas-regional-theatre-movement-cha nged-the-game/.
2. D. Tran, "The Top 20* Most-Produced Playwrights of the 2019–20 Season," *American Theatre*, September 18, 2019, www.americantheatre.org/2019/09/18/ the-top-20-most-produced-playwrights-of-the-2019–20-season/.
3. "Winners and Finalists by Category: The Pulitzer Prizes: Drama," The Pulitzer Prizes, www.pulitzer.org/prize-winners-by-category/218; O'Quinn, "Going National."
4. Z. G. Voss, G. B. Voss, D. Fonner, I. B. Rose, and L. Baskin, *Theatre Facts 2018* (Theatre Communications Group, 2019), p. 4, www.tcg.org/pdfs/tools/ TCG_TheatreFacts_2018.pdf.
5. T. C. Davis, *The Economics of the British Stage, 1800–1914* (Cambridge University Press, 2000), p. 2.
6. J. Poggi, *Theater in America: The Impact of Economic Forces, 1870–1967* (Cornell University Press, 1968), pp. 211–12.
7. M. Gottfried, *A Theater Divided: The Postwar American Stage* (Little, Brown & Company, 1967), pp. 103–27.
8. V. Landro, "The Mythologizing of American Regional Theatre," *The Journal of American Drama and Theatre,* 10 (1998), p. 76.
9. Gottfried, *A Theater Divided,* pp. 104–5, 127; J. Novick, *Beyond Broadway: The Quest for Permanent Theatres* (Hill and Wang, 1968), pp. 8, 21; J. W. Zeigler, *Regional Theatre: The Revolutionary Stage* (University of Minnesota Press, 1973), pp. 170–71.
10. J. M. Harding and C. Rosenthal, "Pulling the Curtain on False Dichotomies: The Importance of the Theatrical Mainstream in the 1960s," in J. M. Harding and C. Rosenthal (eds.), *The Sixties, Center Stage: Mainstream and Popular*

Performances in a Turbulent Decade (University of Michigan Press, 2017), pp. 6–8.

11. R. Schechner, "Intentions, Problems, Proposals," *The Tulane Drama Review*, 7 (1963), p. 21.

12. Schechner, "Intentions, Problems, Proposals," 20–21.

13. Schechner served as editor of *The Tulane Drama Review* (which became *TDR*, then shifted to *The Drama Review: TDR*, then to *TDR* again) from 1962 to 1969, and then again from 1986 to the present. Harding and Rosenthal, "Pulling the Curtain," p. 6.

14. R. Schechner, "Ford, Rockefeller, and Theatre," *The Tulane Drama Review*, 10 (1965), pp. 23–24; Schechner, "Intentions, Problems, Proposals," p. 7.

15. D. Galella, *America in the Round: Capital, Race, and Nation at Washington DC's Arena Stage* (University of Iowa Press, 2019), p. 22.

16. H. K. Chinoy, "Art versus Business: The Role of Women in American Theatre," *The Drama Review: TDR*, 24 (1980), pp. 6–7.

17. B. Atkinson, "Stage Folk Study Theatre in Dallas," *New York Times*, August 1, 1947, p. 21.

18. Qtd. in H. Sheehy, *Margo: The Life and Theatre of Margo Jones* (Southern Methodist University Press, 1989), p. 132.

19. M. Jones, *Theatre-in-the-Round* (McGraw-Hill, 1965), p. 3.

20. B. J. Hopkins, "'The Mind of an Adult, the Heart of a Girl': Constructing Margo Jones in Rehearsal," *Theatre Symposium*, 22 (2014), p. 34.

21. Jones, *Theatre-in-the-Round*, p. 61.

22. Ibid., p. 62.

23. Sheehy, *Margo*, p. 137.

24. Atkinson, "Stage Folk," p. 21.

25. A. L. Fliotsos and W. Vierow, *American Women Stage Directors of the Twentieth Century* (University of Illinois Press, 2008), pp. 419–20, 424.

26. T. Ravas, "The Nina Vance Alley Theatre Papers at the University of Houston Libraries Special Collections," *Theatre Survey*, 49 (2008), p. 123.

27. Zeigler, *Regional Theatre*, p. 26; Ravas, "Alley Theatre Papers," p. 127.

28. N. Vance, "Alley Theatre: First Legitimate Playhouse on Main Street, Houston, Texas (We Hope)," in T. London (ed.), *An Ideal Theater: Founding Visions for a New American Art* (Theatre Communications Group, 2013), p. 296.

29. Vance, "Alley Theatre," p. 295.

30. Qtd. in Ravas, "Alley Theatre Papers," p. 123.

31. Vance, "Alley Theatre," p. 294.

32. R. M. Treser, "Houston's Alley Theatre," unpublished PhD dissertation, Tulane University (1967), pp. 28–29, 68–69.

33. Treser, "Houston's Alley Theatre," pp. 59–60; H. Roussel, "Houston 'Circle': New Theatre in Texas," *New York Times*, February 18, 1951, p. X3.

34. N. J. Stanley, "Nina Vance: Founder and Artistic Director of Houston's Alley Theatre, 1947–1980," unpublished PhD dissertation, Indiana University (1990), pp. 65–66; Zeigler, *Regional Theatre*, p. 29.

35. Qtd. in M. Kakutani, "Nina Vance, Leader of Alley Theater," *New York Times*, February 19, 1980, p. B5.
36. Fliotsos and Vierow, *American Women Directors*, p. 420.
37. Stanley, "Nina Vance," pp. 165–66.
38. Edward Mangum, qtd. in B. Coyne, "A History of Arena Stage," unpublished PhD dissertation, Tulane University (1964), p. 14.
39. D. Galella, "Making Art and Making Money: Arena Stage in the 1960s," in J. M. Harding and C. Rosenthal (eds.), *The Sixties, Center Stage: Mainstream and Popular Performances in a Turbulent Decade* (University of Michigan Press, 2017), pp. 274–75.
40. Qtd. in Galella, *America in the Round*, p. 33.
41. B. Cameron and J. Lee, "Arena Stage: Interviews with Zelda Fichandler, David Chambers, and Thomas Fichandler," *Theater*, 10 (1979), p. 29.
42. Galella, "Making Art and Making Money," p. 278.
43. Zeigler, *Regional Theatre*, p. 198; Z. Fichandler, "Theatres or Institutions?," *Theater*, 3 (1970), p. 114.
44. Galella, *America in the Round*, p. 62.
45. Ibid., pp. 63–64; S. Zolotow, "Arena Stage Fails in 'White Hope' Bid," *New York Times*, October 11, 1968, p. 38.
46. Poggi, *Theater in America*, pp. 213–15.
47. *Theatre Facts* does not differentiate between TCG theatre members and not-for-profit theatres that filed IRS form 990 or provided data through SMU DataArts' Cultural Data Profile, so these numbers are significantly higher than previous years. Voss et al., *Theatre Facts 2018*, p. 1; R. Rothschild Mayleas and Theatre Communications Group, *Theatre Facts 80* (Theatre Communications Group, 1981), p. 14.
48. Actors' Equity focuses on work weeks in "Liaison Areas," which include theatres with Equity contracts within 100 miles of cities with concentrations of Equity members. Figures include only those actors and stage managers working under Equity contracts. Actors' Equity, *2018 Regional Theatre Report* (Actors' Equity Association, 2019), p. 3, www.actorsequity.org/news/PR/RegionalTheatreReport/ActorsEquity_RegionalTheatreReport_Web.pdf.
49. See Galella, *America in the Round*; S. Engstrom, "Twin Cities Theater in the 1960s: Negotiating the Commercial/Experimental Divide," in J. M. Harding and C. Rosenthal (eds.), *The Sixties, Center Stage: Mainstream and Popular Performances in a Turbulent Decade* (University of Michigan Press, 2017), pp. 251–72; M. Mahala, *Penumbra: The Premier Stage for African American Drama* (University of Minnesota Press, 2013).
50. Gottfried, *A Theater Divided*, pp. 98–100.
51. Poggi, *Theater in America*, pp. 211–12.
52. S. Schmidt, "The Regional Theatre: Some Statistics," *The Tulane Drama Review*, 10 (1965), pp. 50–61.
53. T. Guthrie, *A New Theatre* (McGraw-Hill, 1964), pp. 45–46.
54. Zeigler, *Regional Theatre*, pp. 66–70; Guthrie, *A New Theatre*, pp. 61–62.

55. S. M. Engstrom, "Theatre for the City: Professionalism and Cultural Democracy in Minneapolis, 1946–1976," unpublished PhD dissertation, University of Chicago (2016), p. 155.
56. Engstrom, "Twin Cities Theater," pp. 251, 259–60.
57. "A Theatrical Dream Come True Makes a Miracle in Minneapolis," *Life*, May 24, 1963, p. 41.
58. Engstrom, "Theatre for the City," pp. 193–98.
59. Poggi, *Theater in America*, p. 235.
60. M. Bauerlein and E. Grantham (eds.), *National Endowment for the Arts: A History, 1965–2008* (National Endowment for the Arts, 2009), pp. 5–9.
61. See the speeches of Senators Claiborne Pell, Hubert Humphrey, and Jacob Javits for examples. Bauerlein and Grantham, *National Endowment*, pp. 14–15.
62. W. J. Baumol and W. G. Bowen, "On the Performing Arts: The Anatomy of their Economic Problems," in M. Blaug (ed.), *The Economics of the Arts* (Westview Press, 1976), pp. 218–26, 220–22.
63. B. Cameron, "Numbers and Consequences," *American Theatre*, 16:6 (August 1999), p. 4.
64. P. J. DiMaggio, "Support for the Arts from Independent Foundations," in P. J. DiMaggio (ed.), *Nonprofit Enterprise in the Arts: Studies in Mission and Constraint* (Oxford University Press, 1986), pp. 128–29.
65. While these figures focus on all arts organizations, the authors note remarkable consistency across the performing arts. Helicon Collaborative, with support from the Surdna Foundation, "Not Just Money: Equity Issues in Cultural Philanthropy," July, 2017, pp. 7–9, http://notjustmoney.us/docs/NotJustMon ey_Full_Report_July2017.pdf.
66. N. Salter, "Wednesday Plenary," in *Re: Emergence Part 2: Convening* (Theatre Communications Group Annual Conference, Virtual, 2020), http://howl round.com/happenings/2020-theatre-communications-group-virtual-confer ence-reemergence-part-2.
67. K. Smith, "Love or Money: How about Both?," *American Theatre*, January 24, 2017, www.americantheatre.org/2017/01/24/love-or-money-how-about-both/.
68. S. Carroll, "Alley Board Pressured Artistic Director to Leave," *Houston Chronicle*, January 26, 2018, www.houstonchronicle.com/news/houston-texas/houston/article/Alley-board-pressured-artistic-director-to-leave-125295 22.php.

Select Bibliography

Baumol, W. J., and W. G. Bowen. "On the Performing Arts: The Anatomy of their Economic Problems." In M. Blaug (ed.), *The Economics of the Arts*. Westview Press, 1976, 218–26.

DiMaggio, P. J. "Support for the Arts from Independent Foundations." In P. J. DiMaggio (ed.), *Nonprofit Enterprise in the Arts: Studies in Mission and Constraint*. Oxford University Press, 1986, 113–39.

Fichandler, Z. "Theatres or Institutions?" *Theater*, 3 (1970), 104–17.

Galella, D. *America in the Round: Capital, Race, and Nation at Washington DC's Arena Stage*. University of Iowa Press, 2019.

Gottfried, M. *A Theater Divided: The Postwar American Stage*. Little, Brown & Company, 1967.

Harding, J.M., and C. Rosenthal (eds.). *The Sixties, Center Stage: Mainstream and Popular Performances in a Turbulent Decade*. University of Michigan Press, 2017.

Helicon Collaborative, with support from the Surdna Foundation. "Not Just Money: Equity Issues in Cultural Philanthropy. 2017. http://notjustmoney.us/docs/NotJustMoney_Full_Report_July2017.pdf.

Hopkins, B. J. "'The Mind of an Adult, the Heart of a Girl': Constructing Margo Jones in Rehearsal." *Theatre Symposium*, 22 (2014), 33–47.

Jones, M. *Theatre-in-the-Round*. McGraw-Hill, 1965.

Landro, V. "The Mythologizing of American Regional Theatre." *The Journal of American Drama and Theatre*, 10 (1998), 76–101.

London, T. (ed.). *An Ideal Theater: Founding Visions for a New American Art*. Theatre Communications Group, 2013.

Poggi, J. *Theater in America: The Impact of Economic Forces, 1870–1967*. Cornell University Press, 1968.

Ravas, T. "The Nina Vance Alley Theatre Papers at the University of Houston Libraries Special Collections." *Theatre Survey*, 49 (2008), 119–28.

Schechner, R. "Ford, Rockefeller, and Theatre." *The Tulane Drama Review*, 10 (1965), 23–49.

Schechner, R. "Intentions, Problems, Proposals." *The Tulane Drama Review*, 7 (1963), 5–21.

Sheehy, H. *Margo: The Life and Theatre of Margo Jones*. Southern Methodist University Press, 1989.

Zeigler, J. W. *Regional Theatre: The Revolutionary Stage*. University of Minnesota Press, 1973.

CHAPTER 6

When and Where They Enter
Black and Brown Voices in American Theatre

Faedra Chatard Carpenter

When tasked with exploring the thematic terrain of "Diverse voices in American Theatre," where does one begin – or end? How does one fittingly honor both artists of distinction and significant happenings, while avoiding overly simplified survey summaries or injuries of omission? Such querying underscores the fact that documenting the story of diverse voices in American Theatre is, like all historical narratives, a challenge that is inescapably compromised by archival gaps and silences. Moreover, the facts and figures that tell the story of regional theatre in America reveal both impediments and progress. And so, while we are experiencing a time in American theatre that seems to champion inclusive practices more than ever, the advancements we are witnessing are not simply reflective of miraculous momentum; they are also the consequence of the grind and grit paid up to this point. Accordingly, there is still much work to be done; there still exists the need to conscientiously labor for greater equity in American theatre. After all, "diverse voices" can – and should – be understood in a plethora of ways. Race, ethnicity, gender, sexuality, class, disability, religion, and age are among the many identificatory categories that need to be considered when honoring the politics and experiences of difference. However, simply utilizing expressions such as "diversity and inclusion" will fall flat as trendy phrases unless theatre practitioners and scholars truly value how far we have come while also recognizing, with reflexivity and honesty, how much more we need to accomplish.

Even when considering a single category of difference – racial representation, for example – the ebb and flow of progress within the systematic

---

The title of this chapter pays homage to the words of Anna Julia Cooper: "Only the BLACK WOMAN can say 'when and where I enter, in the quiet, undisputed dignity of my womanhood, without violence and without suing or special patronage, then and there the whole *Negro race enters with me.*'" See Anna Julia Cooper, *A Voice from the South* (Aldine Printing House, 1892), p.31, http://docsouth.unc.edu/c hurch/cooper/cooper.html.

structure of America's regional theatres becomes apparent. The tenuous advent of racial equity in regional theatre is especially noteworthy since the issue of race, amidst other concerns relating to social justice, has historically dominated the dialogues, programs, and policies that purport to address investments in diversity. This is due, in part, to the ways in which theatre informed – and was informed by – the social and political movements during the latter half of the twentieth century. Inspired by the strivings of the civil rights movement (1954–68), the political, social, and cultural movements of the 1960s and 1970s gave birth to artists and activists who were not only fighting for justice and equity for minoritized subjects, but who also recognized that social and political progress was dependent upon "strategic essentialism" – that is, the formation of strategic, unified, and organized fronts working against institutionalized racism and oppression. Thus, the civil rights movement created the fertile field from which the Black Power movement and Black Arts movement grew, alongside the political vigilance and creative innovations of the Chicano movement, the Asian American movement, the American Indian (Native American) movement, women's movement, and gay liberation movement of the 1960s and 1970s.

Among African Americans, the Black Power movement and its ideological sibling, the Black Arts movement, were two of the most pronounced exemplars of the civil rights movement's momentum and productive influence. As repeatedly articulated in the chronicles of contemporary theatre history, the artists and critics of the Black Arts movement argued for sociopolitical leverage propelled by the presence – and performance – of a cohesive and politically astute Black identity. Emblematic of the Black Arts movement's ideologic call to arms was the mission-oriented scholarship of Larry Neal. Neal's definitive essay, "The Black Arts Movement" (1968), became a manifesto for Black artists aspiring to embrace and exercise the movement's nationalist ideals. Asserting that racial inequalities and biases result in social fractures that create "two Americas – one black, one white,"[1] Neal's essay encouraged Black artists to reject the styles and ideals perpetuated by the "Western aesthetic," suggesting that Black American artists should create work that challenges Western racism by building a strong sense of nationhood. Enforcing the belief that "Black people, however dispersed, constitute a *nation* within the belly of white America,"[2] Neal's program for Black artists – and his vision for the Black community – demanded a rigid ideological framework for Black artists/citizens that could claim membership in this nation-within -a-nation. This membership would be paramount in not only affirming their unique contributions and life-perspectives, but it would give them the sense of pride and racial uplift needed to combat the social and political inequities that stifle the progress of Black citizenry.

The communal strategizing that gave birth to the Black Arts movement not only galvanized Black artists, but it also served as reinforcement for other communities and artists of color, among them: the Chicano movement ("El Movimiento"), the American Indian (Native American) movement, and the Asian American movement. Of these various movements, the leaders of the Chicano movement are often recognized as those who most assertively partnered with leaders within the Black Power and Black Arts movements. Following similar principles and practices, the Chicano movement garnered momentum through a variety of communal networks, championing services and structures to augment a sense of nationalism along with community outreach programs. Key to propelling the synergies of this movement were the artists that helped circumscribe and concretize a sense of cultural identity among activists as well as every day citizens. Just as cultural critics such as Larry Neal aided in the dispersal of ideals related to the Black Arts movement, cultural leaders such as Rodolfo "Corky" Gonzales helped to determine and disseminate concepts and curriculum that became tools for the ideological advancement of the Chicano movement and its platform for Mexican American civil rights.

While many of the discriminatory practices against Mexican Americans echoed those faced by African Americans and other marginalized racial/cultural groups (issues related to equitable treatment, voting and political rights, access to education and employment), Mexican Americans wrestled with unique issues such as the struggle to restore land grants and the fight for farm workers' protection and rights. In addition to the struggle to acquire rights and protection under the law, the Chicano movement – in its very name – embraced the desire for a strong, rooted identity. Like the proponents of the Black Power and Black Arts movements, those who championed the term "Chicano" (distinguished from "Mexican American") were also championing an identity that simultaneously embraced an understanding of heritage and cultural traditions alongside one's identity as a full-fledged American citizen. Symbolic of ethnic pride and an empowering merging of cultural experience, the very term "Chicano" became a rallying cry of self-assertion, self-worth, and self-sufficiency. To this end, Gonzales, a Denver-based artist-activist, penned the celebrated poem "Yo Soy Joaquín" ("I am Joaquín"), which served as a poetic and powerful precis on Chicano identity. A man of action as well as words, Gonzales would help lead the Chicano organization, The

Crusade for Justice (1967), as well as help steer the formation and convening of the First Chicano Youth Liberation Conference – a gathering that gave birth to another momentous text, *El Plan Espiritual de Aztlán* (1969). *El Plan Espiritual de Aztlán* was a document which (similar to the Brown Berets's "Ten Point Plan" [1968] and its foregrounding inspiration, The Black Panthers' "Ten-Point Plan" [1966]), emphasized the health and well-being of their cultural communities through affirming strategies in the name of self-defense, community service, entrepreneurship, and education, among other points of address.

While there are many notable Black and Chicano theatre artists that charged – and were charged by – the movements of their corresponding communities, there are specific figures that are recognized as being highly influential and widely studied. Among the countless playwrights whose works forged these early canons, there are – inescapably – names that are habitually cited and rereferenced as forefathers of their respective cultural canons. To that end, Amiri Baraka (formerly known as LeRoi Jones) is often attributed as a key player in the canon of the Black Arts movement, and Luis Valdez as progenitor of the Chicano Arts movement. Each of these celebrated figures are worthy of their repeated recognition; each, through their own artistic genius, fierce determination, and unwavering creative vision, pummeled new paths for artists of color to follow.

Amiri Baraka, who originally penned his literary works under the name of LeRoi Jones, is often framed as the emblematic theatre artist of the Black Arts movement. Larry Neal, in fact, used Baraka's dramaturgy as the model with which he discussed and judged the aims and efficacy of the Black Arts movement. Among Baraka's most studied works is his 1964 Obie Award–winning play, *Dutchman*. Clearly a source of inspiration for Neal's critical conjectures, *Dutchman* dramatizes an encounter between a young Black man named Clay and a young white woman named Lula within the stale and stifling milieu of a New York subway car. Through the course of subway ride, Clay and Lula engage in flirtatious exchanges, witticisms, and retorts that eventually explode into a series of antagonistic exchanges – and lead to Clay's always-intended murder at the hands of Lula. At the heart of this edgy piece is a dramatization of Neal's contention that we live in "two Americas – one black, one white."[3] Rather than representing fleshed-out people, the characters of Clay and Lula are intended to be understood as metaphors; they represent two cultural spheres – Black and White America – and, further, they are drawn to suggest that the dissention between Black and White Americans persists despite temporal illusions of acceptance and cohesion.

Just as the work of Amiri Baraka serves as a foundational text in African American drama, the Chicano playwright Luis Valdez is considered to be the founding father of Chicano theatre; his dramas are synonymous with the canon of early Latinx theatre in America. Raised in a family of migrant farm workers, Valdez intimately understood the political plights facing Mexican Americans, and he merged his interests in theatre-making and political protest to create a distinct oeuvre shaped by agit-prop theatre practices. Valdez founded the still-running *El Teatro Campesino* and created a bevy of works that gave voice to the disenfranchised, all the while expanding the dramatic canon and expectations of dramatic structure.

Among Valdez's notable early works is the play *Los Vendidos* ("The Sellouts," 1967), a theatricalized commentary on the problematics of racist stereotyping and the importance of cultural pride. Set in a odds-and-ends store ("Honest Sancho's Used Mexican Lot and Mexican Curio Shop"), the proprietor, a character by the name of Sancho, is trying to wheel and deal with an anglicized Mexican American woman, Miss Jimenez. Miss Jimenez, we learn, is a secretary for California governor Ronald Reagan, and she is seeking to purchase a human-like, animated mannequin who will pass as an accommodating "Mexican type" employee for the governor's administration. The shop seems to feature an abundance of humanoid robots, and Miss Jimenez dutifully tests three models (the Farmworker, the Pachuco, and the Revolucionario). They fail to pass inspection due to their various shortcomings (all feature what Jimenez considers to be undesirable markers of Mexican/Mexican American identity). Finally, however, Miss Jimenez settles on the Mexican American model called "Eric García," which, happily, doesn't seem to exhibit any troublesome characteristics – that is, not until the Eric García model starts to glitch and begins chanting nationalistic rhetoric ("¡Viva la raza!"). The other models soon join in the chanting, causing an unsettled Jimenez to scream and abruptly vacate the shop. Upon Jimenez's departure, however, the audience learns that "Eric García" is *not* merchandise to be bought and sold – nor are any of the humanoid robots. Rather than being mechanical entities, the shop was filled with *people* who were simply *performing* for Jimenez and, in reality, it was the shop's owner, "Honest Sancho," who was a mechanical puppet while Jimenez, the play's title character, is revealed as "the sellout."

In the aforementioned works of Baraka and Valdez, both playwrights keenly capture the social and political milieu of the time: they are writing with their own communities in mind, cautioning Blacks and Chicanos of the dangers of blind assimilation void of cultural pride and autonomy. Moreover, they are imploring their audience members to reckon with the fact that access into the greater sociopolitical network of American society is not equitable to all. Notably, however, these propositions are offered in vividly artful ways, thus creating dramatic work that is at once entertaining, functional, time-sensitive – and timeless.

The multitude of happenings within the 1960s and 1970s makes it a particularly ripe and prolific era to examine the ways in which the explicit and unapologetic staging of the racial and cultural differences was recognized and produced for commercial consumption. Propelled by political and cultural agendas, these movements advanced the intellectual and creative pursuits of art-makers and influenced the work of theatre artists within community circles as well as in the theatrical circles among universities and colleges, regional theatres, and the stages of Off-Broadway and Broadway.

And yet, while the brief summation of Baraka's and Valdez's contributions offer some insight into their creative fortitude and the potency of their artistic eras, what also needs to be made transparent is that, as products of their time, the works of Baraka and Valdez (and many other writers in the Black Arts and Chicano movements) were not always inclusive in terms of *intracultural* representation. For example, some Black writers and cultural curators expressed bias against other Blacks due to their gender or sexual identities. Case in point: while Neal insisted that "A main tenet of Black Power is the necessity for Black people to define the world in their own terms,"[4] he also aggressively admonished deviations that he considered threatening to the political power of the Black community (namely, homosexuality). If we consider Neal's words now, we are confronted with the fact that "defining the world in one's one terms" seemingly champions the process of *self*-definition. However, by diminishing the role of women and outright castigating gay identities within African American communities, Neal and other leaders within the movement propagated a singular vision about who and what is most valued in Black culture. Thus, while fighting to affirm what should constitute as Black art (or "Blackness"), the delimiting rhetoric, punctuated by sexism and heterosexism, disenfranchised members of the Black community, thereby compromising the full potential of the movement's liberating aims.

In an attempt to combat the problematic residue of such intracultural bias, a number of more contemporary scholars have interrogated the sexism and homophobic aspects of the 1960s and 1970s, offering not only due critique but also revealing the underrecognized and underexamined contributors to the movements at hand. For instance, in *El Teatro Campesino: Theater in the Chicano Movement* (a comprehensive study by Yolanda Broyles-González of Luis Valdez and his historic company, El Teatro Campesino), Broyles-González aptly reminds us of the Chicanas, the Latinx woman in Valdez's company, that were invaluable forces shaping the work and trajectory of the theatre and the Chicano Arts movement.[5] These women were not only initiators of their own ingenious scripts, but their administrative and artistic acumen served to achieve the goals set before the whole. Broyles-González demonstrates that groundbreaking figures such as Baraka and Valdez are vital to our understanding of the development of contemporary American theatre, but her work also cautions that focusing upon the stories of oft-lauded figures in isolation may inadvertently take due attention away from other notable contributors.

Accordingly, while paying tribute to the works of Baraka and Valdez, it serves us well to explicitly acknowledge the invaluable contributions offered by many other writers of the 1960s and 1970s, two of which are the African American dramatist, Adrienne Kennedy, and the Cuban American dramatist, Maria Irene Fornes. Conjuring these women's names prompts the words of activist/journalist Anna Julia Cooper who famously asserted: "Only the BLACK WOMAN can say 'when and where I enter, in the quiet, undisputed dignity of my womanhood, without violence and without suing or special patronage, then and there the whole *Negro race enters with me.*'"[6] Cooper, of course, was insisting that Black people could not find full agency, equity, and liberty unless Black *women* were indistinguishable citizens in the quest for freedom. Her words emphasized the belief that Black women are not mere followers of a political agenda toward justice, but rather they are leaders in the struggle – pathmakers to justice and equality. In the terrain of the American theatre, women of color have tilled, labored, and harvested just like their male counterparts, thereby creating further avenues for those – of various identificatory categories – to follow.

Among these groundbreaking dramatists of note is Adrienne Kennedy, a writer whose play, *Funnyhouse of a Negro*, won a 1964 Obie Award the same year that Amiri Baraka was bestowed that honor. *Funnyhouse of a Negro* is a play that captures the torn psyche of its protagonist, Sarah, an erudite young woman who wrestles with her sense of liminality as she struggles to understand herself amidst American society's unyielding perceptions of "Black" and "white." Animating the maddening effects of racism, Kennedy creates a theatrical world that reflects her protagonist's mental state of fragmentation, contradiction, and confusion through a pastiche of repeated narratives, poetic refrains, and grotesque imagery. In so doing, *Funnyhouse of a Negro* deviates from Aristotelian realism and evinces a tangential, circular, and episodic structure – a hallmark of many Kennedy plays. Thus, in both form and content, the early work of Adrienne Kennedy challenges easy assumptions about what a Black play "should" address – and *how*. Rather than acquiescing to penning storylines that were readily identified to be nationalistic in nature, Kennedy's dramaturgy challenged the assumed parameters of the Black Arts movement, revealing the reality of its permeability and serving as a daring model of independent innovation, then and now.

Just as Kennedy modeled the ability to cultivate a unique voice and vision, thereby inspiring countless dramatists to follow, the Cuban American playwright Maria Irene Fornes – known to many as "The Mother of the Avant-Garde" – was not only a leader in the experimental theatre movement of the 1960s and 1970s, but she has proven to be one of the most impactful figures on America's theatrical landscape. Among the oft-cited plays penned by Fornes (a nine-time Obie winner) is the play *Fefu and Her Friends* (1977).

Noted for both its woman-centered dialogue and innovative dramaturgical structure, *Fefu and Her Friends* is an intriguing example of Fornes's daring imagination. Distinguished by its all-female cast and its characters' unapologetically frank and revealing conversations, the theatrical staging of *Fefu and Her Friends* also marks it as unique. As instructed by Fornes, the audience of *Fefu* is directed to engage in dynamic spectatorship; during the second of three acts, the audience (divided into four groups) literally rotates so that each group witnesses a reenactment of four different scenes (on the lawn, in a study, in a bedroom, and in the kitchen) within the span of the play's second act. Boldly breaking away from traditional theatre conventions, Fornes's directives destabilize audience expectations and literally force them to take on new perspectives while also imploring them to engage with distinctly women-centered subject matter. Focusing on the interrelationships of Fefu and her seven friends, the characters contemplate and converse on a range of different topics, among them: misogyny, marriage, mental illness, disability, sexuality, depression, and friendship. Voicing both typical and taboo topics, Fornes's play aims to liberate female representation from societal expectations.

Paying due attention to Black and Latinx playwrights of the 1960s and 1970s reveals that people of color have always used theatre to address social-political concerns through their artistic activism. Moreover, even in strategically cohesive moments, theatre has served as a platform to explore and reveal the contradictions and complexities within our given communities. Nevertheless, the work of today's contemporary artists of color has become even more self-reflexive, often complicating notions of monolithic paradigms of identity. This is not to say that today's writers are any less strategic, political, or community-oriented, but rather that they are ever more poised to critique and comment upon inscriptions of exclusion and inclusion within both *inter*cultural and *intra*cultural terrain (that is, they not only address issues related to race, but they also explore topics related to identificatory positions such as sexuality, gender, or class). Propelled by our ever-evolving discourse of contemporary identity politics, today's playwrights increasingly animate queries regarding membership and status. In so doing, they not only counter qualitative judgments related to "whiteness" or "blackness" or "brownness" (the list goes on), but they also challenge previously held definitions of what constitutes a culturally specific play. While creating work that interrogates the rigidity of traditional identificatory categories, today's artists challenge the limitations and boundaries that have traditionally restricted the ways in which African American and Latinx dramas have (or have not) been deemed "canonical" within the annals of American drama.

A broadening of what is deemed as American drama (without qualifiers related to cultural specificity) can be witnessed by what regional theatres are producing nationwide. In the past, many of the trailblazing dramas by artists of color were, predominately, debuted and developed within New York City's experimental, Off-Broadway theatres – havens known for developing cutting-edge work. While New York still maintains its reputation for fostering new voices, theatre companies outside and beyond New York are increasingly playing major roles in dispersing and championing the work of diverse voices. Nationwide, regional theatres have clearly committed to staging plays penned by Black writers, as evidenced by *American Theatre's* "Top 10 Most Produced Plays" lists. In fact, in the past four theatre seasons (from 2016 to 2020), two "Black Plays" have made the listing each year and, of special note: all eight of these plays were penned by Black women.[7] Moreover, even more recently, much has been made among critics and scholars about a purported surge of representation, that is, a number of publications have explored the seeming proliferation of plays writing by Black writers for American stages. From city papers with cultural cachet like *The New York Times* and *The Washington Post,* to trade magazines such as *American Theatre* and well-respected journals such as *TDR,* much attention has been paid to Black playwrights who are fostering both inter- and intracultural critiques that make them as ripe and ready for the classroom as they are for the stage.

Furthering this contention is the fact a cursory glance at the Pulitzer Prizes in Drama over the last decade reveals a level of racial and gender diversity that, indisputably, did not exist in previous decades. Not only does *American Theatre's* citing of "top plays" reveal the way in which Black female playwrights are increasingly recognized, but it also proves important to note that from 2009 to 2019, six of the Pulitzer Prize–winning plays were written by women and, out of these eleven plays, five were written by people of color (moreover, four plays out of *those* were written by *women of color* – two penned by the very same author, Lynn Nottage).[8]

Two of the aforementioned women-of-color Pulitzer winners, Lynn Nottage and Quiara Alegría Hudes, are particularly befitting subjects to consider when thinking of the "now and then": how regional theatres are becoming invaluable proponents of Black and Latinx voices and how American Theatre, as a whole, is continuing to develop and dismantle its inner silos. Progenitors of critically acclaimed, innovative, and canon-building work, Nottage and Hudes are present-day examples of writers who are broadening the dramatic landscape through their theatrical inter-ventions. These artists befittingly represent the place and space we are in now – they defy easy categorization: they are interdisciplinary in their creative expressions, and wide-ranging in their topics and life/art-shaping experiences. They proudly assert their womanhood and cultural back-grounds, yet resist in having these particulars curtail the subject or design of their work.

Lynn Nottage

Brooklyn-born and raised, the playwright Lynn Nottage – informed by myriad experiences – gives proof to the fact that distinctively disparate experiences yield intellectual and creative riches. One of Nottage's own literary missions has been to "sustain the complexity"[9] of her characters and their worlds and, without a doubt, she dutifully navigates through the world of theatre with an indefinable ingenuity. For even the casual observer of Nottage's plays, one is struck by the breadth and range of her oeuvre, revealing an inherent defiance against easy categorization. Devising works that would satisfy a wide range of theatrical palates is a celebratory consequence of Nottage's familial upbringing, formal educational experiences, rigorous artistic training, and manifold global ventures.

While Nottage's artistic pursuits and political advocacy would eventually take her all over the world, her craft as a playwright began, she has said, at the kitchen table of her childhood home: "Down there was a gathering place for so many women. To come home from school, and my grandmother would be sitting at the table, and my mother would be sitting at the table. The woman from across the street would be sitting at the table. And they all had stories to tell."[10] She listened to the women that surrounded her – they were teachers (like her mother, who also was a principal), as well as nurses, artists, and activists, who, alongside her father (a child psychologist), honed Nottage's nuanced understanding of the human condition in all its triumphs and challenges.

Nottage gives special credit to the women in her family for shaping her creative senses and political sensibilities: "Sometimes, I think about what an incredibly privileged life I have because of the courageous choices that that woman made. And, I also think that's true of my mother, who was a feminist, and in many ways, it's her brave choices that gave birth to me as a writer."[11] The stories that were birthed by Nottage's familial inspirations and crafted during her childhood within the pages of her personal journal eventually led her to pursue art-making with a sense of certainty and pointed direction.

When praising Nottage, critics and audience members routinely celebrate her sharp, resonant dialogue and vivid characterizations, applauding her fluency with comedy and satire, as well as searing, soul-searching drama. Evidenced again and again is the fact that Nottage has the uncanny ability to capitalize on both the weight *and* levity of a given scenario, whether it is inspired by conventional day-to-day routines, anomalous life-or-death predicaments, or the sheer ubiquity of life's unpredictability. This artistic versatility has led to Nottage's notable success within regional theatres. Not only does Nottage consistently create the kind of compelling work that finds a ready home in regional theatres, but she also continuously manages to surprise audience members with her constant refashioning. The astounding variety of subjects and styles found in Nottage's writing has also resulted in a recurring refrain among those familiar with her canon. Artists and scholars alike frequently refer to Nottage's "complexity," readily observing the absence of an identifiable writerly voice among her plays. Addressing this, director Kate Whoriskey rightly noted that Nottage simply "has more range than other playwrights, and she has the ability to be very specific," thereby creating a situation in which "the material she's writing about finds the style."[12]

This is not to say, however, that Nottage's works are void of any commonality – quite to the contrary. In an interview with the *Washington Post's* Celia Wren, Nottage acknowledged both the diversity and central focus of her writing: "My plays are stylistically different yet thematically similar. … What ties them all together is, by and large, women from the African diaspora, women who, in some regards, are marginalized by the culture at large."[13] This truism is frequently underscored by those who study, write, and teach about Nottage, and succinctly referenced by the theatre scholar Sandra Shannon when she observes that Nottage creates "unapologetically female centered plays." Shannon goes on to assert that Nottage's works often feature a prototypical character "who is well ahead of the times in her stubborn will to define her own terms which often means that she breaks the mold society has set in place for her race and gender." Breaking societal expectations, these female characters "trample stereotypes and create more individualized portraits of African American womanhood."[14]

But beyond shattering stereotypes, Nottage is also driven by the desire to write the stories of everyday "sheroes" whose grit and perseverance, whose survival as Black women, is a feat in itself that deserves our attention:

> My plays are about ordinary, extraordinary women. I'm fully aware of that. Many people like to imagine that their ancestor was a prince or a king. But what I recognize is that I come from a long line of really hard-working women who did not write books, and who tended to other people's children. Who washed laundry and sewed clothing, and picked cotton, and cut sugar cane, but who were extraordinary in their own right, and were the building blocks for who I am, and the building blocks for this country itself because they were raising white children, who became the leaders of this country. These women, in their own remote way, helped shaped the sensibilities of this country.[15]

These "sheroes" are not espousing heroism through superhuman acts, nor are their actions necessarily or wholly admirable. Rather, as Jocelyn Buckner explains, Nottage's stories repeatedly disclose "a tale of unsung struggle for survival and personal happiness among individuals living along and beyond the margins of society. The heart of Nottage's dramaturgy lies in nuanced negotiations of complex stories, where individuals are neither good nor bad, but rather valiantly seeking to better their lot in life."[16]

By theatricalizing the personal and collective histories of her characters, Nottage works to fill long-standing voids in American theatre. She also fills these voids in another palpable way: by serving as a teacher and guide for new, up-and-coming writers. Her active presence in this way is particularly important, of course, for playwrights of color:

> I continue to mentor a number of playwrights of color, who are becoming important writers in their own right. I think in some ways, they probably may not exist if there weren't writers like us who cracked open the regional theaters with plays that became incredibly successful and allowed artistic directors to say, "Hey, we have an audience for this work." I feel proud to be part of the frontline of change in the theatrical landscape.[17]

As a beacon for the next generation, Nottage has penned innumerable works that captivate and inspire. Among these works is the widely acclaimed and frequently staged play *Intimate Apparel*.

Jointly produced by South Coast Repertory and Center Stage (now known as Baltimore Center Stage), *Intimate Apparel* was honed within the walls of two regional theatre companies in 2003 before making its New York debut at Roundabout Theatre Company in 2004. Originally helmed by Kate Whoriskey (Nottage's frequent collaborator), *Intimate Apparel* would go on to be the most produced play in the 2005–6 theatre season (with sixteen productions). The play managed to maintain notable popularity the following theatre season by tying as the fourth most produced play in 2006–7 (with nine regional productions to its credit).[18]

A poignant drama that recasts the thematic concept of The American Dream through the toil and yearnings of an eclectic assortment of characters, *Intimate Apparel* offers familiar tropes of self-making, belonging, immigration, ownership, and communal ties through the eyes and lives of minoritized citizens. Among the play's characters: the central protagonist, Esther, a Black seamstress whose personal grit and entrepreneurial impetus grants her the possibility of independence (but whose misplaced trust wounds her emotionally and fiscally); Mr. Marks, a Jewish immigrant and store owner whose business relationship with Esther percolates with sincere, but futile affections; Mayme, a Black woman who trades her body – and forlorn dreams of being a concert pianist – to survive; and George, the Barbadian immigrant who swindled his way into Esther's life to chase his own dubious desires.

Each character within *Intimate Apparel* has pursued a unique path toward attaining material security, thereby highlighting the various ways The American Dream may be envisioned and pursued – and achieved and lost. Inclusive of differences in race, gender, class, nationality, and religion, the play's host of characters explicitly encompass a wide range of vantage points, yet foreground the experience of Esther, a Black woman. In doing so, Nottage models a Black Feminist strategy, one that affirms and recognizes the matrixes of identity and the necessity to address the intersectional ways in which oppressive systems function. Unsurprisingly, the source of this artistic commentary was directly inspired by Nottage's own biography.

When speaking of the origins of *Intimate Apparel,* Nottage disclosed that the play spawned from the discovery of an old photograph, that of her great grandmother. She found the photograph while cleaning out her grandmother's house. The picture features her serious-looking great grandmother holding two little girls (one, presumably, being Nottage's grandmother). Nottage knew that her great grandmother had been a seamstress in New York, but she knew little else of her life. In an effort to, ostensibly, restore her own history, Nottage decided to research what her grandmother's life may have been like – and then wrote a play about it. Accordingly, *Intimate Apparel* – in origin and content – vividly illustrates Nottage's acclaimed practice of giving voice to the underexamined populace. She gives silenced, forgotten, and underexplored lives the attention they deserve, prompting new stories to be staged, and old histories to be documented.

Quiara Alegría Hudes

Like Lynn Nottage, the incomparable Quiara Alegría Hudes – a playwright, lyricist, and essayist – is an artist that defies easy categorization. Be it penning plays, staged musicals – or playing or penning music – Hudes has honed a bountiful assortment of talents. Self-described as a "a writer, strong wife and mother of two, barrio feminist and native of West Philly, U.S.A.,"[19] Hudes was born into a close-knit family whose influence on her artistic crafts and creative subject matter is palpable. Raised primarily in the household of her Puerto Rican mother and stepfather, while also remaining close to her Jewish father and his kin, Hudes grew up in West Philadelphia. There she was gifted with unique experiences and exposures, shaped by her culturally rich, artistically infused, and politically active family members and community happenings.

Whether it was listening to the Afro-Caribbean music her mother religiously played at home "every morning, volume eleven"[20] or the lessons she gleaned from the professional musicians that surrounded her, Hudes's musical sensibility was shaped by a number of valuable confluences and influences. Crediting her family with infecting her with enthusiasm for music and, importantly, introducing her to a bevy of artists and musical genres throughout her youth, Hudes carried this instilled passion through her journey studying classical music (her instrument, piano) at the celebrated Settlement Music School in Philadelphia, and up to her later training while pursuing a BA degree in music composition at Yale University.

Hudes has shared that during her undergraduate studies, she found herself less invested in using words, invariably leaning on the composition of music rather than the writing of text to express herself. As a young adult, however, Hudes began to realize that "something was not clicking into place."[21] It was not until her mother pointedly *reminded* her of how writing had been so central to her, reminding her that she is a writer just as much as a composer, that prompted her to recognize how imperative it was that she exercise both talents with equal vigilance. Hudes reflected on this pivotal realization with the *Broadway.com*, "Tales from the Script" journalist Beth Stevens in 2016:

> My mom looked me in the eye and said, "This is our history: it's not written down, it's not recorded, it could disappear." So she gave me a task to do, and I would not have done that task if it did not resonate deeply within my core. Sometimes I wish I could just write plays that don't have that social context of what happens if this particular story never gets told, but I haven't been able to escape that yet. There's still more to say.[22]

Propelled by the fervent encouragement of her mother, Hudes ended up pursuing an MFA in playwrighting at Brown University. This grounding was then complemented by the critical attention she received with *Yemaya's Belly* (2003) – a piece that earned her the 2003 Clauder Competition for New England Playwrighting, the Paula Vogel Award in Playwrighting, as well as the Kennedy Center–sponsored ACTF Latina Playwriting Award. Following this notable success, Hudes went on to captivate even broader audiences when her play *Elliot, A Soldier's Fugue* (a play inspired by her "real-life" cousin, Elliot) premiered at Atlanta's Alliance Theatre in 2006 and became a finalist for 2007 Pulitzer Prize in Drama. The success of *Elliot, A Soldier's Fugue* led to the development of a second play based on Elliot's life, *Water by the Spoonful*, which premiered at yet another regional theatre, Hartford Stage – and ended up earning Hudes the coveted Pulitzer Prize in 2012. Rounding out Hudes's aspiration to create a dramatic triptych (and demonstrating the fertile grounds of regional theatre) was her third play in her Elliot trilogy, *The Happiest Song Plays Last*, which premiered at Chicago's Goodman Theatre in 2013.

Gifted with her nuanced understanding of dialogue, lyrics, and music, Hudes's ability to oscillate between these related, yet distinctly different forms of artistic expression, has buoyed her ability to not only pen her own plays, but to also partner with a number of notable entities and artists. Among Hudes's more well-known collaborations are those achieved through sizable partners such as The Cleveland Orchestra, as well as singular – but unquestionably paradigmatic – partnerships as evidenced through the work created with fellow Pulitzer Prize– and Tony Award–winning creator, Lin-Manuel Miranda (her co-creator for the Tony Award–winning musical, *In the Heights*).

At the heart of Hudes's artistry is the connecting tissue of music, and although music does not always play a central role in her dramatic work, Hudes attests to the ways in which music is always a determining factor in how she *hears* her plays, their characters, and the settings in which they live. Similarly, another recurring element within Hudes's dramaturgy is the imprint of cultural roots and communal sensibilities within the worlds she creates. Lin-Manuel Miranda attributes this thread to the same impulse and influences that compelled Hudes to seriously devote herself to writing in the first place: "You have to remember, this is a woman who went into playwriting because she sensed that her family stories – those in Puerto Rico, those in Philadelphia – would fade if she did not give them language."[23] Significant in this conjuring is Miranda's acknowledgment of Hudes's Latinaness *and* Jewishness. While Hudes understands herself as a Latinx woman, she also understands herself as a bi-cultural person and resists the limiting nomenclature often associated with the simple label of being a "Latina writer," noting "I think 'playwright' is the larger family I feel most at home with."[24] This is a not a diminishment of her Puerto Rican heritage, but rather the embrace of her own lived complexities – complexities that have informed how she experiences and navigates the world – in real life and within her plays:

> I feel that my writing reflects my own multi-cultural sensibilities and is that totally mainstream yet? I don't know. But I think it puts people at ease, because it lands somewhere in between. In fact as I've been dealing with some characters that are bi-racial, mixed ethnicity, and it really strikes a chord with a lot of people with a mixed cultural background and I think it reverberates to a larger philosophical question. Which is . . . "Where do I belong?" "Where do I fit in?" It's fascinating how I found that to strike a chord. I think it's something of a new frontier. But it asks an age-old question.[25]

To be sure, questions of belonging are seeded within the landscape of Hudes's life and the lives of those to which she is closest. Case in point is

Hudes's play, *Elliot, A Soldier's Fugue.* As frequently shared, the writing of *Elliot, A Soldier's Fugue* was informed by Hudes's relationship with her uncle, George, and her cousin, Elliot. While Hudes used her own dramatic imagination to sculpt the story, places, and people fictionalized in *Elliot,* she paid homage to her family by using their first names in the piece, crediting the fact that "their candid stories are woven into the heart and soul of this play."[26]

Like the multitude of American theatre's impactful dramas, *Elliot, A Soldier's Fugue* began its professional journey away from Broadway's lights; an early version of the play was initially produced at Miracle Theatre in Portland, Oregon (also known as Teatro Milagro) in 2005 before moving to its official world premiere production at New York's Page 73 in 2006. Initially produced amid America's entanglement with the Iraq War (2003–11), the play reverberated with layered, contemporaneous relevance. The title character, Elliot, was a soldier in the Iraq War while the play's other male leads, Pop and Grandpop, fought in Vietnam and Korea, respectively. Paying tribute to American veterans and the consequences (physical and emotional) of battles waged to defend American ideals, *Elliot, A Soldier's Fugue* not only dramatizes intergenerational connections within the play, but it also offers common ground among audience members outside distinctions such as race, culture, age, or gender.

The memories that besiege the three generations of *Elliot's* Puerto Rican family are, as conveyed by the title, reminiscent of a fugue composed by Johann Sebastian Bach. The collection of perspectives, the varying vantage points and experiences, and the distinct individual voices collide and harmonize to create the play's contrapuntal narrative. When the character of Grandpop extemporaneously elucidates on the artistry of Bach, he speaks of fugues – but is also speaking on the very construct of the play's dramaturgy:

> The fugue is like an argument. It starts in one voice. The voice is the melody, the single solitary melodic line. The statement. Another voice creeps up on the first one. Voice two responds to voice one. The tangle together. They argue, they become messy. They create dissonance. Two, three, four lines clashing. You think, Good god, they'll never untie themselves. How did this mess get started in the first place? Major keys, minor keys, all at once on top of each other. *(Leans in)* It's all about untying the knot.[27]

Untying the knot – giving the attention and time needed to release each strand, thereby allowing each voice to be heard – proves to be Hudes's charge. Though her play focuses on the lives of three men, *Elliot, A Soldier's*

Fugue relinquishes any impulse to cloak these men's vulnerabilities with overt masculinity; the characters are real and raw, determined and emboldened, wary and wounded. Time is equally fluid in *Elliot* – Hudes lets us know that the play defies chronological logics; it "ping-pongs back and forth between scenes," ricocheting between past and present. Likewise, the space described in the play also oscillates: some moments are staged in an "empty space," a space that feels forlorn and weathered while at other times we see the men in the "garden space" – a space that is "teeming with life."[28]

The preponderance of elements that speak to a refusal of singularities and fixed perspectives is further accentuated by the ruminations of the play's lone female character, Ginny, when she speaks of her garden:

> I planted bearded irises next to palms. I planted tulips with a border of cacti. All the things the book tells you: "Don't ever plant these together," "Guide to Proper Gardening." Well I got on my knees and planted them side by side. I'm like, You have to throw all preconceived notions out the window, You have to plant wild. . . . It doesn't matter what the seed is. So long as it grows. I plant like I want and to hell with the consequences. I planted a hundred clematis vines by the kitchen window, and the next thing I know sage is growing there. The tomato vines gave me beautiful tomatoes. The bamboo shot out from the ground. And the heliconia! Each leaf is actually a cup. It collects rainwater. So any weary traveler can stop and take a drink.[29]

Not only does the presence of Ginny help juxtapose the imagery of war and death-filled battle fields against the life-affirming, generative vision of a prolific garden, but her sentiments echo Grandpop's reflections on fugues. Relishing in the freeing integration of different plants, Ginny celebrates the diversity found in her garden; she recognizes the unexpected delight, comfort, and satiation that come from bringing together that which may originally have seemed too disparate or incompatible. All her words also echo the familiar frames associated with The American Dream: the rewards of ingenuity when one "makes something out of nothing," the affirmation gained from seeding and harvesting one's labors, and the security that comes from laying claim and possessing ownership.

Conclusion: Opening the Door Wider

Lynn Nottage's *Intimate Apparel* and Quiara Alegría Hudes's *Elliot, A Soldier's Fugue* are distinctly different dramas, forged by distinctively different dramatists, yet, notably, both Nottage and Hudes, as women of color, share a sociopolitical vantage point that imbues them with perspectives that consciously and directly engage in the recognition of multiple identificatory positions. Nottage, an African American woman, and Hudes, a Latinx woman, are writing in culturally specific ways, but also in ways that reveal a cultural mélange of references and influences – in this way, they both activate Black Feminist Principles of inclusion and really do speak to the promise of an *American* experience, one that is culturally rich and experientially varied and reflected in the textures of their own personal lives, as well as in the worlds they are creating. The fact that these writers were also born and raised in cities – New York and West Philadelphia – which are, in themselves, shaped by diasporic networks, also gives rise to their ways of knowing the lived reality of diversified communities. As such, Nottage and Hudes are particularly primed to represent the multifarious viewpoints that are now, more routinely, adapted and presented on the regional stage.

In highlighting Nottage and Hudes as playwrights whose work symbolize a growing openness to presenting the textured fabric of American culture and identities, we can see two artists whose works not only aim in expanding how we frame the American Dramatic Canon, but they also give us a means to recognize the way in which regional theatre in America has been key in creating audiences – commercial and scholarly – to propagate a fuller understanding of what constitutes American drama and what qualifies as a canonical classic.

In citing this shift, it is important to recognize that while Nottage and Hudes are both recipients of the Pulitzer Prize, their Pulitzer-winning plays are not the ones that receive focus in this chapter. Rather, it feels especially apropos to examine (as is done here) the works that have not achieved what some may perceive as the ultimate honor. In choosing to turn to other notable work rather than simply pay homage to the most highly honored dramas of Nottage and Hudes, one opens up the chance to cogitate on the politics related to publicly touted honors and, moreover, to consider how the act of bestowing them is simultaneously a source of celebration and an expression of the limitations and biases embedded in America's award-giving systems. As is the case for all award systems, potential nominees and winners are championed through mechanisms of exposure – and exposure not only depends upon whether artists are invited and/or included in particular networks, but it is also determined by whether or not an artist's work ascribes to subjective rubrics or the preferences of selected adjudicators. With this understanding, audiences must always weigh awards (like any formal review or evaluative procedure) carefully, understanding that social, political, and cultural politics inform how accolades are granted or withheld. Likewise, audiences must actively pursue the discovery of artists beyond the bounds of familiar theatre-producing circles if we are truly prioritizing diversity, equity, and inclusion.

And thus, a problematic paradox confronting many acclaimed writers of color is the tenuous joy of personal affirmation amidst the knowledge that fellow artists are still experiencing diminishment or dismissal due to the lack of systematic equity. Befittingly, Hudes and her sister, Gabriela Serena Sanchez, shed light on this tension when they shared the stage and offered their keynote speech, "Pausing and Breathing" at the 2018 ATHE conference in Boston, Massachusetts. With refreshing honesty, Hudes spoke of the precarious experience of critique that all theatre artists are subjected to – and how these are often exacerbated for artists of color. While affirming her gratitude and love for the industry that has celebrated her contributions, Hudes openly acknowledged the anxieties and fears she grapples with when confronted with the sexism and racism that stills permeate the world of theatre, in venues large and small. With biting frankness, Hudes noted that

> Theatre, at least at the upper echelons of the professional field, is frequently elitist, expensive, exclusive, and nondemocratic. Our biggest-budget theatrical institutions purport to encourage equality and champion the underdog, but in fact must appease wealthy patrons and subscribers, disproportionately feature male leadership, and carry stubborn institutional memory beholden to the white aesthetics and values they have built themselves upon for decades . . .
>
> Can institutional theatre not hold multiple worldviews and paradigms? Do multimillion-dollar capital projects lead to fancy theatres that reinforce a single aesthetic mode? . . .
>
> Perhaps the greatest revolution I can imagine is to insist that no matter how "other" my characters are in the white wealthy spaces of theatre, to nonetheless affirm that they are not guests on the American stage. To insist that I am a center, I am a hostess. New hostesses are required. My art is hospitality and an open door.[30]

What made Hudes's keynote remarks especially resonant was the source of the commentary. Again, Hudes is a Pulitzer Prize–winning playwright and, thus, represents an apex of success for many. Likewise, her sister, Gabriela Serena Sanchez, is accomplished in her own right in the world of efficacious art-activism. By presenting their differing vantage points (yet shared perspective) regarding the potential for theatre to activate inclusive practices and bring forth greater sociopolitical shifts, Hudes and Sanchez are powerful models for others to follow. But Hudes's words, and her resolution to share her sentiments – as difficult as they may have been to reveal or receive – speak to the need for more work to be done. Indeed, new – and more – hosts are required.

The theatre world not only needs more writers of color to be heard, but it needs more beacons and facilitators of color involved in all aspect of theatre administration and production in order to actualize stated efforts toward diversity, equity, and inclusion. This latter point has been made time and time again; it is an age-old declaration and obvious truism, but one that has yet to be sufficiently realized. Despite the marked progress that has been made, the pervasive homogeneity in American regional theatre has yet to be deconstructed and, in fact, at the time of this writing (penned in the midst of history-making protests), we are starkly confronted with the challenges before us.[31] Hopefully, however, with the aid of advocating guides and innkeepers such as Quiara Alegría Hudes and Lynn Nottage, creatives of color and their allies (cited and uncited) will harness the potential of regional theatre to break down barriers and open doors – while further widening the threshold.

Notes

1. L. Neal, "The Black Arts Movement," *The Drama Review: TDR*, 12:4 (Summer 1968), p. 29.
2. Ibid., p. 39.
3. Ibid., p. 29.
4. Ibid.
5. See Y. Broyles-González, *Teatro Campesino: Theater in the Chicano Movement* (University of Texas Press, 1994).
6. Cooper, *A Voice from the South*, p. 31.
7. For the 2016–17 season, *A Raisin in the Sun* by Lorraine Hansberry and *Intimate Apparel* by Lynn Nottage made the list; for the 2017–18 season, *A Raisin in the Sun* by Hansberry and *Skeleton Crew* by Dominique Morisseau made the list; for 2018–19, *Skeleton Crew* by Dominique Morisseau and *Sweat* by Lynn Nottage made the list; and for 2019–20, *School Girls or, The African Mean Girls Play* by Jocelyn Bioh and *Pipeline* by Dominique Morisseau made the list. See www.americantheatre.org/tag/top-10-most-produced-plays/.
8. To lay claim in even clearer terms: last year, in 2019, the Pulitzer Prize in Drama was awarded to Jackie Sibblies Drury and her play *Fairview*. Drury was the third Black woman to be named a Pulitzer Prize winner in Drama, joining the company of Lynn Nottage, who won the award in 2017 for *Sweat*, while also securing the award in 2009 for *Ruined*, and Suzan-Lori Parks, who won the prize in 2002 for *Topdog/Underdog*). Lin-Manuel Miranda became the second Latinx playwright to win the prize in 2016 for *Hamilton* (following the trail

blazed by Nilo Cruz, who won it in 2003 for *Anna in the Tropics*), and Quiara Alegría Hudes, the first Latina to win the Pulitzer for Drama, won the award in 2012 for *Water by the Spoonful*, followed by Ayad Akhtar – the first South Asian playwright to win the Pulitzer for Drama – who took home the coveted honor in 2013 for his play *Disgraced.* Thus, in a single decade, half of the Pulitzer Prizes for Drama were awarded to playwrights of color, and six out of ten were penned by women (three of which are *women of color* – Nottage claiming two of the awards in a single decade's time).

9. J. Buckner, "'Sustaining the Complexity' of Lynn Nottage," in J. Buckner (ed.), *A Critical Companion to Lynn Nottage* (Routledge, 2016), p. 185.

10. "Lynn Nottage, 1964," *Contemporary Black Biography,* January 3, 2020, www .encyclopedia.com/education/news-wires-white-papers-and-books/nottage-l ynn-1964.

11. Buckner, "'Sustaining the Complexity' of Lynn Nottage," p. 185.

12. C. Wren, "Playwright Lynn Nottage Startles Audiences," *Washington Post,* April 22, 2011, www.washingtonpost.com/theater-dance/playwright-lynn-nottage-startles-audiences/2011/04/15/AF8XPpPE_story.html.

13. C. Wren, "Playwright Lynn Nottage Startles Audiences."

14. S. G. Shannon, "Freedom Is a Debt to Repay; a Legacy to Uphold," in Buckner, *A Critical Companion to Lynn Nottage*, p. 1.

15. J. Buckner, "On Creativity and Collaboration: A Conversation with Lynn Nottage, Seret Scott, and Kate Whoriskey," in Buckner, *A Critical Companion to Lynn Nottage*, p. 184.

16. Buckner, "'Sustaining the Complexity' of Lynn Nottage," p. 9.

17. Buckner, "On Creativity and Collaboration," pp. 198–99.

18. *American Theatre* Editors, "The Top 10 Most-Produced Plays: 1994–2014," *American Theatre,* September 23, 2014, www.americantheatre.org/2014/09/2 3/top-10-most-plays-1994–2014/#2005.

19. Q. A. Hudes, "Bio – Quiara Alegría Hudes," https://tdps.berkeley.edu/reso urces/playwrights-color/quiara-alegria-hudes.

20. D. Pollack-Pelzner, "Quiara Alegría Hudes Rewrites the American Landscape," *New Yorker,* April 5, 2018, www.newyorker.com/culture/per sons-of-interest/quiara-Alegría-hudes-gives-the-american-landscape-a-puert o-rican-voice.

21. M. Gardley, "Music Is Her Muse: Quiara Alegría Hudes and Her Path to the Pulitzer," *The Brooklyn Rail,* July–August 2012, http://brooklynrail.org/2012/08/ theater/music-is-her-muse-quiara-alegra-hudes-and-her-path-to-the-pulitzer.

22. B. Stevens, "Quiara Alegría Hudes on Why She Wrote *Daphne's Dive* & How Lin-Manuel Miranda Is Like *Seinfeld's* Kramer," *Broadway.com,* May 19, 2016, www.broadway.com/buzz/184898/quiara-Alegría-hudes-on-why-she-wrote-d aphnes-dive-how-lin-manuel-miranda-is-like-seinfelds-kramer/.

23. Pollack-Pelzner, "Quiara Alegría Hudes Rewrites the American Landscape."

24. A. Soloski, "A Family's Story Spans a Trilogy, and Beyond," *New York Times,* November 28, 2012, www.nytimes.com/2012/12/02/theater/for-quiara-alegria -hudes-plays-are-family.html.

25. Quoted in F. Piantadosi, "Lisa Loomer & Quiara Alegría Hudes," *The Dramatist*, p. 58.
26. Q. A. Hudes, *Elliot, A Soldiers Fugue* (Theatre Communications Group, 2012), p. vii.
27. Ibid., p. 35.
28. Ibid.
29. Ibid., pp. 22–23.
30. Q. A. Hudes and G. S. Sanchez, "Pausing and Breathing: Two Sisters Deliver the ATHE 2018 Conference Keynote Address," *Theatre Topics*, 29:1 (March 2019), pp. 1–13.
31. As I write this, it has been three weeks since the May 2020 death of George Floyd, an African American man who was killed by a white Minneapolis police officer despite the victim's belabored exhortations of "I can't breathe" – the very words uttered by another African American man, Eric Garner, when he died in a police chokehold in 2014. Floyd's murder served as a tipping point for activists and supporters of the Black Lives Matter movement (a movement founded in 2013 in response to the acquittal of the racially motivated murderer of seventeen-year-old Trayvon Martin), leading to both national and international upheaval in the quest for racial justice.

Select Bibliography

Broyles-González, Y. *Teatro Campesino: Theater in the Chicano Movement.* University of Texas Press, 1994.

Buckner, J. (ed.). *A Critical Companion to Lynn Nottage.* Routledge, 2016.

Carpenter, F. C. *Coloring Whiteness: Acts of Critique in Black Performance.* University of Michigan Press, 2014.

Cooper, A. J. *A Voice from the South.* Oxford University Press, 1988.

Hudes, Q. A. *Elliot, A Soldiers Fugue.* Theatre Communications Group, 2012.

Hudes, Q. A., and G. S. Sanchez. "Pausing and Breathing: Two Sisters Deliver the ATHE 2018 Conference Keynote Address." *Theatre Topics*, 29:1 (2019).

Kennedy, A. "Funnyhouse of a Negro." In *Adrienne Kennedy in One Act.* Minneapolis: University of Minnesota Press, 1998.

Mahala, M. *Penumbra: The Premier Stage for African American Drama.* University of Minnesota Press, 2013.

Neal, L. "The Black Arts Movement." *TDR*, 12:4 (1968), 28–39.

Nottage, L. *Intimate Apparel and Fabulation, or the Re-education of Undine.* Theatre Communications Group, 2006.

CHAPTER 7

El Jardín Mágico

Commissions, Collaboration, and New Play Development in American Regional Theatre

David A. Crespy

At the heart of new play development in the regional theatre in America is the collaborative relationship between artistic directors, dramaturgs, literary managers, playwrights, directors, actors, and designers. Often this collaboration begins with an artistic director commissioning a play and providing a "magic garden" of collaborating artists and audience, where a playwright can develop an idea into a fully realized script through levels of workshop up to and including theatrical production. Yet the regional theatre was not actually created as a place for new plays and new play development. While it might be argued that this realm of American theatre has become one of the most fertile environments for new work, with many original plays growing from regional premieres to national success, the regional theatre was originally created with idea of bringing "classic" works of the theatre to America's theatre communities outside of New York, Chicago, and Los Angeles. From its conception in the late 1940s until 1967, regional theatre was designed to populate the United States with resident acting companies bringing a repertoire of theatre classics (mostly European and some American) to audiences who would otherwise not experience live professional performance. Theatres like the Guthrie Theatre, the Mark Taper Forum, The Goodman Theatre, and the Arena Stage, which now have become synonymous with uniquely successful new play production, were not founded to support new plays. That new plays have had rather stunning success with regional audiences is more a serendipitous accident than the end result of a planned process.

The Disconnect: Challenges for Playwrights and the New Play

Because of this, the fertile explosion of new plays and new playwrights – which has grown up in a kind of organizational improvisation – has created unique challenges for the regional theatre in creating a place where playwrights can write, develop, and ultimately see their plays produced. These challenges have included a disconnect between playwrights and regional theatre artistic directors. For playwrights, there is a lack of coherent programs for new play development, with far more plays commissioned than produced. There is also tension between artistic directors trying to please audiences and playwrights attempting to create innovative theatre. Finally, there is a lack of sustainable salary and health insurance for writers, and a patchwork of commissions, grants, and residencies for playwrights that shifts constantly – offering none of the stability that nearly every regional theatre employee enjoys. Yet despite these daunting facts, since 1960, the American regional theatre has indeed been a magic garden for the ongoing collaborative creation of new work across the United States, bursting the traditional notions of America's centralized theatre in New York.

This chapter provides an overview of how some American resident theatre artists have developed new work through collaboration within the unique ecological system of regional theatre. This includes the wildly successful, frequently produced playwright Lauren Gunderson, who writes traditional plays that appeal to America's heartland; avant-garde director/playwrights like Carey Perloff and JoAnne Akalaitis, who develop challenging new work from both classic and contemporary sources; and mid-career Latinx playwright Elaine Romero, who has navigated the network of new play development over the past twenty years.

The Beginnings of the US Regional Theatre

The regional theatre in the United States grew up in the early 1950s postwar boom and expanded into the 1960s through the efforts of visionaries such as Margo Jones and Theatre '47 in Dallas, Zelda Fichandler at the Arena Stage in Washington (established in 1950), Nina Vance at the Alley Theatre in Houston (founded 1947), Tyrone Guthrie who founded the Guthrie Theatre in Minneapolis with Oliver Rea and Peter Zeisler in 1959, and Gordon Davidson at the Mark Taper Forum (founded in 1967). Joseph Zeigler went on to write what has become the definitive text on the regional theatre movement, *Regional Theatre: The Revolutionary Stage.* Though it was published over forty-six years ago, it still points to some of the forces that led to new work being developed regionally rather than on Broadway. Regional theatres (or "winter stock companies") grew out of an earlier Little Theatre movement that included older not-for-profit theatres, which still exist today like the Goodman Theatre in Chicago

(1925), the Barter Theatre in Virginia (1933), McCarter Theatre in Princeton (1930), and the Cleveland Playhouse (1915). These theatres were following the tide of the European avant-garde and its independent theatre movement exploring experimental work that was not commercially oriented. Some later served as tryout houses for Broadway, roadhouses for national touring companies, or places of employment for theatre professionals in the Great Depression in the 1930s. Many were simply built upon local theatre communities that were off the beaten path and had developed a strong production reputation that veered toward professional theatre.

The regional theatre movement was also fueled by a desire to create a national theatre, not unlike France's Comédie-Française, England's National Theater, or the Moscow Art Theatre in Russia, with a resident company that would remain in place for years, training new generations of acting talent through professional mentorship by older company members. W. McNeil Lowry of the Ford Foundation was instrumental in providing funding for this initial growth of resident companies in the regional theatre, noting that the "first order of business" was to "stabilize the workforce" and providing "substantial" grant monies to "sustain a company of actors." Once Lowry had laid this foundation, he was prepared to take the next step and focus on new work in the regional theatre, once again modeling his program on the European ideals:

> With actors on yearly contracts for the first time, he could pursue his second dream; putting these ensembles at the service of the new play – as did Gaston Baty, Charles Dullin, Louis Jouvet.[1]

European playwrights like Molière, Shakespeare, and Chekhov had written specifically for members of their own companies, such as the roles written by Molière for Madeleine Béjart, by Shakespeare for Richard Burbage, or by Anton Chekhov for Olga Knipper. The idea of a national theatre company performing shows in repertory, with plays written by American dramatists specifically for resident actors of that company, never fully came into being, though instances of that did occur. However, some of those instances were not in the regional theatre – instead this could be found in the New York not-for-profit Off-Broadway theatre, which was and remains an important source of new work. A prime example of that was the work of playwright Lanford Wilson, who wrote many roles specifically for members of the not-for-profit Circle Repertory Theatre in New York City's Off-Broadway theatre where Wilson had been a founding member. Steppenwolf Theatre, which had close ties to Circle Repertory Theatre, did and continues to maintain a remarkably resilient resident company, and

was originally mostly known for stirring revivals of the plays of Lanford
Wilson, Sam Shepard, Tennessee Williams, and John Guare until the
premiere of Frank Galati's 1988 adaptation of *The Grapes of Wrath* and
Tracy Letts's Pulitzer Prize–winning *August: Osage County* in 2007; these
plays were written with specific Steppenwolf company creating those roles
in ensemble performance.

Carey Perloff: Collaboration and the Dream of a Resident Company

The notion of a resident ensemble still lives as an ideal in the regional
theatre, however. In their article, "In Company We Trust," Gregory Boyd
and Paul Tetreault, both formerly of the Alley Theatre, raise a number of
important positives about a resident company:

> A resident company of actors creates a continuum. In the context of
> company, each actor – playing a variety of different parts over time, in
> plays from different periods and styles – can grow and evolve and can
> exercise different aspects of his or her imagination and technique.[2]

They note that at the Alley Theatre, the audiences take ownership of these
companies, watching the actors develop and transform from play to play,
and exclaim that "acting companies have been at the center of the art
form's highest achievements"[3] including the development of major playwrights like Bertolt Brecht at the Berliner Ensemble and Clifford Odets
working with the Group Theatre. Boyd and Tetreault acknowledge that
the "jobbed-in" mentality still predominates the casting of actors in the
regional theatre because of the perceived expense of maintaining
a company.

Carey Perloff, the indomitable force who ran the American
Conservatory Theatre (ACT) in San Francisco as its artistic director
from 1992 to 2018, presided over one of the success stories in resident
companies, holding together its core company from 2001 to 2012 and ultimately providing some of the best compensation for its performers in the United
States as a highly collaborative creator of new work for the stage. Even then,
however, she mourned that ultimately ACT could not maintain it:

> In the end, we were defeated by the cost of living in San Francisco. What
> I was saying to our core company is, you have to be ours 52 weeks of the year.
> Even though I felt I was paying them a really good wage, better than
> anywhere in the country in terms of a permanent acting job, they had to
> live here, and they couldn't do film, and they couldn't do TV. Ultimately it
> wasn't sustainable. I couldn't make the numbers work.[4]

The challenge for Perloff was to get funding for the core company, and after going to the Mellon, Duke, and Ford Foundations, she discovered that "there is no appetite in the funding community in America to support long-term relationships with actors."[5] In Perloff's amazing twenty-five-year tenure at ACT, she was able to transform the notion of a resident company into a venture that maintained long-term commitment to collaboration and artistic partnerships that led to a major $300,000 Andrew W. Mellon Foundation Award for new work and the premiere of many new works for the theatre including Perloff's own *The Colossus of Rhodes* (2003) and *Higher* (2012). Despite this inability to hold onto the notion of a resident company, Perloff has been one of the nation's finest creators of new work. One of her last successes at ACT, the adaptation of Khaled Hosseini's *A Thousand Splendid Suns*, was originally developed under Perloff's direction and written by Irish Indian playwright Ursula Rani Sarma. The collaboration between herself and Sarma provides a particularly unique model of how artistic partnerships can work in the regional theatre, despite the lack of a resident acting company.

In 2017, partnering with Theatre Calgary of Canada, Perloff commissioned Sarma with task of translating a novel taking place over thirty years, several generations, and multiple points of view into an evening's performance. *A Thousand Splendid Suns* focuses on the experiences of two Afghani women of different classes: Mariam, born out of wedlock to a once-wealthy man and his housekeeper, and Laila, a young urban, educated woman who has been nursed back to health by Mariam, after losing her family and her lover, Tariq. Perloff was fascinated by the female friendship and how the two women deal with Laila's abusive husband. Perloff's partnering with David Coulter, a musician whose unusual and unique use of found instruments, such a handsaw, contributed to the creation of a performance that rose above literal interpretation, and, instead of a history lesson, became a visceral theatrical experience. Perloff, who is an accomplished playwright herself, was particularly proud that the ACT adaptation of Hosseini's *A Thousand Splendid Suns* went on to a busy life at many other regional stages including the Old Globe Theatre, the Arena Stage, and Seattle Rep.[6]

A New Approach to New Work: JoAnne Akalaitis

As a creative collaborator of new work, Perloff is an intriguing figure, because she was a transfer herself from New York City, moving to American Conservatory Theatre after serving as the artistic director of the Classic Stage Company Off-Broadway. One other particularly intriguing theatre artist, who had her beginnings in New York's Off-Off-Broadway work, and made a name for herself in the regional theatre for creating new work in the theatre was director, playwright, and artistic director JoAnne Akalaitis. Akalaitis's story points to the precarious nature of building and maintaining a career in the realm of developing new work, but it also suggests that Akalaitis's model for developing risky and adventurous new work grows out of creative nontextual influences, such as the bodies of the actors in rehearsal, as much as it relies on reinterpretation and reimagining of text. In addition, her approach engages the director/designer as a creative artist rather than solely as an interpretative collaborator on a play's text. It was the Mabou Mines, the avant-garde New York theatre group she cofounded Off-Off-Broadway with Lee Breuer, David Warrilow, Ruth Maleczech, and Philip Glass, that established her as a creator of new work for the theatre. Retreating to Glass and Akalaitis's home near Mabou Mines, Nova Scotia, to create their first theater piece, *Red Horse Animation*, the ensemble redefined the nature of theatre work in America. Initially working as an actor in the Mabou Mines performance pieces such as Samuel Beckett's *Play* and *Come and Go*, she became the leading director of the group. Each of the new works that Akalaitis directed for the Mabou Mines went on to receive an Obie Award including *Cascando* (1975), *Dressed Like an Egg* (1977), *Dead End Kids* (1980), and *Southern Exposure* (1979). Even while maintaining her relationship with Mabou Mines and directing their projects at the New York Shakespeare Festival, Akalaitis went on to build a career directing larger productions of classical and contemporary works in the regional theatre. As she worked with these kinds of revivals, Akalaitis's interpretations were essentially akin to creating a new work for the stage. She received particular notoriety with her run-in with the Samuel Beckett estate over her production of *Endgame* at Boston's American Repertory Theatre (ART), which was set in an abandoned subway station, set to the music of Philip Glass, and featured two African American actors. Though they eventually permitted the show to continue, the Beckett estate responded negatively, calling the production a "parody" of the play. Critics disagreed with the Beckett estate's assessment, giving it strong reviews, and the production continues to reverberate in the annals of the regional theatre.[7]

Akalaitis's work reinterpreting both traditional and modern theatre classics was particularly revelatory; her 1989 production of Jean Genet's *The Screens* at the Guthrie was much lauded, with its blend of the Algerian revolution and the Palestinian Intifada. The production received national acclimation, praised by Jack Kroll of *Newsweek* as "one of the major events of the decade in American Regional Theatre," and she went on to direct other productions of Genet's work including *The Balcony* at ART in 1986 and *Prisoner of Love* at the New York Theatre Workshop in 1995.[8] After bringing her production of John Ford's *Tis Pity She's a Whore* to the New York Shakespeare Festival, which she originally staged at Chicago's Goodman Theatre, Akalaitis's brief, controversial stint as artistic director of the New York Shakespeare Festival from 1991 to 1993 did nothing to slow down her continued presence in the regional theatre. She had a particularly positive relationship with the Guthrie, and directed several new works there, including her new vision of Georg Büchner's *Leon and Lena (and Lenz)*, produced at the Guthrie in 1987, which adapted Büchner's irreverent fairy tale, "Leonce and Lena," moving the story to a fictional, corporate kingdom in the American southwest. Her revivals of plays are in essence new works. When she directed *The Screens* at the Guthrie in October 1989, Akalaitis re-visioned the play through her research in the culture of North Africa, exploring "death, near-death experiences, and Islamic death rituals" and transformed the play into a kind of "human bazaar under a huge mustard-tarped circus tent."[9] In 1997, she went on to direct *The Iphigenia Cycle* at Chicago's Court Theatre, including Euripides' *Iphigenia at Aulis* and *Iphigenia.*

Having trained with Jerzy Grotowski and in particular with his leading actor Ryszard Cieslak, Akalaitis developed a series of physical exercises that would become one of the defining methods in her work with actors which she calls "pure actor-research." This physicality of performance has become the signature aspect of her work as a director:

> Even first time audience members sense, on some level, that the in-the-flesh presence of the actor's body is vital to any theatrical event: the text is spoken by the voice which comes out of the body, costumes go on the body, scenery exists in relation to the body, sweat and spirit are excreted by the body. In Akalaitis's work the actor's body is the central nervous system of the production.[10]

Akalaitis's unique approach of working with actors' physical exploration of texts to create remarkable new theatre pieces has been accentuated by her ability to collaborate intensively with designers as creators of new work. In particular, her collaborations with Ming Cho Lee, the much-awarded set designer, on Harold Pinter's *The Birthday Party*, *The Trojan Women*, and *The Iphigenia Cycle* set a high mark in Akalaitis's career in the regional theatre. Lee's famously transparent and minimalist designs provided the

canvas for Akalaitis's often subversive reimagining of classic works, allowing her to create radically new versions – which, growing out of her actors'
embodied creativity, changed the notion of directorial "interpretation" of
a play into essentially an entirely new work.[11] Lee, inducted into the
American Theatre Hall of Fame in 1998, and awarded the National
Medal of Arts in 2002, shaped a generation of designers as professor of
design at the Yale School of Drama, and his designs and the designs of his
former students in the regional theatre become a kind of text working
along with the language of the playwright, actors, and other collaborating
designers in theatrical production.

Like her collaborator Ming Cho Lee, JoAnne Akalaitis became an
important teacher of theatre artists, serving as the head of the directing
program at Juilliard and later teaching at Bard College. In more recent
years, Akalaitis has been creating new site-specific works such as *Bad
News! I was there ...*, which is described as an "oratorio of messenger
speeches collaged from classic Greek plays." *Bad News!* was first produced at the Guthrie, which has supported many of Akalaitis's innovative new works. Created originally to be performed outdoors at the
Poets House, at a location on River Terrace in Manhattan, *Bad News!*
was written when Akalaitis was not feeling particularly supported by
the New York theatre, even contemplating giving up entirely. This
moment in Akalaitis's career was particularly shocking, considering that
Akalaitis had been the former artistic director of the New York
Shakespeare Festival. But once again, the opportunity to create new
work rekindled Akalaitis's desire to revisit classic Greek theatre. The
invitation to create the piece came shortly thereafter and drew upon
many voices including, from Akalaitis's perspective, "from the Gods":

> While that is certainly possible, it is equally likely that it arose from
> Akalaitis's deep study of Greek tragedy over her 50-year career in the theatre,
> and from her work with classicists, not to mention her perceptions of the
> current political moment.[12]

Written with classicist Greg Taubman, playwright Kate Atwell, and Ashley
Tata, an opera and theatre director, the play is pastiche of important
translations of Greek tragedies, including Nicholas Rudall's *Medea*, Anne
Carson's *Antigonick*, W. B. Yeats's *Oedipus Rex*, Ellen McLaughlin's *The
Persians*, and the Paul Schmidt translation of Racine's *Phaedre*. For
Akalaitis, the Guthrie was the home she needed when she created this
piece, even as she eventually brought *Bad News!* to New York, as it allowed

her to work on the play over a number of years, perfecting the piece with the actors' physical work for which she is famous.

New Plays: The Shift from New York to the Regional Theatre

It is intriguing to consider Perloff's and Akalaitis's careers as New York-based theatre artists who moved into regional theatre careers, since new play development itself shifted from the Off-Broadway and Broadway theatre in New York to the not-for-profit regional theatre starting in the late 1960s. New York simply became too expensive a place for a new play to fail. This change has not been a process without its trials and tribulations, and the challenges facing playwrights and new plays because of those harsh realities were rather soberly documented in *Outrageous Fortune: The Life and Times of the New American Play*, a 2008 study funded by the Theatre Development Fund and written by Todd London (along with Ben Pesner and Zannie Giraud Voss), then the artistic director of New Dramatists. In the early part of the twentieth century, the number of plays opening on Broadway in a year was staggering; there were over 200 new plays produced in 1927. This number started dwindling with the advent of the "talkie"/ motion picture in the 1920s, and continued to decline until, by the 1960s and 1970s, the number of nonmusical plays dwindled to mere double digits, and by 2017, only approximately seventeen to twenty musical and nonmusical plays (including revivals) were opening on Broadway. The high cost of producing theatre in New York, where a highest priced Broadway ticket can be as much as $400, and more than a hundred for a lower priced ticket, makes the economics of developing new work there daunting. Even Off-Broadway, where prices run as high as $75 for its lowest cost tickets, has made developing and producing new work any-where in New York an ongoing near impossibility.[13] Douglas Anderson, in his 1988 *TDR* article *The Dream Machine: Thirty Years of New Play Development in America*, written exactly twenty years prior to *Outrageous Fortune*, noted, "the escalation of real estate valuations and operating costs … triggered the collapse of off-Broadway," and subsequently, "by the early 1970s, New York has abandoned its traditional role of the incubator of new work."[14] Once New York lost its preeminence in devel-oping new work, that role became the primary function of the regional theatre. With the success of the Arena Stage's production of *The Great White Hope*, discussed later, new problems have arisen, and questions raised by both London and Anderson get at the serious challenges to producing new work in the American regional theatre. These include the rarity of commissioned plays actually coming to full production, the financial hardship and lack of support for working professional playwrights (relative to the salaries and benefits of other regional theatre employees), the disconnect between what artistic directors believe their subscription audience wants versus the avant-garde and adventurous plays playwrights actually are interested in writing, and the lack of connection between playwrights and institutional gatekeepers in the regional theatre.

Despite the previously mentioned challenges facing these regionally based playwrights, there have been many success stories including the original "dream" transfer to Broadway, cited in Anderson's *The Dream Machine,* Howard Sackler's *The Great White Hope.* Its production originated at the Arena Stage in Washington, DC in 1967, and was considered "the great leap forward" initiating the idea of regional theatre as an important source for new plays for the New York Stage. Zeigler considered *The Great White Hope* the fourth major change in the regional theatre "revolution" noting that it "proved the national power of new plays." Yet *The Great White Hope* was not the success for the Arena Stage that it could have been. After the triumph of the transfer, the Arena did not contractually share in its financial success on Broadway, even though the production "was a gargantuan undertaking for Arena Stage – scores of actors, hundreds of costumes, many thousands of dollars."[15] In the years following the 1960s fruitful transfer of *The Great White Hope* at the Arena Stage, there would be many major transfers from the regional stage to major New York productions on Broadway. Some of these, moving through the decades since, include the Alley Theatre's production of Paul Zindel's *The Effect of Gamma Rays on Man-in-the-Moon Marigolds* (1965); Sam Shepard's *Buried Child,* which premiered at the Magic Theatre in San Francisco (1978); Actors Theatre Louisville's *Crimes of the Heart* by Beth Henley (1979); the Mark Taper Forum's productions of *Angels in America, Part I: Millennium Approaches* by Tony Kushner (1990), and *The Kentucky Cycle* by Robert Schenkkan (1992); South Coast Repertory's production of *Wit* by Margaret Edson (1995); the Goodman Theatre's production of Lynn Nottage's *Ruined* (2007); the Arena Stage's musical *Next to Normal* (2008) and *Sweat* by Lynn Nottage (2016); and Steppenwolf Theatre's *August: Osage County* by Tracy Letts (2007), to name just a few transfers which were also Pulitzer Prize–winning plays.

Lauren Gunderson: America's Most Produced Playwright

However, success with new plays in regional theatre is being redefined and is swiftly moving beyond the New York transfer. An example of this is

Lauren Gunderson, who has been lauded and documented as one of the most produced playwrights in the United States by *American Theatre,* the primary publication of the Theatre Communications Group, which is the major organization of the regional theatre movement. She is a playwriting phenomenon whose incredible accomplishments in sheer number of plays produced has happened mostly outside of the New York theatre. She is representative of a new kind of success story for the field of playwriting in the regional theatre, as noted in *The New Yorker* in 2017:

> Increasingly, theatres are banking on Gunderson, who, at thirty-five, has already had more than twenty of her works produced: among them witty historical dramas about women in science ("Emilie," "Silent Sky," "Ada and the Engine"), giddy political comedies ("Exit, Pursued by a Bear," "The Taming," "The Revolutionists"), and wildly theatrical explorations of death and legacy ("I and You," "The Book of Will").[16]

Gunderson's extraordinary triumph at connecting to regional audiences has suggested that the New York dream of success is not necessarily the only way a playwright can achieve a sustainable existence in American theatre. In fact, Gunderson has not had a major Broadway or even Off-Broadway coup in New York. However, in sheer number of productions in the regional theatre, Gunderson has beat playwrights like Tennessee Williams, Arthur Miller, and August Wilson despite the mixed reviews of her several productions in New York theatre (though Gunderson is no stranger to Manhattan, she completed her MFA at NYU). Ironically, success like Gunderson's in new play development outside of New York sometimes guarantees just the opposite when one's work finally hits the Big Apple, as demonstrated in the case of Robert Schenkkan's Pulitzer Prize–winning *The Kentucky Cycle*, which received its world premiere at the Intiman Theatre in Seattle. The eight-hour epic was roundly panned by the New York critics – as if punishing the play for having won the Pulitzer outside of the purview of New York.[17]

Elaine Romero and El Jardín Mágico

While not the phenomenon that Lauren Gunderson has become, Elaine Romero is an example of yet another reality in the regional theatre – a playwright connecting with specific regional audiences and communities with a success story that has nothing to do with being a New York theatre sensation. Romero is perhaps a more down-to-earth example of a working, successful playwright making a living from her chosen field. She is a kind of everywoman of dramatists, finding a convergence in her regional audiences of those attracted to her work because of issues she raises that often tie into Latinx culture, style, community, and aesthetics – though her work continues to move beyond Latinx culture with her recent broader focus on war. For Romero, a Latinx playwright residing in Tucson, Arizona, who graduated with her MFA in playwriting from the University of California at Davis in 1987, this artistic home was Arizona Theatre Company (ATC) where she first worked in the development office. Romero is considered a very successful and busy mid-career playwright, having written ninety plays, many of which have had full productions in the regional theatre. Particularly interesting has been her ability to navigate the waters of new play development into the full production, in addition to building a career as a teacher and as a mentor for other Latinx playwrights. She had notable early successes, including her plays *¡Curanderas! Serpents of the Clouds* (1995), *The Fat-Free Chicana and the Snow Cap Queen* (1997), *Barrio Hollywood* (1998), *Before Death Comes for the Archbishop* (1998), *Undercurrents* (1999), and *Secret Things* (1999), several of which not only received production, but also publication, a rare thing in the world of playwriting. One of her most well-known plays, *Barrio Hollywood,* is about Alex Moreno, a Mexican American boxer, who dreams of fighting his way out of poverty and finds his dreams deferred when he is injured. This bi-cultural romance has received premieres in both English and Spanish and is one of Romero's most produced plays. *Secret Things* explores the mysterious history of Mexican Americans with crypto-Jewish roots, and follows the experience of a journalist, Delia, who is uncovering this unusual past and, in the process, discovers challenging secrets about herself.

While Romero is not a household name, and she has not been a major force in New York or the regional theatre, she has crafted an influential career in the middle of America, as she explains:

> I feel I built my career from the middle of the country out instead of focusing on the coasts. I let people fight over the edges, while I drove straight to the middle, in communities like Dallas, Austin, and San Antonio TX or Independence, KS. When a community had no playwright, I reported for duty to be that playwright.[18]

Her career has focused, in part, on her heritage as a Chicanx playwright, and she has been committed to elevating the status of Latinx playwrights in general. Establishing herself early on as a mentor and dramaturg for countless other playwrights, Romero has made a name for herself in the

National New Play Network, the Playwrights Center of Minneapolis, Chicago Dramatists, and most recently at the O'Neill Theater Center in Connecticut. One of Romero's major areas of focus includes her US–Mexican border trilogy plays including *Wetback* (2009), *Mother of Exiles* (2013), and *Title IX* (2014). *Title IX* was initially developed at the prestigious National Playwrights Conference at the Eugene O'Neill Theater Center – one of the areas of attention in this essay. With each level of new play development or production, Romero's career has taken specific turns and peaks, moving her closer to national recognition as a writer.

Romero's collaborations with multiple directors, theatres, and developmental organizations has led to her creating a tetralogy of plays which include *Graveyard of Empires* (2012), *A Work of Art* (2011), *When Reason Sleeps* (still in process at this writing), and *Revolutions/Revoluciones* (2019), which explore the subject of war and its cross-cultural ramifications. As is the case with many new works, Romero's plays are often commissioned at one theatre and produced elsewhere. The third play, *When Reason Sleeps*, is a good example of this – the ten-minute inceptive idea of this play was called *Rain of Ruin* and was originally commissioned by Curious Theatre Company in Denver. It later was produced in Boston and internationally in Sydney, Australia, where it appeared on Australian Television alongside works by Suzan-Lori Parks, Paula Vogel, and Tony Kushner in a program titled *The War Anthology* (and Romero was also interviewed by the Australian Broadcasting Corporation). Hopscotching various theatres in new play development before the play premieres at yet another theatre is fairly typical in terms of new play development patterns, and continued with all the plays of Romero's war tetralogy. The first play, *Graveyard of Empires*, won the Blue Ink Playwriting Award at American Blues Theater and was developed there and at Rivendell Theatre Ensemble before being picked up at 16th Street Theater. The success of *Graveyard of Empires* and *A Work of Art* has brought important recognition to Romero's work as she has hit a nerve in an American society exhausted by unending war in Iran and Afghanistan. Latinx and African American communities have been particularly hard-hit by the interminable nature of our involvement because these wars are fought by the working poor. Because of the ongoing controversies about immigration, war, and class-based economics across the Obama and Trump administrations, Romero's plays are finding more venues and larger audiences.

However, Romero's trajectory as a mid-career writer is a particularly perilous time for a playwright, as London notes in his *Outrageous Fortune*:

> To some the rubric of "emerging playwright" is a life raft that keeps them from drowning in the treacherous waters of middle career. Mid-career tends to be a time when grants dry up, teaching beckons, television becomes more alluring, and the ambitions of career and the demands of daily life grow less compatible, even as the small money of playwriting becomes less sufficient.[19]

The reality is that American theatre, and entertainment culture in general, does not sustain consistent careers; it idolizes an emerging writer, becomes enthralled with a work or two, and then it's on to the next big thing. The tastes of American theatre audiences and critics have a short attention span and "lack the mechanisms to support bodies of work and lifelong careers."[20] And it is here that teaching quite often fills the gap; it comes at a time when a writer needs to rethink who they are, fill a creativity gap with connection to young minds, and have the stability to recharge their own imaginative juices. With teaching, there are perils, however, as there are in any day job – long service requirements, endless committee meetings, course preparation, and grading, all of which take away from precious hours writing new plays. As a result, the writer is taken out of the brisk, challenging world of professional theatre. Because of the lack of connection to the newest, brightest trends, the writing becomes less engaged, and the writer finally retreats to older themes and safer zones. It can be a form of death and drying up of that same creative energy.

The Economics of the American Playwright

Of course, without an academic roost, survival by grants, commissions, and the occasional teaching/residency, no playwright can live what London refers to as a "middle-class lifestyle," and it is still very rare that playwriting provides enough income to purchase, for example, health insurance or is sustainable enough for playwrights to place a down payment on a home.[21] Even Tony Kushner, perhaps one of America's most well-known living playwrights, has been quoted often about the fact that he can't support himself with his playwriting career, noting,

> I make my living now as a screenwriter! Which I'm surprised and horrified to find myself saying, but I don't think I can support myself as a playwright at this point. I don't think anybody does.[22]

Kushner is one of many playwrights who have found a sustainable career writing in the film and television medium; the catch has always been that, once shifting careers to film and television, those playwrights rarely come back to writing for the stage. The recent and growing need for writers in the new Wild West of streaming television, which demands more and more new content, has turned playwriting into a marketable commodity:

> In this era of so-called peak TV, the demand for strong storytellers on the small screen has sparked a new love affair: Television adores playwrights, and the feeling is mutual. In unprecedented numbers, playwrights are essentially answering an industry personal ad that might as well read: Seeking skilled writers with a keen grasp of character development, nuanced dialogue, narrative structure and emotional realism.[23]

Showrunners looking for new writers are reading plays rather than screenplays, and young writers still in professional training programs are contemplating a kind of "polygamy" of writing for both the stage and the small screen. Yet the reality of doing both is more of a dream, and playwrights who want to focus primarily on writing for the stage are still at an economic disadvantage.

It was notable then that in 2015, Playwrights Horizons decided to offer playwrights partially covered health insurance premiums as well as compensation for their preproduction efforts. In "Want My Time? Please Pay for It," Diep Tran writes that Playwrights Horizons became one of the few theatres that supported its playwrights in the same manner as its salaried employees. It is ironic, of course, that playwrights in the regional theatre rarely have the level of financial support that a theatre technician or administrator might have. Tran notes that because of the lack of consistent compensation, "only half of an average writer's income came from playwright-related activities (with a meager 15 percent of that half coming directly from their plays)."[24] To deal with this inequity, some theatres, such as Yale Repertory Theatre, are providing residencies for playwrights that include "a salary, health insurance, and artistic support" though such residencies are rare. In recent years, the Andrew W. Mellon Foundation has created thirty new residencies for playwrights at theatres across the country. This has been especially important, as playwrights have been leaving the field and turning to writing for streaming television. While these new Mellon residencies have created incredible opportunities for playwrights, they have had limited effect, mostly because, as soon as the funding ends for these individual residencies, the same "catch as catch can" conditions of surviving from grant to grant return for playwrights.[25] Because of this, most playwrights working in the regional theatre who only receive one to two productions per year on average have to choose one of two major options if they want to work in their profession of dramatic writing: either to write for television or film, or seek a university position.

Working as a Resident Playwright: Arizona Theatre Company

So it is all the more notable that, because of her long-term commitment and residency at Arizona Theatre Company (ATC), Romero has retained her commitment to professional theatre, has had a major resurgence in her career, and has accomplished all of this while achieving tenure as a professor of playwriting at the University of Arizona. Keeping her residency alive at ATC has led Romero to the Chicago theatre scene with her play *A Work of Art*, to the Los Angeles Latinx audiences with *Revolutions/Revoluciones*, and then on to the prestige and glow of New York audiences through her successful development of *Title IX* at the O'Neill. If anything, Romero's experience working through the promotion and tenure process ignited her playwriting career and prevented the kind of stagnation that faces many playwrights when they accept an academic roost.

The Arizona Theatre Company is considered the state theatre of Arizona and is the premier LORT (League of Resident Theatres) theatre there, serving an audience base of over 130,000 subscribers. With two locations in the state, and a multi-million-dollar budget, it is one of the major regional theatres in the country. Receiving a 1998 TCG/Pew playwriting residency, Romero crafted her early career working closely with David Ira Goldstein, ATC's long-serving artistic director.[26] There was a small service requirement of Romero's 1998 TCG/Pew National Theatre Artist in Residence Program grant, which funded her to administer the National Latinx Theatre Award as well as running a mentorship program that brought together Latinx and Native American Writers. The National Latinx Theatre Award has jumpstarted the careers of many Latinx playwrights; Kristoffer Diaz's *The Elaborate Entrance of Chad Deity* was later a Pulitzer finalist.

Romero's residency at ATC focuses primarily on commissions to support her writing and her work as a theatre artist. However, as the resident playwright at ATC, she has at times assisted with season planning, programming, education, and community engagement. Romero has collaborated with most of ATC's artistic directors, including Gary Gisselman, the aforementioned David Ira Goldstein, David Ivers (who is currently the Artistic Director of South Coast Repertory Theatre), and, more recently, Sean Daniels, the current ATC artistic director (who has taken on a unique focus on new work). Though she carefully parcels her times to focus on her writing, Romero has felt "embedded" in all aspects of ATC's efforts in context with community development, season selection, dramaturgy, new play development with a special focus on Latinx playwrights many of whom, under her mentorship, have gone on to major careers of their own. Romero has specifically advocated for her ATC family of Latinx dramatists, helping to "close the deal" on specific productions. In 2019, Benjamin Benne's *Alma*, a play that Romero specifically advocated for, was picked up by American Blues Theater in Chicago and won its Blue Ink Award. While she refuses to take full credit on the Latinx shows she has supported, she notes what she does is not unusual:

> I think people of color often become ambassadors of sorts. That's because we have a commitment to rise together as a community, and in order to do that, we can't only be focused on ourselves or our work, even though we work so hard to perfect that and believe in ourselves most of all. The best advocate for a playwright is often not the person themselves. In the end, it can't ever be just about us or our work.[27]

It is remarkable that Romero feels this way – after writing ninety plays and authoring fifty publications, and receiving important national awards in playwriting. Her personal connection to the ATC also extends to actors who have come back repeatedly to the theatre to work on her plays, as well as resident designers who have come to understand her work and have become part of the conversation as she develops her plays. However, one of most important ways that ATC has supported Romero is through commissioning her plays.

Commissions and the Working Playwright

When beginning at ATC and in her early work with David Goldstein, Romero recalls that Goldstein had a specific goal in commissioning her plays, which was "Let's keep you writing." Romero, in her conversations with this author, noted several times that, while commissions are the bread and butter of the playwrights' profession, not all commissioned plays are produced, a fact noted by London in *Outrageous Fortune*: "relatively few writers … have plays commissioned and produced by the same company."[28] Commissions average around $3,000–5,000, though some can range up to $25,000 with the idea that once the play is in production, the playwright will also then benefit in royalties. However, it is extremely rare that the same theatre will commission and then produce the play, so "plays that bring in both commission and royalty from the same theatre are rarer than rare."[29] Romero was the recipient of multiple commissions, including those at ATC, the

Goodman Theatre, Ford's Theatre, the Alley Theatre, Center Stage, American Blues Theater, National Theatre Action, Kitchen Dog Theater, ZACH Theatre, and Borderlands Theater. Grants, however, provide larger amounts and a more sustainable living for playwrights – in Romero's case, she has been the recipient of multiple grants and fellow-ships, including the previously mentioned TCG/Pew Grant, a National Endowment for the Arts (NEA) Arts Work Grant with ATC, Goodman Theatre Playwrights Unit, and Carl J. Djerassi Fellow in Playwriting, among many others.

Most of Romero's plays were commissioned by one theatre, developed by another, and produced by yet another theatre. A case in point is the development and workshop production process of Romero's play *Modern Slave*. Originally a Ford's Theatre Commission in 2014, it received staged readings at Victory Gardens Theatre in Chicago and the Road Company in LA in 2015, and then was accepted to the Seven Devils Playwrights Conference McCall, Idaho, where it was directed by Amy Saltz. Saltz worked with Lloyd Richards at the O'Neill Theater Center for seventeen years and the artistic director, Jeni Mahoney, started Seven Devils to reflect Richards's vision of the O'Neill. Mahoney had attended as a playwright, and when she founded Seven Devils, she hired Richards's people, followed his development process, and invokes Richards every conference. *Modern Slave* has been developed further at A Contemporary Theatre in Seattle, Washington.

Working Together: The Playwrights Unit at the Goodman Theatre

Romero, like many American playwrights, has established her career working with these organizations which link playwrights to regional theatres. In particular, Romero's work with the Goodman Theatre's Playwrights Unit provided her with an important commission to develop her play *A Work of Art*, which was subsequently produced at Chicago Dramatists in association with the Goodman Theatre. Because of this experience, Romero established herself as a nationally recognized playwright, and the experience led, at least in part, to her hire at University of Arizona. The Goodman Theatre's Playwrights Unit is a relatively new organization, which like many of the projects and productions at the Goodman Theatre, has been presided over by Robert Falls, whose own generosity of spirit as an artistic director has loomed large over the Chicago Theatre community. Falls's aesthetic embraces Goodman's mantra of "quality, diversity and community," and his own journey as a working-class, relentlessly industrious director grows out of his own storied connection to the Chicago Theatre:

> I'm the usual Chicago thing. . . . I don't come from a polished place. I didn't go to Juilliard or Yale. I came out of the Midwest and my growth as a director is mirrored by other Chicagoans' growth as actors or writers. Some of those connections are mythological, but they also represent a shared past.[30]

Falls's appreciation for a "rougher" theatre seems to be the idea behind the Goodman Theatre's Playwrights Unit, which is a collaboration with Chicago Dramatists (a playwright development organization). It provides four commissioned writers with bimonthly meetings with members of the Goodman's literary staff to develop and workshop their plays-in-progress. This process culminates with concert readings of each of the new plays. Plays developed in the Goodman Theatre's Playwrights Unit have gone on to receive readings and workshop productions in the New Stages series, as well as full productions at the Goodman. Romero's work at the Goodman provides a useful example of how playwrights can be fed by a long-term commitment to their work and their process by a major regional theatre. It also illustrates how connected these theatres are – and how the new play development process doesn't just happen at one theatre, but becomes part of a chain of opportunities for the care and feeding of playwrights.

For Romero, the experience at the Playwrights Unit was one in which she was fully embraced by the Chicago Theatre community, and developed important relationships with her fellow 2011–12 Goodman playwrights – Philip Dawkins, Nambi E. Kelley, and Martín Zimmerman. The Goodman Theatre's Playwrights Unit dramaturg is Tanya Palmer, the Goodman's Producer and Director of New Play Development who served as the dramaturg on Lynn Nottage's *Ruined*, commissioned by the Goodman and first performed in 2007 in the Goodman Theatre New Stages Series, later winning the Pulitzer Prize in 2009. Romero describes the experience of working with Palmer at the Unit:

> We would gather from around the city and get together regularly and discuss the work, and do readings of the work and they might or might not move forward with the writing, but just the community of it, to be a part of such a creative ensemble of writers was amazing. . . . Working with Tanya Palmer who is one of the country's top dramaturgs, who is very interested in how the process of dramaturgy helps writers. . . . It was so different from writing alone.[31]

From this fascination with time and the nature of war, Romero, while a member of the Goodman's Playwrights Unit, developed *A Work of Art*, which would gestate to become an entire tetralogy of plays about the nature of war.

Romero's decision to wrestle with the reality of war grew out of a profoundly personal experience:

> I had lost my uncle in the Vietnam War when I was five. My aunt was pregnant at the time and they already had two children. I had always figured if I could fold time, I could see him again, and the injustice of that one loss in a war could be undone if even for just a moment. It was his death that inspired *A Work of Art*, but also the entire tetralogy. I had to answer the question of war. Each of the plays wrestles with a question. With *A Work of Art*, I ask, "What do we ask families to live with when we send their loved ones to war? As a person who had watched the death of one soldier play out over my lifetime, I felt uniquely qualified to embark on these plays."[32]

The play came to her in the form of a fever dream, an imagistically poetic piece, that she felt was fueled by the responses of her cohort with the Unit, with Henry Godinez as director. The development process at Chicago Dramatists was under the supervision of the late Russ Tutterow, who, as artistic director of Chicago Dramatists, provided the inspiration and support Romero needed to write the play:

> In the embrace of Chicago Dramatists and its supportive realm, under the genuinely warm and encouraging presence of Russ Tutterow, I found myself very interested in the malleability of time and I wondered how audiences would experience *A Work of Art*, a play whose structure echoes its theme. If I could write the full experience of time, then time could be folded like Origami and we could take what we know now and bring it into the past.[33]

The play was the last work Tutterow chose before dying. He passed away of cancer that season, but his influence was crucial in the sustenance of the entire community of Chicago playwrights. For Romero, Tutterow not only supported *Work of Art*, which was ultimately produced by Chicago Dramatists as the first collaboration between itself and the Goodman Playwrights Unit, but also fostered readings of her plays *Wetback, Mother of Exiles*, and *Title IX*. Tutterow and Chicago Dramatists became an important connection for Romero as a mid-career playwright, and had a profound influence on the growth and flowering of her career in this mid-career stage of her work as a writer. She maintains her connections with Chicago Dramatists.

Lloyd Richards, Architect of the National Playwrights Conference

One other major theatre figure who figured in Elaine Romero's career was director Lloyd Richards, the American director most famous for his work interpreting the plays of August Wilson and directing Lorraine Hansberry's *A Raisin in the Sun* on Broadway, but who was credited for transforming the National Playwrights Conference at the O'Neill Theater Center in 1968 from a wonderful idea that was rapidly descending into chaos under its well-meaning, gregarious producer/benefactor George C. White. White was known for creating O'Neill Center out of thin air, securing the Hammond Estate, raising funding, truly a profound theatre lover, but "without a master plan," as O'Neill veteran, Jeffrey Sweet notes:

> So the idea of a theater that might produce some plays transformed into a meeting among some handpicked writers, and that became a season of two produced plays augmented by some staged readings and that became a season of staged readings, and that – in 1968 – became a season of whatever the writer, directors, and actors could throw together, given the circumstances. And that, as Ron Cowen observed, almost sank the whole thing.[34]

Richards's calm magisterial presence at the O'Neill transformed it into the organized, playwright-focused organization that it has become. He understood its mission from the start and transformed a generation of directors into dramaturgical guides. He trained those directors on how new play development was "to allow problems to surface, not to cover them up with the tricks of our trade," at the same time delving deeply into the text, stimulating fine performances which teased out challenges, encouraging the writer to "play" and "to find things."[35] Richards's techniques of managing the inevitable fiery conflict between playwrights and directors were so instinctively calming and innovative that Michael Feingold, the *Village Voice* theatre critic, compared him to Abraham Lincoln. Richards, because of his unique position of being not only the artistic director of the National Playwrights Conference but also the Dean of the Yale School of Drama, and thereby the artistic director of Yale Rep, had uncommon power and influence in the world of new work, and his ideas transformed that landscape in the regional theatre – moving these organizations from simply producing new work to creating a process of new play development to sustain new plays and playwrights.

Romero had her play accepted to the O'Neill long after Richards had passed, but she had been profoundly touched by the rejection letter she had received in one of her earlier submissions, *¡Curanderas! Serpents of the*

Clouds: she had received finalist status, and Richards had taken the time to reach out to her, letting her know "how much he had liked what was at the heart of her play."[36] When she was finally accepted in 2017 after many years of submitting her work, she writes that

> I cried out of joy when I was accepted and I knew the quality of work being done there – and I wanted this place to touch my work. My work is a tad ahead of itself. I often end up with one too many regional theatres saying that my work is ahead of its time. However, I am patient. It really has to do often with the content of my plays – and their predictive nature. My plays prognosticate so much, I begin to get worried when I embark on something dark, because I have too often later seen that thing happen. As it was, Latinx writers were not being done at the O'Neill back then, but the world has changed. Time wins over all of us.[37]

She did eventually meet Richards at the Last Frontier Theatre Conference in 2001, actually taking a glacier cruise with him in Valdez, Alaska, and was charmed by how down to earth and accessible he was, despite his legendary status in the American theatre. It was Richards's encouragement and his own belief in the development process he had created that inspired Romero to continue submitting her work to the O'Neill.

Revolutions/Revoluciones: Innovation in Process

While the O'Neill represents the primary model of new play development, Romero's ability to engage with different models of play development is exemplified in her development of her 2019 play *Revolutions/Revoluciones*. After many years of wrestling with notions of war in her shorter works, and with the success of *Graveyard of Empires* and *A Work of* Art, upon her return to Arizona, she revised a short play *Revolutions/Revoluciones* into a larger work, developing the notion of tetralogy of plays on war. Having originally written *Revolutions/Revoluciones* as a ten-minute play that initially received production in New York and later internationally, in Panama, she reconceived it as a full-length play at the Hermitage Artists Retreat (with a personal goal that the play would be first presented in Spanish). Collaborating with Romero on the project was Bruno Bichir, one of the bright stars of Mexico's theatre and film community. Bichir hoped to realize Romero's dream of presenting the play in Spanish in Mexico, and attracted fellow Mexico City artists for the project. Bichir comes directly from a family of artists, where all of its five members (his parents and his two older brothers) are also well-recognized actors and directors. Among this tight Mexican celebrity group of friends were the best and most celebrated Mexican artists such as Salma Hayek, Diego Luna, Gael García Bernal, Alfonso Cuarón, Guillermo Del Toro, and Alejandro González Iñárritu. Bichir's involvement with *Revolutions/Revoluciones* assured that Romero's work may reach audiences in both the United States and in Mexico. Bichir's vision of Romero's play was realized in Spanish by the Latino Theatre Company in association with Mexico's Foro Shakespeare, at the Los Angeles Theatre Center in May 2019, under the artistic direction of José Luis Valenzuela. The production represented one more step to Romero's larger project of a tetralogy of plays dealing with war – and each of the plays in her tetralogy has had a similarly unique development process. The story of Elaine Romero's personal journey as a Latinx playwright navigating the waters of new play development and production in America's regional theatre offers some important insights into its history and ongoing change.

Of course, producing new work has always been enormously risky, whether following the somewhat rarefied careers of Carey Perloff, Robert Falls, Lloyd Richards, and JoAnne Akalaitis in the high atmospheres of major institutions like the American Conservatory Theatre, the Goodman Theatre, the O'Neill Theater Center, or the Guthrie, or traveling alongside busy, hardworking Latinx playwright Elaine Romero, resident playwright at Arizona Theatre Company, one of America's larger regional theatres. In some ways, hamstrung by subscriber audiences, and yet continuing to successfully educate those same audiences, artistic directors and playwrights in both realms struggle, recommit, and continue to prove there is a fertile and magic garden in the American regional theatre for challenging, adventurous new work.

Notes

1. D. Anderson, "The Dream Machine: Thirty Years of New Play Development in America," *TDR*, 32:3 (1988), p. 57.
2. G. Boyd and P. R. Tetreault, "In Company We Trust," *American Theatre*, 19:4 (2002), p. 6.
3. Ibid.
4. R. Avila, "Carey Perloff: Left Coast, Right Time," *American Theatre*, 38:4 (2017), www.americantheatre.org/2017/09/26/carey-perloff-left-coast-right-time/.
5. Ibid.
6. E. Milvy, "For 'A Thousand Splendid Suns,' a Well-Timed Journey from the Page to the Stage," *LA Times*, January 19, 2017, www.latimes.com/entertainment/arts/la-ca-cm-thousand-splendid-suns-20170122-htmlstory.html.
7. A. Fliotsos and W. Vierow, *American Women Stage Directors of the Twentieth Century* (University of Illinois Press, 2008), p. 49.

8. Fliotsos and Vierow, *American Women Stage Directors*, pp. 41–42.

9. A. J. Nouryeh, "JoAnne Akalaitis: Post Modern Director or Socio-Sexual Critic," *Theatre Topics*, 1:2 (1991), pp. 177–91.

10. D. Saivetz, "An Event in Space: The Integration of Acting and Design in the Theatre of JoAnne Akalaitis," *TDR*, 42:2 (1998), p. 138.

11. Ibid., pp. 132–56.

12. E. B. Mee, "JoAnne Akalaitis Bears 'Bad News!' The Visionary Director Returns to the Stage with Timely Messages from the Greeks," *American Theatre*, 36:7 (2019), pp. 42–43.

13. T. London et al., *Outrageous Fortune: The Life and Times of the New American Play* (Theatre Development Fund, 2009), pp. 24–26.

14. Anderson, "The Dream Machine," pp. 55–84.

15. J. W. Zeisler, *Regional Theatre: The Revolutionary Stage* (University of Minnesota Press, 1973), pp. 193–94.

16. D. Pollack-Pelzner, "You've Probably Never Heard Of: America's Most Popular Playwright," *The New Yorker*, October 16, 2017, www.newyorker.com/books/page-turner/youve-probably-never-heard-of-americas-most-popular-playwright.

17. W. Harris, "How a Lone Producer Gambled on an Epic," *New York Times*, November 7, 1993, p. 2:5.

18. E. Romero, interview with author, March 4, 2020.

19. London et al., *Outrageous Fortune*, pp. 80–81.

20. Ibid., p. 83.

21. Ibid., pp. 61–62.

22. A. Feldman, "Q&A: Tony Kushner the Master Wordsmith Reflects on a Busy Season of Work," *TimeOut*, May 24, 2011, www.timeout.com/newyork/film/q-a-tony-kushner-drama.

23. J. Geltstaff, "The Peak TV Era Has Sparked a New Love Affair between Playwrights and the Small Screen," *LA Times*, November 17, 2017, www.latimes.com/entertainment/arts/la-ca-cm-playwrights-on-tv-20171119-story.html.

24. D. Tran, "Want My Time? Please Pay for It," *American Theatre*, 32:1 (2015), pp. 86–91.

25. H. Sidford and A. Frasz, "Assessment of the National Playwright Residency Program," report prepared for HowlAround, Hellicon, 2017, https://helicon collab.net/our_work/national-playwright-residency-program-assessment/.

26. K. Lengel, "Exit Interview: Arizona Theatre's David Goldstein," *The Republic*, May 22, 2017, www.azcentral.com/story/entertainment/arts/2017/05/22/exit-interview-david-ira-goldstein-arizona-theatre-company/331925001.

27. E. Romero, interview with author, December 17, 2019.

28. London et al., *Outrageous Fortune*, p. 59.

29. Ibid.

30. C. Jones, "The Man and the Challenge," *American Theatre*, 16:6 (1999), p. 16.

31. Romero, interview with author, December 17, 2019.

32. Romero, interview with author, December 18, 2019.
33. Romero, interview with author, July 3, 2019.
34. J. Sweet, *The O'Neill: The Transformation of Modern American Theater* (Yale University Press, 2014), p. 55.
35. Ibid., p. 59.
36. Romero, interview with author, March 4, 2020.
37. Romero, interview with author, July 3, 2019.

Select Bibliography

Anderson, D. "The Dream Machine: Thirty Years of New Play Development in America." *TDR*, 32:3 (1988), 55–84.

Fliostos, A., and W. Vierow. *American Women Stage Directors of the Twentieth Century*. University of Illinois Press, 2008.

London, T., et al. *Outrageous Fortune: The Life and Times of the New American Play*. Theatre Development Fund, 2009.

Nouryeh, A. J. "JoAnne Akalaitis: Post Modern Director or Socio-Sexual Critic." *Theatre Topics*, 1:2 (1991), 177–91.

Saivetz, D. "An Event in Space: The Integration of Acting and Design in the Theatre of JoAnne Akalaitis." *TDR*, 42:2 (1998), 132–56.

PART III

Experimental Theatre and Other Forms of Entertainment

Experimental Collectives of the 1960s and Their Legacies

Timothy Youker

American ensemble-based play composition emerged in the 1960s as a reaction against the repressive norms of Cold War-era culture. Working against the rigid, homogenizing structures of the corporation, the nuclear family, and the military, a wave of experimental theatre ensembles explored alternative modes of community and nonhierarchical approaches to making plays. Influential ensembles such as the Living Theatre, The Performance Group, the Open Theater, and the San Francisco Mime Troupe each offered their own models for such processes, which influenced contemporary collective creation as well as contemporary playwriting. At the same time, these groups and their successors demonstrated the core challenges and pitfalls of collective playmaking. Modeling utopian social praxis while also making formally innovative art that rigorously analyzes urgent political issues is a very tall order. Many avant-garde ensembles founded in the 1960s and 1970s split or dissolved because of tensions among members about how to pursue and balance those aims. Groups from later decades that built on the work of 1960s ensembles have often had to develop new organizational and dramaturgical strategies to find their own balance and adjust to changing times.

The United States was not the only country where companies experimented with collective playmaking styles in the 1960s, but the social, economic, and political circumstances in the United States at that time made it a particularly germinal environment for such work. In the 1960s, the United States saw both a rapid increase in institutional arts funding and the growth of a youth counterculture that rejected capitalist and fine arts institutions, choosing to make do instead with found materials and repurposed spaces. The chief targets of this counterculture's critiques were capitalist individualism, racial segregation, sexual repression, and the US invasion of Vietnam.

In 1961, the nonprofit Ford Foundation launched a massive initiative to fund new repertory theatre companies in cities across the United States. In 1965, the US government created the National Endowment for the Arts to help support experimental artists. At the time, these and other cultural initiatives were seen as a key front in the Cold War. Leaders argued that greater funding for American artists would help spread American ideals and close the "culture gap" that led Europeans to view the United States as culturally backward. Alternative theatres in the 1960s arose both because of these new institutions and, at times, in opposition to them. As theatre historian Theodore Shank notes, many 1960s theatre companies were part of the "drop-out culture" of the 1950s and 1960s, which was itself a response to the affluence and conformity of the postwar middle class.[1] "Drop-out culture" valorized not working within or profiting from established institutions, even when that meant accepting a life of poverty and obscurity. For example, R. G. Davis, founder of the San Francisco Mime Troupe, refused to seek money from the NEA or Ford on the grounds that companies that accepted such funds would "end up selling capitalism, or at least accepting its framework, no matter what promises company members made to each other."[2] The Open Theater applied for and received money from the NEA, Ford, and the New York State Council for the Arts, but the Open Theater's co-founder Joe Chaikin frequently fretted about the Open's artistic mission becoming compromised by money and success.

For many experimental ensembles, community building and formal experiment mattered more than conventional measures of artistic success. As performance historian Sally Banes put it, 1960s avant-garde theatre, in content and practice, "supplied images of alternative communities that changed power relations, creating intimacy outside the family and equality among members."[3] Mainstream American culture during the Cold War generally portrayed individualism as morally superior to the collectivism of communist societies. Styles of art that critics could easily identify with individualist ideology and the Romantic figure of the lone, toiling artist tended to receive the most institutional support in the 1950s. Erasing divisions of labor, flattening hierarchies, sharing credit for creative work, and resisting the allure of "selling out" were seen not only as methodological choices but also as acts of rebellion.

American experimental theatre makers often replaced dominant norms of professionalism with an embrace of popular culture and collective ritual. Alfred Poland and Bruce Mailman distinguish the 1960s American avant-garde from earlier forms of experimental theatre in the United States on the basis of the former's extensive engagement with American pop culture:

"One need only be familiar with general American sociology to understand the new syntax: the movies on Saturday nights, popcorn, Cokes, the radio, TV, comic strips, drugs, etc."[4] Poland and Mailman argue that while Broadway playwrights were mostly content to build off of the work of Ibsen and Chekhov, the American avant-garde drew on "the mythology of American folk art," by which they did not mean "folk art" as an art historian or anthropologist would define the term, but rather the iconography of American popular culture and entertainment.[5]

In the theatre, this interest in popular and folk culture often dovetailed with a desire to return the theatre to a (partly imagined) primal state, in which theatre was neither high art nor a diversion for the wealthy but a communal ritual and bonding activity. Julian Beck of the Living Theatre wrote in 1964 that their collective's goal was "to aid the audience to become more what it was destined to be when the first dramas fanned themselves on the threshing floor; a congregation led by priests, a choral ecstasy of reading and response."[6] Political theatre scholar Henry Lesnick, writing in 1973, saw contemporary street theatre as a return to "the communal festival of primitive society," which the emergence of a class society had turned into "the play produced by professionals for consumption by an audience."[7] While mixing ancient rituals with Coca-Cola, hot dogs, comic strips, and soap operas might seem counterintuitive, many 1960s artists saw both ritual and pop culture as inclusive and equalizing alternatives to "highbrow" culture.

With this thematic interest in equality and boundary-breaking, there also came an interest in approaches to production that equalized the elements of theatre – text, speech, music, movement, light, space, imagery – and removed the imaginary "fourth wall" separating performers and spectators. A key influence in this regard was the Epic Theatre of German writer-director Bertolt Brecht, who also called for a separation of theatrical elements and the demise of the fourth wall. Though Brecht himself lived and worked in California from 1941 to 1947, his impact on American theatre was only indirect until the early to mid-1960s, when popular English translations of his plays and essays began to appear. Brecht encouraged spectators to treat theatrical events not as artful illusions produced for passive consumption but as self-consciously slanted and contestable acts of showing performed by actors occupying the same space as them. In "The Street Scene" (1938), Brecht argued that theatre, at its most primitive level, should be like an eye-witness account of a traffic accident, in which the witness presents their own partial account, demonstrating what they thought had happened and contesting the accounts of other witnesses; at a more advanced level, the different "witnesses" might include actors as well as other production elements: projected media, music, or prewritten text, each of which communicates to the audience in its own formal language. Brecht believed that critical analysis of lived situations could improve the human condition, and he wanted his epic theatre to give spectators an occasion to hone their analytical skills.

Another key European influence was French director Antonin Artaud, whose germinal book of essays *The Theatre and Its Double* (1938) was translated into English in 1958 by Mary C. Richards. Artaud rejected the idea that the primary purpose of theatre was to enact or interpret the vision of a playwright as encoded in a dramatic text, arguing that theatre should instead be a physically and emotionally overwhelming multisensory event, in which text is not the controlling element or even necessarily an element at all. Artaud argued that theatre should aspire toward "cruelty," an uncompromising portrayal of human existence pushed to sensory and moral extremes. Such a "Theatre of Cruelty," as Artaud called it, would force audiences to confront and accept their own inner darkness and, consequently, reject the banality and conformity of their lives outside the theatre. Artaud's writing is shot through with a dark personal vision of the human race as universally depraved, but American interpreters of Artaud tended to elide or discard the pessimistic strains in Artaud's thinking, focusing instead on the liberating potential of a theatre that could spur social change through shock tactics. The ease with which Americans detached Artaud's aesthetic ideas from his social views is best evidenced by how many American artists in the 1960s treated Artaud's ideas as a complement to Brecht's, despite how much their politics and views on the human condition differed.

One of the first groups to synthesize these various social and theoretical influences was the Living Theatre, a New York-based group organized in 1947 by Judith Malina and Julian Beck. Malina and Beck learned about Brecht via Malina's teacher, former Brecht associate Erwin Piscator, and were exposed to Artaud in 1958, when composer John Cage gave them a copy of Richards's translation of *The Theatre and Its Double*. Their efforts to Americanize Brecht and particularly Artaud resulted in their productions of Jack Gelber's *The Connection* (1959) and Kenneth Brown's *The Brig* (1963).

The Connection (1959) follows the fictional premise that a playwright and producer have paid a group of real heroin addicts to perform a play about their lives for an audience and film crew, with a live jazz quartet providing musical accompaniment. The Living Theatre production adopted a hyperrealistic acting style – the cast mumbled, meandered, and tossed away their lines – that left some audience members wondering whether they were actually watching real junkies onstage (the Freddie Redd Quartet, who performed the music, actually had all lost their cabaret licenses for drug-related reasons). The production was Epic insofar as it estranged the common artistic practice of treating stories about the poor and marginalized as fodder for melodrama and cultural tourism. Its cruelty lay in its unflinching depiction of the grinding boredom and anxiety experienced by addicts perpetually waiting for another fix. In the play's notorious concluding scene, a character shoots himself up and nearly dies of an overdose onstage. The overdose sequence proved so convincing that it routinely caused audience members to faint.[8] Lastly, the production's embrace of jazz and junky culture participated in what Poland and Mailman called Off-Off-Broadway's embrace of popular "folklore." The critic Kenneth Tynan, an important early proponent of the Living Theatre, noted that *The Connection* became such a sensation that "there are few prominent Broadway figures who would admit, with anything like pride," to not having seen it.[9]

The Brig (1963) was inspired by Kenneth Brown's experiences as an inmate in a US Marine Corps brig in Japan. The Living's set recreated a Marine Corps brig as described by Brown, complete with a chain link fence separating most of the stage space from the audience. Cast members studied the Marine Corp Handbook as preparation for the performance. While *The Brig* was performed from a fixed text, Brown's play offers little in the way of plot or characterization. The brig inmates and guards are flat types, and the action consists of little more than their everyday routine, with minimal disruption and no developing conflict. If *The Brig* has a meaning, then, its meaning derives not from its linguistic content but from the sensory and emotional experience that it evokes in performance. A key part of that emotional experience was the naturalistic depiction of the violence that brig guards regularly inflicted on inmates, from shouted verbal abuse to gut punches dealt out as punishment for minor infractions. According to Malina's director's notes, the goal of *The Brig*'s extreme violence was to make the audience "know violence in the clear light of the kinship of our physical empathy,"[10] which the Living Theatre hoped would wake audience members up to the intolerable violence happening around them in the world outside the theatre. "The immovable structure is the villain," Malina wrote, "whether that structure calls itself a prison or a school or a factory or a family or a government or The World as It Is."[11]

The brig offered one possible synecdoche for that cruel, immovable structure, which the Living Theatre wished to explode to pieces.

According to Beck's observations of Malina in rehearsal, she also tried to avoid erecting immovable structures within the production process: "The careful directing books we had used at the beginning were quite gone. She began to suggest rather than tell, and the company began to find a style that was not superimposed but rose of their own sensitivities. The director was resigning from the authoritarian position."[12] By the time *The Brig* opened, the Living Theatre had become an anarchist commune as well as a theatre company. Being part of the Living was not just an artistic avocation for its members; it increasingly became a way of life, and many of its members left the country along with Malina and Beck when they went into self-imposed exile in 1964 after a legal dispute over back taxes.

The Living Theatre was just one of the first of many companies of its type to appear in Greenwich Village, a neighborhood encompassing the west side of Manhattan between Fourteenth Street and Houston Street. The Village has been associated with bohemian culture and experimental theatre since the 1920s, and in the 1950s and 1960s, it was home to a host of jazz clubs, bars, and coffee houses that served as gathering places for artists, as well as several key institutions that supported artistic experimentation. The left-leaning congregation at Judson Memorial Church offered free space for the Judson Poet's Theatre, Judson Dance Theatre, and Judson Gallery, along with a promise never to censor the content of the art made and displayed by those groups. The Church of St. Mark's in-the-Bowery lent space to Theatre Genesis and later to Richard Foreman's Ontological-Hysteric Theatre. Ellen Stewart's Café La Mama (later renamed La MaMa Experimental Theatre Club) and Joe Cino's Caffé Cino offered small but lively venues for experimental playwrights. The theatre produced in these and other spaces in and around the Village came to be known as Off-Off-Broadway theatre.

Off-Off-Broadway theatre's relationship to space was determined not only by aesthetic and political preferences but also by the fact that performances tended to happen in spaces that were not designed for theatre. Performances happened in cafés, church basements, and converted industrial spaces, as well as outside in parks and on street corners. The Performing Garage, home to The Performance Group and its successor, the Wooster Group, is a converted flatware factory with a motorized garage door at one end of the space. The Caffé Cino required playwrights to create texts that could play on a tiny stage for an audience mere inches away from the performers. Café La MaMa's original space was a basement with a dirt floor that Ellen Stewart covered with fruit crates. The modernist vision of the performance space as an empty black box was simply not practicable in these spaces, nor was the realist convention of an invisible fourth wall particularly suited to them. Not only did Off-Off-Broadway venues often lack physical boundaries between playing place and audience space, but they also often lacked rigging for the kinds of lighting technology that modern designers use to evoke the illusion of a fourth wall.

In his essay "Six Axioms for Environmental Theatre" (1968), director and performance scholar Richard Schechner offered a theoretical justification for Off-Off-Broadway theatre's practical relationship with space. Schechner defines theatrical performance as "a set of interrelated transactions" among performers, spectators, a space, and nonhuman production elements.[13] In other words, a theatrical performance is not a unified work but a collection of coinciding and overlapping moments of interaction in which all elements are equal and, as Schechner asserts later in the same essay, "all production elements speak in their own language."[14] In conventional Western theatre, a playwright and director arrange these theatrical transactions to evoke a bounded, seamless onstage "world" in which a linear plot unfolds, and every member of the audience has more or less the same experience. Schechner believed that by instead using unconventional spatial arrangements to create unpredictable interactions among performers and spectators, environmental theatre could make its audiences reconsider the politics of space in everyday life.

Schechner put his ideas to the test as director of The Performance Group, which operated out of the Performing Garage in Manhattan's SoHo neighborhood from 1967 to 1980. In *Dionysus in '69* (1968), adapted from *The Bacchae* of Euripides, the audience was permitted to occupy any space in the theatre, including anywhere on a set of multilevel wooden towers and platforms designed by Michael Kirby and Jerry Rojo. In enacting the conflict between Dionysus, God of wine and theatre, and his prudish, misogynistic mortal cousin King Pentheus, the actors recited their lines from positions all over the space, and during many scenes walked among the spectators naked or nearly naked. To promote confusion between fiction and actuality, performers addressed and referred to each other both by their characters' names and by their real names. Midway through each performance, Dionysus would challenge Pentheus to try to "pick up" a female spectator and experience free love for himself. Pentheus's efforts at seduction almost inevitably failed – and in fact had to fail in order for the play's central conflict to unfold as scripted – but during at least one performance someone said yes, bringing the performance to an abrupt halt.[15]

The text of *Dionysus in '69* modernized much of Euripides' original dialogue, drawing clear comparisons between the play's central conflict and the clash between "hip" and "square" cultures in the 1960s. Dionysus and his nude Bacchae stood in for a liberated life promised by the hippie counterculture, a life free of the "immovable structure" that Malina decried. At the same time, as the Bacchae's orgy ends with them devouring Pentheus (an event that happens offstage in Euripides' play but occurs in front of the audience in The Performance Group's version), the Bacchae also stand in for the darker side of the counterculture, the threat of descending into violent anarchy. By allowing the cast and spectators to intermingle, *Dionysus in '69* evoked both the freedom and the vulnerability of bodies in a world without boundaries.

While The Performance Group sought liberation and a sense of community through eliminating conventional spatial and social boundaries in the theatre, another ensemble headquartered elsewhere in Lower Manhattan, the Open Theater, was exploring a more physically rigorous approach to personal liberation. The Open Theater began when a collection of actors, directors, and writers, many of whom had been students of the acting teacher Nola Chilton, met in a loft in Greenwich Village in 1963 to continue the work on nonnaturalistic acting that Chilton had begun with them in her classes. This group included former Living Theatre members Joe Chaikin and Peter Feldman and playwrights Megan Terry and Sam Shepard (Jean-Claude van Itallie, the playwright most closely associated with the group, joined a few months later). While the Open initially only gave public performances to showcase their workshop findings, they transitioned over the mid-1960s into a company that produced both conventionally authored and collectively created plays.

The Open sought to strip theatre down to its most essential element: what Chaikin, who emerged as the Open's de facto leader, called "the presence of the actor," the actor's "deep, libidinal surrender" of themselves to a live audience.[16] The Open developed a minimalist approach, in which the actor's expressive body took the place of scenery and props, and in which prewritten dialogue was only one of many forms of sound through which actors revealed their inner lives. Many of the Open's foundational exercises involved breath control, learning how to breathe and speak in unison, and learning how to stage scenes in which actors engaged in multiple simultaneous dialogues. Sound-and-movement exercises, derived from Chilton's acting games, asked actors to employ their whole bodies and full vocal ranges to communicate feelings or concepts nonverbally.

A key element of the Open's acting style was what they called transformations. In transformation-based acting, the actor's primary commitment is not building a role or embodying a single coherent character but following a set of rules or patterns that govern their onstage transformations from one persona to another. As Schechner explains in his writing on the Open, "Each unit within a set of transformations is (or can be) as 'real' as any bit of naturalistic acting; but the quick changes from one bit to another give the overall effect of kaleidoscope, fluidity, and scenic explosion."[17] Alternatively, a transformation may leave the performer within the same situation but ask them to shift their point of view on that situation. In his book *The Presence of the Actor* (1973), Chaikin uses the example of a burning house, inviting actors to imagine themselves first as a person inside a burning house catching fire, then as a neighbor witnessing the fire, then a reporter reporting on the fire, and finally a someone listening to a report of the fire on the radio, exploring how the nature of their emotional investment in the situation changes as their role shifts.[18]

In Megan Terry's play *Viet Rock* (1966), which she developed with the original cast through a series of workshops at the Open, the "burning house" is the war in Vietnam. The cast (Terry's text specifies no number, but the original cast consisted of seven men and seven women) embodies characters occupying various positions in relation to the war: draftees sent overseas to fight, their anxious families, the jingoistic sergeant who trains them, policy experts at a congressional hearing, Vietcong fighters, Vietnamese villagers, and a North Vietnamese radio propagandist. In some cases, such as the congressional hearing, actors in the original production had to switch roles rapidly mid-scene. The play's first scene consists of an extended sound-and-movement sequence: the cast performs sounds associated with infancy and childhood innocence while arranged on the floor in a circle like petals on a flower, then gets up and acts out wordless scenes evoking boyhood and motherhood, which culminate in a scene of seven mothers sending their sons to war. The play ends with the entire cast dying in combat in a formation resembling a ruined version of the flower from the beginning. Then the dead rise and exit the theatre through the audience, lightly touching audience members on their way out. This process of transforming from child to soldier to corpse to risen ghost – while embodying a variety of other characters in between – is the "story" of *Viet Rock*.

Another foundational Open Theater practice was "jamming," a practice inspired by jazz music. In a jamming session, a single actor begins an improvisation based on a single theme or "emblem" (a word, phrase, or gesture that evokes an abstract concept or feeling). Chaikin explains: "One actor comes in and moves in contemplation of a theme, travelling within rhythms, going through and out of the phrasing, sometimes using just the gesture, sometimes reducing the whole thing to pure sound."[19] A second actor steps in to build off of it, and then another. Each new actor that steps into the scene must make sure that their personal contribution complements what is already happening in the playing space, until a complex stage image has emerged.

The Open's most acclaimed production, *The Serpent* (1968), included several scenes built through jamming. *The Serpent* began with a lengthy exploratory workshop process inspired by the first five chapters of the Book of Genesis. At one point, Chaikin asked the cast to improvise scenes inspired by their own personal visions of Eden:

> [The] premise was that everyone had his garden-in-the-mind, this place that the world isn't, this utopia – where creatures are themselves. ... An authentic image came; somebody got on the stage and introduced it. ... One actor will get up and do his garden and if another actor is sensitive to it, he will join him so that they make a little world. A third actor may or may not join, depending on whether this garden does or does not signal anybody else. ... Soon somebody will start a world with its own logic, its own rules, and its own sense. Then we have a garden.[20]

The Open followed a similar process in creating *Terminal* (1970), a piece focused on death, dying, and those who care for the terminally ill, drawing on such source material as research into the physiology of dying, performers' personal experiences caring for dying loved ones, and various religious perspectives on death. The performers, referred to as The Dying in Susan Yankowitz's script, channeled spirts of the dead – most memorably, New Orleans Voodoo Queen Marie Laveau, who "took over" the body of cast member Paul Zimet.

A generation of major American playwrights got their start in Off-Off-Broadway, and their playwriting was often shaped by collaborations with ensembles such as the Living and Open Theatres and Performance Group. In addition to Terry and van Itallie, Sam Shepard, Maria Irene Fornes, Adrienne Kennedy, Ed Bullins, and Lanford Wilson all spent time working in this creative crucible. Shepard, who was a founding member of the Open and worked with The Performance Group on a production of his play *The Tooth of Crime* (1972), continued to incorporate transformation-based structures into his plays for the remainder of his career, while Fornes's most famous play, *Fefu and Her Friends* (1977), has a nonlinear, compartmental structure that recalls environmental theatre. Van Itallie also influenced many later playwrights in his work as a writing teacher at Yale and New York University, most notably Tony Kushner, whose *Angels in America* duology (1991–92) requires cast members to switch roles repeatedly and to shuttle between naturalistic and hallucinatory worlds.

While the Open Theater saw rigorous formal innovation as politically transformative in itself, not everyone agreed with that argument. On the other side of the United States, another influential 1960s collective – the San Francisco Mime Troupe (SFMT) – was working toward its own answer to the question of how to balance aesthetics and community engagement. SFMT began in 1959 as the R. G. Davis Mime Troupe, under the direction of R. G. "Ronny" Davis, an assistant director at the Actors' Workshop of San Francisco, a major regional theatre. Davis's troupe began as an experimental wing of the Actors' Workshop, giving late-night performances in the theatre's small basement space. Inspired by his studies with noted French mime Étienne Decroux but unhappy with French mime's purism and traditionalism, Davis sought to fuse European mime and clowning traditions with American-style modern dance and left-wing politics. By late 1963, Davis had already heard of the Open Theater and begun to incorporate some of the Open's exercises in rehearsals, but Davis saw the Open as part of "the right wing of the Radical Independent Theatres" because of its plays' lack of direct engagement with concrete political issues.[21]

The troupe, soon renamed the San Francisco Mime Troupe, began giving free Commedia dell'Arte performances in parks in 1962. While they performed traditional scenarios in traditional costume, they adapted the texts or added topical ad libs to connect the action to current social issues such as the war, racism, homelessness, or public health. They also performed premodern songs with new lyrics commenting on current events, often as a prelude to the main performance, to attract the attention of passersby. All performances ended with "the pitch," in which a performer would explain what members of the audience could do about issues raised in the performance and ask for donations.

In describing the relationship with its public that the SFMT developed through their park performances, Davis coined the term "Guerilla Theatre," which he defined as revolutionary theatre that "travels light and makes friends of the populace," prioritizing mobility and community engagement.[22] Over the remainder of the decade, their guerilla approach expanded to include other types of performances. The Gorilla Marching Band, dressed in outfits made of rags, would march in local parades, following every song by flashing signs that read "GET OUT OF VIETNAM." Following the example of Peter Schumann's Bread and Puppet Theatre and the San Francisco Women's Street Theatre, they began creating works for portable puppet theatres and "crankies," a crude form of moving picture in which words and images are written on a single long sheet that a crank-operated device then causes to scroll past the audience. They also made their own defiance of legal authorities a spectacle in itself. In 1965, Davis staged his own arrest in a public park for playing without a permit, to protest the Parks Commission's efforts to censor theatre performed in public spaces; after gathering a sizable crowd, Davis announced his own arrest and leaped into the arms of a group of police officers.

While Davis favored work inspired by Commedia and music-hall theatre, the collective that SFMT became after his departure in 1970 draws on the styles and iconography of melodrama, B-movies, comic books, pulp fiction, and commercial musicals. Joan Holden explained this change by stating that workers should be given stories in which "an underdog fights an overlord and wins" and issues are clear "matters of right and wrong."[23] For example, stagings of *Hotel Universe* (1977), SFMT's musical about a group of elderly residents protesting the demolition of their residential hotel, represented an apartment fire with orange paper streamers, while the riot police who disperse the protesting tenants were simply drawings on large sheets of paper that actors carried across the stage. The post-Davis troupe's composition process begins with picking a topic and style for the performance by group consensus, followed by a period of research by the full group. Then a small group of members writes the material, and a single director runs rehearsals and guides revisions of the text.

While the rise of experimental ensembles in America is inextricably tied to the social and political context of the 1960s, new companies and new techniques continued to emerge in subsequent decades, and those companies have often built on the work of 1960s companies. These parallel developments have included: the proliferation of ensembles expressly founded to center women's, LGBTQ+ or ethnically minoritized perspectives; a retreat by some other companies away from programmatic politics and toward formalism and irony; and a growing tendency to frame theatre as the practice of (re)building and navigating social worlds via practical frameworks such as Viewpoints and Moment Work.

A key pitfall for theatres that follow collective creation processes is that collaborations that seem equal on the surface may in fact reproduce inequalities prevalent in the outside world. Roberta Sklar, discussing her work as a dramaturg and assistant director in the Open Theater, said: "I worked much in the same way women did in the peace movement and the student movement. We did a lot of the work, got little of the credit, and didn't realize that there was a major section missing in the political analysis – the section that was about us."[24] Artists of color working in white-dominated ensembles also felt at times like they were being exploited or not being fully heard, or that the part of the political analysis that was about them was being neglected. Realizing that a purely formalist rigor often renders artists blind to what's missing from supposedly "universal" forms and stories, many female, queer, and nonwhite theatre artists decided in the 1970s and 1980s that they needed to form companies that centered their own experiences.

In 1976, Muriel Miguel, who had performed as part of the Open Theater in *Viet Rock, The Serpent,* and *Terminal,* cofounded Spiderwoman Theater with her sisters Gloria Miguel and Lisa Mayo. Spiderwoman's creation process, called Storyweaving, resembles the Open's process, but it draws its organizing metaphors from Native American storytelling and Indigenous women's collective textile-making practices. "We translate our personal stories, dreams, and images into movement," they explain in a group statement. "We usually begin with a theme, someone tells a story, another repeats it, and we work together to transform it into movement and reduce it to its essence. Muriel Miguel, as director, makes the final decision as to what works and what doesn't with an eye toward the creation of an entire production, but everyone in the group has a voice and doesn't hesitate to use it to express herself."[25] While earlier Off-Off-Broadway ensembles used analogous methods and promoted a craftwork-based ethos, Spiderwoman does so in a way that treats Indigenous and female perspectives as central rather than secondary. Major works by Spiderwoman include *Sun, Moon, and Feather* (1981), *Winnetou's Snake Oil Show from Wigwam City* (1988), and *Power Pipes* (1992).

Lois Weaver, who participated in Spiderwoman's early productions, later split off from the company to form Split Britches with Peggy Shaw and Deb Margolin. Starting with the self-titled show, *Split Britches* (1981), and continuing with works including *Beauty and the Beast* (1982), *Little Women* (1988), and *Lesbians Who Kill* (1992), the trio produced works blending personal experience and pop culture pastiche, staged in a rough, low-cost style inspired by the aesthetics of Off-Off-Broadway and Shaw's clown training. Split Britches performers were also among the founders of WOW Café, a Lower Manhattan venue that bills itself as a "collectively-run performance space for women and/or trans artists,"[26] and has offered space to many practitioners of devised theatre. Artists that venue helped to launch included the Five Lesbian Brothers (Maureen "Moe" Angelos, Lisa Kron, Babs Davy, Dominique Dibbell, and Peg Healey), who achieved notoriety for their collectively authored plays *Brave Smiles … another lesbian tragedy* (1992) and *Secretaries* (1993), both dark comedies that send up Hollywood stereotypes about lesbianism. Both Split Britches and Five Lesbian Brothers continue the downtown avant-garde's engagement with what Poland and Mailman called the mythology of American folk art, but their pop culture collages often reveal and remedy the absence or distortion of lesbian experience in that mythology.

A second, roughly simultaneous trend was a retreat by certain ensembles from direct political and social engagement in favor of formally playful, interpretively open-ended, and often ironically toned compositions. The political disillusionment of the 1970s (the Watergate scandal, economic malaise, a backlash against the civil rights movement) caused many artists to shed the optimism that characterized 1960s theatre. It is common, therefore, for scholars to describe the 1970s as a period when experimental artists retreated from utopian politics into more formalistic, introspective work. One can see signs of such a retreat in the supplanting of The Performance Group by the Wooster Group (1975–present), an offshoot of The Performance Group led by Schechner's former assistant Elizabeth LeCompte.

While The Performance Group sought to produce moments of unmediated exchange between performers and spectators, the Wooster Group has become known for investigating the many artificial means through which human presence and knowledge can be mediated. As Arnold Aronson discusses at length elsewhere in this volume, the Wooster Group was one of the better-known pioneers in using home video technology and audio and video matching (having actors move and speak in synch with recorded media) in devised performances. They were also influential practitioners of a type of theatre devising that prioritizes formal play with nondramatic media and pop culture artifacts over explicit thematic content or social engagement. *House/Lights* (1997) mashes up Gertrude Stein's verse play *Doctor Faustus Lights the Lights* (1938) with video-matching sequences inspired by the notorious pornographic film *Olga's House of Shame* (1964). *Poor Theatre* (2005) features the company's doomed effort to enact an exact recreation of scenes from Jerzy Grotowski's famous 1968 production of Stanisław Wyspiański's *Akropolis* based on studying and copying film footage. *La Didone* (2010) alternates scenes from Francesco Cavalli's seventeenth-century opera of the same name with live recreations of scenes from the shoddy English dub of an Italian science fiction film about space vampires.

While many of the Wooster Group's performers have backgrounds that include rigorous physical and vocal training, LeCompte favors an informal style of delivery that can read as glib or emotionally flat to audiences not accustomed to it. Making an engaging performance out of video- and voice-matching requires considerable skill and practice, but it can seem simplistic or superficial to a spectator who associates good acting with lifelike performances that index characters' psychological depths. Consequently, while the Wooster Group's work avoids any politically programmatic content, it rebels against conventional definitions of "good" acting and "fine art." Since the 1990s, many more groups with similar approaches have emerged. These groups make devised pieces centered on the puzzle of making theatre out of texts that don't "belong" in the theatre, or that would be judged as "bad" according to traditional aesthetic norms, and often do so while projecting an air of practiced awkwardness.

Elevator Repair Service (ERS), directed by former Wooster Group associate John Collins, is one such group. In *Room Tone* (2002), ERS made theatre out of the dense academic writing of psychologist William James and used video matching to devise dance breaks inspired by scenes from Stanley Kubrick's film *The Shining* (1980). Their pieces *Gatz* (2006), *The Sound and the Fury* (2007), and *The Select (The Sun Also Rises)* (2008) all explore ways to adapt classic novels into theatre while preserving what Collins calls their "bookness."[27] *Arguendo* (2012) dips into verbatim theatre by making a performance out of the oral arguments in *Barnes v. Glen Theatre*, a 1991 US Supreme Court case concerning the First Amendment rights of exotic dancers. ERS performances are full of intentional elements that feel mistaken or out of place: lurching movements, meandering or stuttered conversations, props that look like someone pulled them out of a closet at random. As scholar Sara Jane Bailes notes, ERS's dance breaks "function as disarticulatory interludes and are constituted out of well-practiced movements made to retain their clumsiness."[28] The resulting tension between virtuosity and awkwardness brings the audience back, over and over, to the immediacy of performance. It also forces one to reevaluate how one distinguishes correctness from mistakenness, both in art and in everyday life.

Another, comparable New York ensemble is the Nature Theater of Oklahoma (NTO), a group founded by director Pavol Liska and dramaturg Kelly Copper in 2006. According to their mission statement, NTO is devoted to "making the work we don't know how to make, putting ourselves in impossible situations, and working from out of our own ignorance and unease."[29] NTO's magnum opus is the ten-part cycle *Life and Times* (2009–16). Over the course of ten recorded phone conversations, musician Kristin Worrall narrated the story of her life to Liska and Copper. Instead of editing Worrall's sixteen-hour account into a neatly structured drama, Copper left the text largely intact, preserving all of Worrall's digressions and filler words. Each episode of *Life and Times* adapts a portion of Worrall's story in a different style. Part 1 resembles the calisthenics demonstrations and propaganda rallies that Liska watched as a child in Czechoslovakia, with actors in gray and red uniforms singing the text in a recitative style while dancing with balls and hoops. Part 2 is performed by an ensemble in striped tracksuits, in a style that resembles a 1980s music video. Parts 3 and 4 are staged as an Agatha Christie-style murder mystery play, with Worrall's reflections on puberty and high school delivered like lines from a crime thriller.

Another contemporary company that uses devising mainly for an occasion for formal play is the Saratoga International Theatre Institute (SITI), cofounded by American director Anne Bogart and Japanese director and acting teacher Tadashi Suzuki in 1992. Bogart worked with former members of the Open Theater in the 1980s and has often cited Chaikin as a key influence, but the two pillars of the SITI Company's practice are Suzuki's rigorous physical theatre training and the Viewpoints Method originally devised by dancer and choreographer Mary Overlie. Overlie developed her Six Viewpoints as a way to deconstruct theatre, to replace the conventional hierarchy in which all other elements serve the text with a system in which Space, Shape, Time, Emotion, Movement, and Story were coequal. "Instead of beginning with the idea of making theatre," Overlie writes, "this approach begins by taking theatre apart. To accomplish this task, it is necessary to be practiced at deconstruction or separating the whole into its essential parts."[30] With fellow director Tina Landau, Bogart developed a revised and expanded list of Viewpoints for the theatre and made the Viewpoints the foundation of a production process called Composition. Though Composition also includes phases of collective research and improvisation like the Open and SFMT, the Viewpoints add an extra analytical dimension to the process by breaking scenes down into thirteen key elements: Tempo, Duration, Kinesthetic Response, Repetition, Shape,

Gesture, Architecture, Spatial Relationship, Topography, Pitch, Volume, Silence, and Timbre. While Viewpoints is often called a "method," it does not offer formulas or recipes; it furnishes a rehearsal vocabulary and a heuristic for determining what might need to be added or adjusted in a particular scene. The Composition process can be used to create new plays from scratch or as a way to develop new interpretations of existing plays.

One of the SITI productions that exemplifies its Composition approach is *bobrauschenbergamerica* (2003), a play developed with and scripted by frequent SITI collaborator Charles L. Mee Jr. Drawing on visual motifs from the art of Robert Rauschenberg and a collage of texts by Rauschenberg, Walt Whitman, the Beats, John Cage, and texts produced by participants in a workshop at Skidmore College, *bobrauschenbergamerica* presents a sequence of thematically linked scenes that riff on American pop culture imagery. Though Mee's text contains named characters, these characters are little more than "types" – suburban housewife, trucker, hobo, and so on. The SITI Company performed the play on a set consisting of an American flag painted onto the rear and floor of the stage, so that the stripes run from up to down and then from upstage to downstage. The flag creates a simple set of geometric boundaries for the actors to play with, while chairs, ladders, and a small window high up the rear wall add vertical levels.

For all the opportunities for free play that it affords, Bogart and Landau's Composition also participates in a third trend that has become particularly prominent among companies founded since the early 1990s: using the relative formal freedom of devising methods to represent the institutional and technological structures that define (post)modern life in the developed world. Where Malina, Davis, Schechner, and Chaikin all saw their work as a struggle to shatter what Malina called "the immovable structure," contemporary artists often see their project as navigating and finding meaning within structures that never seem to stop moving. In practical terms, this often means deeper engagement with new media and/ or documentary sources and the use of site-specificity to connect theatrical performance with how our institutions and infrastructure "perform" (or fail to perform) in everyday life.

Another example of this trend is Tectonic Theater Project. Moisés Kaufman, co-founder and artistic director of Tectonic, was a student of Mary Overlie and influenced by her Viewpoints model. However, while Tectonic's method, called Moment Work, also begins with breaking theatre down into coequal expressive elements, Tectonic, in works such as *The Laramie Project* (2000), *I Am My Own Wife* (2004, with playwright Doug Wright), and *The Tallest Tree in the Forest* (2013), builds ad hoc structures for works centered on conventional forms of storytelling, often using primary documents to tell true stories. Kaufman rejects the idea, which many in the American avant-garde inherited from Artaud, that the dramatic text is "a tyrant" that needs to be overthrown. "If the 1990s and 2000s were about deconstruction," Kaufman states, "then perhaps our time now is about reconstruction."[31] When Tectonic devises a new play from scratch, the company begins by creating a catalog of Moments – brief, simple actions improvised around objects, gestures, texts, or ideas related to the piece's topic. The piece then takes its form through the company stringing and layering Moments together into scenes, connecting smaller units into larger units until a greater whole forms.

Philadelphia-based Pig Iron Theatre also combines ad hoc devising with an exploration of the systems that structure our lives. Founded in 1995, Pig Iron builds on a foundation inspired by the company members' backgrounds in French clowning and physical theatre (specifically the methods of Jacques Lecoq). Chaikin, who collaborated with them on their piece *Shut-Eye* (2001), was also a major influence. Though most of their pieces have some amount of text, Pig Iron often uses dance and mime as substitutes for written dialogue. Several Pig Iron pieces also make use of outdoor and built spaces not normally marked as "theatrical," such as the derelict industrial sites that dot the poorer parts of Philadelphia, which form the backdrop for *Anodyne* (2001), and the various sites used to stand in for bombed-out buildings in their World War I drama *Gentlemen Volunteers* (1998). Their more recent piece, *Zero Cost House* (2012), a collaboration with Japanese playwright Toshiki Okada, weaves together Okada's biography and thoughts on housing and ecology with those of Henry David Thoreau, producing a meditation on art's power to stage alternative ways of fashioning a society. *Superterranean* (2019), a collaboration with designer Mimi Lien, explores human relationships with urban infrastructure on a set designed by Lien to evoke the concrete interiors of waste treatment facilities and other similar public buildings.

Viewpoints and Moment Work both add an analytical framework on top of the more freeform process of jamming that 1960s groups such as the Open followed. This doesn't necessarily mean that either company is less committed than its predecessors to exploring what theatre can tell us about the practice of freedom. Bogart and Landau's productions of Mee's plays – even his darker, more violent works – are marked by an exuberant air of controlled chaos that recalls many Off-Off-Broadway productions of the

1960s. Tectonic's original production of *I Am My Own Wife*, a play about writer Doug Wright's friendship with the openly transgender German antiquarian Charlotte von Mahlsdorf, was both a masterclass in transformations (Jefferson Mayes single-handedly portrayed Wright, von Mahlsdorff, and dozens of other minor characters) and a poignant meditation on the compromises that people with marginalized identities often have to make to retain their freedom. As Tectonic's documentaries and Pig Iron's site-specific productions often suggest, a society without any reliable structures (housing, infrastructure, a fair justice system) is a society in which only the socioeconomically privileged are genuinely free.

In the contemporary theatre, the influence of radical devising ensembles of the 1960s and 1970s has diffused to the point where they can no longer be considered solely features of leftist or anarchist theatre, nor can the label of "devised theatre" or "ensemble-based theatre" be seen as connoting any specific staging style. The commonalities that remain are: striving for an egalitarian rehearsal space, equalizing the expressive elements of theatre, seeking a dramatic structure that fits the thematic and aesthetic goals of a specific piece instead of defaulting to a linear dramatic plot, and, in many cases, treating audience and space as components of a performance rather than external to it. While companies have devised many different systems, methods, and disciplines to help ease the composition process, collective ensemble creation remains, in many essential respects, a practice defined by freedom, however imperfect and perilous.

Notes

1. T. Shank, *Beyond the Boundaries* (University of Michigan Press, 2002), p. 2.
2. R. G. Davis, *The San Francisco Mime Troupe: The First Ten Years* (Ramparts Press, 1975), p. 10.
3. S. Banes, *Greenwich Village, 1963: Avant-Garde Performance and the Effervescent Body* (Duke University Press, 1993), p. 35.
4. A. Poland and B. Mailman, *The Off-Off Broadway Book: The Plays, People, Theatre* (Bobs-Merrill, 1972), p. 12.
5. Ibid.
6. J. Beck, "Storming the Barricades," in Kenneth Brown (ed.), *The Brig: A Concept for Theatre or Film* (Hill & Wang, 1965), p. 21.
7. H. Lesnick, *Guerrilla Street Theater* (Aron Books, 1973), p. 12.
8. Beck, "Storming the Barricades," p. 27.
9. K. Tynan, "Preface," in J. Gelber, *The Connection, a Play* (Grove Press, 196), p. 7.
10. Malina, "Directing *The Brig*," in Brown, *The Brig*, p. 106.

11. Ibid., p. 83.
12. Quoted in Banes, *Greenwich Village 1963*, p. 42.
13. R. Schechner, "Six Axioms for Environmental Theatre," *TDR*, 12:3 (Spring 1968), p. 41.
14. Ibid., p. 59.
15. Shank, *Beyond the Boundaries*, p. 96.
16. J. Chaikin, *The Presence of the Actor* (Theatre Communications Group, 1991), p. 20.
17. R. Schechner, "The Playwright as Writer," in M. Terry (ed.), *Viet Rock and Other Plays* (Touchstone, 1971), p. 11.
18. Chaikin, *Presence of the Actor*, p. 9.
19. Ibid., p. 116.
20. Ibid., pp. 62–64.
21. Davis, *The San Francisco Mime Troupe*, p. 130.
22. Ibid., p. 150.
23. S. V. Mason, *The San Francisco Mime Troupe Reader* (University of Michigan Press, 2005), p. 83.
24. R. Babb, "Ways of Working: Post-Open Theater Performance and Pedagogy," in J. Harding and C. Rosenthal (eds.), *Restaging the Sixties: Radical Theatres and Their Legacies* (University of Michigan Press, 2006), p. 112.
25. L. W. Jenkins, "Spiderwoman," in H. C. Chinoy and L. W. Jenkins (eds.), *Women in American Theatre*, Rev. and Exp. 3rd ed. (TCG Books, 2006), p. 292.
26. WOW Café Theatre, www.wowcafe.org/story/.
27. S. J. Bailes, "Elevator Repair Service – *Cab Legs* (1997) to *Gatz* (2006)," in J. Harvie and A. Lavender (eds.), *Making Contemporary Theatre: International Rehearsal Processes* (Manchester University Press, 2010), p. 84.
28. Ibid., p. 82.
29. Nature Theater of Oklahoma, *Life and Times Episode 1* (53rd State Press, 2013), p. 125.
30. M. Kaufman and B. Pitts-McAdams, *Moment Work: Tectonic Theater Project's Process for Devising Theatre* (Vintage Books, 2018), p. 11.
31. Ibid., pp. 13–14.

Select Bibliography

Banes, S. *Greenwich Village, 1963: Avant-Garde Performance and the Effervescent Body.* Duke University Press, 1993.
Bogart, A., and T. Landau. *The Viewpoints Book: A Practical Guide to Viewpoints and Composition.* Theatre Communications Group, 2004.
Bottoms, S. *Playing Underground: A Critical History of the 1960s Off-Off-Broadway Movement.* University of Michigan Press, 2006.
Kaufman, M., and B. Pitts-McAdams. *Moment Work: Tectonic Theatre Project's Process for Devising Theatre.* Vintage Books, 2018.

Malzacher, F. (ed.). *The Life and Work of Nature Theater of Oklahoma*. Alexander-Verlag, 2020.

Mason, S. V. *The San Francisco Mime Troupe Reader*. University of Michigan Press, 2005.

Quick, A. *The Wooster Group Workbook*. Routledge, 2007.

Shank, T. *Beyond the Boundaries: American Alternative Theatre*. University of Michigan Press, 2002.

Syssoyeva, K. M., and S. Proudfitt (eds.). *A History of Collective Creation*. Palgrave Macmillan, 2013.

Tytell, J. *The Living Theatre: Art, Exile, and Outrage*. Grove Press, 1995.

CHAPTER 9

Post-Avant-Garde Theatre

Arnold Aronson

The historical avant-garde emerged in Europe in the late nineteenth century as a significant development of the Romantic project.[1] Following World War II, the center of the avant-garde, in almost all genres, moved to the United States, in part because of the influx of artists escaping fascism and totalitarianism in Europe. It flourished in the United States in the postwar decades. But by the end of the millennium, the avant-garde was no longer a vital creative source of new performance; it was no longer sustainable in the age of postmodernism. The historical avant-garde had, in fact, succeeded in its goals of reshaping the dominant structures of artistic production and reception. Furthermore, the economics of a voracious culture industry had whole-heartedly absorbed the avant-garde as one more component of a vast and malleable mainstream to such an extent that a defining aspect of the avant-garde – a continuously evolving revolt against, and challenge to, the status quo – had been subverted. Almost every strategy advanced by avant-garde artists was instantly absorbed, often becoming transformed into tropes of everything from pop music to fashion. And at the same time, the rapidly rising costs of urban life, particularly a real estate market that used artists as pawns and then forced them farther and farther from centers of creativity while driving the costs of even the most basic resources out of reach, all sapped the vitality of a once thriving art world. Some would say the avant-garde was dead.[2]

Of course, this analysis was not new. Peter Bürger, as far back as 1974,[3] asserted that "since now the protest of the historical avant-garde against art as institution is accepted as *art*, the gesture of protest of the neo-avant-garde becomes inauthentic. Having been shown to be irredeemable, the claim to be protest can no longer be maintained."[4] Hal Foster, while disagreeing with Bürger's contention that the contemporary avant-garde was merely empty repetition, nonetheless situated the art world within historical stages of capitalism and acknowledged that "the structural codes which the modern avant-garde sought to transgress no longer exist as such or are no longer defended as such by the hegemonic culture. In this new, all-but-global reach of capital, there may be no natural limit to transgress."[5] And in a 1988 essay about two Wooster Group productions, critic Elinor Fuchs referred to the company as "this purest surviving example of our all but vanished theater avant-garde."[6]

But to suggest that the avant-garde was "dead" was not to announce the end of experimentation, innovation, the search for new forms of expression, or attempts to alter our perception of the world. It just meant that the framework, the methodologies, the structures, and perhaps certain goals had changed. But the newer forms of art that were still identified by some critics as avant-garde had, at best, a tenuous connection to the Romantic project. Unlike the historical avant-garde in which distinct movements such as Futurism or Dadaism emerged with some regularity, often announced by manifestos rejecting previous iterations of the avant-garde, and distinguished by unique attributes, the work of recent decades tended to be more eclectic and amorphous, resisting attempts at easy classification. Already by the 1960s – a period when the American avant-garde was flourishing – the terms neo-avant-garde and post-avant-garde were being applied by various critics and scholars.[7] For the purposes of this essay, I will use the term "post-avant-garde" as the simplest way of aggregating all the developments of the past twenty-five or thirty years. After all, what better descriptor could there be for a movement that follows the avant-garde?

Establishing a coherent narrative for the post-avant-garde, though, is complex if not impossible since there are many threads to follow, some overlapping, some contradictory. Furthermore, at least from certain perspectives, the avant-garde was still breaking new ground. Rebecca Schneider, for instance, has argued that the notion of an avant-garde that has ceased to function may be a particularly male perspective. "I nevertheless find it telling (as have many before me)," she states, "that the avant-garde and the option of 'shock' that it championed should die just as women, artists of color, and gay and lesbian artists began to make critically incisive political art under their own gender-, race-, and preference-marked banners."[8] And, in fact, work by these various groups has been and continues to be more socially and culturally disruptive than much of the avant-garde. But even if one accepts the idea of a post-avant-garde distinct from the historical avant-garde, it is not as if there was a sudden break when one movement came to an abrupt end and a new one began. Many genres, forms, and techniques continued in parallel with newer developments, with a fairly fluid movement of ideas and practices among them.

For this essay, I want to focus on a particular aspect of post-avant-garde performance: the technological, which incorporates electronic and digital media into live performance often coequal with or dominant over the human actors. Theatre has always been fascinated with technology, of course, with examples dating back to the *apò mēkhanês theós* of ancient Greece. Obviously, there are other categories and other ways of categorizing the post-avant-garde, too numerous to include here. One could look at theatre companies that draw heavily from popular culture such as Vampire Cowboys and the Rude Mechanicals or the plays of Charles Busch. There is the migration of directors who came out of experimental theatre working in both opera and not-for-profit theatres reimagining classics such as JoAnne Akalaitis, Andrei Serban, Anne Bogart, Julie Taymor, Peter Sellars, and perhaps in his own category, Robert Wilson. (And we seem to have reached a moment when the classic avant-garde itself is being reimagined – notably the Rude Mechanicals' restagings of The Performance Group's *Dionysus in 69* from 1968 and Mabou Mines's *The B. Beaver Animation* from 1974.) There is, however, one stream of the avant-garde that has persisted into the post-avant-garde – performance art. And despite its emphasis on the centrality of the solo performer, and the body as the site of artistic creation and meaning, there are several artists who have adopted technology as well. I will return to performance art later.

I want to propose that a significant body of post-avant-garde theatre in the United States – at least in New York City-based performance – can be traced largely to the work of Richard Foreman and his Ontological-Hysteric Theatre (O-HT) and to the Wooster Group (WG) under the direction of Elizabeth LeCompte.[9] Between them, they drew upon ideas and practices derived from the visual arts, performance art, American avant-garde cinema, video art, modern philosophy, popular culture, contemporary psychology (notably Lacan), and dramatic theories of Brecht and Gertrude Stein, to cite but a few influences, to create work that was essentially unlike anything that came before and that rejected the highly physical, ensemble-based theatre that had dominated the experimental theatre world of the 1960s. That in itself had a significant effect on the subsequent path of post-avant-garde theatre. But their influence went beyond that: they both nurtured a new generation of artists through internship programs as well as sponsored developmental workshops that provided space and resources for theatre artists: the Incubator Series at the O-HT and the Emerging Artist Series at the Performing Garage. Among the people who participated with one or both of these groups as interns or technicians and designers, or who participated in either of the workshop programs, were John Collins, co-founder of Elevator Repair Service; Jim Findlay, co-founder of Collapsable Giraffe; David Herskovits, artistic director of Target Margin Theater; Eric Dyer, co-founder of Radiohole; Pavol Liska, founder of Nature Theatre of Oklahoma; Richard Maxwell, founder of New York City Players; Young Jean Lee, founder and artistic director of Young Jean Lee's Theatre Company; Marianne Weems, co-founder and artistic director of The Builders Association; and performance artist Andrew Schneider. These artists and companies then continued to build upon and transform the aesthetics of their precursors and mentors, and they in turn trained the next generation of theatre artists and expanded the audience for these works.[10]

Technology

Technology, particularly electronic and digital media, was a major factor contributing to the end of the Romantic-based avant-garde. A great many of the strategies and goals of the historical avant-garde were actually achieved in the techniques and structural vocabulary of television and newer digital technologies, building on the precedents of film and even radio. Narrative continuity gave way to continuously shifting points of view and the rapid juxtaposition of images and sound; the natural boundaries of time and space dissolved as past, present, and future could exist simultaneously, and the physical limitations that had constrained live theatre since its origins evaporated. As I have noted elsewhere, almost overnight the Aristotelian-based model of the linear narrative and unified frame was largely supplanted by an image-driven associative structural model.[11] While there were certainly avant-garde genres of film and video, it was in the commercial and popular sphere that electronic media thrived and became pervasive. Thus, while the historical avant-garde often borrowed techniques and tropes from popular entertainments, the situation was now reversed, and the techniques of the avant-garde were significantly realized in popular media.[12] The very structure of digital communication achieved a transformation of consciousness, the way in which the human brain accessed and stored information and the way in which we perceived the world: everything that the avant-garde had spent more than a century attempting to achieve. And it is precisely these same technologies that formed the foundation for a significant aspect of the post-avant-garde.

This shift was already being recognized by the early 1970s, decades before the digital revolution. One observer noted, "it goes without saying that the technological revolution and its immediate effect upon everyday life, and the great experience of cybernetics which offers glimpses of hitherto unexplorable territories, greatly contributed to the rise of the neo-avant-garde waves."[13] And, of course, landmark books such as Janet Murray's *Hamlet on the Holodeck* (1997) were examining the way in which communication was being restructured by such technologies, and in particular the way in which traditional narrative was being reinscribed in computer gaming. Inevitably, in the first wave of a mediatized theatre, many artists were dazzled by the new toys at their disposal and created work more focused on the versatility of the technology than the artistic content. There was a touch of what theatre historian Brooks McNamara often referred to, in regard to nineteenth- and twentieth-century realism, as "gee-whiz naturalism" in which the audience was astonished by the recreation of everyday mechanisms on the stage. In this case, such elements as video monitors, cell phones, complex projections, holograms, and so on, often seemed to be employed for their own sake – a "gee-whiz futurism" as it were – with little attention to how the vocabulary of cybernetics or electronic media functioned within the language of the physical stage.

In fact, what the new technologies were doing was fueling a move toward the dematerialization of the stage (to paraphrase the term popularized by art critics Lucy Lippard and John Chandler who, in 1968, described a phenomenon they labeled the "dematerialization of art", resulting in the devaluation and even elimination of the art object).[14] The increasing adoption of digital media began the process of negating the millennia-old borders and constraints of the physical stage – although the nature of these media still required an essentially static physical relation between spectator and image. And at the same time, there was a rise in stagings of environmental, site-specific, and immersive theatre that rejected conventional theatres for alternative spaces, and often enveloped the spectators within more fluid, less-defined environments. While this latter approach often rejected cutting-edge technologies, both these trends – the technological and the physical – aimed to disrupt the conventional relationship of spectator to performance. Furthermore, the introduction of the televisual and the digital to the theatre allowed for the disintegration of temporal and visual continuity and coherence – all of which constituted a crucial aspect of the post-avant-garde.

Mediatized Theatre

Philip Auslander, in his landmark book, *Liveness*, defines mediatized performance as "performance that is circulated on television ... and in other forms based in technologies of reproduction."[15] He goes on to cite Fredric Jameson who discusses spatial arts (which, of course, would include theatre) in regard to postmodern spatialization, which "plays itself out in the relationship and the rivalry among the various spatial media" such as video versus film, or photography versus painting. Mediatized fine arts, he says, "come to consciousness of themselves as various media within a mediatic system in which their own internal production also constitutes a symbolic message and the taking of a position on the status of the medium in question."[16] If we acknowledge the use of projections as the introduction of media into theatre, then the history of media on the stage dates back to at least the Renaissance in Europe, while the use of cinematic or moving images is generally attributed to Erwin Piscator in Germany in the 1920s. Up through the mid-twentieth century, these projections tended to function variously as special effects, a substitute for painted and constructed scenery, or, significantly, as a means of visually conveying information more powerfully and efficiently than language alone could achieve.[17] Especially with the use of film, no matter how effective it may have been in achieving certain goals, it almost always read as the superimposition – even intrusion – of one medium on another: two different sign systems or vocabularies in uneasy symbiosis.

A major step that led to the development of video art and the use of video in performance came in the mid-1960s with the Sony Portapak,[18] a portable and relatively affordable video tape recorder. These were bulky, heavy, and awkward by present standards, and the quality and capabilities were nowhere near current-day smart phones, but the new device allowed nonspecialists the possibility of easily recording live events on-site and playing them back immediately. The major pioneer in the growth of video art was Korean-born artist Nam June Paik, but it began to appear in the performative work of Fluxus and other conceptual artists.[19] In 1971, video artists Woody and Steina Vasulka founded The Kitchen at the Mercer Arts Center in Lower Manhattan, described as "a theater utilizing an audio, video, and electronic interface between performers (including actors, musicians, composers and kinetic visual artists) and audience."[20] The Kitchen continues to the present day (in a different location) as one of the premiere interdisciplinary performance spaces in New York.

Perhaps the first substantial integration of video art and conventional theatre came when the California-based video collective, Video Free America, teamed up with the Off-Broadway Chelsea Theater Center in Brooklyn in 1970 to create "video sets" for several productions over the next few years, beginning with Heathcote Williams's *AC/DC*. Utilizing multiple television sets integrated into the scenographic architecture, Video Free American utilized live feeds, prerecorded material, instant replays, slow- and fast-motion in order, in the words of Chris Salter, "to show multiple perspectives on the stage, to have the camera's point of view influence a live event."[21] The 1973 production of Peter Handke's *Kaspar*, directed by Carl Weber, was probably the most ambitious use of video in theatre to that time. The stage was framed by fifteen monitors showing live, delayed, and prerecorded images of Kaspar. Crucial to the performance was the ability of the actor Christopher Lloyd to interact with his video self throughout the show – a technique soon to be picked up by other companies. Video was being used not merely for effect but as an integral aspect of the production, one that created a vital dialectic among visual, spatial, and temporal components of the performance. Supposedly, some critics at the time, particularly German ones, were upset by the intrusion of video into the "sacred space of the stage," which seemingly negated the liveness that defined theatre.[22]

By the late 1970s, more experimental theatre groups began to explore the use of electronic media, primarily video, which became central to the creation of the work and an inextricable component of the performance text. It is important to remember that flat-screen monitors did not yet exist at this time, and thus any of these theatre productions required the presence of cathode-ray-tube (CRT) monitors – old fashioned televisions, though without the enclosures or casings of commercial models – as part of the scenographic landscape. One of the first such theatre companies to explore the visual and performative use of video, in provocative and even shocking ways, was Squat, a Hungarian troupe that emigrated to the United States in 1977. The first work they performed in the United States was *Pig, Child, Fire!*, which had originally been created earlier that year in Rotterdam and included live-feed images on a TV screen (including a scene in which performer Anna Koós stood on the street reading Artaud's "Letter to André Breton" while a camera under her skirt focused on her naked crotch). For their next production, *Andy Warhol's Last Love* (1978), a video camera on the street outside the storefront theatre transmitted live images from the street to a monitor in the theatre. And the 1981, *Mr. Dead and Mrs. Free* incorporated extensive use of film as well as a twelve-foot tall *papier mâché* baby with video monitors for eyes. For Squat, film and video was an extension of their performances, a tool to both disrupt the experience of theatrical spectatorship and to break down the boundaries – literal and metaphorical – between life and art, between inside and outside. The image on video monitor "was yet another device to mirror reality, to make visible that which was hidden," explained Gautam Dasgupta.[23] Its function was "to superimpose another order of reality on the theatrical reality presented before our eyes on stage ... or else to make insubstantial through the medium of a filmed image that which was visible and tangible."[24]

At about the same time, Laura Farabough, co-founder of the San Francisco company Snake Theatre, which had been in the forefront of site-specific theatre, began to explore video in her productions. *Her Building* (1977), co-written with co-artistic director Chris Hardman, combined site-specific performance in front of the Sausalito City Hall along with several video monitors placed throughout the audience showing scenes not otherwise visible. In 1982, with Nightfire Theatre which she founded in 1980, she created *Obedience School* in which video set up a dialectic between performer and character.[25]

The Wooster Group

But the company most closely associated with the development of video in theatre is the Wooster Group. This was in part due to their longevity as a company and the evolution of their work over time. From their first production, *Sakonnet Point* in 1975, based on personal memories of actor Spalding Gray, analog technology played a role, but, in a sense, they were creating a dialectic with technology. In the decidedly lo-tech *Sakonnet Point*, sound, in the form of vinyl records played on an onstage phonograph, was a crucial component. Phonographs and other analog sound technologies were a feature of much of their subsequent work. In fact, while the Wooster Group is most often associated with their pioneering use of video, their exploration of sound – recorded music, miked voices, amplified, dislocated, or recorded dialogue, and so on – is equally if not more important.

Their introduction and exploration of video emerged organically as they gradually integrated what was becoming, by the 1970s, the defining technology of the era. The scenographic incorporation of video, especially as an active component in dialogue with the performers – and often as a site in which the performers existed imagistically – embodies what Phaedra Bell calls "dialogic media" that employs "inter-media exchange" which is "the mutual acknowledgement of images produced by separate media and their accompanying interchange of dialogue, glance, attribute, equipment or other currency such that the images cohere and appear to coincide in the same time and space."[26] Film first appeared in *Point Judith* (1979); video was first used in *Route 1 &*

9 (1981). Partly a deconstruction of Thornton Wilder's *Our Town, Route 1 & 9* was controversial for its use of blackface. The production employed four television monitors hanging above the stage which could be lowered to be in the direct sightline of the audience, as well as one monitor on a table in the playing space. In the third section of the production, elegiac enactments of *Our Town* played out on these screens in contrast to the often-raucous scenes that preceded them. And in the final part of the production, two of the four overhead monitors showed an explicit porno film made by the company while two others showed a monotonous Warholesque "road trip" through the industrial landscape along the New Jersey Turnpike. Throughout the performance, the videos had served to fragment the spectators' view and the tonalities of the production, but the final sequence posed a challenge for the viewers, creating a tension between the contrasting onscreen images, a dichotomy between the images and the ostensible subject of the production, and the substitution of electronic images for the presence of the actor. And the physical movement of the monitors themselves, as simple as it was, made them performative elements.

Their next production, *L.S.D. (... Just the High Points ...)* (1984), which Marianne Weems declared a "watershed for cross-media work,"[27] continued the use of analog and electronic sound but included two video monitors. Happenstance led to a use of video that began to truly break down the boundaries of onstage/offstage, past and present, live and recorded. When Michael Kirby, one of the performers, could not join the company on tour, they recorded him and played it on a CRT monitor in place of the live performer.[28] When he rejoined the production, sections of the video were kept and Kirby interacted with himself onscreen. Although video has been used in almost all subsequent Wooster Group productions, perhaps the most thematically complex use of video can be found in their 1991 piece *Brace Up!*, based on Chekhov's *The Three Sisters*. The production included two monitors that moved back and forth on tracks on the stage floor of the industrial looking set by James Clayburgh (with lighting by Jennifer Tipton), another smaller monitor that could be placed at different places on the stage, and a fourth monitor upstage left. The latter showed the translator Paul Schmidt who sat onstage, back to audience, commenting on the performance but whose face was visible only via live video feed. On the other monitors, one might see close ups of actors' faces – either live offstage or prerecorded. Also interspersed were scenes of kabuki dances and a Godzilla film. But none of the overpowering video imagery we have come to expect from the use of large flat-screen monitors in many current productions was present. There were simply the relatively small CRT screens, functioning as performative and sculptural elements.

Phaedra Bell perceptively places this work in the context of Una Chaudhuri's concept of "geopathology": the "characterization of place as a problem."[29] The concept of place is essential to Chekhov's play, yet the Wooster Group transposed the Prozorov household to the Performing Garage, the group's home[30] and then deconstructed not merely the text but the home itself through their use of video. By the time the piece was revived in 2003, both actor Ron Vawter and translator/performer Paul Schmidt had died. As with Kirby, their images were included on video. However, other actors now replaced them on the stage so that, unlike Kirby performing with himself, live actors stepped into roles created by others who now continued to perform as video-ghosts. As scholar Matthew Causey has noted, "televisual actors [in the Wooster Group productions] fall under a separate ontological regime, which is more absent than present, more image than substance."[31]

Critic Bonnie Marranca points out that the Group's use of video was strongly influenced by the pioneering video artist Joan Jonas who also appeared in two of their productions. Jonas employed what Douglas Crimp called "de-synchronization" – the disruption of the signals between the monitor's receiving and transmitting frequencies as in her landmark *Vertical Roll* (1972),[32] but that term could also be applied to any disjunction between visual and aural or action and perception, as well as the juxtaposition of live performance and video. "The process of image-making," noted Marranca, "was a part of the performance, duplicating and altering the information of the performance as it was being performed."[33] Marranca also cites Carolee Schneemann's performance/installation "Up to and Including Her Limits" (1973), which included the projection of film and slides as well as the playing of audiotapes, all containing her image and voice so that she was present in multiple media as well as live.

The Wooster Group was certainly not the only avant-garde company experimenting with video and other technologies in the 1980s. Several groups in the San Francisco area including Soon 3, Antenna Theatre, and especially, George Coates Performance Works explored film, video, and projection, as well as the intersection of performance with the internet. In New York, Mabou Mines created *Hajj* (1983), a production with a triptych of mirrors that seemingly transformed into television monitors showing both live and prerecorded images along with a collage of music and sound. It was more technically sophisticated and complex than anything the Wooster Group was doing at the time, although unlike the

Wooster Group, the intent was not so much to create a dialectic between presence and absence as much as to explore the psyche of the character portrayed by Ruth Maleczech.

Because of the high visibility of the Group within the American avant-garde, their influence was profound. And this influence was amplified by their extensive touring especially in Europe where their use of video influenced a generation of young theatre artists.[34]

The Post-Avant-Garde Progeny

For the Wooster Group, video monitors were relatively small objects within the greater stage space, like jewel boxes, or windows into other times and spaces – wormholes in the space of the stage. Video was an aesthetic tool, one that often existed in counterpoint to both the actors and the three-dimensional stage, but the productions were never *about* video or the social construct of a society pervaded by the televisual or digital image. But for the artists who passed through the WG/O-HT universe, and who used video and digital technology in a significant way in their own work, the technology was often both the thematic and visual center of their productions in which the screen often came to visually dominate the stage. (Part of this, of course, was a result of developments in technology itself which allowed ever larger and larger screens and greater flexibility in the transmission of images.) As indicated above, numerous theatre groups emerged out of the aesthetics and praxis of the Wooster Group and the Ontological-Hysteric Theatre. While thematic concerns, dramatic structures, scenographic and technological elements, acting styles, and so on from those two companies can be discerned to one degree or another in their offspring, each new group developed a particular approach and focus – some clearly descended from the source, others only faintly recognizable.

Among the first "alumni" of the Wooster Group to create her own theatre was Marianne Weems who had served as the company's dramaturg from 1988 to 1993. She founded The Builders Association (TBA) in 1994 and the company has been at the forefront of digital technology in the theatre ever since, often teaming up with architects and technology organizations such as Diller + Scofidio, DBOX, and motiroti. There are two significant differences between the Wooster Group and The Builders Association. First, TBA usually uses multiple large video screens that often occupy the entire rear of the stage and are the dominant visual component. Second, many of their pieces are a commentary on the digital and web-based world that has come to be a primary mode of information and communication over the past few decades. Thus, TBA does not utilize video simply as one more tool within a conceptual framework; it draws attention to itself so as to make the audience aware of the media – both how it functions on the stage as well as its role in society at large. In fact, the video can be understood *as* the text, or at least a significant element of it, while the physical components of the technology – computers, monitors, sound equipment, and so on – hold a place in the scenography equal to the images they project along with the human performers.

Two of their most acclaimed productions were *Jet Lag* (1998) and *Alladeen* (2002). The former, created in collaboration with Diller + Scofidio, deals with travel, staged reality, video communication, and electronic surveillance, among other things, employing the deft editing of live and prerecorded video, live performers, and digital images. Part 1 is based on the true story of a British electrician who set off as part of a solo round-the-world sailing race in 1969 despite being inexperienced and ill prepared. Unable to complete the race, he sailed in circles off the coast of South America for ten months, all the while sending back reports purporting to document his progress. He ultimately threw himself overboard and presumably drowned. His written logs and the film and reel-to-reel tapes he left behind documented his mental deterioration and delusional state. In The Builders Association production, an actor portraying a fictionalized version of the character sat on a stool in front of a video camera with a small screen behind him depicting seascapes. This, in turn, was captured by another camera and a very large combined image was projected on a large upstage screen, providing a reasonable illusion of a man on a boat at sea. Downstage, on a level below the actor, was a liquid crystal display that could hide or reveal a table behind which were performers as TV reporters chronicling the supposed journey.

Part 2 depicted another true story about an American grandmother who, in a period of six months, flew back and forth across the Atlantic 167 times with her fourteen-year-old grandson in order to elude the pursuit of the boy's father and psychiatrist. During this time, they never left the space of air travel – planes or terminals. The grandmother finally died of jet lag. The large screens depicted a digitally animated airplane as well as video of the interior of airports including a scene in which the two performers, though stationary, appeared to ascend an escalator.

Alladeen was an exploration of the international corporate call centers in Bangalore, India – the site that most people unwittingly encounter when calling for hotel or airline reservations or computer technical support. The entire upper half of the back wall of the stage was a projection screen that showed everything from excerpts from Bollywood films to faces of call center operators. Scholar Shannon Jackson provided an excellent description.

> Kaleidoscopic digital squares zoom in and around a video screen, forming grids that constantly change, their internal patterns lining up to form new symmetrical patterns. The images dance to the steady beat of techno music, accelerate, and refigure into new arrangements of luminous, multicolored eye candy. More blocks slide in and fit together with a satisfying synthetic click. ... The synthesized whooshes, plops, and kerchunks mimic the soundscape of a high-end website search. Suddenly, a mailbox, a phone booth, and a fire hydrant digitally slide onto the set . . . by the transit systems of a software program as electronically mediated objects. Digitally rendered human silhouettes begin to appear and move through the mise-en-scène. By the same means, a vendor's food cart drops from the sky with a synthesized crash.[35]

"The impetus for me," explains Weems, "is not the technology but the human story and, in the twenty-first century, stories are inevitably bound up with some kind of network. Technology comes as part of the story-telling package because people's lives are complicated by it, and because those are the tools we use. It's a way of holding a mirror up to our society to express something that's part of the contemporary moment."[36]

Two other groups with connections to Foreman and the Wooster Group are Collapsable Giraffe (founded 1995) and Radiohole (1998). In 2000, the two groups inaugurated a shared performance space in Williamsburg, Brooklyn, called the Collapsable Hole whose rough indus-trial aesthetic was reminiscent of the Performing Garage, the home of the Wooster Group.[37] The space also hosted many artists and companies including Young Jean Lee, Joseph Silovsky, Mallory Catlett, Big Dance Theater, and Elevator Repair Service. That space closed in 2013 and was resurrected at Westbeth in Manhattan in 2016 as a partnership of nine artists/companies: Mallory Catlett, Annie Dorsen, Jim Findlay, Findlay// Sandsmark, Daniel Fish, Immediate Medium, Aaron Landsman, Okwui Okpokwasili, and Radiohole.

One stylistic element of both the O-HT and the WG was sudden shifts from a quiet or contemplative state to raucous and manic activity and music. Collapsable and Radiohole absorbed that aesthetic but took it into more extreme, anarchic, and outrageous territory. Part of this extended to the use of technical equipment. The founders of the Wooster Group were mostly early baby boomers and preboomers. They came to video technology gradually when the equipment was still expensive and thus needed to be treated with care. Although exploring new technology in innovative ways, they nonetheless treated the equipment with respect. The next generation, however, grew up with early iterations of personal computers and home video equipment and were thus totally relaxed around the equipment – it was part of their daily lives. Thus, in performance, they would literally toss a video camera or small monitor across the stage to be caught by someone else. A performer might be operating a control panel one minute and performing the next. The productions created by both Foreman and LeCompte were intensely rehearsed and exquisitely precise, whereas Radiohole actually welcomes the mistakes that can arise through a less-than-rigorous approach as well as the glitches that come with electronic equipment. Eric Dyer observed that,

> technological catastrophes are rarely apparent to the audience but happen on a fairly regular basis. Sometimes they are purely technical failures, but more often than not it's a mistake in executing the technical score. Part of what we do is set ourselves such a complex series of tasks that it's almost impossible to actually do all of them. There have been instances of wrong buttons pushed or right buttons pushed at the wrong time, resulting in sonic somersaults and instant, on-the-spot rewrites. In our first show, *Bender*, I tripped over an extension cord and unplugged the whole show.[38]

However, Jim Findlay of Collapsable Giraffe, who has also created his own work separate from the group and in collaboration with others,[39] sees it somewhat differently. Discussing *Dream of the Red Chamber* (2014), he noted that "there is constant video presence in a truly epic way. But a deceptively large portion of that video is live. The technology's main function in the world of the piece isn't its content. Rather, its most essential function is that it occupies the performers' actions. I enjoy watching people struggle to do something difficult; using technology in performance in a rigorous way is difficult, especially when it's largely controlled by the performers themselves."[40]

From the earliest theatrical experiments with video, it was the "live feed," the recording and simultaneous projection of video in real time, that was the most provocative – the ability to introduce other locations or points of view onto the stage. This took the fundamental element of theatre, its living presence, and mediatized it, setting up a dichotomous, even oppositional, relation between actor and image, lived space and projected space. For the first time in theatrical history, onstage and offstage (a limitless offstage) could be present simultaneously. Scholars David

Bolter and Richard Grusin, in an important study of new media, coined the term "remediation," which they define as "the formal logic by which new media refashion prior media forms."[41] They identify this as one of the three traits of new media, the other two being "immediacy" – "a style of visual representation whose goal is to make the viewer forget the presence of the medium (canvas, photographic film, cinema, and so on)," and "hypermediacy" – "a style of visual representation whose goal is to remind the viewer of the medium."[42] All three terms seem useful in approaching the mediatized work of post-avant-garde theatre, particularly the work of Big Art Group, founded 1999 by Caden Manson and Jemma Nelson.

Somewhat like Weems, Manson and Nelson are very concerned with the role of media and technology in the postmodern world. They have stated that "it's not possible to create art or indeed meaning without technology, since technology is integrated into our society and increasingly into our own bodies. It's not just a matter of light instruments and video projections: our perceptions and self-conceptions are blended with the information we receive through the channels of our own choosing." However, their work tends to focus more on the performance of technology than on using technology to comment on social issues.

Manson invented a mediatized form he called "Real-Time Film," defined on their website as "a hybrid of film and theatre in which actors recombined formal ideas of performance through the use of simultaneous acting on stage and for live video using complex choreography, digital puppetry and live video framing."[43] Their performances tend to consist of very frontal stagings with live actors in front of video cameras and composite images created from an amalgam of individual images projected on a large screen or screens above or behind the performers. Because the audience perceives both the corporeal actors in three-dimensional space and the mediatized composite images created by their actions, "the audience is forced to undertake a continuous semiotic analysis," according to Marvin Carlson, "not only receiving the flow of filmic signs presented on the screens in the manner of familiar video or cinematic practice, but also being simultaneously aware of these signs as signs by witnessing the specific and conscious process of their construction."[44] Discussing *Flicker* (2002), Jason Farman proposes a "dialogic relationship between fragmented bodies on the analogue stage and cohesive bodies staged through digital reproduction on three stage-front screens. The relationship between these two modes of stage production posits an embodied and situated performer (and audience member) in relationship to the voyeuristic tools of visual media and surveillance technologies."[45]

Jay Scheib, a theatre artist with no direct connection to either the Wooster Group or the Ontological-Hysteric Theatre, has also been at the cutting edge of the amalgamation of live video and theatre. *World of Wires* (2012), which he developed at the Massachusetts Institute of Technology, was based on a science fiction novel adapted to film by Rainer Werner Fassbinder and entails characters who may be living in a computer simulation. Actors exist simultaneously onstage and in live video. One of Scheib's trademarks is to insert himself as the videographer in his productions, as a kinetic presence with a video camera, moving around the stage providing a continuous live stream of images from angles or spaces not available to the seated audience. Jennifer Parker-Starbuck notes that the onstage filming is "always framed by the lenses of simulation. ... By foregrounding the film-maker, and always questioning the spaces between bodies on stage and those on screen, the immersion of the potential simulation remains a plot device."[46]

Troika Ranch, a dance and media company, founded in 1994 by choreographer/media artist Dawn Stoppiello and composer/media artist Mark Coniglio, integrates theatre, dance, and new media in its works. Coniglio wrote the widely used real-time media manipulation software program, Isadora. The software was developed, explained Coniglio, in response to the "convergence of creative choreographic investigation, computer instability, the complexity of existing interfaces, the absence of an integrated tool for real-time media manipulation."[47] In the *Future of Memory*, for example, dancers perform in front of a projected montage of morphing images accompanied by sometimes distorted voices and music. One critic observed that the live video feed gave it "a voyeuristic feel. ... It's a chilling reminder of the world we live in and that pervasive video surveillance makes us invisible to no one."[48] *16 [R]evolutions* (2006) used motion-capture software combined with Isadora to track the dancers' movements and transform them into complex patterns of images that move across the stage and the performers, or reduplicate shadows of dancers into multiple configurations. Even the sound is affected. Thus the scenography of the work is directly connected to, even generated by, the movements of the performers. If the work of the Wooster Group or The Builders Association was intended to foreground a visual dialectic of live and video, the work of Troika Ranch blends performer, imagery, and technology seamlessly.[49]

Nonmediated Post-Avant-Garde

Not all the descendants of Foreman and LeCompte moved into the technological and digital realm. Elevator Repair Service (ERS), founded in 1991 by
John Collins who worked as a sound designer with both the Wooster Group
and the O-HT, has been one of the most well received Off-Off-Broadway
companies of recent decades. But the majority of its work would seem to have
little in common with either the O-HT or the WG. The ERS website
describes their work as "built around a broad range of subject matter and
literary forms; they combine elements of slapstick comedy, hi-tech and lo-
tech design, both literary and found text, and the group's own highly
developed style of choreography."[50] Somewhat like Wooster Group productions, the work they did over their first fifteen years or so took fragments of
literary sources and sometimes mashed them up with elements of pop culture.
But whereas the Wooster Group tends to use classical texts as a source for
exploring other ideas, ERS tends to explore the texts themselves. The work
took a significant turn in 2006 with *Gatz* which was a word-for-word
enactment of the novel, *The Great Gatsby*. Directed by Collins, the actor
Scott Shepherd, depicted sitting in a drab office, picks up a copy of the novel
and begins to read it out loud. Slowly he transforms into the narrator and
other office personnel morph into the other characters. As dull as that may
sound, it became one of the most acclaimed and mesmerizing performances
of the first decade of the new century. But aside from a subtle sound score and
evocative lighting design, it was "merely" actors and text. No video in sight.

Richard Maxwell, founder of the New York City Players, though
another Wooster Group alum, eschews not only the technological but
the emotive. The acting style of his productions – that he writes, directs,
and composes – is stripped to its essence, with actors embodying a neutral,
detached affect. *New Yorker* critic Hilton Als has compared him in this
regard to German filmmaker Rainer Werner Fassbinder. One of his plays
was even called *Neutral Hero* for which, Maxwell declared, he had to "find
the essence of the verb, communicating no adjectives."[51] And yet, according to *New York Times* critic Ben Brantley, Maxwell is "asking us to
perceive the mythic in the mundane and to feel as if what is happening
at this moment, in this country, were occurring in eternity."[52]

Performance Art

Performance art constituted another major category of the historical avant-
garde and has continued as a significant component of the post-avant-garde

as well. And just as so much of the avant-garde has been subsumed by mainstream theatre and art, so too have some performers achieved fame beyond the art world and been eagerly welcomed into museums and commercial galleries. The most notable example, of course, was "The Artist is Present" (2010) at the Museum of Modern Art in New York in which Marina Abramović sat at a table in the museum's atrium for eight hours a day, over two and a half months, as people lined up for hours for a chance to sit opposite her. But most performance art tends toward the conceptual and minimalistic. It is the centrality of the body – often the body *in extremis* – that is the crucial element. The classic works of performance art by artists such as Yoko Ono, Linda Montano, Chris Burden, Vito Acconci, Tehching Hsieh, Adrian Piper, and Lorraine O'Grady employed a minimum of scenographic elements. That tradition was continued by newer waves of performance artists including Holly Hughes, Spalding Gray, Ron Athey, Karen Finley, Tim Miller, John Fleck, Carmelita Tropicana, William Pope.L, Dread Scott, Coco Fusco, and Guillermo Gómez-Peña. A few, like Suzanne Lacy, staged site-specific works with many participants, and some occasionally employed video and sound, but that was rarely at the heart of the work. Meredith Monk and Ping Chong, though not performance artists in the sense of creating primarily solo work, both worked with sound, projections, and film, and their works were often described as mixed media.

Nonetheless, there are some performance artists who created their work around technology. First and foremost was Laurie Anderson. From her earliest pieces such as *Duets on Ice* (1974) that included her tape-bow violin in which prerecorded magnetic tape replaced the bow strings and was pulled across a magnetic tape head in the bridge to generate sound, she has used various technical devices, notably a vocoder that alters her voice. From the 1980s on, most of her performances included projections, often on a large screen behind her – a visual format echoed decades later by The Builders Association and Big Art Group. Many of her works contain original music and have also been released as recordings. Her most ambitious mixed media performance was the four-part *United States* in 1983 that included music, electronic inventions, projections, and film. Images sometimes reinforced the text, sometimes seemed like an ironic commentary, and sometimes had little overt connection to the material. There were seldom single sequential images; instead, there were montages and complex interweaving of images. While the technology was less sophisticated than current-day equipment, and much of what Anderson achieved would be much simpler to do today, it was cutting edge for the time, and perhaps the most ambitious mediatized performance art ever undertaken.

Anderson continues to explore new avenues of technological performance. In 2017, together with new media artist Hsin-Chien Huang, she created a VR piece, *Chalkroom*. Her website describes it as a piece in "which the reader flies through an enormous structure made of words, drawings and stories. Once you enter you are free to roam and fly. Words sail through the air as emails. They fall into dust. They form and reform."[53] For Anderson, this meant giving up absolute control over the narrative because the spectators could now at least partially shape the experience. She and Huang created another VR piece in 2019 called *To the Moon*.

Among the performance artists whose work is most closely aligned with electronic and digital technology is Andrew Schneider, another Wooster Group alum (and TBA intern). Reviews of his work are fairly consistent in observing that the content is usually the weakest aspect of his productions, but that the technology is extraordinary. In *You Are Nowhere* (2015), critics talked about a technologically driven *coup de théâtre*, perhaps related to Schrodinger's Cat, so astonishing they refuse to divulge it for fear of spoiling the show. He invents light, sound, and robotic devices, many of which can be worn on his body during a performance and from which he can control aspects of light and sound.

Director and MacArthur "Genius" grant fellowship awardee Annie Dorsen has, in one of her pieces, *Hello Hi There* (2010), eliminated human actors and created a performance for two computers running a chatbot program. The material is drawn primarily from a 1971 debate between Noam Chomsky and Michel Foucault, supplemented with material from Shakespeare, the Bible, comments on YouTube about the debate, and some material written by Dorsen, among other things. Dorsen introduces the show, then starts the program, which runs for forty-five minutes or so. The text of every performance is radically different. Similarly, for *A Piece of Work* (2013), she took the text of *Hamlet* and allowed it to be reconstituted by computer codes and chatbots, what she calls "algorithmic theatre." The five acts are each structured by different algorithms. The third act is the only one performed by a human actor – reciting the material as fed to them through an earpiece from the computer. Dorsen continued this exploration with subsequent works, though *The Slow Room* (2018) took material from online sex chatrooms and had them read by human actors who never interacted with each other.

Schneider's work can in some ways be categorized as transhuman – the augmentation of the human through technology, something that the

Cypriot-Australian artist Stelarc has been doing since the 1970s. However, Schneider is not augmenting and extending his body as such. Rather, he is using technology placed on the body to create or control a digital environment that constitutes the performance. In this way, he can be understood as part of the movement toward posthuman performance. Dorsen is also part of this movement. Explaining her view of theatre, she said,

> Over the course of its long history, theatre has generally served to reflect, invoke or extend what we understand a human to be. We rig the mirror held up to nature to tilt towards man, displayed within an ever-changing diorama alongside the various institutions of his time: the gods, God, society, the state, the family. One could say that part of the cultural work theatre does is to preserve a collective understanding of what a human is and to assure us that we are as we have always been. Theatre's continual investment in its own history erases difference, sustaining and affirming comprehension across decades and centuries. . . . I have been trying to reconcile this assessment of theatre with my sense that the vision of eternal man is no longer defensible, and certainly not useful. I began thinking about a theatre without human actors, in which that timeworn mirror becomes a glossy screen onto which human audiences project themselves, mediated by data, algorithms and interfaces.[54]

In some sense, posthuman performance relates to the dematerialization of the stage. The constraints of the physical world and human limitations, and even the human actor, are being dissolved, replaced by machines and digital imagery, which have no concrete existence. Theatre, as noted, has always been fascinated by technology. And of course, most traditional narrative theatre asks the audience to believe that the actions are occurring in a different time and place than the actual stage on which it is performed. If the conventional requirements of theatre – a performer and a spectator in shared real space – are being challenged and eradicated, then the post-avant-garde may be more radical than anything that has preceded it.

Notes

1. *Romanticism*, a term created by critics and applied retroactively to a wide range of work, is notoriously hard to define, and even the dates of the movement are hard to pin down. In broad terms, Romanticism valorized emotion and individuality as well as a return to nature, at least in part as reaction to the Enlightenment. The emphasis on the individual allied it with certain nationalist revolutionary movements. The avant-garde, in the sense of a rejection of the

status quo and a striving for an ideal society, can be seen as an outgrowth of these tendencies, especially in the writings of Richard Wagner.

2. See A. Aronson, *American Avant-Garde Theatre: A History* (Routledge, 2000).

3. The date of the original German edition.

4. P. Bürger, *Theory of the Avant-Garde*, trans. M. Shaw (University of Minnesota Press, 1984), p. 53.

5. H. Foster, *Recodings: Art, Spectacle, Cultural Politics* (Bay Press, 1985), p. 152.

6. E. Fuchs, *The Death of Character: Perspectives on Theater after Modernism* (Indiana University Press, 1996), p. 185.

7. The earliest use of the term *post-avant-garde* in news media in English seems to be 1979, *neo-avant-garde* 1986, though the terms can be found in academic publications since at least the early 1960s.

8. R. Schneider, *The Explicit Body in Performance* (Routledge, 1997), p. 4. Schneider pays particular attention to performance artists Annie Sprinkle and Ann Magnuson and the indigenous women's company Spiderwoman. One could add Split Britches, The Five Lesbian Brothers, much of the work presented at the WOW Café, and many, many others.

9. Parallel to the growth of New York–based art and performance, there was – and continues to be – a strong West Coast art world, mostly located in and around Los Angeles and San Francisco. Historians and critics, myself included, have all too often ignored the California branch of the family in creating a historical narrative. Nevertheless, the influence of the Ontological-Hysteric Theatre and the Wooster Group, internationally as well as within the United States, has been profound.

10. Critic and editor Bonnie Marranca situated Foreman together with Robert Wilson and Mabou Mines within a movement she termed the "theatre of images." While Wilson became the avatar of the avant-garde, he is sui generis, mostly working at a scale that other American theatre artists could not achieve and thus, I would argue, his direct influence was felt more abroad than in the United States. Mabou Mines was, and is, a collective of artists with often distinct aesthetics. Directors Lee Breuer and JoAnne Akalaitis were important catalysts in popularizing the reimagining or deconstruction of classic texts, but, again, their immediate influence on specific theatre artists was less direct than that of Foreman or the Wooster Group.

11. Aronson, *American Avant-Garde Theatre*, p. 202.

12. Examples include montage, collage, the elimination of linearity, simultaneity, alogical structures, and dissociative juxtapositions.

13. M. Szabolcsi, "Avant-Garde, Neo-Avant-Garde, Modernism: Questions and Suggestions," *New Literary History*, 3:1 (1971), p. 65.

14. The "disintegration of art," declared Lippard and Chandler, "is implicit in the breakup . . . of traditional media, and in the introduction of electronics, light, sound, and, more important, performance attitudes into painting and sculpture – the so far unrealized intermedia revolution whose prophet is John Cage." L. Lippard and J. Chandler, "The Dematerialization of Art," *Art International*, 12:2 (1968), p. 218.

15. P. Auslander, *Liveness: Performance in a Mediatized Culture* (Routledge, 1999), p. 5.
16. F. Jameson, *Postmodernism; or, The Cultural Logic of Late Capitalism* (Duke University Press, 1991), p. 162.
17. For historical overviews of these developments, see C. Salter, *Entangled: Technology and the Transformation of Performance* (MIT Press, 2010), and G. Giesekam, *The Use of Film and Video in Theatre* (Macmillan, 2007).
18. It was introduced in 1965 as a nonportable 110v device; a battery-powered version was introduced in 1967. Salter, *Entangled*, p. 115.
19. Artists such as Andy Warhol, Les Levine, and Wolf Vostell were using video more or less the same time. See ibid., p. 117.
20. Qtd. in ibid., p. 120.
21. Ibid., p. 128.
22. Ibid., p. 130.
23. G. Dasgupta, "Squat: Nature Theatre of New York," *Performing Arts Journal*, 7:1 (1983), p. 17.
24. Ibid.
25. The piece toured to New York City, where it performed at the Performing Garage, home of the Wooster Group. Phaedra D. Bell, who wrote the entry on Farabough for the *Dictionary of Literary Biography*, is at great pains, with some justification, to point out that Farabough's video work preceded that of many New York–based theatre artists. But she also claims that the Wooster Group artists were "scandalized" by the introduction of video onto the stage – an odd claim given that the Group had introduced video into its own work in 1981. Perhaps she confused it with the response to *Kaspar* noted above.
26. P. Bell, "Dialogic Media Production and Inter-media Exchange," *Journal of Dramatic Theory and Criticism*, 14:2 (2000), p. 44.
27. M. Weems, "Weaving the 'Live' and Mediated," in C. Svich (ed.), *Trans-Global Readings: Crossing Theatrical Boundaries* (Manchester University Press, 2003), p. 51.
28. For much of the performance, most of the actors were seated at a table facing the audience, so Kirby was recorded essentially as a "talking head."
29. U. Chaudhuri, *Staging Place: The Geography of Modern Drama* (University of Michigan Press, 1997), p. xii.
30. See my discussion of the production in *American Avant-Garde Theatre: A History*, pp. 186–90.
31. M. Causey, *Theatre and Performance in Digital Culture: From Simulation to Embeddedness* (Routledge, 2006), p. 100.
32. D. Crimp (ed.), *Joan Jonas: Scripts and Descriptions 1968–1982* (University Art Museum and Stedelijk van Abbesmuesum, 1983), p. 9.
33. B. Marranca, "The Wooster Group: A Dictionary of Ideas," *PAJ: A Journal of Performance and Art*, 25:2 (2003), p. 9.

34. Belgian director Ivo van Hove, one of the most influential directors in the contemporary theatre, acknowledged the influence of the Wooster Group after seeing their production of *Point Judith* in Brussels in 1981. *New Yorker*, October 26, 2015.

35. S. Jackson and M. Weems, *The Builders Association: Performance and Media in Contemporary Theater* (MIT Press, 2015), pp. 196–97.

36. V. Patel, "Wired Connections," *Span Magazine*, 50 (May–June 2009), p. 53.

37. The Performing Garage, a former industrial space in the Soho section of Manhattan, was created in 1968 by Richard Schechner and The Performance Group.

38. B. Browning, "Radiohole," *Bomb*, 2012, p. 118, http://bombmagazine.org/articles/radiohole/.

39. Findlay was projection designer for *Fun Home* at the Joseph Papp Public Theater and winner of several awards for set and projection design for *The Slug Bearers of Kayrol Island* at the Off-Broadway Vineyard Theatre. He has worked with Bang on a Can, Ralph Lemon, Daniel Fish, and Ridge Theater.

40. Odyssey Works, "Jim Findlay on the Desire for Connection and the Dexterity of Art," 2017, www.odysseyworks.org/blog-library/jim-findlay-on-the-desire-for-connection-and-the-dexterity-of-art.

41. J. D. Bolter and R. Grusin, *Remediation: Understanding New Media* (MIT Press, 1999), p. 273.

42. Ibid., pp. 272–73.

43. Big Art Group, http://bigartgroup.com/about/big-art-group/.

44. M. Carlson, "Mixed Media and Mixed Messages: Big Art Group's Exploration of the Sign," *Journal of Dramatic Theory and Criticism*, 22:2 (2008), p. 122.

45. J. Farman, "Surveillance Spectacles: The Big Art Group's *Flicker* and the Screened Body in Performance," *Contemporary Theatre Review*, 19:2 (2009), p. 181.

46. J. Parker-Starbuck, "Cyborg Returns: Always-Already Subject Technologies," in S. Bay-Cheng, J. Parker-Starbuck, and D. Saltz (eds.), *Performance and Media: Taxonomies for a Changing Field* (University of Michigan Press, 2015), p. 81.

47. A. Horwitz, "Talking to Troika Ranch," *Culturebot*, July 8, 2014, www.culturebot.org/2014/07/21972/talking-to-troika-ranch/.

48. S. Yung, "Into the 'Future' with Troika's Smart Video Dance," *The Dance Insider*, Flash Review 2:3–4 (2003), www.danceinsider.com/f2003/f0304_2.html.

49. Critic D. Jowitt, in her *Village Voice* review (www.villagevoice.com/2006/01/17/our-primal-future/), wistfully observed that choreographer Alwin Nikolais, a pioneer in the use of multimedia in dance, would have appreciated the work.

50. Elevator Repair Service, www.elevator.org/about/bio/.

51. R. Maxwell, "Writing & Performance," *PAJ: A Journal of Performance and Art*, 34:1 (2012), p. 128.
52. B. Brantley, *New York Times*, October 23, 2012.
53. Laurie Anderson's website, http://laurieanderson.com/?portfolio=chalkroom.
54. A. Dorsen, "On Algorithmic Theatre," 2012, htp://anniedorsen.com/userup loads/files/on_algorithmic_theatre.pdf.

Select Bibliography

Aronson, A. *American Avant-Garde Theatre: A History*. Routledge, 2000.

Auslander, P. *Liveness: Performance in a Mediatized Culture*. Routledge, 1999.

Auslander, P. *Performing Glam Rock: Gender and Theatricality in Popular Music*. University of Michigan Press, 2006.

Bolter, J. D., and Richard Grusin. *Remediation: Understanding New Media*. MIT Press, 1999.

Chaudhuri, U. *Staging Place: The Geography of Modern Drama*. University of Michigan Press, 1997.

Dixon, S. *Digital Performance: A History of New Media in Theater, Dance, Performance Art, and Installation*. MIT Press, 2007.

Foster, H. *Recodings: Art, Spectacle, Cultural Politics*. Bay Press, 1985.

Jackson, S., and M. Weems. *The Builders Association: Performance and Media in Contemporary Theater*. MIT Press, 2015.

Parker-Starbuck, J. "Cyborg Returns: Always-Already Subject Technologies." In S. Bay-Cheng, J. Parker-Starbuck, and D. Saltz (eds.), *Performance and Media: Taxonomies for a Changing Field*. University of Michigan Press, 2015.

Salter, C. *Entangled: Technology and the Transformation of Performance*. MIT Press, 2010.

CHAPTER 10

Populist Provocations and Commercial Cavalcades
Popular Entertainments and the Rise of Mass Mediated Performance

Chase Bringardner

When most theatre historians craft the narratives of theatre and performance in the twentieth and twenty-first centuries, they often relegate popular entertainments to a token chapter at best or a footnote at worst. Popular entertainments challenge notions of what constitutes theatre and blur the boundaries of theatre and performance. Over the course of the twentieth and early twenty-first centuries, popular entertainment forms, like circus, themed entertainments, spectacles, and living history museums, have grown from small-scale localized events to mass market performances with national and global audiences. These entertainments, almost always, insist upon a direct engagement with commercialism and the audience as consumer. Success for artists in these entertainment forms involves attaining a level of popularity – whether through turning out large crowds and/or yielding large box-office revenues. Within most forms of popular entertainment, what once might have been regarded as experimental or avant-garde becomes mainstream and commercial. What some may see as selling out, others see as expanding audience or tapping into new forms of audience engagement.

In many ways, popular entertainments offer large-scale performances that directly reflect the complex identities and contradictions of America itself. Popular entertainments perform America in ways that document its history, encapsulate its narratives, and highlight its constructions. Just as experimental theatre practices influenced generations of performance makers across the twentieth century, popular entertainments engage with contemporary media to craft big, bold performances that shape twenty-first-century theatrical production.

This chapter looks at how a variety of twentieth-century popular forms – circus, Las Vegas spectacles, the modern pop/rock concert, living history museums, and theme parks – created new languages of performance and expanded the realm, scale, and scope of spectacle by borrowing and reshaping past forms and methodologies. These new languages of popular entertainment performance engage most directly with threads of technology, narrative, authenticity, and audience engagement. These threads in turn come to characterize the popular and influence contemporary traditional theatre practice, both nationally and internationally.

Popular entertainments anticipate and directly engage with trends in new technologies providing fertile testing grounds for their possible uses in other performance environments. Popular entertainments foreground the relationship between the human and the machine in overt and less overt ways and force the larger fields of theatre and performance to expand and contract in accordance. How they use new technologies often impacts how more traditional theatrical entities might adopt such technological advances. Concert lighting for example, with the financial backing of more traditional capitalist market forces, often precipitates advances in theatrical lighting. What might initially appear in a Taylor Swift or U2 concert might also subsequently appear in a Broadway musical in a similar or slightly altered state. In many ways, technology or engagement with technology emerges as a primary defining characteristic of popular entertainments across the late twentieth and early twenty-first centuries. Even those forms that rely on a less obvious technologically heavy apparatus – reenactments or street performances, for example – still engage in technology through their incredibly selective or strategic use.

The primacy and centrality of technology in popular entertainments permeate the genre and shape each form's other central defining characteristics: narrative, authenticity, and audience engagement. For example, in one of the genre's earliest and most popular iterations, melodrama explicitly presented narratives that highlighted human engagement with technology: damsels in distress tied to logs heading into sawmills or active train tracks, people escaping burning tenements, and even horses racing on elaborate treadmills. These narratives staged technological change for a rapt audience drawn in by the staged spectacle. Popular entertainments offer audiences opportunities to question not only the relation between humans and technology but also larger questions of authenticity and identity through their narrative. They directly engage with concepts of authenticity, challenging what is "real" and fabricated and creating discourse around the space in between.

Popular entertainments also narrate the popular itself, offering up complex and layered performances of American identity wrapped up in the mechanisms of consumerism and capitalism. The quest to entertain an audience remains intrinsically tied to the quest to amass financial capital, which allows for a reinvestment in the spectacles and technology that will continue the cycle. Popular entertainments thus often seek to outdo or exceed a previous iteration in scale and spectacle, desiring to stay afloat within the swirl of capitalism. Considering a handful of popular entertainment forms – circus, Las Vegas spectacles, modern rock and popular concerts, living history museums, and theme parks – and their engagement with technology and audiences will illustrate how economies of spectacle and fiction affect the ways in which theatre and drama are made in the twenty-first century. Moreover, such a consideration will also assert popular entertainments as a vital component of and critical contributor to historical narratives of theatre and performance of the late twentieth and early twenty-first centuries.

Circus

From its earliest iterations, the circus staged conversations about technology and the changing relationship between human and animal performance. Staging elaborate narratives showcasing authentic talent/s for enthralled audiences, the circus in many ways laid the groundwork for all subsequent forms of popular entertainment in the United States. From the Ringling Brothers and Barnum and Bailey Circus in the late nineteenth and twentieth centuries to Cirque du Soleil in the late twentieth and twenty-first centuries, the form expanded and contracted while navigating the ups and downs of retaining its popular status, both economically and culturally. Each of these iterations of the circus embraced different trajectories in how they incorporated experimental techniques and technologies. The specific choices each offered useful examples of how, even within a specific form, notions of the popular are mutable and subject to a host of economic, artistic, and other factors.

From its inception in the United States in the late nineteenth and early twentieth centuries, the circus relied heavily upon technology both onstage and off. Circuses spread rapidly, and their popularity grew in direct relation to the rise and proliferation of the railroad. As Janet Davis states in her book *The Circus Age: Culture and Society Under the American Big Top*, "at the turn of the century, the gigantic railroad circus descended upon a community, shut it down, and then moved on."[1] Circus not only became intrinsically linked with this form of technology but also became synonymous with technological innovations. Circus acts incorporated technology both onstage and backstage. Acts like Mademoiselle Mauricia de Tiers's "L'Auto Bolide" or "The Dip of Death" for Barnum and Bailey combined new technologies with performance techniques resulting in "a highly dangerous automobile act in which the driver raced down a steep track, ending in a free-falling summersault before the car landed upright on different track."[2] Yet even the less complex, more traditional circus acts like the flying trapeze or the tight trope showcased the exciting tension between the capabilities of the human body and changing technologies. These acts after all still incorporated the use of theatrical lighting, staging, and sound to set the scene and raise the tension.

Additionally, the circus also grew hand in hand with changes to the structures of business and economics in the United States. Like almost all popular entertainments, the circus most definitely operates as a commercial endeavor, intrinsically tied up within US capitalist systems and dependent upon audience for revenue. The continual consolidation of various circuses into new companies – Ringling plus Barnum plus Bailey to create Ringling Brothers and Barnum and Bailey Circus for example – illustrates the many ways the circus operated squarely within a corporate model. As Davis remarks, "as a corporation on wheels, the circus's labor performances of the new-industrial order, its variegated exhibitions of human and animal relationships, and its spectacles of America's growing power in the world affairs heralded the arrival of a new modern age."[3] At the height of its popularity at the turn of the twentieth century, the circus staged the complexities of a rapidly modernizing world "framed around an unsettling matrix of bodily celebration and prudery, social conformity and marginality, jingoism and internationalism, racial hierarchy and racial fascination."[4] The circus employed these whirling, seemingly contradictory concepts in its narratives to expand its audience base and engage as many paying customers as possible. By staging the thrill of the precarious, the circus, like other popular entertainments, challenged notions of authenticity, simultaneously seeming, for example, to embrace racist tendencies while also teasing a fascination with the other or create a sense of a strong patriotic celebration alongside a global fantasia. The circus offered stark juxtapositions wherein representations in performance blurred lines of "real" and fabricated, challenging audiences to interrogate authenticity as a construct. Was the purported alligator wrestler really from Zaire? How did he and his Black body relate to the display of the "native African village" located outside the main tent? Moreover, was the unicorn an actual unicorn?

At that height of popularity, as the circus continued to crisscross the United States on a growing number of railway lines, it increased its offerings and types of acts even expanding from one to three rings. Yet by the 1930s, traditional circus audiences declined as "urban development and the rise of suburbs pushes the show grounds away from the vicinity of rail yards, making it difficult for those large railroad shows to navigate efficiently."[5] Moreover, the circus found greater competition in other entertainment forms like radio, movies, and, eventually, television. Circuses had to respond to changing audience expectations and rapid advances in technology. Some circuses created new acts like the Globe of Death – a metal globe inside which up to five motorcycles would perform tricks. Others doubled down on other kinds of spectacle promising unicorns and alligator wrestling – not so different from the golden age of the circus only now amplified through the power of modern media technologies. So even after a period of audience decline, the circus continued to try and reinvent itself with some now filling arenas instead of tents in rural and urban areas alike. Tractor trailers even joined the railroad as a major component of circus transportation infrastructure. Yet the irony of the development of the circus comes from both changing attitudes toward human engagement with animals alongside increases in theatrical technology. Changing societal behaviors around issues of animal welfare led circuses like Ringling Brothers and Barnum and Bailey, in an attempt to continue to attract audiences, to eventually, in the early twenty-first century, abandon the signature circus animal, the elephant, and finally shutter altogether. Ringling Brothers and Barnum and Bailey Circus ultimately could not resolve its classic three ring format and reliance on the spectacle of animal performers with the demands of changing theatrical technology. Without their signature nonhuman performers and narrative structure to provide the expected spectacle, they simply could not adapt.

Just as the traditional three ring circus began to fade in popularity in the 1980s and 1990s, a small French-Canadian troupe of street performers founded Cirque du Soleil in 1984. Upstart Cirque du Soleil did away with animals and the additional two rings, doubling down on the use of innovative technologies to put a sharp emphasis on the fantastic possibilities of the human body. Cirque "charted a more aesthetically innovative circus, combining circus with dance, theatre and music, as well as fantastic costumes, lighting, and sets."[6] Whereas those circuses like Ringling Brothers and Barnum and Bailey used technology like the railroad to reach a truly national audience, Cirque du Soleil harnessed new technologies to increase its reach globally, blending the roots of traditional circus with a more sophisticated European aesthetic stemming explicitly from their founding city of Quebec and its legacies of street performers, festivals, and café culture.[7] Moreover, Cirque expanded upon the traditional circus's fabricated "global" reach by actually, and mostly ethically, seeking out and employing performers from around the world. As Davis remarks, while Cirque du Soleil harkens back to the earliest form of the one-ring circus, it appeals primarily to adults, not children, as their primary audience, and through its high-ticket prices, global aesthetics, and even posher food and beverage options, Cirque does "not aspire to 'instruct the minds of all classes' like the railroad circuses of old."[8]

Importantly, Cirque du Soleil also, at least initially, relied upon creative processes more frequently reserved for artistic forms outside of popular entertainment traditions. Cirque creative directors "would initiate a creation phase by providing performers with a loose and adaptable concept, rather than a formal script to follow, and performance acts would be forged 'in action.'"[9] The show itself would form organically from the amalgamation of acts, and the performers contributed to the overall formation of the ideas, theme, and story. Shifting away from a roster of revolving acts modeled on late nineteenth-century popular forms like Vaudeville or burlesque that might change from city to city, a Cirque show existed as an entity to itself with each act serving a dramaturgical function to shape the overall narrative. Rejecting a hasty blend of acts based solely on availability and popularity, a Cirque show evolved through a process that "could last up to nine months" that "allows performers an opportunity to perfect their act, and in the case of potentially dangerous acts, to feel safe and confident about their delivery."[10] In other words, their narrative placement afforded a more structured sense of rehearsal that allowed space for the incorporation of greater, more complicated technologies and increased the autonomy of the performer to advocate for themselves in the creative process. Unlike the traditional circus, performers "were given space to realize their vision for a particular project and develop their own sense of character, often pushing the boundaries of their individual (and collective) competencies through enhancement of their informal, embodied knowledge."[11] Cirque du Soleil's particular collaborative process that seamlessly weaved together new technologies, unconventional performance forms (extreme sports like BMX, skateboarding, and trampoline), and innovative reimaginations of traditional circus acts revitalized and redefined the popular form of circus. From a small troupe in Montreal, Cirque has grown to a truly global phenomenon with ten different stage productions on tour in twenty-nine countries and seven permanent shows in Florida, Las Vegas, and Mexico. The corporation employs over 5,000 people worldwide and reports over $900 million in revenue.[12] Just as Ringling Brothers joined forces with Barnum and Bailey to improve their financial lot by creating a national circus conglomerate, Cirque built upon its success to fashion a multileveled, modern performance corporation.

Cirque's success relied upon their wedding of the traditional circus with a decidedly modern sensibility; the performance architecture of each traveling show, for example, consisted in part of a single ring housed under their modern iteration of the classic circus tent, harkening back to the golden age of the circus while simultaneously using technology both "offstage" (robotic lighting, digital sound) and directly "onstage" through innovative acts and performances. Each show, even in their most recent performances, reconfigures that single ring to fit the specificities of that given show.

At present, instead of chasing Ringling Brothers and Barnum and Bailey, those circuses that wish to survive seek to emulate Cirque du Soleil. Troops like The Big Apple Circus (with only horses and dogs) and the Universoul Circus each now try and mirror Cirque du Soleil eliminating or downgrading the use of animals, reducing to one ring in a portable tent, and increasing the use of innovative theatrical lighting and narrative development. Even Ringling Brothers and Barnum and Bailey Circus, in its last efforts to survive the changing performance landscape, consolidated to a single ring and tried to adopt many of Cirque's aesthetic principles. Yet major challenges exist for Cirque du Soleil, and those remaining circuses that attempt to emulate their success. As technologies advance rapidly and audience tastes expand to incorporate vibrant new physical and digital landscapes, Cirque du Soleil must strive to stay on top of those technologies to maintain their audiences, which requires significant financial resources. And while their corporate structure affords them multiple revenue streams, as with many entertainment and performance related corporations, over time Cirque du Soleil has become increasingly less risk averse, and that emphasis on creative process that afforded their initial success has shifted. While Cirque du Soleil in the past "attempted to maintain a balance between experimentation and control, there is a shift away from an unregulated creation space and the open and adaptable script" toward a process where "input is limited except at the very earliest stages and spaces in the creation process" resulting in an increased emphasis on "conformity" and a "loss of creativity throughout the process."[13] As one performer remarked in an interview with Deborah Leslie,

> Cirque du Soleil has contributed to a lot of the evolution of circus, but it's
> been thirty years. For 10–15 years they haven't done anything new in the
> sense that it's the same formula. It's always the same thing. Yes they build
> new apparatus and things like that, but it's still the same music, décor, big
> CDS make-up. Before it was nouveau cirque, but now I find it's become
> more like traditional circus. … They are really good technically, but in
> terms of the artistic component, I feel that that's missing.[14]

This performer's remarks illustrate the challenges of popular entertainments to maintain their popular moniker. Within the form of circus, the nature of the performance form and its itinerant nature fundamentally shaped the ways the form could evolve. From trains, tents, and three rings to big rigs, planes, and single rings, the traveling nature of the form, like many popular entertainments of previous centuries, can limit innovation and technological advancement.

Yet Cirque, in its expansion, carved out a number of permanent venues that afforded them the possibility to design the performance spaces with the technological demands in mind and to explore new possibilities. Making their show a destination as opposed to bringing the show to the audience mirrored some of the practices of earlier popular forms like Vaudeville and burlesque (which both had traveling companies and permanent houses in major cities). While Cirque du Soleil currently maintains permanent venues in Florida and Mexico, their primary home for their most technologically advanced creations is Las Vegas. As Davis remarks while contemplating the legacy of the circus,

> the circus's imperative to discover the world through consumerism has also
> been reincarnated at Las Vegas … amid the city's constant slot-machine
> clatter, one can … sit next to an opulent Roman fountain at Caesar's Palace,
> visit the Luxor, a sleek black pyramid hotel outlined in neon … or stroll the
> streets of "New York, New York," a cluster of hotels replicating the
> New York skyline.[15]

These permanent monuments of performance innovation further blur the line between circus and other genres creating, even within the lexicon of Cirque, a different style of truly modern popular performance.[16]

Las Vegas

Throughout its storied history, Las Vegas maintained a reputation as a very particular kind of entertainment destination. Carved out of the Nevada desert by Bugsy Malone and his fellow mobsters, Las Vegas built its reputation as a kind of adult playground full of gambling, spectacle, and a variety of entertainment offerings. From its inception as an entertainment destination in the early 1930s, Las Vegas provided stages for a variety of popular acts from musicians like the Rat Pack (featuring Frank Sinatra, Dean Martin, Sammy Davis Jr., among others), Elvis, Cher, Wayne Newton, and countless others to magicians and show girl spectacles. Casinos invested heavily in constructing elaborate performance spaces to attract the next great residency that would appeal to potential gamblers from across the globe. These performances became as synonymous with Vegas as the game floors and cocktail rooms.

As Las Vegas labored to expand its brand in the 1980s and early 1990s, casino owners sought to attract more families in addition to the traditional adult audiences. Marketing strategies presented Las Vegas not just as an exciting, vibrant adult mecca but also as rife with safe, sanitized spaces perfect for families. At the forefront of this concerted effort was an investment in establishing Las Vegas as a popular entertainment destination. Some casinos like Circus Circus and the Mirage relied on traditional forms such as the circus and magic acts, while others like the New York-New York, Stratosphere, and MGM Grand constructed roller coasters or entire theme parks. Yet perhaps the most lasting changes to the entertainment offerings at this time came when the creators of Cirque du Soleil decided to invest in the city. Starting in 1993 with *Mystère* at Treasure Island casino, Cirque over the course of the next twenty-five years refurbished old or constructed new performance venues in seven different Las Vegas casinos.

The Cirque du Soleil shows in Las Vegas incorporate the same languages of technology – narrative, spectacle, authenticity, and audience engagement – as other popular entertainments and most of the other Las Vegas entertainment offerings. These shows, similar to their circus roots, blur (and sometimes explode) the lines between the authentic or "the real" and the fabricated or constructed, challenging the ways spectacle conveys meaning. Treasure Island boasts a pirate ship that sinks on the hour while the Bellagio's fountain dances to music on the quarter hour. Yet these other popular entertainments do not achieve the sheer reach of Cirque's presence on the Strip. Cirque maintains seven shows on the Strip, each distinctly different in their content and approach but each undoubtedly possessing the distinctive stamp of Cirque. In addition to *Mystère* still running at Treasure Island, Cirque offers *Kà* at MGM Grand, *Zumanity* at New York-New York, *Michael Jackson: One* at Mandalay Bay, *O* at the Bellagio, *The Beatles: Love* at the Mirage, and the newly opened *R. U.N.* at the Luxor (which recently replaced another Cirque show, *Criss*

Angel: Mindfreak following a ten-year run). Each of these seven productions showcases the very latest in theatrical technologies. Performing within more permanent spaces than the transitory tents of the traveling show, these shows invest in greater technical infrastructure that allows creators to incorporate more advanced technologies into the shows. While some shows, like *Zumanity*, borrow directly from past popular entertainment forms like burlesque, the great majority of the Vegas Cirque productions took advantage of new technologies to redefine popular performance. When *Kà* opened in 2005, for example, it set a record at the time for the most expensive and technologically advanced show ever created with a - $220 million construction budget. The 1,950-seat theatre offers a massive scale: "The stage is 120 feet across. From the high grid rigging at the ceiling to the pit (the lowest floor level), it's 149 feet (about 15 stories). It's 98 feet from the stage level to that high grid. And it's 120 feet from the stage level to the pit."[17] Within this enormous space they placed

> five stage lifts moving 25 feet up and down transport[ing] props and performers during the show. The rear stage segment (the Tatami Deck) slides forward 50 feet and weighs more than 37 tons. Finally, the Sand Cliff Deck (a 25-foot by 50-foot platform that weighs 40 tons) is controlled by a vertical gantry crane and a robotic arm attached to four 75-foot-long hydraulic cylinders running along two support columns.[18]

Even more impressive, that gantry crane and robotic arm "can lift the Sand Cliff Deck 72 feet, rotate 360 degrees and tilt from flat to 110 degrees – all at the same time ... powered by five 250-horsepower pumps and a 4,000-gallon oil reservoir."[19] The robotic arm and Sand Cliff Deck function as an additional character in the performance, providing maximum spectacle and making a strong argument for the performative nature of technology itself. For with the context of the narrative of *Kà*, this technology works in tandem with other sophisticated lighting, sound, and projection systems to create a truly immersive theatrical experience – one that blends more traditional theatrical practices with technology heretofore not seen within theatre contexts.

As early as October 1998, just down the Strip, Cirque du Soleil opened *O* within the newly constructed Bellagio casino. Building off the successful integration of technology and performance, *O* took inspiration from the Bellagio's Italian theme and its signature fountains which perform their own show every fifteen or thirty minutes for all walking down Las Vegas Boulevard. Unlike the creators of *Kà* who seven years later would retrofit an existing theatre, the creators of *O* built their space from the ground up to achieve similar spectacular goals. As Christopher Hoile remarked in his review for *Stage Door*, "the 1800-seat auditorium is built to look like the interior of an ornate Baroque opera house surmounted by a huge oval watery blue dome that suggests that the theatre itself is submerged."[20] Taking its cue from a completely different trajectory of popular entertainment, *O* borrows heavily from the aquacades of the World's Fairs and early cinema as well as from the sport of synchronized swimming and diving to create a performance space of both land and sea, solid and liquid. As Hoile describes, "the theatre has a proscenium but the center of the stage consists of an elliptical 1.5 million-gallon pool – 150 feet in length, 100 feet in width and 25 feet deep – with water access upstage via two canals."[21] Within this large pool, the stage consists of four platform lifts "that can move from 17 feet below the surface to 18 inches above it, either separately or together in various configurations. Drilled with thousands of holes for rapid movement, the stage can, within seconds, change from a pool to a solid surface."[22] The flow of the lifts allows for the sudden entrances and exits of performers, harnessing technology to create magical stage moments where it appears like performers are walking on water or diving into a solid mass. *O* incorporates these technologies along with extensive safety technology (e.g., underwater breathing apparatus) and lighting, sound, and projection equipment to create a seamless thematic experience. While the narrative is front and center in *Kà* alongside the technology, *O* resists a clear narrative emphasizing theme and perhaps borrowing more heavily from the "concept" musical. Moreover, *O* relies upon a huge technological infrastructure to convey its ideas but weaves its technology more seamlessly into the performance, not drawing particular attention to the technology itself but instead allowing the performers and performances to pull focus. Both *Kà* and *O* demonstrate the pinnacle of popular entertainments in Las Vegas that incorporate advanced technologies in new theatrical contexts and illustrate an evolution of the formula Cirque du Soleil honed through its traveling shows. Both *Kà* and *O* also incorporate into the popular entertainment form traces of other artistic movements outside of more traditional popular forms bringing these techniques to a broader, popular audience. For example, they include elements of both the avant-garde movements of the early twentieth century (Surrealist dreamscapes and Futurist *sintesi*) and postmodern performance (like those of Robert Wilson playing with duration, time, language, and movement).

Building on the success of shows like these, Cirque du Soleil expanded its offerings in Vegas beyond the narrative driven or thematically linked show to bridge their approach with another legacy of Vegas performance.

With shows like *Michael Jackson: One* at Mandalay Bay, *The Beatles: Love* at the Mirage, and the now closed *Viva Elvis* at the Aria Casino,[23] Cirque du Soleil strayed from their typical formula and leaned into those previously mentioned Vegas histories of storied musical performances and residencies. For these particular shows, Cirque remastered the original recordings of these musical artists and used their songbooks as the chief inspiration. Rather than providing an original score and live vocal performances as in previous shows, acts emerged organically from the individual songs, and while there was a general arc, they lacked true narrative. This shift allowed Cirque to court new audiences of Vegas tourists who might embrace these popular songs but might fear the more esoteric, abstracted nature of their usual shows, with loosely drawn plots and invented languages. In many ways, these shows were appealing to an even more "popular" audience by directly incorporating the most popular music possible alongside their more conceptual French-Canadian roots. They create a productive, lucrative tension that often exists within popular entertainment; just as the circus staged the space between respectability and scandal, these Cirque shows exist in the space between the popular and the highbrow. These popular songs appeared fresh and could be heard anew through the incredibly engineered remasters of the original tracks that accompanied these shows. The in-the-round Mirage theatre that houses *The Beatles: Love* even installed three speakers into each of the 2000 seats for an intimate, technologically advanced sonic experience on top of the Cirque spectacle. This decision to incorporate popular music directly into the performance not only sought to broaden Cirque's appeal to new audience members, but also paid homage to the performance histories of the city itself and the famed residencies of its lauded performers like Wayne Newton, Elvis, Dean Martin, Donny and Marie, and eventually Elton John, Celine Dion, and Lady Gaga.

Vegas spectacles highlight another aspect of technologies, focusing on the mechanics of production and the technologies of transportation that popular entertainments rely upon. While Vegas shows, like Cirque du Soleil's many offerings, inhabit one particular venue, and audiences travel to that space, other popular entertainments, like their early nineteenth-century predecessors, travel from city to city bringing their production to the audience in their location. Often these Vegas spectaculars provide a testing ground for new technologies like automated robotic lighting and projection technologies that eventually find their way into these traveling or touring productions. Creative teams and engineers gain valuable information from witnessing new lighting instruments or sound systems on an existing stage show before figuring out creative ways to incorporate them into a new arena concert. These popular forms with their high profit margins allow for investment and reinvestment in the creation of such new technologies and experimentations and thus play a vital role in the performance ecosystem of American theatre practice and other popular performance forms.

Arena and Stadium Concerts

The advancement of the popular music concert over the twentieth and twenty-first centuries provides another example of how popular entertainments evolve and change in accordance with developments in technologies and the symbiotic relationship that exists within the various forms. Contemporary arena and stadium concerts illustrate the complex relationship found in popular entertainments between spectacle and consumerism and often provide an amplified stage for new technologies and techniques. From 1945 on, developments in technology within and outside of the music industry had dramatic impact upon many elements of popular music. Bob Dylan plugging in at the Newport Folk Festival in 1965, for example, dramatically changed not only the trajectory of Dylan as a musical artist but changed the narrative of what popular music sounded like. Changing recording technologies from long playing records to cassette tapes to 8-tracks to compact discs to digital files to streaming platforms radically altered what it means to be a recording artist. With each change in technology came a reevaluation of the mechanisms of the industry as a whole. While artists could make money off the sales of recordings for a large part of the twentieth century, the proliferation of digital and streaming platforms necessitated a reassessment of the sources of revenue. Artists could no longer make the same kinds of money selling albums as sales of physical copies decreased. Increasingly artists had to make their primary money off of touring. As a result, an artist's live performances gradually assumed a much more significant role in their financial outlooks. This emphasis on performance then provided an opportunity for musical artists to embrace not only the technologies associated with other popular entertainments but to adopt a host of theatrical elements to strengthen the impact of their stage shows.

Musical artists throughout the history of musical performance engage with questions of performance and theatricality whether implicitly or explicitly, particularly around issues of authenticity. A musical artists' genre generally dictates certain parameters surrounding authenticity, the delicate tightrope of "real" to fabricated they must walk to bolster their performance persona. If an artist strays too far outside an acceptable range, they risk losing their credibility and thus their audience. For example, for a country artist to reside primarily in a large city and incorporate more traditional pop music fabrications brings with it risk of losing their legitimacy or credentials. Conversely, for a rock artist to embrace a more produced, commercial sound with carefully constructed imagery and spectacle brings with it risk of that artist violating rock music's traditional obsession with edgy, rebellious, unaffected, unfiltered presentation. Concerns of authenticity explicitly dictate part of that engagement with theatrical elements and technologies. Depending upon the genre of music, those theatrical elements and technology may remain more or less visible depending upon the desired image (a pop singer may choose lavish costumes and robotic lighting to highlight the fantasy while an alt-country artist may strip away elements and purposefully scale back their apparel to appear more "real"). Some genres like glam rock even play explicitly with such representations seeming to celebrate the showmanship of 1950s rock and roll culture while at the same time undermining rock's adherence to the ideology of authenticity in the late 1960s through calling direct attention to the theatricality.[24]

Examples of performers adopting a stage persona to cultivate audiences and sell records trace back to the beginnings of musical performance. From Wolfgang Mozart to Bob Wills and the Texas Playboys to Elvis and The Beatles, performers (and their management and record labels) have taken advantage of the space of live performance to connect to their audiences and court loyalty. While musical artists of all levels of popularity and genre engage with theatrical elements and technology in their performances, those performers who tour large arenas by necessity of space create the largest scale spectacles and, as a result, attract the most massive audiences, earning large amounts of money. The increased spectacle aligns with increased ticket prices that in turn increase expectations of fan experience. These concerts, in a similar vein to the Las Vegas Cirque du Soleil shows, become the economic engine for the development of new performance and theatre technologies (new lighting equipment, hazers, special effects, sound equipment). That technological equipment then circulates throughout different performance forms, locations, and venues, like the Broadway musical. The hazer that emits atmospheric fog as Beyoncé appears on an arena stage also helps create the ice effect as Elsa builds her ice castle in the *Frozen* musical.

The scale of financial investment in these large stadium and arena shows makes them ideal for the development and testing of new technologies. The relative financial flexibility and scale also allow for an atmosphere that supports creativity. These musical artists seek to connect to their audiences and deliver their music in such a way in concert that makes audiences not just want to purchase the music (which doesn't benefit the artist usually) but to return repeatedly to their concerts, tour after tour spending hundreds of dollars a ticket rather than a dollar or two a song (of which usually a very small percentage reaches the actual artist). As a result of this system, the artists are incentivized at this level of popularity to enhance their concerts with large and spectacular elements and to incorporate theatricality as a means of making that necessary connection.

Two of the earlier pioneers of these arena spectacles are Madonna and U2. Madonna adopted a highly theatrical stage persona relatively early in her career. As she gained popularity, the size and scale of her tour performances grew. While there had always been a strong emphasis on the theatrical in her live performances (see her infamous performance of "Like a Virgin" at the MTV Video Music Awards in 1984 as just one example), starting with *The Drowned World Tour* in 2001, Madonna invested more fully in crafting a theatrical narrative by dividing her shows into thematic segments and creating completely different visual experiences within each segment. These concerts incorporated elaborate costumes, advanced theatrical lighting, pyrotechnics, wire work, digital projections, and a variety of platforms (hydraulic and otherwise) and set pieces not to mention nearly twenty dancers, a bevy of backup singers, and a band. These shows also pointedly often incorporated previous popular entertainment traditions explicitly within those narratives – moments of burlesque, variety acts, vaudeville shtick, and so on. As Madonna's albums became less and less commercially successful, her concerts increased exponentially in spectacle and theatricality.

A similar trajectory can be seen with the band U2 who began as a quintessential anthem arena band, filling stadiums with their musicianship. As the economic realities of the music industry began to shift and while their popularity remained, they invested heavily in increasing the theatricality and technological experiences of their concerts. Like Madonna, U2 became synonymous in the late 1990s, 2000s, and 2010s with technologically advanced stadium shows. Unlike Madonna, U2 continues to push their use of technology to find new ways to connect with their audiences more intimately even within a large venue. Their most recent tour, *Experience and Innocence,* uses something called "'the barricage,' a 29-metre long, double-sided LCD screen" that sits on a walkway and spans the entire length on the arena floor "linking the main stage and a smaller, circular platform at the far end of the arena."[25] The performers can actually walk in between these two screens that also "rise and fall throughout the show, transmitting live footage, political slogans and colorful animations."[26] Moreover, these screens "can also go transparent at the flick of a switch, allowing U2 to appear and disappear behind the wall and even tussle with the images around them."[27] While this apparatus allows for any number of impressive tricks and magical moments, perhaps, most importantly, it also allows the band access to their audience.

Another contemporary popular artist, Taylor Swift, has similarly incorporated technology in her stadium tours that functions to both create spectacle and fabricate intimacy. For both her *1989* and *Reputation* tours, Swift partnered with a company called PixMob to create a unique prop gifted to every audience member. When entering the venue, every fan received "an LED wristband – a translucent silicone bracelet that lights up and changes color perfectly in time to the music."[28] Every audience member transforms (whether they chose to or not) into an active participant and leaves with a souvenir of the experience. The technology works to directly engage the audience and offer the concertgoer an authentic experience that connects them both to the overall experience and specifically to Taylor Swift herself. Technology here provides not just spectacle but connectivity between performer and audience. Unlike with Cirque and the spectacle of circus or Vegas, the use of technology within this kind of large stadium concert makes the experience feel somehow smaller and more intimate while at the same time huge – the productive tension that typifies popular entertainments. Further highlighting the interconnectedness of these large-scale popular entertainments' use of technology, the technology PixMob used to fabricate the wristbands they originally developed for ponchos for . . . Cirque du Soleil.[29]

Living History Museums

While a Taylor Swift or Beyoncé concert may be the epitome of contemporary spectacle and compel redefinitions and reconsiderations of performance, there also exists another strand of popular entertainments that aim to recapture or represent a more "accurate" or "authentic" slice of American history and in doing so still exhibit that unique tension of human and technology that so often characterizes popular entertainments. While they may seem far removed from the large-scale spectacles of stadium concerts, living history museums similarly use technology in implicit and explicit ways to convey narrative and engage directly with their audiences.

Living history museums gained popularity across the twentieth century and grew out of more traditional museum culture. Rather than confining artifacts to display cases surrounded by signage and labels that place those items in historical context, living history museums seek to immerse the individual in an approximation of the historical moment. Within the recreated moment, that individual, at least in theory, can then connect to that history in a more embodied manner making use of all their senses. Old Sturbridge Village in Sturbridge, Massachusetts and Colonial Williamsburg, two of the most established of this type of popular entertainment, both founded in the first half of the twentieth century, exemplify the purpose of this form. Both Colonial Williamsburg's and Old Sturbridge's stated missions – "to feed the human spirit by sharing America's enduring story"[30] and "to find meaning, pleasure, relevance, and inspiration through the exploration of history,"[31] respectively – emphasize the importance of the personal connection to that history. Successfully accomplishing the goal of providing visitors with that meaningful experience relies on immersion, placing the visitor inside an approximation of the "actual" history. In turn, that immersion relies upon both technology and theatrical elements to recreate those places in such a way as to illicit that desired effect.

One of the primary ways living history museums accomplish these effects using technologies and theatrical elements is through the crafting of narrative. As Scott Magelssen states in *Living History Museums: Undoing History through Performance*, "these museums engage in the narrative contract in order to fit lived events into a story through which visitors may comprehend those events. ... Old Sturbridge Village employ[s] themes of social conflict."[32] These narratives provide the visitor a role to play within the story and suggest possible ways for them to engage with the history surrounding them. Technology in living history museums functions to support these narratives; thus, unlike in Las Vegas, those mechanisms may very well remain hidden from view with the desired effect on display but not how it was created. The use of "theatrical magic" works to shape the guests' experience and provide the illusion of historical accuracy where actual accuracy cannot be achieved.

As living history museums depend heavily on narrative, they also must continually adapt and revise those narratives to take into account the contemporary moment and the continual process of history itself. The historical understanding of Colonial America, for example, drastically changes over time as historians discover new information and craft new interpretations but also as societal contexts evolve. Colonial Williamsburg explicitly deals with this in terms of slavery and how to represent the "reality" of enslaved peoples in the late eighteenth century, a historical fact within the community the museum purports to represent. In this particular instance, as well as in other examples of living history museums trying to stage these moments of social conflict, issues of representation – explicitly theatrical representation – arise. In this case, theatre and performance provide a much different useful framework outside of the technological realm. Many of these living history museums have taken to hiring theatre professionals not only to perform roles but also to draft scripts, conduct research, and stage historically accurate performance offerings. Theatre professionals portray both actual historical figures as well as amalgamations or composite characters. The Jug Broke Theatre Company at Colonial Williamsburg, for example, performs "actual" theatre within the larger theatrical context of the entire site. They perform a combination of actual eighteenth-century texts alongside original texts they have composed, inspired by the historical archive. Moreover, Colonial Williamsburg has a department of "Education, Research and Historic Interpretation" that not only focuses on crafting accurate historical representations but also engages in scholarly archival research and audience engagement and outreach in a dramaturgical sense. These sites ultimately view these reenactments as performance, and as such, they exist solidly within popular entertainment frameworks.

More recently, the concept of living history museums has expanded as demands for immersion have grown alongside advances in technologies, incorporating increasing levels of spectacle in their design to engage audiences. Magelssen in his later book *Simming: Participatory Performance and the Making of Meaning* contends that in the past, living history museums have "sought to convince visitors in the programming and publicity that walking through the gates of their simulated versions of the past is an exercise in stepping back in time."[33] He contends that in the contemporary moment several museums "have explicitly revised their exhibits and programming to downplay this notion, in favor of experiential learning that emphasizes how our understanding of the past is a construction informed as much by popular culture and values as it is by historical research."[34] This development allows those theatrical elements and technologies to emerge from the shadows through interactive elements like kiosks, for example, and to foster more explicit and transparent conversations about the processes of history and the connections between the present and the past.

Such technologies engage audiences directly in an experience that blurs the past and the present, the past with the modern. As Rebecca Schneider contends in *Performing Remains: Art and War in Times of Theatrical Reenactment*, such reenactments of history always contain "a battle concerning the future of the past."[35] These living history museums "flummox those faith-keepers who hold that the present is fleeting and entirely self-identical, or who hold that the movement from the present to the future is never by way of the past, or who believe firmly in absolute disappearance and loss of the past as well as the impossibility of its recurrence."[36] The presence of enhanced immersive technologies works further to disrupt the presumed relationships between past and present. These encounters position the audience differently in the narrative and allow them in many cases a more active, disruptive role in the shaping and reception of that history.

The recently opened Legacy Museum in Montgomery, Alabama, located next to the National Memorial for Peace and Justice and part of the larger Equal Justice Initiative, for example, certainly does not function as a traditional living history museum. The Legacy Museum differs in two critical ways and potentially highlights a future trajectory for these kinds of immersive performance. Rather than purporting to represent a specific historical moment, The Legacy Museum offers a very specific narrative contained overtly in the museum's subtitle: "The Legacy Museum: From Enslavement to Mass Incarceration." In their publicity, they go to great lengths to lay out their narrative clearly and make their argument. They even go as far as to state that "our new museum is the physical manifestation of that research."[37] Visitors here immerse themselves in a different kind of living history museum becoming part of a process, being led through exhibits that build upon one another to craft an argument. Technology plays a critical role in this process as well. Toward the end of the experience, visitors have the opportunity to engage directly with a prisoner on death row through advanced projection. The individual sits down at a replica of a prison visiting room, and once they pick up the phone, they come face to face with the hologram of an actual death row inmate who shares their story. Technology supports narrative and allows near complete immersion. As Bryan Stevenson, founder and executive director of the Equal Justice Initiative, remarked, "at the Legacy Museum, we want to employ every narrative tool that can deepen our commitment to human rights and human dignity."[38]

Conclusion/Theme Park Entertainments

Placed exactly in the middle of the World Showcase at Walt Disney World's EPCOT, the United States of America pavilion, referred to as the host pavilion, recreates detailed colonial architecture complete with resplendent white columns and a soaring atrium. As Disney marketing describes it, "the stunning building … was intended as a 'people's mansion,' taking design cues from the classic Georgian style of the late 1700s, Colonial Williamsburg, Independence Hall, Thomas Jefferson's Monticello and the Old State House in Boston."[39] Workers within the pavilion don colonial attire harkening back to the late eighteenth century around the signing of the Declaration of Independence. An acapella group, known as The Voices of Liberty, regales audiences with patriotic music, taking audiences on a journey through the American song book. The highlight of the pavilion is a show entitled *The American Adventure* that occurs continuously every twenty-nine minutes. In the performance, which features "35 Audio-Animatronics figures, digital rear-projection images on a 72-foot screen and stirring patriotic songs, you'll watch firsthand as America's story unfolds."[40] In every description of the performance, Disney highlights the combination of technology and narrative: "pivotal moments in history appear and disappear seamlessly through the use of a massive computer-controlled movable device. Ten different sets are stored under the stage and are moved forward or backward on cue by this American technological marvel."[41] The show reflects American exceptionalism at its finest: "It truly is a show like none other – just like the country that inspired it!"[42]

The American Adventure is only a small microcosm of the large-scale popular performances happening across the globe in theme parks. In many ways, the theme park represents the future of popular performance even with soaring ticket prices. Theme parks incorporate the latest technologies in a creative and theatrical manner and dedicate a massive amount of capital in creative development both in terms of people and technology. At Disney, their division of Imagineers works to realize the impossible, creating technologies to solve creative problems, from the recent *Avatar: Flight of Passage* ride, which recreates a "living," "breathing" fantastical creature from the film for visitors to ride, to the recently opened *Star Wars: Rise of the Resistance* ride that places you directly in a Star Wars narrative as you traverse the galaxy in at least three different ride vehicles. Additionally, Disney's Magic Band system, similar to the wristbands at Taylor Swift concerts, not only allows visitors to access the parks and hotels and to pay for meals and souvenirs, but it also has the potential to allow for even more immersive experiences wherein Snow White, for instance, could address you by name or a Storm Trooper could compliment you on your score on the Millennium Falcon ride. In the case of theme parks, technology functions to make the experience ever more immersive and to submerse the guest in total narrative experiences. As Jenny Kokai and Tom Robson posit in their new anthology, "in immersive Disney, 'show' is everything the guest encounters, and the tourist often has the ability to collaborate in the writing of their own show."[43]

Popular entertainments, regardless of the specific form, engage in a critical conversation of the twentieth and twenty-first centuries – the relationship between the human and technology. Popular entertainments stage interactions between technologies and humans, re/performing history, challenging the limits of the body, and re/defining and re/creating spectacle. Popular entertainments generate new languages of performance, engaging directly with technology to craft narratives that productively trouble authenticity and navigate tensions and ruptures all while finding new and innovative ways to engage audiences. Popular entertainments through their engagements with technologies and audiences, influence theatrical forms and vice versa. These forms deserve careful attention as they continue to force conversations about technology, commercialization, and identity construction while simultaneously entertaining the masses.

Popular entertainments illustrate the continual cycles present within histories of performance forms, wherein what once might have been regarded as experimental or avant-garde becomes mainstream and commercial. But just as what was once peripheral becomes central, the process dictates not a linear progression but a cyclical one, always circling, always spiraling back to the center. For example, whereas the circus embraces the avant-garde, the postmodern also embraces the circus (Peter Brook's *Midsummer Night's Dream* or Nick Hytner's recent production at The Bridge Theatre). The modern dancer debuts a piece in Chicago that a pop artist incorporates into their concert tour that becomes a focal point of a digital ad campaign only to return in a slightly newer form in another dance piece. Popular entertainments incorporate and influence, borrow and loan, expand and contract. As creative engines contributing to these cycles, popular entertainments stand at the forefront of many of the chief concerns of American theatre practice since 1945. Through a language of performance, popular entertainments engage most directly with threads of technology, narrative, authenticity, and audience engagement that categorize the major shifts in American theatre practice. The experimental and radical are appropriated and adopted in the popular for mass consumption through use of these very threads. As a result, popular entertainments exist at the forefront of developing and redeveloping theatrical techniques and practices in front of mass audiences, incorporating experimental techniques and ideas and thus contributing to the process of moving them from the periphery to the center.

Notes

1. J. M. Davis, *The Circus Age: Culture and Society Under the American Big Top* (University of North Carolina Press, 2002).
2. Ibid., p. 103.
3. Ibid., p. 227.
4. Ibid.
5. Ibid., p. 229.
6. D. Leslie and N. Rantisi, "Deskilling in Cultural Industries: Corporatization, Standardization and the Erosion of Creativity at the Cirque du Soleil," *Geoforum*, 99 (2019), p. 259.
7. Ibid.
8. Davis, *The Circus Age*, pp. 234–35.
9. Leslie, "Deskilling in Cultural Industries," p. 260.
10. Ibid.
11. Ibid.
12. Ibid., p. 257.
13. Ibid., p. 261.
14. Anonymous Cirque performer, qtd. in Leslie, "Deskilling in Cultural Industries," p. 262.
15. Davis, *The Circus Age*, p. 230.
16. Recent financial difficulties, exacerbated by the COVID-19 pandemic, led Cirque in June 2020 to file for bankruptcy protection. As the production company emerges from this moment, seeking new financial partnerships to stabilize its growing debt, the company will once again wrestle with these modern forces. Time will tell how their modern popular performance style transforms under these new pressures.
17. J. S. Lewinski, "Cirque du Soleil's Sophisticated *Kà* Evolves with New Tech," *Wired*, February 16, 2010, www.wired.com/2010/02/cirque-du-soleils-sophisticated-ka-evolves-with-new-tech/.
18. Lewinski, "Cirque du Soleil's Sophisticated *Kà*."
19. Ibid.
20. C. Hoile, "Las Vegas, NV: *O*," *Stage Door*, January 17, 2012, ww.stagedoor.com/Theatre/Elsewhere/Entries/2012/1/17_Las_Vegas,_NV__O.html.
21. Ibid.
22. Ibid.
23. Interestingly, *Viva Elvis* was replaced at Aria by a short-lived show entitled *Zarkana* (2012–16), which found inspiration in the older popular

entertainment form of the variety show and was structured around a story of a magician in an abandoned theatre.

24. P. Auslander, *Performing Glam Rock: Gender and Theatricality in Popular Music* (University of Michigan Press, 2006).

25. M. Savage, "How U2's Technology Is Changing Concerts for the Better," *BBC News*, October 18, 2018, www.bbc.com/news/entertainment-arts -45864368.

26. Ibid.

27. Ibid.

28. M. Martinelli, "How Do the Light-Up Bracelets on Taylor Swift's 1989 Tour Actually Work?," *Slate*, July 17, 2015, http://slate.com/culture/2015/07/pix mob-the-company-behind-the-led-bracelets-on-taylor-swift-s-1989-tour-expl ains-how-they-work.html.

29. Ibid.

30. "Our Mission," www.history.org/foundation/mission.cfm.

31. "Mission and Narrative," www.osv.org/about/mission-narrative/.

32. S. Magelssen, *Living History Museums: Undoing History through Performance* (Scarecrow Press, 2007), pp. 40–41.

33. S. Magelssen, *Simming: Participatory Performance and the Making of Meaning* (University of Michigan Press, 2014), p. 11.

34. Ibid.

35. R. Schneider, *Performing Remains: Art and War in Times of Theatrical Reenactment* (Routledge, 2011), p. 4.

36. Ibid., p. 53.

37. "The Legacy Museum," http://museumandmemorial.eji.org/museum.

38. T. Dafoe, "A First Look inside the New Alabama Museum Boldly Confronting Slavery and Its Brutal Legacy," *Artnet News*, April 25, 2018, http://news .artnet.com/art-world/legacy-museum-memorial-peace-justice-1272686.

39. "The American Adventure," http://disneyworld.disney.go.com/attractions/e pcot/american-adventure/.

40. Ibid.

41. Ibid.

42. Ibid.

43. J. A. Kokai and T. Robson (eds.), *Performance and the Disney Theme Park Experience: The Tourist as Actor* (Palgrave Macmillan, 2019), p. 15.

Select Bibliography

Budd, M., and M. H. Kirsch. *Rethinking Disney: Private Control, Public Dimensions.* Wesleyan Press, 2005.

Kokai, J. A., and T. Robson (eds.). *Performance and the Disney Theme Park Experience: The Tourist as Actor.* Palgrave Macmillan, 2019.

Magelssen, S. *Living History Museums: Undoing History through Performance.* Scarecrow Press, 2007.

Magelssen, S. *Simming: Participatory Performance and the Making of Meaning.* University of Michigan Press, 2014.

Magelssen, S., and R. Justice-Malloy (eds.). *Enacting History.* University of Alabama Press, 2011.

Schneider, R. *The Explicit Body in Performance.* Routledge, 1997.

Schneider, R. *Performing Remains: Art and War in Times of Theatrical Reenactment.* Routledge, 2011.

Smoodin, E. (ed.). *Disney Discourse: Producing the Magic Kingdom.* Routledge, 1994.

Sorkin, M. (ed.). *Variations on a Theme Park: The New American City and the End of Public Space.* Hill and Wang Press, 1992.

Printed in the USA
CPSIA information can be obtained
at www.ICGtesting.com
LVHW061245200823
755745LV00002B/202